the cinema of ANG LEE

DIRECTORS' CUTS

the cinema of
ANG LEE

the other side of the screen

SECOND EDITION

whitney crothers dilley

 WALLFLOWER PRESS LONDON & NEW YORK

A Wallflower Press Book

Wallflower Press is an imprint of
Columbia University Press
Publishers Since 1893
New York   Chichester, West Sussex
cup.columbia.edu

Library of Congress Cataloging-in-Publication Data
Dilley, Whitney Crothers.
   The cinema of Ang Lee : the other side of the screen / Whitney Crothers Dilley. — Second edition.
        pages cm. — (Directors' cuts)
   Includes bibliographical references and index.
   ISBN 978-0-231-16772-7 (cloth : alk. paper) — ISBN 978-0-231-16773-4 (pbk. : alk. paper) —
ISBN 978-0-231-53849-7 (ebook)
   1. Lee, Ang, 1954—Criticism and interpretation.   I. Title.
PN1998.3.L438D55 2014
791.4302'33092—dc23   2014022600

Columbia University Press books are printed on permanent and durable acid-free paper.
This book is printed on paper with recycled content.
Printed in the United States of America

c 10 9 8 7 6 5 4 3 2 1
p 10 9 8 7 6 5 4 3 2 1

Book design by Rob Bowden Design
Cover image: © Getty

CONTENTS

ACKNOWLEDGMENTS

THE AUTHOR HAS incurred personal and professional debts to more people than can be named here, and owes the successful publication of this book primarily to Kai-chong Cheung, whose support of this research has been invaluable, and Milan V. Dimić, whose timely counsel and enthusiasm helped propel this work forward. Thanks to friends and colleagues Peng-hsiang Chen, Chen-ching Li, John Hu, Tien-en Kao, Heidi Yu, Yung-aun Li, Charlene Chen, Peter Lin, Alex Rath, Yvette Huang, Irene Wang, Stephanie Pu, Kelly Weng, Song Hwee Lim, Kien Ket Lim, Ru-Shou Robert Chen, Ivy I-Chu Chang, Li-Chun Hsiao, Hsiu-Chuang Deppman, Song-Yong Sing, Che-ming Yang, Hui-Fen Chin, George Huang, Peng Hsiao-yen, Chang Hsiao-hung, Wenchi Lin, Eileen Cheng-yin Chow, Emilie Yueh-yu Yeh, Darrell W. Davis, and especially Ching-hsien Wang at the University of Washington, Douglas Kellner at UCLA, and Jerome Silbergeld at Princeton for academic inspiration.

Jennifer Crewe, director at Columbia University Press, and Yoram Allon, consulting editor to Columbia University Press and founder of Wallflower Press, have offered their illimitable support to this work and have been instrumental in its successful completion. Columbia University Press senior manuscript editor Roy E. Thomas also deserves commendation for his detailed attention and expertise. The author is grateful to the many individuals, particularly Jacqueline Downs, Curtis Quick, and Linda Theriault, whose insightful critiques aided in preparing early drafts of the manuscript, and to the anonymous reviewers for reading the manuscript and providing valuable input and suggestions. Staff at the Chinese Taipei Film Archive in Taiwan, under the directorship of Winston T. Y. Lee, have been extremely helpful in unearthing resources from Ang Lee's early filmmaking days, including the earliest published version of Lee's award-winning screenplay for *Pushing Hands*. Shih Hsin University generously awarded the author a sabbatical leave and two substantial research grants, which allowed for the completion of much of this research.

To Larry, a great husband, and to Michelle Kupé, a faithful friend. Thanks to Robert, Judith, and Tim Crothers.

Finally, this is for Liza, Stephen, and Chris, and all those who vividly remember New Canaan's ice storm of 1973.

NOTE ON TRANSLITERATION

THE TITLES OF all Chinese-language sources in the notes and bibliography are rendered in pinyin according to the system of romanization for Chinese written language based on the pronunciation of the northern dialect of Mandarin Chinese. Since most readers know more of the standard pinyin romanization than the Wade-Giles or Yale systems used in Taiwan, all Chinese-language names and terms are romanized in pinyin, except in cases where the person's name is widely known in a different romanization system, or the transliteration is already available in Yale or Wade-Giles. For clarity and consistency in discussion of the films, all actors' names from Ang Lee's films are romanized according to cast lists accompanying the films, and all Chinese-language characters' names are romanized to match the names as they are rendered in the films' subtitles.

the cinema of ANG LEE

ONE

Introduction: *Ang Lee—A History*

Repression is a main element of my movies. It's easier to work against something than go along with something.[1]

The Auteur

ANG LEE HAS been referred to as an auteur and it is not difficult to see why—he is an artist with his actors, and seems to draw amazing work out of his cast, from the smallest to the greatest, while continuing to reiterate common themes of family, culture, and identity in an astonishing variety of genres. Keeping in mind that he has made films in Mandarin Chinese, Taiwanese, British English from the time of Jane Austen, high-school drop-out cowboy English, American English from the Civil War era, and 1960s American hippie slang—with six languages (Mandarin, English, Japanese, Hindi, Shanghainese, and Cantonese) represented in *Lust/Caution* (*Se jie*, 2007) alone—this is no small feat. He has drawn performances of the highest quality out of actors as diverse as Kevin Kline, Joan Allen, Chow Yun-fat, and Tony Leung, as well as defining and prodigious early work from a young Tobey Maguire, Christina Ricci, Katie Holmes, and, at 19, Kate Winslet and Zhang Ziyi. As Jake Gyllenhaal reflected after the making of *Brokeback Mountain* (2005), Ang Lee is also "fluent in the language of silence."[2] This has been proven by his films from his earliest 15-minute dialogue-free scene between Deb Snyder and Sihung Lung (Lang Xiong) in *Pushing Hands* (*Tuishou*, 1991), to the paean to noncommunication and 1970s angst, *The Ice Storm* (1997), and finally, to the tortured secrets of repressed souls in *Brokeback Mountain*. Indeed, the use of silence is so effective for this director that the last fifteen minutes of *The Ice Storm* were virtually a silent movie; similarly, 16-year-old first-time actor Suraj Sharma had to carry much of *Life of Pi* (2012) with nothing but a blue screen to share his soliloquies. While Lee uses language and silence to tell his stories, he also narrates them through physical posture and facial expression. Thus, he brought out such memorable performances as Heath Ledger's clenched-jaw repression, Sigourney Weaver's languid and vampish physicality, Joan

Allen's erasing of her own identity, Michelle Yeoh's fathomless loyalty, Hugh Grant's internalized awkwardness, Tony Leung's brutal indifference, and Tobey Maguire's passage from boyhood to maturity. The nuanced performances in *Brokeback Mountain* were widely recognized as the three young actors in the film, all just in their twenties, were each nominated for Academy Awards, one of the youngest casts in history to receive such recognition.[3]

Ang Lee's talent for drawing out the best from his actors is mixed with his flawless incorporation of the natural environment, utilizing breathtaking vistas and frames. In *Sense and Sensibility* (1995), animals, hedges, and the natural effects of wind create subtleties in mood; in *Ride with the Devil* (1999), sun-dappled woods filmed on location in Missouri coupled with peaceful scenes of farmstead domesticity contrast markedly with the bloody and violent battles that take place in that setting. In *Crouching Tiger, Hidden Dragon* (*Wohu canglong*, 2000), he utilizes the startling green bamboo grove and the grid of old Beijing; in *Brokeback Mountain*, the hundreds of sheep stumbling up a mountainside, the headlights of a lone truck moving at a distance down a country road; in *The Ice Storm*, the cool metallic look of ice-encased branches and snow-slick streets. All are extremely evocative and unforgettable, almost haunting, images. It is the style of Ang Lee: emotionally resonant (in human relationships) and visually splendid (in the natural world).

After the critical and commercial failure of *Hulk* in 2003, Lee faced a grueling depression. During an introductory speech at the Toronto International Film Festival in September 2005, where *Brokeback Mountain* was previewed, Ang Lee said that after *Hulk* he wasn't sure if he wanted to continue to be a filmmaker. He considered quitting the profession, and giving up directing entirely. Ironically, it was his father, a conservative high school principal and teacher who had always longed for his son to follow in his footsteps and settle into a more stable career, who pushed Ang Lee back into the game. Ang Lee's father, who had never encouraged him to be a filmmaker, stunned his son by telling him "You need to go and make a movie."[4]

Lee elaborates in Michael Berry's *Speaking in Images*, a 2005 volume of interviews with contemporary Chinese filmmakers:

> [My father told me] he wished that I would continue making movies even though I told him I wanted to stop. That was in February 2004. He saw *Hulk* and loved it—I don't know why. He was very old. I told him I wanted to retire, or at the least, take a long break from filmmaking. He asked me if I wanted to teach, but I told him I didn't think so. He warned me that I would be very depressed if I stopped. So he told me to just put on my helmet and keep on going. That was the very first time he encouraged me to make a movie. In the past, he would always try to talk me out of making movies.[5]

Tragically, Lee's father died two weeks after this crucial conversation, which was the first time he had been supportive of his son's dream of being a director.

Ang Lee took his father's advice. The film that he went to make was *Brokeback Mountain*. Regarding this film, Lee says, "In some ways, it was a movie I didn't dare to make, for both economic and subject-matter reasons."[6] He had read the script several years earlier and found it extremely moving, especially the ending, but he felt it would be very difficult to bring the story to the screen. (Instead of pursuing it, he turned his attention to *Hulk*.) Finally, after his father's nudge, in late spring 2004 Lee began filming *Brokeback Mountain* in a remote part of Canada. In contrast to the multimillion-dollar *Hulk*, it was a return to the simpler, small-budget, independent-style filmmaking he had enjoyed in the past. Little did he know that his simple film with a small cast of young and (at the time) lesser-known actors would put him on the road to the Academy Awards.

The Outsider

The whole of Asia was held in thrall on the morning of Monday, the 6th of March, 2006, during the live presentation of the Academy Awards (broadcast at 9:00 a.m. in Taiwan), while waiting to see if Ang Lee would be named Best Director, thereby becoming the first Asian in history to win the award. At the ceremony in 2001, when *Crouching Tiger, Hidden Dragon* had been nominated in the Best Film and Best Foreign Language Film categories, Lee's disappointment was palpable when *Crouching Tiger, Hidden Dragon* won the latter award. The film had taken America by storm in 2001 and arguably was more deserving of the Academy Award that ultimately went to *Gladiator* (2000). *Crouching Tiger, Hidden Dragon* had dominated the headlines that year, and all who saw it were claiming it was something really special: not only was it the most popular subtitled Mandarin film ever to be received in the West, but it spawned imitators hoping to capitalize on the new popularity of the martial arts genre (*Hero*, 2002, and *House of Flying Daggers*, 2004, are just two examples).[7] Within a year of its release, *Crouching Tiger, Hidden Dragon* became the highest-grossing foreign-language film ever released in the United States,[8] and it triggered a cultural phenomenon, much the way *Brokeback Mountain* did following its release in 2005. There was hardly a moviegoer in America that year who did not see the film, or make a joke about "Crouching Something, Hidden Something-else."[9] While the film took home four Academy Awards, Lee's disappointment was evident as his movie won for Best Foreign Language Film; he was clearly upset that the top award, Best Film, was going to elude him. Even while delivering his acceptance speech on the Academy stage, the bittersweet look on his face revealed his true feelings. The filmmaker who had unstintingly championed the cause of the outsider, the alienated, and the foreigner was still considered a foreigner/outsider himself, and it clearly irked him.

Ang Lee was 37 years old when he began his career as a professional filmmaker. He had lived in America since he was 23. Ironically, although Lee had to overcome numerous obstacles due to his "outsider" status in America, he initially did not find himself quite "fitting in" with Asian society, either. Born on October 23, 1954, in Ping-tung County, Taiwan, and growing up both in Hualien and later in Tainan City, he faced increasing difficulty conforming to his own culture's expectations, particularly that of the model Chinese son. His father, Lee Sheng, a traditionalist in his Confucian emphasis on education as well as subjection to authority and conformity, was disappointed by his son's failure in the important national university entrance exams (Lee twice failed this exam that every Taiwanese youth spends his middle school and high school years preparing for—both times he developed a mental block after panicking on the mathematics section). He had attended his father's own high school, Tainan First Senior High School, the best in the city. Lee Sheng was frequently disappointed by his son's lack of attention to books and poor performance at school; in the summer, during the school holiday, he would have both his sons practice calligraphy and study Chinese classics. Tainan First Senior High School was a strictly-regimented place where students wore the standard school uniform—identical khaki pants and short-sleeved shirts embroidered with their student number—and studied in crowded classrooms in sweltering tropical heat. Lee frequently escaped to the Chin Men Theater to watch movies, the only thing he was "good at."[10]

After his repeated failure at the university entrance examination, Lee finally enrolled in the Theater and Film program at the Taiwan Academy of Arts (now the National Taiwan University of Arts) which, when he attended in 1973, was a three-year vocational school rather than a prestigious university, a real step down in status in the eyes of his father.[11] Worse, he was majoring in Theater and Film, a field not considered gentlemanly and respectable, and in the conservative 1970s environment of Taiwan, one viewed with a jaundiced eye. People in the entertainment business in Taiwan at that time were considered somewhat akin to vaudeville entertainers in early American theatrical history—one step above prostitution and debauchery. Lee's proper, highly-educated father was appalled and shamed by this career choice; friends of Ang Lee's parents would deliberately not ask about him—and instead ask about his younger brother, Khan—to avoid embarrassing Lee Sheng. It was almost unthinkable in Chinese culture for the son of a high school principal to go into acting.

Nevertheless, Lee was delighted with his experiences at the Taiwan Academy of Arts and felt immediately at home acting onstage. In his own words, "My spirit was liberated for the first time."[12] Clearly, this type of cathartic experience had not been available to him growing up in a heavily academic environment, where his father was often a silent, fearsome presence (according to childhood friends, Lee's father did not speak at the dinner table and relaxed, casual conversations would take place there only when his father had left the room). One of his most memorable roles was Tom Wingfield in Tennessee Williams' *The Glass Menagerie*—a drama best-known for its intergenerational conflicts, and the son's ultimate flight from parental control. While originally he had entered the Academy to avoid conscription into Taiwan's mandatory military service—he was planning to take the college entrance exam again, for the third time, to transfer to a better school—he instead fell deeply in love with drama. His father allowed him to stay at the Academy, with the appended promise that after graduation he would go abroad for further study. Lee was clearly a gifted performer; he acted in numerous roles, and in his second year at the Academy he won a top acting prize in a national competition. In his third year, he made a Super-8 film as a graduation project—the film was called *Laziness on a Saturday Afternoon* (*Xingqiliu xiawu de lansan*, 1976), an 18-minute black-and-white silent film about a kite. This film would later be included in the application materials that would gain him acceptance into New York University's film school.[13]

In 1978 Ang Lee went to the United States and, with financial support from his family, entered the University of Illinois at Urbana-Champaign as a theater major.[14] Within a few months of beginning his studies there, he turned 24; thus he was considerably older than his fellow students, since he had been obligated to complete his two years of government-required military service in Taiwan following his time at the Academy. In addition to the drawback of being older, his English was heavily accented and far from fluent. Therefore, he faced inevitable difficulties with his drama performance courses because it took him longer to read scripts and memorize his lines than it did his American classmates.[15] However, during his time at the University of Illinois, he began experimenting with directing rather than acting and discovered a way to use his artistic vision that rendered his accented and grammatically imperfect English less of a problem. Although he had enjoyed acting and performing, he now threw himself into this new medium. He directed a production of Ionesco's *The Chairs*, and studied the plays of Bertolt Brecht, Harold Pinter, Tennessee Williams, and Eugene O'Neill. Describing his experience from that period, he says: "the look of Western theatre struck me in a big way. . . . I got very good at it."[16]

Lee graduated from the University of Illinois with a B.F.A. (Bachelor of Fine Arts) in Theatre/Theatre Direction in 1980. After graduation, he went on to the Tisch School of the Arts at New York University to complete a master's degree in Film Production. At NYU, Lee enjoyed a very prolific early period producing student shorts. These films included *The Runner* (1980), *Beat the Artist* (1981), *I Love Chinese Food* (1981), and *Shades of the Lake* (1982). *Shades of the Lake*, also known as *I Wish I Was By That Dim Lake*, won Best Short Film in Taiwan's Golden Harvest Film Festival. This second-year film project also won a full scholarship for Lee to continue his studies at NYU. In addition, during this early period in New York, Ang Lee had the opportunity to work with fellow NYU classmate Spike Lee. The two worked together on Spike Lee's student film *Joe's Bed-Stuy Barbershop: We Cut Heads* (1984), with Ang Lee acting as assistant cameraman.

In 1983, Lee married Jane Lin, a fellow Taiwanese student at the University of Illinois who was majoring in microbiology. The two had met for the first time in August 1978 (a week after he had arrived in the United States) on an international student outing to a Little League game in Gary, Indiana—they happened to sit next to each other in a car full of Taiwanese students. They continued to get to know each other during their time together at the university. Lin, interviewed by John Lahr in the *New Yorker* in 2003, described their courtship: "He just talks—about everything. I fall asleep, I wake up, he's still talking."[17] The year they married was also the year Lee's father retired. Lin's mother questioned the match. According to Lin, her mother said, "Why did you pick this one, with all the other nice boys around—engineering and regular people?"[18] Married in New York City, the two said their vows in a civil ceremony reminiscent of the famous courthouse marriage in *The Wedding Banquet* (*Xiyan*, 1993) which so embarrassed Lee's mother just as it had the mother in the film. In addition, again echoing *The Wedding Banquet*, Lin became pregnant on their wedding night, but she would not permanently join her husband in New York until January 1986, when she finally graduated with her Ph.D. from the University of Illinois.

During his time at NYU, Lee spent two years making the lengthier film *A Fine Line* (1985) as a master's thesis. This film, which is the story of a young Chinese girl, Piu Piu (Ching-Ming Liu), and a rough-neck Italian boy, Mario (Pat Cupo), was an earlier, more rudimentary version of the East-meets-West formula in his first trilogy of feature-length films, especially *Pushing Hands* and *The Wedding Banquet*, for which he later became known. Made over a period of two years, this film displayed Ang Lee's nascent talent for the East/West cultural dialectic, and also his eye for location (the film was shot largely in New York's Chinatown and Little Italy, as well as in New Jersey, and on and around the Jersey River). He also worked with the then-unknown actor Chazz Palminteri on this film. The 43-minute *A Fine Line* won the New York University Film Festival's top two awards for Best Director and Best Film—a great honor for the new Master of Fine Arts in Film Production—and was later aired on PBS. In addition to garnering the praise of both the NYU community and the larger film community in New York, Lee's film attracted the attention of the top U.S. film agency William Morris. As Lee related in Stephen Lowenstein's *My First Movie*:

> I decided to go back to Taiwan. . . . But before I went I wanted . . . at least to show the film at the school's film festival. I realized later that it was a big deal because a lot of people were from outside film school and a lot of Asians were watching. Anyway, I was packing up all my stuff. . . . I got a phone call and they said, "This guy from William Morris is looking for you." And I said, "William who?"[19]

Although he had not heard of the agency, the William Morris agent tried to convince him to stay in America and pursue whatever opportunities he could to develop screenplays and work on films. Lee relates how, having decided the prospects for a Chinese filmmaker in the United States were slim, he was intending to head back to Taiwan to make a name for himself in his native country. At the time he received the phone call from William Morris, he had already packed everything he owned into eight cardboard boxes to be shipped to Taiwan the following day. As a result of the last-minute offer from the William Morris agency, Lee decided to take the gamble of staying another half-year in New York while waiting for Jane to finish the final semester of her doctoral program. It was a fateful decision.

Reversal of Fortune

Ang Lee has described the next six years of his life as "development hell."[20] His eldest son Haan had been born in 1984, and his son Mason followed in 1990. Lee spent the six years between *A Fine Line* and *Pushing Hands* being a house husband of sorts, cooking, and looking for filmmaking opportunities. He wrote screenplays, and his agent occasionally found him work as a production assistant on other films while he tried unsuccessfully to pitch his own. It was a lonely and difficult time for Lee, living in the New York suburbs with sometimes very little to do: much the same way actor Sihung Lung does in the film *Pushing Hands* (more can be found on this topic in chapter 3). John Lahr details how at one point Lee in desperation would go nearly daily to hit a tennis ball around at the local tennis court. When he became overly distraught, his wife would take him to his favorite restaurant, Kentucky Fried Chicken.[21] Lee has often praised his wife and family publicly for not giving up on him and his dream during this period, saying that he would not have become a film-maker if it had not been for Jane's support. During the six years Lee was not working, she brought home the salary from her job as a microbiology researcher while Lee stayed at home taking care of their children. While somewhat more common in the United States, this situation (a wife supporting the family as the main breadwinner) is considered an embarrassment in Chinese culture. Neil Peng, screenwriter on *The Wedding Banquet* and close friend of Lee from these early days, observed that "the artist has a tempo of his own," implying that the six-year break gave Lee a chance to prepare himself for his directing career. "During those six years, Ang Lee never gave up his film dreams. He kept a huge movie database in his brain and would work on dozens of scripts at the same time."[22]

In 1990, with the birth of his second son, Lee was 36 and had little to show for his years of effort. It is difficult to imagine the now world-famous director languishing through his thirties as year by year he grew no closer to his goal. With his poor English, no one was interested in financing his movies. James Schamus and Ted Hope at Good Machine had seen Lee's graduate thesis film *A Fine Line*; in 1991, when they began to organize Good Machine as a firm to help worthy directors finance good projects with less-than-Hollywood budgets, they connected with Lee. According to Schamus, who met him just as his luck was changing:

> It was clear when Ang left the room why he had not made a movie in six years. . . . The idea of flying this guy to Los Angeles for a story meeting—forget it. When he left the office, I turned to Ted and said two things. One was "Boy, this guy can't pitch his way out of a paper bag." And two: "He wasn't pitching a movie; he was describing a movie he'd already made. He just needs somebody to realize it."[23]

In the meantime, Lee had entered a screenwriting contest held by the Taiwan govern-ment in order to strengthen the fledgling Taiwanese film industry. As the principal submission, he sent the screenplay "Pushing Hands," and, almost as an afterthought, he included in his submission a three-year-old screenplay that had never excited any producer's interest entitled "The Wedding Banquet."[24] Unbelievably, the break-through for Lee occurred as a result of this contest. In late 1990, these two screen-plays won the two top prizes in the contest, and as a result, Lee was given US$16,000 in prize money to make the winning script, "Pushing Hands," into a film. The new head of Taiwan's Central Motion Pictures Corporation threw his support behind the new film and gave Ang Lee an additional US$400,000 to make it.[25] *Pushing Hands* was filmed entirely in New York; apart from the main actors, most of the crew was American. The culture-straddling experience of this early "international" production foreshadowed Lee's future career trajectory. *Pushing Hands* was hugely successful in Taiwan; it was the third-highest-grossing Mandarin-language film of 1991, and won two major Golden Horse awards (Taiwan's version of the Academy Awards) as well as the Asian-Pacific Film Festival's Best Film award. Nevertheless, despite the popularity of *Pushing Hands* in Taiwan, the film is little known in the West. This is due to the fact that since Lee wrote the screenplay with a Taiwanese audience in mind (in order to win the contest), the film enters deeply into Chinese cultural psychology and, due to its centralized theme of filial piety, sits more comfortably in the Taiwanese film aesthetic. However, because of the huge success of *Pushing Hands* in Taiwan, Central Motion Pictures Corporation offered Lee a small budget to make the second film, *The Wedding Banquet*, with the stipulation that the movie be made in under six weeks. The newly-formed film company Good Machine stepped in to help with the financing for both films, and James Schamus began what would be a decades-long collaboration with the director.[26]

All three of Ang Lee's early films continued his fascination with the East/West dialectic. *Pushing Hands*, completed in 1991, tells the story of an aging tai chi master forced to adjust to living in America with his son, who is married to a Caucasian woman. *The Wedding Banquet*, released in 1993, is a comedy/drama about a young Taiwanese-American in New York who tries to hide his homosexuality from his tradition-bound parents by agreeing to marry a Chinese woman who wants to obtain U.S. citizenship. This screenplay, written with Neil Peng, was based on the similar experiences of a Taiwanese friend. The low-budget (US$750,000) *The Wedding Banquet* was a huge hit, bringing in a worldwide profit of US$32 million—thus becoming the most proportionately profitable film of 1993, surpassing even *Jurassic Park*.[27] This film also garnered Lee his first Academy Award nomination for Best Foreign Language Film.[28]

In 1994, Lee followed the success of *The Wedding Banquet* with the globalization and feminist treatise *Eat Drink Man Woman*, set, for the first time, in Taipei. This film combined Chinese cooking—a hobby which he claims "strengthens my spirit"—with a tender and nuanced story about the relationships between a widowed father and his three daughters.[29] After the phenomenal success of *The Wedding Banquet*, Lee was approached by many Hollywood studios; however, he was interested in pursuing instead a more personal mission: "I felt a desperate need to establish myself as a Chinese filmmaker, so I needed to go back home. . . . *Eat Drink Man Woman* was actually the first movie—and so far the only movie—I have made in my [birthplace], Taiwan."[30] Lee discusses how during his six years as a house husband, cooking for his family, he dreamed of making a film that would use food to make people's mouths water—a sumptuous feast that would tempt and arouse the audience with food in the same way movies often use sex.[31] The film brought Ang Lee his second Academy Award nomination for Best Foreign Language Film.[32]

Taiwanese scholar Ti Wei explores the importance of economics and location in Ang Lee's early trilogy. He quotes Lee:

> Making *Eat Drink Man Woman* was my first experience of the [dual] pressure for artistic achievement and box-office performance. I had never thought much about that when I was making *Pushing Hands* or *The Wedding Banquet*. . . . After *The Wedding Banquet* was a hit, distributors from all over the world offered high prices for my films. The international

market model for my films was formed: the "mainstream popular market" in Taiwan and Asia plus the "art-house cinema" in the U.S. and Europe.... I began to think much more about the taste of the global art film market.... Therefore I found myself caught between the Chinese and the Western.[33]

The success of Lee's early trilogy attracted the attention of major studios in Hollywood. His next three films would be English-language films made with access to international funding and audiences. Producer and director Sydney Pollack of the Mirage production company was among those who admired how *The Wedding Banquet* and *Eat Drink Man Woman* managed to be touching and romantic without being maudlin or sentimental. When he was seeking a director to bring the Jane Austen novel *Sense and Sensibility* to the screen, he and colleague Geoff Stier turned their attention to Ang Lee. When producer Lindsay Doran and screenwriter Emma Thompson heard this choice, they were struck by how right it seemed, and became even more convinced after finding the same line in the *Eat Drink Man Woman* screenplay as Thompson's own—when the older sister says to the younger sister "What do you know of my heart?" For his part, Lee was surprised to be asked to direct this British classic (he confessed later that when he saw Jane Austen's name on the screenplay, he thought the producers must be crazy), but he agreed to do it; one of his first acts as director was to ask Emma Thompson to play the lead role of Elinor Dashwood.[34] Directing an entirely British cast in period dress on location in Britain was no small feat; more is detailed in chapter 6 on *Sense and Sensibility*.

The success of *Sense and Sensibility* in 1995, with its seven Academy Award nominations and a win for Emma Thompson (Best Adapted Screenplay), moved Ang Lee from the marginalized category of "foreign-language film director" to a leading force in Hollywood. His next film, *The Ice Storm*, explored another culture and period in time—suburban America during the post-Watergate era of the 1970s. The critical success of *The Ice Storm*, which starred A-list Hollywood actors, followed by *Ride with the Devil*, a U.S. Civil War film sympathetic to the plight of Southerners, further demonstrated Lee's ability to penetrate the essence of whatever subject he tackled, no matter how unique or how remote.

Taking Flight—International Celebrity

While Chinese audiences lamented the lack of public recognition for his English-language films' achievements, Ang Lee was about to pull his biggest coup yet—the film he'd been dreaming about making since childhood. At the beginning of his career almost ten years earlier, when making *Pushing Hands* on a shoestring budget in 1991, Lee was quoted in an interview published by the Taipei International Film Festival: "The thing I'd most like to do is make a classical Qing-dynasty-style martial arts film—I already have my eye on a novel I'd really like [to base it on]."[35] In a later interview, Lee admits he had wanted to work with the Chinese martial arts genre since boyhood, and a friend of his, knowing of his fondness for the work of Wang Dulu, recommended this particular series in 1994. When he read *Crouching Tiger,*

Hidden Dragon, with its strong central protagonist, Jen, he was convinced that there was a movie in the material.[36] In 2000, his hopes were realized (he jokingly describes this movie as the result of a midlife crisis): he was able to assemble an astounding group of Chinese cast, crew, and musical talents, drawing top performers and artists from China, Taiwan, and Hong Kong (from Asian A-list actors Chow Yun-fat and Michelle Yeoh to Hong Kong–American pop singer Coco Lee and world-renowned cellist Yo-Yo Ma) and filming in China, in places as diverse as the Gobi Desert and the Taklamakan Plateau north of Tibet, near the Kyrgyzstan border. Lee has mentioned in an interview that his fight choreographer, Yuen Wo Ping, had doubts about the Western audience's ability to accept physical flight in a martial arts film:

> I had long talks—no, *debates*—with Mr. Yuen [Wo Ping] about whether or not to do the *qinggong* [a martial arts skill which enables practitioners to defy gravity] flying thing. From his experience, he [didn't] think the West would take to it, but to me it's a metaphor, and it's visually very interesting. [So] I worked his team to death.[37]

Lee decided to gamble on the flight sequences, with actors suspended from wires so they could appear to fly up walls and over rooftops, with a particularly challenging and hard-to-film scene in the treetops of a bamboo forest. It was a difficult shoot, as Michelle Yeoh, a female lead, broke her knee in the first fight sequence and had to be sidelined for three months out of the five-month shoot. Also, during filming, the cast and crew experienced difficulties like poor weather (in the driest place on earth—the Gobi Desert—it rained for days) and freezing cold. The film cost US$12 million to make, a record-breaking cost for a Chinese film; Lee contributed his own salary to get the film finished. The film, advertised in a trailer that did not include spoken dialogue so that audiences would not necessarily be aware that it was a subtitled film in Mandarin, became an international sensation. However, it did not win the Oscar for Best Film in 2001 (as noted, this award went to *Gladiator*—another film evoking the culture of a remote time and place; critics have even noted the similarity between the astonishing replica of old Beijing, with its warren of alleyways, and *Gladiator*'s computer-enhanced evocation of ancient Rome).

Lee turned his attention to his next project, the big-budget film *Hulk* (US$150 million), with jubilant enthusiasm, joking that it was "my next 'Green Destiny,'" a reference to the name of the sword in *Crouching Tiger, Hidden Dragon*.[38] The film signaled a crossover for Lee to the domain of American pop culture connected with Marvel Comics, animated movies, and various television series. Little did he know that he would soon be caught in the morass of script difficulties—he and James Schamus wanted to emphasize the Greek tragedy in the plot while Universal Studios insisted on a "whammo" (a car chase or an explosion, according to producer Joel Silver) every ten pages.[39] These competing interests in the screenplay led to a narrative, tone, and pacing that was neither big-budget blockbuster nor small-budget art-house, but an awkward combination of the two. Computer-generated imaging (CGI) problems (for creating a realistic-looking Hulk) would cause the budget to spiral out of control. Depressingly capitalistic marketing ploys (including 150 items with the *Hulk* logo, from garbage bags to skateboards) added to the enormity of the problem: "They're marketing everything that's green."[40] *Hulk* was an artistic and financial disaster, and for Lee, an emotional ordeal as well. After two years of work on the film, longer than any other he had worked on previously, he saw the film become his first major public failure.

Humility and Grace

Time media critic Jim Poniewozik was quoted in 2001: "Lee is able to remake his style for each movie to suit the narrative needs of that movie. In a way, he kind of suppresses his own individuality. There's a certain humility to the way that he directs them . . . to serve the greater interests of what the movie needs to be."[41]

Lee has a tremendous humility, in that he seems to disappear into his films with no brash directorial presence.[42] He has a gentle touch with his art, which has led film critics to make "chameleon-like" a common phrase used to describe his style. It is true that his films have been amazingly diverse, each requiring an enormous amount of strenuous preparation and labor. He has ruled over the sets of Civil War America—he staged realistically-mounted battles with hundreds of extras for *Ride with the Devil*. He has wrangled many sheep for *Brokeback Mountain*.[43] He has filmed in the poorly-lit conditions of British Heritage–protected mansions for *Sense and Sensibility*. He faced adverse weather conditions in China filming *Crouching Tiger, Hidden Dragon*—and also possible censorship from the Chinese government, which was concerned his film might have "anti-authoritarian" elements. He worked in New Canaan, Connecticut, despite the town's protests during *The Ice Storm*: when residents read Rick Moody's novel and found out the controversial subject matter in the film, many withdrew sites which had been promised for filming. He introduced *wuxia* (martial arts) movies to the Western mainstream and set a new standard for this genre that was followed by other Chinese directors such as Zhang Yimou.

Although Lee projects a soft-spoken air of self-effacement, it can sometimes be forgotten that he has been responsible for bringing out some of the finest performances from the earliest days in the careers of Zhang Ziyi, Kate Winslet, Jonathan Rhys Meyers, Elijah Wood, and a very young Katie Holmes, and has worked with all the giants of Asian film, Chow Yun-fat, Michelle Yeoh (a Bond girl in *Tomorrow Never Dies*, 1997), Tony Leung, and Joan Chen, as well as Tan Dun and Yo-Yo Ma, some of the greatest living Asian actors and musicians. He has brought some of the best performances out of some of the greatest British and American actors, including Emma Thompson, Alan Rickman, Hugh Grant, Hugh Laurie, Gemma Jones, Kevin Kline, Joan Allen, Sigourney Weaver, Jennifer Connelly, and Anne Hathaway, and encouraged astounding turns from the young Tobey Maguire and Christina Ricci. He has a particular talent for bringing the best work out of his younger actors; for *Brokeback Mountain*, his three principal leads, Heath Ledger, Jake Gyllenhaal, and Michelle Williams, were nominated for a range of acting awards. His influence has included meeting Prince Charles (in 1996, following the popular reception of *Sense and Sensibility*), as well as having the president of Taiwan, Chen Shui-bian, visit him at home (at the same time visiting Lee's father Lee Sheng, his former school principal). In Tainan after the success of *Crouching Tiger, Hidden Dragon*, Lee was stunned and deeply moved to be mobbed in the street by fans in his hometown.

In May 2001, Lee was awarded an honorary doctorate from NYU which thrilled him, and above all, thrilled his father. The son that had once brought academic shame now had a Ph.D.

Making History: The Academy Award for Best Direction

When the Academy Awards were broadcast at 9:00 a.m. on March 6, 2006, millions of people in Taiwan sat transfixed around television screens throughout the island. The question of whether the Academy of Motion Picture Arts and Sciences would give the Best Director award to Ang Lee was a topic of discussion nationwide prior to the broadcast. It had been in the headlines of the newspapers for several weeks. When Lee's name was read as the winner of the Best Director award in the Academy Awards live ceremony, a collective cry went out in public places throughout Taipei City. Lynn Lin, an executive at a Taiwanese engineering firm, who was watching the live news coverage of the Academy Awards at a local restaurant that morning, said "My colleagues and I don't usually follow the news, but their eyes were glued to the screen of the television in the restaurant and everybody who was watching the broadcast cried out when they heard [Ang Lee had won]."[44]

When Lee, in the auditorium, heard his name read as the winner of the Best Director Academy Award, he stood up and hugged Jane Lin—the wife who had faithfully supported him and never given up on his dreams—seated beside him. As he made his way to the stage, he gave actor Jake Gyllenhaal a half-embrace, no doubt confident that everyone in the film would soon be honored by a Best Picture win. Arriving at the podium, he said softly, "I wish I knew how to quit you." The audience waited uncertainly; then Ang Lee laughed, to signal the joke. Still, the meaning was obscure; did he mean that he didn't want to compete for Academy Awards anymore, or that he wanted to quit moviemaking?

He continued his speech: "I want to thank two people who don't even exist. . . . Their names are Ennis and Jack, and they taught all of us who made *Brokeback Mountain* so much about not just the gay men and women whose love is denied by society, but just as important, the greatness of love itself." He praised the artistry of Annie Proulx (writer of the original short story), and screenwriters Larry McMurtry and Diana Ossana. In the audience, Diana Ossana had begun to cry; in a gallant display of old-world charm, Larry McMurtry offered her his handkerchief. "Thank you members of the Academy, for this great honor," Lee continued. He thanked everyone at Focus Features, including David Linde and James Schamus. He thanked his wife Jane and his boys Haan and Mason by name, saying, "I love you. On *Brokeback*, I felt you with me every day." Jane beamed at her husband. "I just did this movie after my father passed away. More than any other, I made this for him."

In his acceptance speech, Lee made a point of sharing the honor with the Chinese people around the world, regardless of their country of origin: "And finally to my mother and family and everybody in Taiwan, Hong Kong, and China." In making this statement, he invoked the transnational identity shared by the people of Taiwan, Hong Kong, and China; similarly, he was recognizing his position in a Chinese filmmaking tradition without national boundaries or borders. In addition, following the growing trend at the increasingly multicultural and multilingual Academy Awards, he spoke in Mandarin at the end of his speech, saying *"Xiexie dajia de guanxin,"* which means "Thank you for caring."

In Taipei that morning the euphoria could be felt in the streets, in convenience stores, in restaurants, in parks; even the taxi drivers grinned widely and said, "I'm so happy to hear the great news about Ang Lee." Asia celebrated with great pride and joy.[45] Newspapers praised his win for days, calling him, "The Glory of Asia."

Brokeback Mountain—*After the Academy Awards*

The peace on Lee's face as he won the Academy Award for Best Director belied the controversy that had surrounded *Brokeback Mountain* both prior to and following the awards ceremony. Immediately following the Best Director win, *Brokeback Mountain* went on to lose to *Crash* (2004) for Best Picture of 2005. It was a startling upset—*Brokeback Mountain* had been heavily favored to win—so unexpected that even the *Crash* producers were visibly caught by surprise (demonstrated by their stunned appearance and seemingly unrehearsed acceptance speech). *Brokeback Mountain*'s loss stirred up a new wave of controversy almost immediately. For example, after the ceremony, just minutes after Lee won his Best Director award, reporters in the postshow interviews bombarded him with questions about whether *Brokeback Mountain*'s loss was a snub against homosexuals. It was a familiar topic—James Schamus and Ang Lee, as well as the principal actors, Heath Ledger and Jake Gyllenhaal, had continually dealt with the homosexuality controversy since the film had been released. In this case, without taking the reporters' bait, Lee replied with utter grace: "You're asking me a question and I don't know the answer . . . Congratulations to the *Crash* filmmakers."[46]

When *Brokeback Mountain* lost as Best Film in 2006, critics of the Academy's decision were up in arms. For example, Annie Proulx wrote a sour-grapes rant for *The Guardian* in Britain, accusing the Academy of homophobia and caustically skewering the entertainment industry of Los Angeles, which kept the *Brokeback Mountain* controversy going on into its second week.[47] CNN picked up the story " 'Brokeback' author: We Were Robbed," in which Proulx described Academy voters as "living cloistered lives behind wrought-iron gates or in deluxe rest-homes, out of touch not only with the shifting larger culture and the yeasty ferment that is America these days, but also out of touch with their own segregated city."[48] Even Lee's own brother, Khan Lee, who runs a Taiwan-based company in television production and film distribution, weighed in with the claim that America "kept the top award at home" for reasons of "nationalism." This charge of not giving the top award of Best Film to an Asian-directed movie was made under the premise that the award, if given to Lee's film, would be perceived as going "abroad" to Asia, rather than being given to the all-American, LA-produced *Crash*. This theory seems far-fetched, however, because of the thrust of the film's narrative—what could be more American than a story about two cowboys? If the film had won Best Picture, it surely would not have been viewed as a distinctly "Asian" victory.

In addition to these arguments, the film continued to be caught between the agendas of gay advocacy groups and American conservatives. Gay activists praised the cultural breakthrough represented by *Brokeback Mountain*, which they described as "frankly gay love in a mainstream movie starring A-list actors"[49]— conveniently omitting the fact that Heath Ledger, Michelle Williams, Jake Gyllenhaal, and Anne Hathaway were not A-list when they were cast. Meanwhile, conservatives actively condemned the film. In a particularly biting polemic, Stephen D. Greydanus, film reviewer for the online Decent Films Guide, said that *Brokeback Mountain* "may be the most profoundly anti-Western film ever made, not only post-modern and post-heroic, but post-Christian and post-human."[50] Conservatives accused Lee of making a "gay western *Wuthering Heights*,"[51] and claimed that liberal media and critics were using *Brokeback Mountain* as an excuse to "shove the gay agenda down people's throats."[52] The 78th Academy Awards ceremony was labeled "the year of the gay agenda"[53] because the top two contenders for the Best Actor award were both actors playing homosexuals: *Brokeback Mountain*'s Heath Ledger was in a very close contest with Philip Seymour Hoffman (star of the biopic *Capote*, 2005) for Best Actor.

In addition to the ongoing polemical debate, *Brokeback Mountain* continued to face censorship, not only in the U.S., where it was banned by towns in several states including Washington and Utah, but in countries abroad as well. On the eve of its scheduled opening, the Bahamian government's Plays and Films Control Board banned the showing of *Brokeback Mountain*, sparking off protests by gay activists, free-speech advocates, and theater owners in the Caribbean country. Chavasse Turnquest-Liriano, liaison officer for the control board, was quoted by the Associated Press as saying, "The board chose to ban it because it shows extreme homosexuality, nudity and profanity, and we feel that it has no value for the Bahamian public."[54] *Brokeback Mountain* was also completely banned in China (where, until 2002, homosexuality was considered a mental illness), and in Turkey the film was given a strict rating limiting its audience to viewers over 18.

To add to *Brokeback Mountain*'s woes, another attack came from the inside: actor Randy Quaid, who had played the fairly minor role of Joe Aguirre in the film, sued Focus Features and *Brokeback Mountain*'s producers James Schamus and David Linde, claiming he had been tricked into taking a low salary for the film. At the end of March 2006, Randy Quaid filed a $10 million lawsuit against the producers, claiming they misled him into believing that the film was "a low-budget art-house film with no prospect of making any money" so that he would sign on for a nominal sum. Quaid said he agreed to "donate" his performance rather than request his customary seven-figure fee plus a percentage of the box office gross, because the filmmakers convinced him it was a low-budget picture with no commercial potential. Quaid said in the lawsuit that he originally was approached in 2004 by Ang Lee, who told him, "We have very little money; everyone is making a sacrifice to make this film." The film then went on to become a box office hit, grossing around US$160 million worldwide. Quaid charged in the lawsuit that he was the victim of a deliberate, preplanned "movie laundering scheme" intended to obtain his services as an actor in *Brokeback Mountain* "on economically unfavorable art-film terms."[55]

This is an ungrounded charge, since the film's makers historically faced repeated obstacles in raising backing for the screenplay, the rights to which were purchased by the screenwriters themselves. All producers considered the film a risk; screenwriter Diana Ossana became one of the producers herself. Having finally received tentative backing, the small group consisting of screenwriters Diana Ossana and Larry McMurtry, along with James Schamus and Ang Lee, set out to make a small film that no one else had dared to make for eight years previously—they clearly were not expecting the film to be a financial success. Diana Ossana, in an essay entitled "Climbing *Brokeback Mountain*" published before the charge was brought, confirmed that "*Brokeback Mountain* was filmed on a tight, modest budget."[56] She even relates how her family and friends pitched in to help with details around the set. In addition, Lee has said this film is the first he had made with such a small budget since making *Eat Drink Man Woman* in 1994. No one expected the film to make any money. The lawsuit was finally dropped in May 2006, with Quaid claiming to have been paid a bonus, and Focus Features denying any settlement had been made.

Despite the Academy Award loss to *Crash* for Best Film, *Brokeback Mountain* was still a record-breaking film and an international phenomenon. During the awards' season leading up to the Academy Awards in early March, the film became one of the most honored movies in cinematic history. The list of the awards won by the film is long; it had more Best Picture and Director wins than previous Academy Award–winners *Schindler's List* (1993) and *Titanic* (1997) combined. Just to name a few, it won various awards at the Golden Globes, the British Academy (BAFTA), the Producers, Directors, and Screen Actors Guilds, the Writers Guild of America, the NY Film Critic's Circle, the LA Film Critics Association, the National Board of Review, and the Film Independent Spirit Awards. In addition, indicative of its cultural importance, *Brokeback Mountain* may ultimately be remembered for its parodies—one of the clues that the film truly penetrated the national consciousness and left a lasting legacy. The parodies include countless late-night television skits, over 150 YouTube videos satirizing the trailer and film which have been uploaded by viewers in an irrepressible online homage, and a fake Marlboro advertisement with two cowboys saying to their cigarettes "I wish I knew how to quit you." Host of the ceremony, political wit Jon Stewart, added his voice to the mix when he said: "Not all gay people are virile cowboys. Some are actually effete New York intellectuals."[57]

Indeed, there has been an explosion of scholarship on *Brokeback Mountain* in academic circles, and the cultural impact of this film, nine years after its release date, has yet to be fully measured. Two full-length volumes of scholarly essays have appeared thus far. The first, Jim Stacy's *Reading Brokeback Mountain: Essays on the Story and the Film* (2007), is a collection of fifteen critical essays and a selected bibliography of nearly 130 scholarly sources on the film compiled from various disciplines, including literature, anthropology, sociology, psychology, and popular culture. The second, *The Brokeback Book: From Story to Cultural Phenomenon* (2011), is an eclectic collection of both scholarly and personal essays edited by William R. Handley, in which the contributors situate *Brokeback Mountain* in relation to gay civil rights, the cinematic and literary western, the Chinese value of forbearance, male melodrama, and urban and rural working lives across generations and genders. Unquestionably, few films have inspired as much passion and debate—or produced as many contradictory responses—as writers, journalists, scholars, and ordinary viewers continue to explore the film's ongoing cultural and political significance.[58]

After Brokeback: Lust/Caution *and* Taking Woodstock

After his astonishingly diverse forays into English-language film with *Hulk* and *Brokeback Mountain*, Lee returned to Chinese-language cinema with the film *Lust/Caution*, based on a 26-page short story by noted twentieth-century Chinese author Eileen Chang (Zhang Ailing, 1920–1995). Set in Shanghai's golden period between the 1930s and 1940s, the story focuses on a young secret agent who tries to seduce and assassinate a pro-Japanese collaborator working for the Wang Jingwei government, a puppet government set up during the Japanese occupation of Shanghai during World War II. The film is shot in a film noir style appropriate to the time period it portrays, representing Ang Lee's first experimentation with the genre of film noir and espionage-thriller.

Previously, Ang Lee purchased rights to the Eileen Chang short story "Lust, Caution," which is relatively unknown in the West. Coincidentally, the publisher New York Review Books, teamed with well-known American translator Karen Kingsbury, brought out a translation of Chang's works entitled *Love in a Fallen City* in October 2006. Eileen Chang, who has been listed alongside Chekhov, Hawthorne, Balzac, Auden, and Colette, is already renowned in China for her prolific essays, short stories, and novellas which reflect her experience growing up in a wealthy but dysfunctional family. As a young woman in Japanese-occupied Shanghai, she was able to publish the stories and essays (collected in two volumes, *Romances*, 1944, and *Written on Water*, 1945) that quickly established her as a literary phenomenon. The rise of Communist influence made it increasingly difficult for Chang to continue living in Shanghai; she moved to Hong Kong in 1952, then immigrated to the United States three years later. She never returned to China for the rest of her long life. Eileen Chang is a famously rich and complex stylist who is now considered one of the greatest Chinese authors of the twentieth century. According to Kingsbury:

> "Lust, Caution" is a rather unusual story within Chang's oeuvre, because it's indebted to Cold War spy fiction and the Hollywood tradition of the action-suspense thriller. . . . Chang's early-period storytelling takes place at the intersections of late-Qing and early modern cultures. Her story "Lust, Caution" crossed those earlier divides. It's more entirely, less ambiguously modern.[59]

Eileen Chang's work has attracted other directors in the past; two well-known film versions of her stories are *Red Rose White Rose* (*Hong meigui, bai meigui*, 1994) and *Love in a Fallen City* (*Qing cheng zhi lian*, 1987). However, these films have never garnered much attention outside of Asia. While Lee's *Lust/Caution* seemed a timely opportunity to give Eileen Chang's brilliant fiction a greater audience beyond Asian borders, the unexpected result was that the film instead touched off a major controversy in China about patriotism (by contrast the film was revered in Taiwan and Hong Kong), and the main actress, Tang Wei, was excoriated for her anti-patriotic actions in the film and banned from the film industry (she was finally allowed to make a film again in late 2010). Since Lee had weathered the now-historic controversy over *Brokeback Mountain*, it was a shock to once again be at the center of a maelstrom over another one of his films.

Not surprisingly, following the challenging experiences of making *Brokeback Mountain* and *Lust/Caution*, Lee pointedly stated that after making a series of brutally emotional films, he needed to choose a ligher topic. *Taking Woodstock* is Ang Lee's "happiest" film, a film that meditates on the meaning of nostalgia and transformation. Lee has said he wanted to make a film that "bookends" with his bleak view of the 1973 aftermath of 1960s excess—this is the prequel to *The Ice Storm*. *Taking Woodstock* tells the story of a Greenwich Village artist, Elliot Tiber, who inadvertently helps to spark a cultural revolution by offering the organizers of the Woodstock Music and Arts Festival a venue at his family's Catskills motel. Emboldened by the burgeoning gay rights movement yet still tied to tradition in the form of the family motel business, Tiber steps in to help after Woodstock Ventures loses its permit from the nearby town of Wallkill, New York. The venue is switched to Max Yasgur's adjacent farm near White Lake, which becomes the center of the counterculture celebration that would ultimately be remembered as one of the greatest events in the annals of rock and roll history. Lee wanted to capture the innocence of the time, a time of naïve hope and spirit, absent of political cynicism. Producer and screenwriter James Schamus has attributed the film's relatively tepid reception to the fact that the movie did not attempt to restage any of the musical performances of the Woodstock concert itself, and he added humorously that when people see an Ang Lee film, they want to be "sublimely depressed."[60] The film also became known as Lee's third foray into the topic of homosexuality as Stephen Holden has stated "the movie explicitly connects Woodstock to the gay-liberation movement," although as Holden admits "[it is] a relationship that is made much more emphatically in Mr. Tiber's memoir."[61]

The Second Academy Award for Best Director: Life of Pi

Seven years after winning the Academy award for *Brokeback Mountain*, Ang Lee found his film *Life of Pi* nominated for an astonishing eleven Academy Awards. This had not seemed likely at the beginning of the filmmaking process. *Life of Pi* was a huge gamble for Lee and Fox 2000, with a budget of over US$100 million, and another US$25 million for the 3D alone. Lee has said in interviews that he was motivated to do the impossible: to make a film out of a novel that was unfilmable. In *Life of Pi*, Lee took on an entirely new technology and revolutionized the field—again. Lee has said: "I wouldn't have been able to do this without doing *Hulk*"[62]—referring to the fact that he was again a pioneer in a new cinematic language (3D), the language of the future of technological development in film that was just in its beginning stages (as CGI was when Lee made *Hulk*):

> It was really intimidating, more so than *Hulk* I believe . . . [I knew it would] be just as expensive and with technology that's unknown to me and I didn't know if it would work or not. . . . Rolling such a big dice and not really knowing whether it would work or not in the mainstream, it was pretty scary.[63]

Some of the challenges Lee faced were framing the story, a first-person narrative, as a third-person narrative, which he solved by using the framework of the story told by Pi to the Canadian writer, and the challenges of the "fantastic" or nonrational elements of the story:

> The book provides you a grand illusion and it defends it. It's very hard to do in movies so I thought of a narrator that has a first-person sort of feeling but also a third-person perspective. So I thought that it could be the older Pi telling the writer his story. That was a break for me. Then I thought if I do it in 3D, maybe people will be more open to something new (chuckles).[64]

The filming of *Life of Pi* began with a two-week shoot in India in March 2011. After ten days in Pondicherry, where the story opens, Lee moved the crew to Munnar, a small town in the hills of South India. He also shot for several months in Taiwan, in a huge water tank created in an airport hangar in Taichung, where Lee designed a pool for the film's ocean scenes nearly on the scale of *Titanic* (1997). He also faced the practical concerns of finding a 16-year-old boy actor to star in the film: Suraj Sharma's final monologue involving violence, murder, and cannibalism was an extremely challenging piece of acting for an untrained actor, reminiscent of the performances Lee pulled out of his young cast in *The Ice Storm*. In addition, Lee spent an entire year on the editing process alone, seamlessly weaving the tiger from both a real one and a digital creation.

Lee's efforts paid off—again. When he was called to the stage for the Best Director Academy Award in 2013 for *Life of Pi*, the entire audience rose to their feet in a standing ovation. Lee bowed deeply before them, with typical modesty, before beginning his speech. During his acceptance speech, Lee first thanked the "movie god," then author Yann Martel for "writing this incredible, inspiring book" and then the 3,000 people who worked on *Life of Pi* with him, including crews from India, Canada, and Taiwan. He gave special thanks to Taiwan, where over 90 percent of the film was made. "I [could not] make this movie without the help of Taiwan," Lee said in his speech. "I want to thank everybody there [who] helped us, especially the city of Taichung." He thanked the audience, saying, "Thank you [for] believing this story and sharing this incredible journey with me." Poignantly, along with his family in Taiwan and his sons, Lee thanked his wife Jane Lin in his speech, saying, "We will have been married thirty years this summer. I love you." For those familiar with the history of support Lin offered her husband at the beginning of his career to achieve his dreams, this was very touching, indeed. Lee concluded his speech with a salutation in Hindi: "Namaste."

Following the ceremony, Ma Ying-jeou, the president of Taiwan, sent a telegram to congratulate Lee, and Jason Hu, mayor of Taichung, pledged to award him an honorary citizen's medal from the municipal authorities of Taichung, and thanked Lee for bringing more recognition to Taiwan by making his film there. Lee won Best Director for *Life of Pi* over the highly-favored Steven Spielberg for *Lincoln* (he had also won over Spielberg, up for *Munich*, in 2006). Interestingly, just as *Brokeback Mountain* lost to *Crash* in the same circumstances seven years before, *Life of Pi* did not win Best Picture; that award went to Ben Affleck's Iran hostage-crisis drama *Argo*.

Conclusion: Security/Insecurity

Taiwan has produced an "autobiography" of Ang Lee in Chinese, entitled "A Ten-year Dream of Cinema." This book, edited by Zhang Jingpei in 2002, was put together from interview notes and written as a first-person account. By Zhang's indication, Lee does not like to sit for interviews and rarely grants them, suggesting instead that "If you want to understand me, it's all in my films."[65] John Lahr echoes this in his interview where Lee describes himself as "lacklustre" in real life, a man who only comes to life when working. "I don't have a hobby," he says, "I don't have a life."[66] Ang Lee thus asserts that he cannot be fully known or understood apart from his films—that the films he has made are the most articulate record of who he is and what his motivations are.

His films have always been full of risk, both topically and stylistically. His willingness to walk the line between the known and the unknown, and his humility in making his art with a seeming detachment from the outcome, is what makes his work so extraordinary. A quotation from Lee sums up the Taoist-inflected thought behind his filmmaking:

> Nothing stands still. That's important in my movies. People want to believe in something, want to hang on to something to get security and want to trust each other. But things change. Given enough time, nothing stands still. I think seeking for security and lack of security is another [important theme] in my movies.[67]

The singlemost remarkable aspect of Lee's career—besides its success—is that it almost never started. It now seems nearly incomprehensible that the world-famous director did not make his first feature-length film—basically did not begin his career—until the age of 37. It is even more astonishing to consider that from the age of 31 to 37, while living in New York, he could not find work. Six years is a long time to hold on to a dream of filmmaking, especially when all evidence points to its impossibility: Lee's wife was supporting the family financially, his father had given up hope on his eldest son's future, and Lee was already in his thirties, growing older and older, without any prospects or hopeful signs. It is interesting to think about Lee at the age of 37, just before his luck changed—his life going nowhere, shuttling back and forth from New York to California chasing endless possibilities, with dozens of half-written or fully-completed screenplays that no one in America would produce. The turnaround had yet to come for this quiet man with a foreign accent who could not find anyone in Hollywood to take him seriously.

Despite the apparent hopelessness of these early days, when things changed, they changed dramatically. Although Lee got his foot in the door when he won the Taiwan government's contest to make his first movie, *Pushing Hands*, his international career did not truly begin until *The Wedding Banquet*, when he won the top prize in the Berlin International Film Festival and realized his life would never be the same again. After *Sense and Sensibility*, Lee's work was praised but almost no one knew his name (and those who saw his movies thought they must have been directed by a woman). *Crouching Tiger, Hidden Dragon* made his name recognizable on a wide scale for the first time, and finally he achieved world renown with the Best Director win for *Brokeback Mountain*. Thus, from the age of 37 to the age of 51, the director emerged from humiliating obscurity, rejection, and failure, to become the most celebrated Asian filmmaker in history.

Ang Lee's example is one of tenacity and sheer determination; he made almost a film a year for the first six years of his career: 1991, 1993, 1994, 1995, and 1997. He is a director who dared to imagine the impossible; even while making *Pushing Hands* on a shoestring budget in 1991 he was dreaming of making a martial arts epic that would redefine the genre. He is a director who is not afraid of failing; he had already failed so often and so completely that he was more able to take risks—like making *Brokeback Mountain*. He is a director unafraid of the powerful emotions evoked by volatile periods in history—Watergate, the Vietnam War, the American Civil War, World War II China—unafraid of the power of a personal narrative despite its political implications—*Brokeback Mountain*, *The Wedding Banquet*—and unafraid to tamper with the time-honored traditional filming of a British classic—*Sense and Sensibility*. His fearlessness has even led him to risk failure on a spectacular level—for example, with the artistically visionary but commercially disastrous *Hulk*. The extravagance of Lee's success and failure comes from his being already inured to failure—he had nothing left to lose.

Lee summed up his directing experience in a *New York Times* interview in 2012:

> My ideas and not me are at the center of attention. A movie seems to have a life of its own. You don't create it, you initiate it because you get a call. It's not about dictatorship. You have to be humble, you have to be tender, communicate sensitively, admit your shortcomings, share your dreams and allow them to be told.[68]

Ang Lee's films are noted for their widely divergent genres and unpredictable subject matter. However, Lee's films share a single thread: his own unique vision; his own dreams. While his films may appear dissimilar to viewers, they are all simply a part of Lee's own imaginative world, a world that he inhabits. Lee lives inside his films, where they are all part of the same world—his own.

TWO

Ang Lee as Director: His Position in Asian and World Cinema

ANG LEE IS a transcendent filmmaker who has not only brought worldwide attention and wider reception to Chinese cinema, but he has also gone beyond his Chinese roots to become a postmodern and post-boundaried artist who moves as easily in Western genres as he does in Chinese. He is a postnational artist because he has crossed and blurred the boundaries not only of the Chinese diaspora (the meaning of the word *diaspora* is, literally, "the scattering of seeds"—a reference to the dispersed and displaced transnational communities of ethnic Chinese living outside of China and all around the globe) but of the cultures of East and West. Lee's duality—this unresolved tension—is his trademark. His films concern themselves with everyday decisions made from a plurality of possible options and intimately connected to the (re)making of self-identity (see Giddens 1990) and his work concerns this crisis of identity in the construction of social forms. The problems of interpreting Ang Lee's films include cultural studies of meaning, discourse, aesthetics, value, textuality, form, and narrativity. In evaluating his films, one must therefore consider the role of meanings, symbols, cultural frames, and cognitive schema in the theorizations of social process and institution; he deals with sweeping cultural and social themes such as tradition, the sacred, feminism, and cultural production.

Historically, Lee has been considered by Chinese scholars as a marginalized and even Americanized director. For that reason, he has been excluded from many major discussions on Chinese film directors, especially those that focus on the distinct styles of directors from mainland China. When his films have been discussed, they have been taken as hybridized culture, and with Westernization associated with marketing transnational China as a globalized culture, blurred for Western tastes. For example, *New Chinese Cinemas* (Browne et al. 1994) did not include Ang Lee, although it included Hou Hsiao-hsien and Edward Yang from Taiwan cinema. This work pointed out the difference between Taiwan New Cinema and the so-called "Fifth Generation" filmmaking in the People's Republic created at a time contemporaneous with it.[1] Despite its title, Lee also did not figure in Rey Chow's *Primitive Passions: Visuality, Sexuality, and Ethnography in Contemporary Chinese Cinema* (1995). Although Lee's work does deal with sexuality and passion, Chow did not choose to include films outside the national boundary of mainland China. A 2001 volume, Tonglin Lu's *Confronting Modernity in the Cinemas of Taiwan and Mainland China*, left him out entirely, even while including Taiwanese filmmakers Hou Hsiao-hsien, Edward Yang, and Tsai Ming-liang, with whom he is often grouped. This book takes into account, of course, differences between the political, social, and economic systems of Taiwan and mainland China, and shows how the process of modernization has challenged traditional cultural norms in both, taking different forms on both sides of the Taiwan Strait.

One of the earliest articles to treat Lee's films as part of the Chinese film tradition was Wei Ming Dariotis and Eileen Fung's "Breaking the Soy Sauce Jar: Diaspora and Displacement in the Films of Ang Lee" (1997). In addition to discussing Lee's early Chinese trilogy, this essay also discussed his Western film *Sense and Sensibility*, applying Chinese critical theory to locate that film in the construct of Lee's "Chinese" filmmaking tradition. Another essay to bring Chinese theory to bear on Lee's English-language work was William Leung's article "Crouching Sensibility, Hidden Sense" (2001), which examined *Sense and Sensibility*'s Romanticism versus Rationalism, and contrasted this cultural dialectic with the Confucianism/Taoism in *Crouching Tiger, Hidden Dragon*. Lee Server's volume, *Asian Pop Cinema: Bombay to Tokyo* (1999) was the first to take Lee's work as representative of Taiwan cinema. Although this book contained only a short chapter on Taiwanese cinema, Lee was featured as the main director from Taiwan. In 2000, a volume produced in China entitled "Ten Chinese Film Directors" (*Huayu dianying shi daoyan*, Yang, ed.) included him in its discussion of ten Chinese—meaning "Chinese-language"—directors. Calling him a "Chinese-language" director is the easiest way to avoid political issues about "China" and "Taiwan"; however, this book's title was not entirely accurate as the writers presented Lee's English-language films as well. Finally, two studies published in 2005 (Chris Berry and Feii Lu's *Island on the Edge: Taiwan New Cinema and After*, and Emilie Yueh-yu Yeh and Darrell W. Davis's *Taiwan Film Directors: A Treasure Island*, 2005) included him in the Taiwanese filmmaking tradition. This lingering difficulty of pigeonholing Lee or fitting his work neatly into a scholarly tradition disappeared in 2006, when Lee won the Academy Award: after this event, China and Taiwan were both eager to claim him as part of their film traditions, and he is no longer overlooked in scholarly studies and edited collections (see, for example, Lim and Ward 2011; Zhang 2012; Rojas and Chow 2013; among others). In 2013, *The Philosophy of Ang Lee* (Arp, Barkman, and McRae, eds.) did not try to categorize him either way, instead opting to analyze his films through Eastern philosophy (Taoist, Confucian, and Buddhist thought) in the first half of the book, and Western philosophy in the latter half, maintaining that Lee's thought is a product of both Chinese and Western influences.

Characteristics of the Cinema of Ang Lee

Globalization and cultural identity. While Lee's three earliest works—*Pushing Hands*, *The Wedding Banquet*, and *Eat Drink Man Woman*—are particularly clear examples of the effects of globalization on cultural identity, his later films such as

The Ice Storm also deal with hybridized identity—or loss of identity—in the face of postmodern global and cultural forms. Lee's films complement the current theoretical orientation of comparative literary and film studies and their focus on the issues of cultural identity and the changes wrought by globalization. This conception of globalization is not only realized as the synthesis and transcendence of opposites but also as the representation of geographic localities and notions of territory—including nationalism, identity, narrative, and ethnicity. The implications of globalization must be considered in light of the relationship between commodity and economic exchange and symbolic and cultural exchange—globalization studies are a continued rethinking of the relation among nations, economies, cultures, social practices, etc. Malcolm Waters (1995) views globalization as fueled by symbolic exchanges, i.e., television, advertising, films, novels, music, fast food—cultural entities that are circulated and recycled simultaneously in many locations throughout the world. The implications of this theoretical paradigm are striking and provide fertile ground for the study of Lee's films, which largely focus on modern or postmodern cultural exchanges, influences, and relationships.

Lee's early trilogy films, *Pushing Hands, The Wedding Banquet*, and *Eat Drink Man Woman*, deal with matters of diasporic identity, introducing issues related to the Chinese diaspora and how they experience networks of communication, commerce, travel, and kinship that connect them. James Clifford theorizes that diasporic identities are formed through hybridization caused by conflict with and intermixture with other cultures, so that "diasporic subjects are distinct versions of modern, transnational, intercultural experiences." He continues: "The centering of diasporas around an axis of origin and return overrides the specific local interactions (identifications and ruptures, both constructive and defensive) necessary for the maintenance of

The effect of globalization: An American fast-food corporation is contrasted with traditional Chinese cooking in *Eat Drink Man Woman* (1994).

diasporic social forms. The empowering paradox of diaspora is that dwelling here assumes solidarity and connection *there*. But *there* is not necessarily a single place or an exclusivist nation."² Thus the Cliffordian model highlights the fluidity of the diasporic identity, both in its formation and in its origin. Lee deals with the changing nature of the Chinese diaspora as well as the conflicting and hybridizing elements between the cultures of China/Taiwan and the United States.

Homosexuality. Ang Lee was the first Taiwanese director, with *The Wedding Banquet* (1993), to deal seriously and sympathetically with the topic of homosexuality. Reasons for this will be explored further, but an easy comparison is the feeling of rootlessness that is reflected in the Hong Kong filmmaker Wong Kar-wai's gay road movie, *Happy Together* (*Chunguang zhaxie*, 1997). Hong Kong's position as a city straddling East and West, with its mixed Chinese and British heritage, contributed to its troubled identity. This identity crisis was made more intense in 1984 when the Sino-British Joint Declaration announced the return of Hong Kong to China, causing worry over the disappearance of Hong Kong's former lifestyle after the 1997 handover. In much the same way, Lee's Taiwan is a nation in transition with an identity crisis of its own. Wong Kar-wai also made *Ashes of Time* (*Dongxie xidu*, 1994), a *wuxia* (martial chivalry) narrative, and his films *Happy Together* and *In the Mood for Love* (*Huayang nianhua*, 2000) have established him as one of the most honored Hong Kong film directors in the arena of world cinema. Wong acknowledged that having his characters escape reality in Argentina (in *Happy Together*) helped emphasize the theme of exile. Stephen Teo observes, "In making his two main characters gay and cutting them adrift in a faraway country, Wong was making a point about the socio-political ramifications of 1997, the fact that the one group in Hong Kong that felt the most anxious and had the most to lose in terms of individual and civil liberties was the gay community."³ While Ang Lee's take on homosexuality has no political overtones, it seems highly plausible that the homosexual theme in both films comes from the sense of rootlessness and lack of identity brought on by the unique political situations in both Hong Kong and Taiwan. Homosexuality is thus a common trope for shifting identity, lack of security, the purposelessness of an unknown future—the lack of direction, alienation, anonymity, and decadence caused by lack of identity associated with postmodern Hong Kong and Taiwan.

Patriarchy. It has been argued that Lee's films reconstruct the traditional patriarchal order. Initially his early trilogy films seem to challenge traditional values, and threaten to render the traditional patriarchy obsolete, presenting the father figure in a position of weakness with slightly comic overtones—i.e., the displaced father facing the derision of his American daughter-in-law in *Pushing Hands*, or the visiting father "deceived" by his gay son in *The Wedding Banquet*. At the same time, the men and women of the younger generation are initially characterized as contemporary and "relevant" in their ability to negotiate the (post)modern world with its Western values, roles, expectations, and institutions. However, by the end of each of the early trilogy films, the father figure redeems himself, winning the sympathy, reverence, and respect that were traditionally accorded him, and reestablishes the conservative patriarchal order. This is especially remarkable in *The Wedding Banquet*, in which the patriarchy is redeemed in the face of gay and women's liberation—the father indeed receives his wish to have a grandchild to carry on the family line. Thus, tensions between patriarchal authority and postmodern globalized society are renegotiated to the benefit of tradition, in such a way as to redeem and honor the father figure. Lee's films ultimately manage to reinstate the patriarchy in a hybridized postmodern economy and culture. In *Sense and Sensibility*, the displacement of the father figure happens in the opening moments of the film, when he is removed from the family by death—what follows is a need to reestablish the patriarchal order so as to recover the dislocated familial and societal harmony. In *The Ice Storm*, the final moments of the film show the remorse of the father for abdicating his position of patriarchal responsibility. In this way it can be seen that reestablishment and reinforcement of the patriarchy are repeated themes not only in Ang Lee's Chinese films but in his English-language films as well.

Feminism. While it may seem to contradict Lee's respect for the father figure, feminism is a topic that is also linked to his films. He often deals sympathetically with the theme of a repressed woman operating within the strict confines of duty in an attempt to fulfill her proper role, while clearly reflecting a lack of fulfillment in, for example, *Sense and Sensibility*'s Elinor Dashwood (Emma Thompson), *The Ice Storm*'s Elena Hood (Joan Allen), and *Crouching Tiger, Hidden Dragon*'s Shu Lien (Michelle Yeoh). Ang Lee's films are known for being female-centered—the roles for actresses in his films are developed and nuanced. From the exploration of sisterly bonds in *Sense and Sensibility* and *Eat Drink Man Woman*, to the dissection of female sexuality in *The Ice Storm*, and the female-driven martial arts film *Crouching Tiger, Hidden Dragon*, Lee is known for his focus on feminine concerns. Often his films have multiple storylines which follow the inner lives of his female protagonists and give them equal or greater screen time than the men. Some examples include the highly complex interweaving of storylines in *Eat Drink Man Woman*, which chronicle six separate accounts of love affairs (two unsuccessful), and *Sense and Sensiblity*'s astounding exploration of two aspects of the female psyche. Special attention is given in *Brokeback Mountain* to the effects of the men's choices on the women in their lives, particularly their wives and daughters. By the same token, Lee has often characterized his principal male figures as weak or indecisive. Some examples of this are *Sense and Sensibility*'s Edward Ferrars (Hugh Grant), *The Ice Storm*'s Ben Hood (Kevin Kline), and even *Crouching Tiger, Hidden Dragon*'s Li Mu Bai (Chow Yun-fat), who becomes distracted by the young Jen (Zhang Ziyi) and waits until it is too late (he is dying) to declare his love for Shu Lien.

The Outsider. Ang Lee's films deal with questions of "the outsider"—a character who is excluded by a difference of language, cultural codes of behavior, race, or even sexual orientation. For example, the three films in his early trilogy invoke representations of the resultant hybridized and postmodernized identity of the younger, Westernized generation, leaving the traditional patriarch as the "outsider." The diasporic global identity of Westernized Taiwanese, such as the Taiwan-American characters of *Pushing Hands* and *The Wedding Banquet*, or the Westernized daughters in *Eat Drink Man Woman*, conflicts with traditional Chinese values, calling into question the legitimacy of the traditional "father figure" role. *Ride with the Devil* chronicles the growing friendship between two "outsiders" fighting on the side of the South in

Civil War America: German immigrant Jake Roedel (Tobey Maguire) and former slave Daniel Holt (Jeffrey Wright) become unlikely friends as they continue to face the disrespect, insults, and abuse of their fellow Southerners. Similarly, in *Brokeback Mountain*, Lee explores the issue of homosexuality in 1960s rural America, where Ennis (Heath Ledger) and Jack (Jake Gyllenhaal) feel like outsiders as they face the restrictions of traditional social expectations; in *Taking Woodstock*, he revisits this idea through Elliot Teichberg's (Demetri Martin) odyssey of self-discovery that takes place under the watchful eye of his more conservative parents. With the topic of "the outsider" or "the foreigner," he taps into a wealth of personal experience due to his own cultural displacement—Lee's empathy for his "unacceptable" characters comes through very strongly in all of his films (although his struggle to win the viewer's sympathy for Hulk proved to be almost too far a stretch).

Family. The theme of the family, especially the different generations within the same family, is one which characterizes each of Ang Lee's films. His early trilogy dealt heavily with father/son and father/daughter relationships. *Sense and Sensibility* had representatives from four different generations of women,[4] *The Ice Storm* was as much about the teenage children as about their parents, and *Ride with the Devil* focused on an entire generation of young, disenfranchised Southern men. *Crouching Tiger, Hidden Dragon* brought generational conflicts to the fore, as the mature older couple differed greatly in codes of conduct from the younger generation. *Hulk* was principally about children trapped by their parents' negative legacies. The screenplay of *Brokeback Mountain* filled in extensive backstory for the characters Ennis and Jack, greatly expanding on Annie Proulx's original descriptions of their parents, wives, and children, including two memorable Thanksgiving dinner scenes contrasting their two families. In *Lust/Caution*, the loss of family ties during wartime, especially the absence of paternal love, drives Wang Chia-chih into the dangerous psychological vulnerability upon which the entire plot hinges. Finally, *Taking Woodstock* and *Life of Pi* are both "coming-of-age" stories that deal heavily with the influence of family: both films feature the protagonist coming to terms with parental control versus the personal freedom to forge a new identity as a mature adult.

The Long Take and Framing. Finally, the signature film techniques of Ang Lee include his use of the long take and framing (positioning the shot within a static frame) to tell the story from a distance. In this way the actors' bodies, gestures, and posture can be used in silence as telling details to advance the narrative. This allows the actors to find their own movements and spaces, and to interact with their quotidian surroundings in the most unexpected ways. This technique of filming is common among Chinese film directors of Taiwan New Cinema, especially Hou Hsiao-hsien, a point which will be discussed further in this chapter. The use of framing to tell the story slows the pace of the film; the shot is measured and deliberate, and the actor in the frame must perform using his or her entire body, from head to toe, rather than just his or her facial expression and voice. The long take also allows the viewer to study and observe the actor, coming to know and being moved by his or her humanity. One example of this is the early sequence from *Pushing Hands* in which the American daughter-in-law, Martha (Deb Snyder), and the Chinese father-in-law, Master Chu

(Sihung Lung), sit with their backs to each other, together and yet apart, expressing an aching loneliness caused by cultural difference. Later, when, without speaking, they clean up the kitchen together, their hands finally work in tandem. Another example is the scene from *Sense and Sensibility* in which Hugh Grant as Edward Ferrars and Emma Thompson as Elinor Dashwood attempt to communicate but their body language nonetheless expresses the social restrictions that subconsciously govern their actions. Lee describes this scene in a 1996 interview: "I insisted they should just sit there for one long shot, with Hugh Grant's face in shadow, not being able to move, or touch each other. . . . I think that's very Chinese."[5] Finally, there are the opening scenes of *Brokeback Mountain*, in which the two young ranch hands stand apart silently in a dusty parking lot, sizing each other up. This silence between two young cowboys, inexpressive because of their habit of never speaking unless they need to, rings very true, and the scene is narrated completely through physical signs and bodily posture.

Lee's early films were considered as part of the rubric of Taiwan New Wave Cinema, largely a movement in the 1980s, which borrows its name from the French New Wave movement. (Later critics have revised the treatment of Taiwan New Wave and, for the sake of clarity, grouped together all of the filmmakers from the Taiwan New Wave period and afterward as "Taiwan New Cinema.") His early films do indeed share characteristics with the works of Taiwanese filmmakers Hou Hsiao-hsien, Edward Yang, and Tsai Ming-liang, which will be explored further in this chapter. However, when Lee began directing mainstream English-language films, he no longer fit neatly into this conceptualization.

Although a 1991 book edited by Chris Berry, *Perspectives on Chinese Cinema*, marginalizes Taiwan and Hong Kong cinema by separating them from the cinema of mainland China and giving them much shorter treatment (two chapters dealing specifically with Taiwan and Hong Kong cinema versus the fourteen chapters devoted to cinema from China), Berry came to the position of wanting to fully include these cinemas within the "Chinese" diaspora. An important article by Chris Berry and Mary Farquhar deals with the topic of Chinese films and the persistence of the "national cinema" (mainland China) paradigm, and the difficulty of fitting "non-nation-state territories" of Hong Kong and Taiwan into that format.[6] Berry argues that Chinese cinema is transnational just as the diaspora is transnational. Coming full circle, Chris Berry published *Chinese Films in Focus* (2003), representing twenty-five individual films from mainland China, Taiwan, and Hong Kong, without differentiating them into categories or separate sections in the table of contents. Instead, the chapters on films from these places show overlap and influence among the films from the entire Chinese-language cinematic tradition.[7]

As Lee's position in world cinema has expanded, so has the academic view of what films fall under the categorization of "Chinese" cinema. In the past two decades, cinema and popular media produced in China, Hong Kong, and Taiwan has been "reimagined" (to use the terminology of Rey Chow, 2000). Chow postulates that Chinese literary and cinematic studies must be reconsidered in light of globalization and cultural trends that have brought the media, celebrities, and films of Hong Kong and Taiwan together into a tradition that must necessarily be also included in the label "Chinese." This is also the position taken by Nick Browne, Paul G. Pickowicz, Vivian Sobchack, and Esther Yau (1994), Sheldon H. Lu (1997), and Chris Berry and Mary Farquhar (2001). While the aforementioned 1994 work (by Browne et al.) used the more hesitant plural *New Chinese Cinemas* before combining different nations and nation-states into the same work, a monograph by Yingjin Zhang does not hesitate to appropriate Taiwan and Hong Kong into an all-inclusive *Chinese National Cinema* (2004). In Sheldon H. Lu and Emilie Yueh-yu Yeh's introduction to their *Chinese-Language Film: Historiography, Poetics, Politics* (2005), the editors also face this difficulty, directly confronting it in the opening paragraph:

> This collection of essays covers the cinematic traditions of mainland China, Taiwan, Hong Kong, and the Chinese diaspora from the beginning of Chinese film history to the present moment. In compiling a highly selective "film historiography," as it were, we editors face once again the dilemma of choice and inclusion—namely, what constitutes "Chinese cinema" or "Chinese-language cinema". As we attempt to come to terms with an ever-evolving phenomenon and a developing subject of investigation, we provisionally define Chinese-language films as films that use predominantly Chinese dialects and are made in mainland China, Taiwan, Hong Kong, and the Chinese diaspora, as well as those produced through transnational collaborations with other film industries.[8]

This passage underscores the difficulty of defining "Chinese" cinema—it is impossible to exactly pinpoint what constitutes a "Chinese" film, not only because "Chinese" diasporas have long been scattered around the globe, but because these groups each may define and document (on film) their own experiences of what it means to be "Chinese." Unlike other countries, too, the very borders of the nation-state known as "China" are under dispute, and often hotly contested. A brief review of more recent academic collections on Chinese cinema show a hyper-awareness of this slippery, changing history: *Perspectives on Chinese Cinema* (Berry 1991), *New Chinese Cinemas: Forms, Identities, and Politics* (Browne et al. 1994), *Transnational Chinese Cinemas: Identity, Nationhood, Gender* (Lu 1997), and more recently, *Reading Chinese Transnationalisms: Society, Literature, Film* (Ng 2006).[9] The founding of the *Journal of Chinese Cinemas* in 2007 and the pluralized title in a recent definitive study, *The Oxford Handbook of Chinese Cinemas* (Rojas and Chow 2013), continue to reiterate the issue.

Finally, Gina Marchetti (2000) and others have attempted to treat Ang Lee's films as the work of an Asian-American artist in the tradition of Wayne Wang, whose feature films on the Chinese-American community—for example, *Chan Is Missing*, (1982), *Dim Sum* (1985), *Eat a Bowl of Tea* (1989), and *The Joy Luck Club* (1993)—have each received attention as Asian-American films. Marchetti concludes that *The Wedding Banquet* daringly serves to bridge the gap between Chinese film and Asian-American film culture:

Wai-Tung and Wei Wei continue to be Chinese, part of a greater China rather than part of a Chinese-American community (let alone an Asian-American body politic) . . . there has been a boom in recent years in films set in American or European Chinatowns, usually produced by Hong Kong or Taiwanese concerns (i.e., Tsai Ming-liang's *What Time is it There?* and Wong Kar-wai's *Happy Together*). Like *The Wedding Banquet*, most of these films deal less with the development of an Asian-American identity among Chinese immigrants than with the creation of a transnational sense of Chinese identity.[10]

Marchetti quotes Lee's characterization of his own experience being Chinese in America: "Wherever you come from, whether it's China or Hong Kong or Taiwan, in New York, you're just Chinese."[11] Emilie Yueh-yu Yeh and Darrell W. Davis (2005) highlight Ang Lee's deliberate preservation/presentation of his Chinese identity: "Lee's outsider status is something he jealously guards, though in the past it was a great burden. He assiduously maintains his Chinese roots, never having applied for American citizenship."[12] Lee also labels himself: "I very much identify myself as a Chinese filmmaker. I was brought up in certain ways that influence my work . . . I lived in a Chinese environment until I was 23 and that is something I cannot change."[13] This statement from a 2005 interview makes it abundantly clear that Lee characterizes himself as Chinese, not Asian-American.

A History of Transnational Chinese Cinema—Some Key Figures

Although the origin of early cinematic history in China dates back to 1896—the year in which the newly-invented medium of film was first exhibited in Shanghai—the most significant developments for the purpose of this book are more recent.[14] One important example is the history of the Shaw Brothers studio, whose films had an influence on the young Ang Lee. Shaw Brothers productions were very popular in the 1950s, 1960s, and 1970s, and their popularity influenced the whole of transnational China. Two of Lee's own cited influences, King Hu and Li Hanxiang, were directors who worked with this studio. The Shaw brothers (originally Xiao) were from Shanghai. They had a studio in the booming film industry of the 1930s in Shanghai, but during the Chinese Civil War and followed by the Japanese invasion of World War II, the film industry was halted and the Shaw brothers moved their studios to Hong Kong. The Shaw Brothers studio, as it came to be known, became the original bedrock of the new film industry in Hong Kong, and went on to become one of the most powerful movie empires in Asia. Almost all the major films from Hong Kong's burgeoning industry, including Li Hanxiang's *The Love Eterne* (*Liang Shanbo yu Zhu Yingtai*, 1963), can credit some involvement from the Shaw brothers. One of the brothers, Run Run Shaw, was knighted by Queen Elizabeth in 1977, ostensibly for his contributions to Chinese and British entertainment.

Ang Lee's major inspiration and influence was a director working mostly in the 1960s and 1970s, King Hu (Hu Jinquan). King Hu's martial arts masterpiece, *A Touch of Zen* (*Xianü*, credited as 1969; actually the film took four years to make, from 1968 to 1972), can be seen as a forerunner for *Crouching Tiger, Hidden Dragon*—Lee has publicly acknowledged his debt to the artistic mastery of Hu in his films. Born in China, King Hu was educated in an arts school in Beijing. During wartime, in 1949, he relocated to Hong Kong, and entered the film industry in 1951 in the art department. In the 1950s he began acting and in 1958 joined the Shaw Brothers studio as a writer and actor (he has a role in *The Love Eterne*), and later a director. In 1967 he left to start his own studio in Taiwan, and returned to Hong Kong in the 1970s. He worked in Hong Kong, Taiwan, and China before his death in Taiwan in 1997. While making his grand opus *A Touch of Zen*, he was criticized for his overly-fastidious and time-consuming working methods. When the film was finished, he was ostracized by the major studios, after which, according to Kwai-Cheung Lo, his career "never fully recovered."[15]

The first major development in film of the transnational Chinese diaspora that garnered the attention of the Western world was the phenomenon Bruce Lee, known in Asia as Li Xiaolong (or "Little Dragon"). Bruce Lee's fame in the West was unprecedented for an Asian; his impact on transnational Chinese culture in the 1970s cannot be underestimated, for his image links Hong Kong and, by extension, the Chinese film industry, with physicality, bodily fitness and prowess, and the martial arts. He is considered a key figure in twentieth-century popular culture, for had it not been for Bruce Lee's kung fu genre movies in the early 1970s, it is uncertain whether the martial arts film genre would have penetrated and influenced mainstream Western cinema and audiences the way it has over the past three decades. Bruce Lee was born in 1940 in the United States when his Cantonese opera-singer father was on tour in San Francisco; as a result he was given dual U.S./Hong Kong citizenship. He spent his childhood in Hong Kong, but when he was a teenager, his parents sent him back to the United States to remove him from gang warfare in Hong Kong, first to northern California and then to Seattle, where he enrolled at the University of Washington to study philosophy. There, he met Linda Emery, whom he later married, and eventually dropped out of school to focus on developing his career as a stunt artist. His stunts eventually brought him to the attention of Los Angeles television producers, and he was contracted to appear in the U.S. television series *The Green Hornet* (1966–67). This constituted the first major visibility for an Asian star in the United States; however, in reality he merely reached cult status among connoisseurs of kung fu action film. Returning to Hong Kong, he made four movies before he died in mysterious circumstances.[16] His last film, *Enter the Dragon* (1973) was released posthumously, cementing his status as a cult hero who died young.[17]

Despite the towering status of Bruce Lee, it was not until the 1980s that the average filmgoer in the West had any interest in or knowledge about Chinese cinema. Interest began in 1985, when Chen Kaige's *Yellow Earth* (*Huang tudi*, 1984), produced at the Guangxi Studio in China, made a significant impact at international film festivals. This is also the same year that the success of Jackie Chan's movies such as *Project A* (*A jihua*, 1983) and *Police Story* (*Jingcha gushi*, 1985) began to bring him a reputation in Asia that was, for the first time, on the scale of Bruce Lee's. In 1987, Bernardo Bertolucci's *The Last Emperor*, while not specifically a "Chinese-made" film, grabbed headlines as a cultural watershed, signifying growing Western interest in China. *The Last Emperor* was the first Western film made in and about China to be produced with full support of the Chinese government since 1949, and the first feature film in history granted permission to be filmed in the Forbidden City. In 1988, it won all of the nine Academy Awards for which it was nominated, including Best Picture and Best Director. The stunning sweep at the Academy Awards, and the beauty of the film itself, raised international awareness and consciousness of China. This film also attracted international interest in actor John Lone (Hong Kong) and the Chinese megastar Joan Chen. Also in 1988, *M. Butterfly*, by David Henry Hwang, won the 1988 Tony Award for best play, the Outer Critics Circle Award for best Broadway play, the John Gassner Award for best American play, and the Drama Desk Award for best new play, again drawing international attention to China, and to the actor B. D. Wong, who played the principal role of Song Liling. (The 1993 film version starred Hong Kong actor John Lone.) The year 1988 was also a watershed for mainland Chinese director Zhang Yimou, whose film *Red Sorghum* (*Hong gaoliang*, 1987) won the Golden Bear at the Berlin International Film Festival, the first film from China to win a top international award. In 1990, Zhang Yimou made *Judou* (with funding from Japan), which won a nomination for Best Foreign Language Film, the first Chinese film to reach this category. The Chinese government, which had banned the film in China, protested the nomination and prevented Zhang from attending the ceremony. In 1991, Zhang followed this with *Raise the Red Lantern* (*Dahong denglong gaogao gua*), with funding from Taiwan. Again, the film was banned in China, but was nominated for an Academy Award for Best Foreign Language Film (this time as the Hong Kong entry). Actress Gong Li became a name known in the West primarily because of her performance in this film.

Beginning in the 1990s, a number of major stars from China, Hong Kong, and other parts of Asia have broken through from regional popularity to international recognition. One example is Jet Li (Li Lianjie), originally from China, and now based in Hong Kong. Jet Li is principally known for his kung fu movies, especially *Shaolin Temple* (*Shaolin si*, 1982), which he made before he was twenty years old; this film is generally credited with starting the 1980s kung fu boom in China. He is also known for *Once Upon a Time in China* (*Huang Feihong*, 1991), based on the legendary Chinese martial artist Wong Fei Hung (Huang Feihong). He began to enjoy limited international recognition after costarring in his first American-produced movie, *Lethal Weapon 4* (1998); this was also the first time he had ever played a villain. *Romeo Must Die* (2000) was made with the plan to give Jet Li crossover status, and with this film he received greater international recognition, especially when his costar in the film, Aaliyah, was killed in a plane crash in 2001. He cemented his international status with *Hero* (2002), a high-grossing and highly-stylized martial arts film that is often compared to *Crouching Tiger, Hidden Dragon*. Li departed from his usual martial arts action films with the drama *Unleashed* (also known as *Danny the Dog*, 2005), a somber, meditative film costarring dramatic actors Bob Hoskins and Morgan Freeman. More recently, he appeared with Sylvester Stallone and other giants of the action film genre in *The Expendables* (2010, with sequels in 2012 and 2014).

Hong Kong–based actor Chow Yun-fat, the male lead in *Crouching Tiger, Hidden Dragon*, made his start in television, but has since become one of Asia's best-loved actors and biggest stars. In 1986, the success of the fast-paced gangster film *A Better*

Tomorrow (*Yinxiong bense*, 1986), directed by John Woo, propelled Chow Yun-fat to international recognition. His enormous popularity in Asia soon made him an icon on the level of Bruce Lee and Jackie Chan. Further hard-edged roles in more John Woo crime films increased Chow's popularity as fans all over the world flocked to see *A Better Tomorrow 2* (*Yinxiong bense II*, 1987), *The Killer* (*Diexue shuangxiong*, 1989), and *Hard Boiled* (*Lashou shentan*, 1992). With the phenomenal global interest in the Hong Kong action genre, Chow Yun-fat decided to try his luck in the United States film industry and appeared in *The Replacement Killers* (1998) with Mira Sorvino, and *The Corruptor* (1999) with Mark Wahlberg. Next he took on his first attempt at a romantic lead in English, starring with Jodie Foster in *Anna and the King* (1999). Chow then returned to the Asian cinema circuit and took on an unusual role (he was not formerly trained in martial arts) in *Crouching Tiger, Hidden Dragon*. Following that, working with renowned director Zhang Yimou, Chow Yun-fat played Emperor Ping in China's *Curse of the Golden Flower* (*Mancheng jindai huangjinjia*, 2006). Again returning to Hollywood, Chow played the demonic pirate captain Sao Feng in the third installment of *Pirates of the Carribbean* (2007).

Chow Yun-fat's costar from *Crouching Tiger, Hidden Dragon* is Michelle Yeoh. Born in 1962 in the mining town of Ipoh, in Western Malaysia, Yeoh's ethnically Chinese parents taught her Malay and English some time before she learned Cantonese. She began ballet dancing at the age of four, and, inspired by *Fame* (1980), she enrolled in England's Royal Academy of Dance, where she eventually earned a Bachelor of Arts degree. Though a back injury ended her career as a ballerina, she had the opportunity while in England to act in student dramas, including productions of Shakespeare. After returning to Malaysia she won a national beauty pageant in 1983. From there, she appeared in a television commercial with Jackie Chan that caught the attention of a fledgling film production company called D&B Films. She continued to produce martial arts films in Hong Kong in quick succession until her career took off internationally following her showstopping performance in *Police Story 3: Super Cop* (1992), where she matched the notoriously fearless Jackie Chan stunt for stunt. At the beginning of the shoot, Chan was skeptical as to whether women could fight, preferring them to look pretty and to sit on the sidelines. By the end of the film, Chan was legitimately concerned that he might be upstaged. Yeoh's hair-raising high-speed motorcycle jump onto a moving train (she learned how to drive the motorbike the day before the stunt) was bested only by Chan's death-defying leap from a minaret to an airborne rope ladder hanging from a helicopter hundreds of feet above Kuala Lumpur. The film was a massive success, making Yeoh the highest paid actress in Asia. From there it was easy to take on the role of the next Bond girl in the eighteenth installment of the 007 series, *Tomorrow Never Dies* (1997). Her success with Lee's film has led to her reprising her leading role of Yu Shu Lien in the Weinstein Company's *Crouching Tiger, Hidden Dragon II: The Green Destiny* (filming in 2014).

Tony Leung Chiu-wai, a Hong Kong actor with ancestry in Taishan, Guangdong, in southern China, is the latest actor to emerge to grand international acclaim under the directorship of Ang Lee. The actor, who plays the complex leading role of a duplicitous government agent in Lee's *Lust/Caution* (*Se jie*, 2007), got his beginnings from partnering with Maggie Cheung in iconoclastic director Wong Kar-wai's films. Leung is known mainly for playing intense, black-sheep characters as a corrupting influence against his upstanding protagonist costars. Tony Leung first gained international exposure through Hou Hsiao-hsien's film *A City of Sadness* (*Beiqing cheng-shi*, 1989), which won the Golden Lion at the Venice International Film Festival. However, many consider Leung's role in John Woo's 1992 action film *Hard Boiled* (where he acted with Chow Yun-fat) his breakthrough role. Leung often collaborates with Wong Kar-wai and has appeared in many of his films: his most notable roles for this director include the lonely policeman in *Chungking Express* (1994), a homosexual Chinese expatriate living in Argentina in *Happy Together*, and a repressed victim of adultery in *In the Mood for Love*, for which he won the Best Actor award at Cannes. He also had a key role in the Zhang Yimou epic *Hero*.

Jackie Chan's career has been unique and far-reaching. Born into a poor family and apprenticed at the age of seven to an opera school, he studied there under a cruel headmaster in Dickensian conditions. Entering stunt work in film after graduation, he sought to replace the vacuum left by the death of Bruce Lee, and eventually hit on the idea to package his martial arts with a self-deferential style of comedy inspired by Charlie Chaplin and Buster Keaton. This proved to be a winning formula, and he made many films and became a popular star in Asia with the trademark of performing his own stunts, allowing no sex or bad language in his films, and including a reel of outtakes of unsuccessful stunts at the end of the film during the closing credits. He desired to conquer Hollywood as he had Asia, but this success proved more elusive as he made two flops with foreign directors; clearly, he had not yet hit on the right timbre to present himself to a Western audience. After studying English for two years in Beverly Hills, he headed back to Hong Kong. His madcap, over-the-top brand of comedy/adventure did not catch on in the West until he made the *Rush Hour* series (1998, 2001, and 2007), partnered with Chris Tucker. Even more hilarious and extreme were the farces *Shanghai Noon* (2000) and *Shanghai Knights* (2003), made with actor Owen Wilson, which lampooned every cliché in the western genre from John Wayne to *Butch Cassidy and the Sundance Kid*–style buddy movies. These films were truly silly, but Jackie Chan's ebullient personality came through to Western audiences. In the first of the *Rush Hour* films, there is a scene in which Chan grabs hold with both hands and hangs from a "Hollywood" street sign in a visual reminder that he has "arrived" in Hollywood.[18]

The style of Jackie Chan's slapstick humor and Hong Kong kung fu movies is distinctly different from the high-minded Asian aesthetic presented by mainland Chinese filmmakers such as Chen Kaige and Zhang Yimou (which Ang Lee and Hou Hsiao-hsien seem to share). Fredric Dannen (1995) argues that these directors are shaped by linguistic forces, i.e., the madcap, cartoonish style of Hong Kong films is driven by the "wildness" of Cantonese, with its earthiness, roughshod humor, and penchant for expletives; the portentous and slow Mandarin-made films produced in China are reflective of Mandarin's more serious, and even elitist, side. Hollywood directors such as Quentin Tarantino and Robert Rodriguez have acknowledged the influence of Hong Kong directors John Woo, Ringo Lam, and Tsui Hark on their work, attracted to the no-holds-barred approach to action, exuberant gags, and excessive stirring up of emotions.[19] Meanwhile, directors from mainland China offer more elitist, highbrow fare; for example, Zhang Yimou's *Judou*, *Raise the Red Lantern*, and *Yellow Earth* are emblematic of the so-called Fifth Generation filmmakers' stylistic and political rejection of the Maoist legacy. Zhang Yimou makes somber films that focus on the lower classes, such as the life of peasants in China. At the same time, Chen Kaige's intelligent and historic Chinese epic *Farewell My Concubine* (*Bawang bieji*, 1993) does a wonderful job portraying the complex and often uneasy love affair between the two stage brothers, while also managing to skillfully express profound themes that resonate throughout the film: fate, loyalty, class struggle, the parallels between opera and life.

From the above we can see how some of the groundwork was laid for the success of *Crouching Tiger, Hidden Dragon*. Performers and directors from the transnational territories of China, Taiwan, and Hong Kong, such as King Hu, Bruce Lee, John Woo, Chen Kaige, Zhang Yimou, Edward Yang, and Hou Hsiao-hsien, have helped pave the way for Ang Lee's stunning success. Lee's work, *Crouching Tiger, Hidden Dragon*, does not exist in a vacuum; the film can be placed within networks of intertextual connections: genre connections, the work of King Hu, and Li Hanxiang's *The Love Eterne*. The films of Ang Lee can also be viewed in conjunction with thematically similar films from the Chinese diaspora (globalization, homosexuality, etc.). The success of *Crouching Tiger, Hidden Dragon* blurs what may be called the boundary between mainland Chinese cinema and a more internationally-based "Chinese-language cinema." The film was made by a Taiwanese director, but its leads include Hong Kong, Taiwan, and mainland Chinese actors and actresses while the funding is from overseas. This merging of people, resources, and expertise from these three regions seems to imply big-budgeted Chinese-language cinema is moving toward an international arena looking to compete with the best Hollywood films.

A Short History of Taiwan Cinema

In understanding Taiwan's history and Taiwanese identity, it is important to understand the short but troubled history of Taiwan in the past century. Taiwan, historically dominated by China, had been colonized by Japan from 1895 to 1945 (previously, Taiwan had been ceded to Japan following China's defeat in the Sino-Japanese War in the Treaty of Shimonoseki in 1895; Japan's control of Taiwan ended with Japan's surrender in World War II in 1945, when Taiwan once again came under Chinese control). Within a few years, Taiwan was under the control of Chiang Kai-shek and the KMT (Kuomintang) government, which had fled to Taiwan (1947–49) to escape the rising Communist army in China. The KMT under Chiang Kai-shek established Taiwan as the "Republic of China" in 1949. The KMT government officials, through the 1950s-1970s, lived in a state of interminable waiting, looking forward to the eventual overthrow of the Communist government on the mainland, and believing themselves to be the repositors of the real China. Thus, the people of Taiwan who had lived first under the colonizing influence of Japan, and then under the strict military rule of the KMT government whose initial focus was to regain power in China, could not easily establish a national identity. To confuse the issue of identity even further, in 1972 the People's Republic of China took over the seat formerly occupied by Taiwan in the United Nations, forcing Taiwan to withdraw. This caused Taiwan to become an international nonentity, as the majority of countries began to recognize the People's Republic of China and shift their allegiance to the Communist government in Beijing. This was the beginning of Taiwan's late-twentieth-century "identity crisis" in the international arena—politically, the island was relegated to a state of international diplomatic nonexistence, a problem that to this day has found no easy solution.

In the 1970s, Taiwan noted the successes of Hong Kong's cinema as a boon to the economy, and this led the KMT government to promote its film industry in the early 1980s. This coincided with the change in the political situation in Taiwan. The strict military rule under Chiang Kai-shek was lessened by his death in 1975, and the son who succeeded him, Chiang Ching-kuo, began to lift the restrictions on cultural and artistic expression. The former government-controlled entertainment—serialized costume melodramas, low-budget kung fu movies, insubstantial comedies, and "Healthy Realist" propaganda cinema promoted by the KMT—had provided mere escapism for Taiwanese audiences; this was a genre cinema producing generic films, utilizing the conventional code and language of the different genres, rather than innovating or speaking with a creative or distinctly Taiwanese voice. Early examples of Taiwan New Cinema were government-financed, and were thus operating under the specter of possible censorship. Taiwanese director Hou Hsiao-hsien ran into this difficulty with *A City of Sadness*, released just two years after the end of the 40-year period of martial law. Despite new levels of artistic freedom, Hou Hsiao-hsien faced government criticism and censorship when he released his most provocative film, dealing with the sensitive events of February 28, 1947 (also known as the 228 Incident, referring to the date). The 228 Incident was an uprising in Taiwan that was brutally suppressed by the Kuomintang government, resulting in the massacre of between ten thousand and thirty thousand civilians. Previously, tensions between the local Taiwanese and mainlanders from China had gradually increased since Taiwan had been placed under the administrative control of the Republic of China from Japan two years earlier. The violence began on February 27, 1947, in Taipei, when a dispute between a female cigarette vendor and an antismuggling officer triggered civil disorder and open rebellion lasting several days; the uprising was quickly and brutally suppressed by the ROC Army. Although Hou Hsiao-hsien's film was censored by the KMT in Taiwan, in September 1989, *A City of Sadness* won the Golden Lion award at the 46th Venice International Film Festival. Only after the film won international acclaim did the government relent and allow the film open distribution in Taiwan.

Taiwanese films are increasingly recognized as an important development in the arena of world cinema, in terms of both aesthetic quality and for their liberalizing effects on Taiwan government and society. The major Taiwan film directors who have won international attention and acclaim are Hou Hsiao-hsien, Edward Yang, Ang Lee, and Tsai Ming-liang. Hou Hsiao-hsien was one of the key figures in the early cinematic movement known as Taiwan New Wave; this term has been used to describe a cycle of socially-critical films from the 1980s which share the characteristics of probing Taiwanese history, society, and identity through dramatizing current sociopolitical and economic tensions. The filmmakers of the Taiwan New Wave, beginning around 1982 and continuing through the late 1980s, shared certain themes and concerns, investigating complex social realities that had been previously ignored or suppressed by rigorous censorship. These directors defined a national Taiwanese cinema as well as defining Taiwanese history and identity. Although a number of Taiwanese scholars and critics still use the term "Taiwan New Wave" to describe a short period of creative cinematic output in the 1980s, this movement has been broadened by subsequent scholarship and is now given the more loosely-based title "Taiwan New Cinema."

Characteristics of Taiwan New Cinema

The clearest example of the phenomenon of Taiwan New Cinema is the work of Hou Hsiao-hsien, whose politically-challenging films were made just as Taiwanese history was in the process of major change. In 1983, in an early project sponsored by the government, Hou directed a segment in a three-story anthology film entitled *The Sandwich Man* (*Erzi de da wanou*, 1983). This film is one of the first post-KMT-rule works of cinema to use native Taiwanese dialect instead of restricting itself to Mandarin—defying a precept of government censorship. Hou followed this film's success with several autobiographical films and personal stories of friends growing up in Taiwan. These films included *The Boys from Fengkuei* (*Fenggui lai de ren*, 1983), *Summer at Grandpa's* (*Dongdong de jiaqi*, 1984), and his own personal story, *A Time to Live and A Time to Die* (*Tongnian wangshi*, 1985). This film courageously deals with the theme of displacement and disorientation felt by people of his parents' and grandparents' generation who had come over from mainland China with the idea of soon returning; instead, they are obsessed with the past and the lost world of old China. Meanwhile, their son, Hsiao, born in Taiwan, is uninterested in these stories since only the life he has known in Taiwan has real meaning for him. This film won the Critics' Award at the Berlin International Film Festival, the first major international recognition for Taiwan New Cinema. Finally, following both the formal establishment of an opposing party, the Democratic Progressive Party (DPP), in 1986, the lifting of martial law in 1987, and the 1988 inauguration of Taiwan's first native-born president, Lee Teng-hui, Hou Hsiao-hsien's most controversial film, *A City of Sadness*, finally found the climate in which it could survive and be made. As noted, the film's Golden Lion award led to the government retracting its suppression of the film. This was a watershed moment in the development of Taiwan New Cinema.

Another striking feature of Taiwan New Cinema that defined it more or less as a cinematic movement was the great amount of shared subject matter, as well as a solidarity of vision and intercollaboration among the filmmakers. Taiwanese critic Hsiung-ping Chiao details these collaborations in a 1990 article about Taiwan cinema; for example, many of the films were based on the screenwriters' own autobiographical experiences. Hou Hsiao-hsien's *A Time to Live and a Time to Die* deals with the director's own childhood; his *Summer at Grandpa's* is the coming-of-age story of author Chu T'ien-wen; his *Dust in the Wind* (*Lianlian fengchen*, 1986) was based on the life story of the film's writer, Wu Nien-chen.[20] In addition, major directors collaborated on film anthologies; two examples are *In Our Time* (*Guangyin de gushi*, 1982), a collection of short narrative films by four directors including Tao De-chen, Edward Yang, Ko I-cheng, and Chang Yi, which is widely credited with establishing the tone and subject matter of what would become Taiwan New Cinema, and *The Sandwich Man*, with segments by three different directors based on three short stories by author Huang Chun-ming. In his excellent study of 1980s Taiwan New Cinema, Douglas Kellner (1998) points out that this focus on rural stories was a result of the burgeoning "rural literature" movement—a growing movement in Taiwanese literature that aimed to preserve stories from Taiwan's agrarian past and expose the harmful impact of urbanization on traditional Taiwanese society. Hou Hsiao-hsien's short film *Son's Big Doll* (*Erzi de da wanou*) in *The Sandwich Man* was influenced by the rural literature movement. *The Sandwich Man* is largely known for its first segment directed by Hou, which showcased his directorial gifts; the film also helped to establish Taiwan New Cinema as a "legitimate artistic movement."[21] As an example of the type of personal commitment these artists contributed to collaborative efforts within the movement, Hou Hsiao-hsien performed the leading male role in Edward Yang's *Taipei Story* (*Qingmei zhuma*, 1985), as well as mortgaging his own home to finance and produce it. (Hou lost his investment when the film, which portrayed the hubris and denouement in the relationship between a young couple, was pulled from theaters within four days.)[22]

A further unique element of Taiwan New Cinema is a distinct cinematic language and style shared among the directors, particularly Hou Hsaio-hsien, Tseng Chuang-hsiang, and Edward Yang. These films all run at a slow, meditative pace, with a choppy or interrupted narrative style consisting of fragmentary scenes and unexpected episodic cuts. The viewer is challenged to construct the narrative to produce the complete story. The Taiwan New Cinema film has a meandering structure without a standard beginning, middle, and end and lacks the narrative pacing of conventional films. Within the films' narrative structure, there are jumps in time—for example, Edward Yang's edits cut from an earlier scene to a later scene months or even years later without an explanation, so that the viewer is forced to fill in the blanks. Also in his films, the actors are often at the screen's periphery, or even off-screen. In terms of technique, Hou Hsiao-hsien commonly uses a static camera setup in a long shot, with few edits and close-ups. Thus the viewers can gradually become familiar with the scene, as an observer would. Taiwan New Cinema uses many outdoor locations to evoke the nostalgia for rural and agriculturally-centered, premodern Taiwan, or to display the contrasting human-less modern cityscape. Another feature of Taiwan New Cinema is that nonprofessional actors are often used, with the filmmakers themselves appearing in each other's movies (see example of Edward Yang's *Taipei Story*, above).

Ang Lee has been classified as a member of Taiwan New Cinema, especially due to his early trilogy films, but he is generally considered to be part of a post-1980s "second wave," together with director Tsai Ming-liang. Both Lee's and Tsai Ming-liang's work can be seen to have roots within the earlier 1980s movement, with similarities in their work to Hou Hsiao-hsien and Edward Yang. For example, Tsai uses long shots, strange fragmentary cuts, and lengthy scenes. He also tends to use the same actors again and again. Meanwhile, Lee uses nonprofessional actors, such as his own son and Winston Chao, and his early films use similar casts, especially Sihung Lung as the traditional Chinese father figure in his early trilogy films. The subject matter of both Lee's and Tsai's films also reflects some of the topics which first intrigued the makers of Taiwan New Cinema in the 1980s. For example, Tsai's film *What Time Is It There?* (*Ni nabian jidian*, 2001) deals with modernity, globalization, and postmodern apprehension of spaces, as the lead character, stagnating in Taipei, becomes obsessed with the faraway city of Paris. Lee's films *Pushing Hands*, *The Wedding Banquet*, and *Eat Drink Man Woman* also deal with the topics of modernity, cultural identity, and globalization.

Below are a series of characteristics that Ang Lee's films share with the filmmakers of Taiwan New Cinema.

Construction of identity. Similar to Lee's recurrent treatment of the topic of identity in his films, the films of Hou Hsiao-hsien are concerned with the exploration and construction of his own personal identity in Taiwan. Hou's family, following his father, moved to Taiwan only two years before the separation from mainland China. As is suggested in his film *A City of Sadness*, Hou has appropriated the island as his homeland because he was born in Taiwan and has lived there all his life; on the other hand, his parents cannot help feeling that they are exiles who cannot return to China, their true home. They reconstruct an identity in the new country where it was once thought they would stay only a few months, after the Nationalist retreat, but now are destined to live the rest of their lives. Taiwan, for Hou, represents an irredeemable place of exile, loss, and emptiness. From his childhood memories, he also longs for the sense of village-life community which, due to modernization and urbanization, has been removed behind thick walls.

Globalization and modernization. Films that are notable for similarity in theme with Ang Lee's work include Edward Yang's *Yi Yi: A One and a Two* (*Yiyi*, 2000), which won him the Best Director award at Cannes that year. This is another film that underscores the question of reimagining self-identity and ethical engagement in the face of change brought on by globalization and modernization. In this film, the grandmother and matriarch of the Wu family has a sudden stroke and goes into a coma on the day of her son's wedding; the story details the effect of this awareness of mortality on the Wu family, especially her daughter, son-in-law, and grandchildren. The bleak urban cityscapes of Taipei, especially scenes of unrelenting traffic and a cold, sterile hotel room where a teenager prepares for her first sexual experience, are used to demonstrate the oppressiveness and inhumanity of the postmodern urban environment. In an earlier Edward Yang film, *The Terrorizer* (*Kongbu fenzi*, 1986),

Fredric Jameson (1994) notes the film's overlap of *traditional* space (an old-style barracks apartment), *national* space (the hospital), *multinational* space (the publisher's office, a glass high-rise in which global media is manufactured), and *transnational* anonymity (in a hotel corridor, the sameness of identical bedrooms). Jameson emphasizes the importance of spatiality in *The Terrorizer* by describing it as "a film about urban space" and "an anthology of enclosed apartments,"[23] demonstrating how Taiwan New Cinema's focus on postmodern spaces reflects an increasingly globalized and postmodern culture that transcends national boundaries.

Homosexuality. Similar to Ang Lee's open treatment of the subject of homosexuality in *The Wedding Banquet*, the films of Tsai Ming-liang, a Malaysian-born director working from Taiwan, are another example to demonstrate the identity confusion and homosexuality which characterize post-"economic miracle" Taiwan. Tsai's *Vive L'Amour* (*Aiqing wansui*, 1994) won the Golden Lion at the 1994 Venice International Film Festival. This film is the second in a three-part series of films, which also includes *Rebels of the Neon God* (*Qingshaonian natuo*, 1992), and *The River* (*Heliu*, 1997), all films which have been discussed at the academic level primarily for their explorations of existential anxiety and loneliness in the millennial metropolis of Taipei. The three films also deal with homosexuality in the wake of this postmodern fragmentation of society and the traditional Chinese family, especially during the significant rise of homosexuality in the 1990s following the Taiwan Kuomintang government's lifting of martial law in 1987.

Autobiography. Just as Hou Hsiao-hsien's *A Time to Live and a Time to Die*, *Summer at Grandpa's*, and *Dust in the Wind* were based on true stories of his own life or the lives of his collaborators, Ang Lee's first three films, *Pushing Hands*, *The Wedding Banquet*, and *Eat Drink Man Woman*, all deal with his own feelings of cultural disconnection (as an outsider living in the United States) or his struggle with his own "father figure." While *Pushing Hands*, *The Wedding Banquet*, and *Eat Drink Man Woman* do not directly tell an autobiographical account of Lee's childhood as other Taiwan New Cinema filmmakers do, the three films in his trilogy do speak about the filmmaker obliquely in an autobiographical way (more on this in the chapters devoted to these films).

Repeated use of actors (also untrained actors). Ang Lee shares this similarity with Tsai Ming-liang, who likes to use his favorite actors again and again in his films, and Hou and the group from 1980s Taiwan New Cinema, who often appeared in each other's films. (Notably, this is also a trait of Hong Kong films, especially those of Wong Kar-wai, which frequently feature Tony Leung.) Lee had Sihung Lung play the central role of the Chinese patriarch in each of his "Father-Knows-Best" trilogy films. (Sihung Lung also appeared as Sir Te in *Crouching Tiger, Hidden Dragon*.) Ah-Leh Gua also appeared in two of Lee's early trilogy films, as did Winston Chao (along with his main role as the gay son in *The Wedding Banquet*, he played a supporting role in *Eat Drink Man Woman*, as the skillful, slightly cynical business associate Li Kai). Similarly, actor Tobey Maguire played a leading role in both *The Ice Storm* and *Ride with the Devil*, and was originally cast in a significant role in *Life of Pi* (he was eventually replaced by Rafe Spall because Lee realized during filming that Maguire's recognizable face would be too distracting to audiences). In his early trilogy films,

Ang Lee also used untrained actors, such as his own son, Haan, who played the role of the young son of Martha and Alex (Bo Z. Wang) in *Pushing Hands*. In *Eat Drink Man Woman*, the young girl Shan-Shan (Yu-Chien Tang) is filmed at her school; the classmates who surround her as she opens her fragrant lunchbox are her real friends. The central actor in *The Wedding Banquet*, Winston Chao, was a retired flight attendant who had never before appeared in a feature film. Jane Lin, Haan, and youngest son, Mason, also appeared in *The Wedding Banquet*. Additionally, it is notable that Lee selected the unknown Suraj Sharma, an untrained teenager who had not even intended to audition for the film, to play the central role in *Life of Pi*.

Historical Context of Ang Lee's Academy Awards for Best Director

As noted, in 2006, Ang Lee became the first Asian to win an Academy Award for Best Director, a distinct achievement on the international stage—and one made even more indelible by his second win in 2013. Though many Asian directors, especially Jackie Chan and John Woo, have tried to storm Hollywood, and others, such as Chen Kaige, Wong Kar-wai, and Zhang Yimou, have achieved honors in the international film community with art-house successes, Lee's history-making first Academy Award for Best Director was for *Brokeback Mountain*, a distinctly un-Asian film. As detailed in chapter 1, while he had previously been overlooked for awards with his English-language films (*Sense and Sensibility* was nominated but only won a single award, for screenwriter Emma Thompson), his Chinese films have always done well at the Academy Awards. Both *The Wedding Banquet* and *Eat Drink Man Woman* in 1993 and 1994 garnered Foreign Language Film nominations, and *Crouching Tiger, Hidden Dragon* won Best Foreign Language Film in the 2001 Academy Awards. Thus, of the first four Chinese-language films that Lee made, only *Pushing Hands* went unmentioned at the Academy Awards. This track record set Ang Lee on a course for success. Disappointed not to be nominated for directing *Sense and Sensibility* in 1995, he apologized to Taiwan for failing to bring his homeland the honor of an Academy Award that year. When he set out to make *Crouching Tiger, Hidden Dragon*, he made no secret of his desire to win an Academy Award with the film.

The only other Asian auteur to reach worldwide recognition at a level similar to Ang Lee was Japanese filmmaker Akira Kurosawa, who never advanced to win the Best Director or Best Film at the Academy Awards. Kurosawa's *Rashomon* (1950) received an honorary foreign-language film award. Because this film was so widely admired for being ahead of its time, yet received so little recognition in the way of international awards, many believe this film was responsible for the creation of the new category, Best Foreign Film, at the Academy Awards. Kurosawa's *Dersu Uzala* (1975) won Best Foreign Language Film in 1976. He was nominated for Best Director with *Ran* (1985), and received an honorary Academy Award in 1990. However, Kurosawa's films never broke into the Best Picture category.

Another Japanese filmmaker, Hiroshi Teshigahara, was nominated in the Best Director category for *Woman in the Dunes* (1964), the first non-Caucasian director ever nominated. The 24-year-old African-American director/writer John Singleton was nominated in 1991 for his directorial debut about South Central Los Angeles gang violence in the ghetto, *Boyz N the Hood* (1991). This film earned two nominations and no wins. Singleton became the youngest nominee for Best Director in Academy history, and the first African-American to be nominated as Best Director.

Back in 2000, before *Crouching Tiger, Hidden Dragon* was nominated for the Best Foreign Film category, an interviewer asked Ang Lee if he hoped for a Best Film nomination. He answered:

> I'll go with the wave. It's an achievement if a Chinese-language film is recognized. There are a bunch of great filmmakers in Asia, but the Oscars is something else. I grew up with subtitles and it's so unfair—it's time for the [American] public to read. There's a big world out there that has a lot to offer. The cultural exchange is so one-way. . . . It would be great satisfaction to me for the film to break outside the art-house into the shopping malls.[24]

While Lee's first win was for a distinctly American subject, in 2013 he won for directing *Life of Pi*, a film (containing subtitles for spoken French) that reflects the influences of globalization (with a boy from India on a Japanese cargo ship with a French cook and a Taiwanese crew bound for Canada), demonstrating how far Lee—and the entire film industry—has come since Lee first voiced these aspirations in 2000. With Lee's second win as Best Director at the Academy Awards in 2013, he became the only Asian to win the award not just once but twice, as well as joining a very select group of directors honored more than once, including John Ford, Frank Capra, William Wyler, Oliver Stone, and Steven Spielberg.[25]

Ang Lee's Influences as a Director

In the March 9, 2001, issue of the *New York Times*, Ang Lee appeared in a series of discussions with noted directors, actors, cinematographers, screenwriters, and others in the filmmaking industry. Some of the previous subjects in the series had been Quentin Tarantino, Janusz Kaminski, Ron Howard, Kevin Costner, Curtis Hanson, and Stephen Soderbergh. The format of the series was to have each subject select and discuss a film that had a personal meaning to him or her. Lee brought up a short list of directors and films from abroad that had emotionally affected him as a young man, including Fellini's *Roma* (1972). Other films he mentioned include Vittorio De Sica's *Ladri di biciclette* (*Bicycle Thieves*, 1948), Yasujiro Ozu's *Tokyo monogatari* (*Tokyo Story*, 1953), Ingmar Bergman's *Jungfrukällan* (*The Virgin Spring*, 1960), and Michelangelo Antonioni's *L'Eclisse* (*Eclipse*, 1962). Another early influence was Mike Nichols' *The Graduate* (1967). As a first-year student at the Academy, Lee saw *The Graduate* three times in a row (staying in the theater for two extra showings), and would never forget the eye-opening inspiration the film was to him.[26] He conceded that, because of the limitations of the film industry in Taiwan both economically and politically in the years he was growing up, he had not seen any films from abroad before the age of 18. Before the rise of Taiwan New Cinema, Italian Neorealism was introduced to Taiwan to great acclaim, demonstrating the high public opinion and official sanction of "realism," and strongly influencing the younger generation of Taiwanese filmmakers, including Lee.[27] Seeing Fellini's *Roma* was the first time he realized that "movies could do more than tell me a story. . . . These are the movies that affect you so deeply that you feel that you are a different person from the one who went into the theater."[28] Ang Lee was being trained in the language, texture, and power of art-house filmmaking.

The film that Ang Lee chose to discuss as a seminal influence was Li Hanxiang's *Liang Shanbo yu Zhu Yingtai* (1963), a Chinese opera also known as *The Butterfly Lovers*. In the interview the film was called *Qi Cai Hu Bu Gui*, as the opera is sometimes titled. This film was produced by the heavily influential Shaw Brothers' Hong Kong studio. The narrative shares similarities with Shakespeare's *Romeo and Juliet*, both in its subject matter and cultural significance. Lee himself translated the title as *Love Eternal*, although the film is more commonly known as *The Love Eterne*; this is the English title that accompanies the film. In May 1963, *The Love Eterne* set records in Taiwan for the longest theater run (186 days), screenings (930), and tickets sold (721,929, approximately 90 percent of the Taipei population at the time).[29] Lee had chosen this film because it reminded him of his "innocence." As a nine-year-old boy living in Hualian in his traditional Chinese household and with dreams of the heroes of traditional China, when he first saw the film it was forever associated in his mind with this type of innocence and sweet, childlike dreaminess.

> I think that for every movie I make, I always try to duplicate that feeling of purity and innocence that I got when I first saw this movie [*The Love Eterne*]. I bring in Western drama. I bring in metaphor. I bring in Jean-Luc Godard. Whatever I bring in to my own films, I am forever trying to update and recapture that feeling.[30]

The unabashedly romantic plot of *The Love Eterne* concerns a young girl, Zhu Yingtai (played by Le Di), from a wealthy family, who wishes to receive a higher education, and so convinces her parents to let her dress up as a boy in order to attend an all-male school. There, she befriends a male student, Liang Shanbo (played by Ling Po), and the two have a close relationship. She falls in love with him and tries to confess her secret, but because of shyness, she can never summon the courage to tell him. When she is suddenly forced to return home, she discovers her parents have arranged her betrothal to another man, the son of a prominent family. She is caught between fidelity to her father's wishes and to her own heart. Meanwhile, the male student she loves has learned the truth about her gender, and, in delight, he sets off to her hometown to propose marriage. However, when he hears of her engagement to another, the blow to his heart sets him in a downward spiral of fatal illness. On the road back to the school he dies, brokenhearted, in a fit of consumptive coughing. The girl hears of this and thus agrees to the arranged marriage, with the stipulation that the wedding party must pass by her former love's gravesite. While passing the grave, she tears off her wedding clothes to reveal funeral garments underneath. A storm pounds the site, splitting open the grave, and she runs to be united with her former love, who appears from the grave as an apparition. The two are buried together in the grave by the force of the storm, but the final image shows them together sailing upward into the clouds to eternal paradise.

This film is crafted in the style of traditional Chinese opera, an art form of heightened theatricality, in which graceful movement is choreographed with music. Chinese opera is an extremely demanding art form of exacting technical training; performers of Chinese opera on the stage must be versed in four separate art forms: singing, acting, dance, and mime. Often these performers are trained from early childhood; only if apprenticed from a young age can the performer master the difficult art. The highly stylized acting and choreography in *The Love Eterne* comes from this tradition, in which an actor must strike a pose, reposition, and strike another pose, all in time to the music. Thus, the emotions are not played at a realistic level, but have a heightened dramatic tone that verges on the melodramatic. Another feature of traditional Chinese opera, that is reflected during the time *The Love Eterne* was made, is having male roles played by females. Indeed, in *The Love Eterne* the two main roles of the girl and her school boyfriend are played by women.

If this movie is a basis for his own films, as Ang Lee claimed in the *New York Times*, then there is evidence of the influence of *The Love Eterne* in his work, especially *Crouching Tiger, Hidden Dragon*. Indeed, Lee himself draws the connection between the suicide leap of the main actress Zhang Ziyi in *Crouching Tiger, Hidden Dragon* and the flight to heaven taken by Le Di and Ling Po in *The Love Eterne*. Truly he is a director that has kept in close touch with his childhood sensibilities. The themes of repressed emotion and sacrificing love in the face of duty are shared by both films.

> It is, I think, the great Chinese theme. For the Chinese audience, it is just in our blood. You must hide your feelings. That becomes the art itself, the metaphor and the symbolism, the use of color and framing.
>
> It is a way of not saying something but of expressing it anyway. And it is such an emotional outlet especially for a repressed society. That is the heart of both films, the repressed emotional wish.
>
> That is the hidden dragon.[31]

The metaphor of being torn between duty and love is most pronounced in the film he had not yet made at the time of the *New York Times* interview, *Brokeback Mountain*. The love unable to find words, the thing untranslatable, the indescribable something in the film that "spoke to you" is what Lee calls "the juice."[32] In *The Ice Storm*, the "juice" comes from a single word, "embarrassment." In *Sense and Sensibility*, according to Lee, it is the moment of transition, when the sisters fully connect in love and understanding to the point where each takes on more "sense" or "sensibility," the best of the other's personality. In *Ride with the Devil*, it is the discovery and clarity that maturity brings. And in *Brokeback Mountain*, which clearly shares roots with *The Love Eterne*, the viewer can see the Chinese theme of hidden, repressed emotion. Lee has stated: "If a topic isn't terrifying enough, or sensitive enough, I won't want to make the movie . . . I like to make movies about conflict, because tension can uncover a person's real humanity."[33]

Lee moves easily among wildly different genres and cultures. He has claimed he likes to return to his Chinese roots for "artistic rejuvenation." Asked what the essence of his filmmaking was by Robert Hilferty Bloomberg, interviewing him in the *China Post* in 2005 after the successful release of *Brokeback Mountain*, Lee replied:

> Repression, the struggle between how you want to behave as a social animal and the desire to be honest with your free will. That's an important subtext in life, and a struggle for me. I also mistrust everything. Things you believe in can change just like that; that's the essence of life. . . . My point of view is a bit Taoist. When things change, you have to adapt to it. That's been our fate. My next film will be Chinese.[34]

Indeed, Lee's next film took the ideas of repression/performance and love versus devotion to duty to a new intensity through the life-and-death struggle of the heroine between her heart and her cause in *Lust/Caution*. *Taking Woodstock* again dealt with the themes of repression and liberation, while *Life of Pi* further integrated these ideas and showed the balance achieved by adapting to and accepting one's fate, each reflecting Lee's continuing exploration of these subjects.

James Schamus

A study of Ang Lee would not be complete without a discussion of American independent film producer James Schamus, who has collaborated with Lee on all of his feature films except *Life of Pi*. In addition to cofounding and serving for twelve years as CEO of Focus Features, the art-house film division of Universal Studios, Schamus is also a professor of film theory, history, and criticism at Columbia University, and a published film historian. He first noticed Lee after seeing his NYU graduate thesis film, *A Fine Line*, and began a collaboration that has been notable both for its success and its longevity. To briefly outline Schamus' most remarkable contributions, he produced *Brokeback Mountain*, cowrote *Hulk*, and cowrote and executive-produced *Crouching Tiger, Hidden Dragon*. He produced *The Ice Storm*, which he also adapted from Rick Moody's novel. He produced and wrote *Ride with the Devil*, coproduced *Sense and Sensibility*, and cowrote and associate-produced *Eat Drink Man Woman*. He produced and cowrote *The Wedding Banquet* and produced Lee's first feature, *Pushing Hands*, for which he also served as an uncredited writer. (Interestingly, his voice is also used in an uncredited cameo; he is the literary agent who leaves an enthusiastic answering machine message about Martha's book.)

Aside from his collaborations with Lee, Schamus has worked with other independent filmmakers such as Todd Haynes (*Safe*, 1995), Nicole Holofcener (*Walking and Talking*, 1996), and Todd Solondz (*Happiness*, 1998). Schamus' original Good Machine production company, which he founded with Ted Hope, produced fiercely defiant films in the early 1990s. Schamus has said, "To be part of the American independent scene in the late 1980s and early 1990s meant that you were defined by, in many ways, your relationship to the early days of queer cinema, which was really the most challenging and the most defining part of that cultural moment."[35] Aside from his early work with Solondz, Holofcener, and Haynes, Schamus' most enduring cinematic relationship has definitely been with Ang Lee.

Lee elaborates on his relationship with James Schamus:

> I brought my first project to him seeking out his help as a producer and the rest fell into place afterward. And on *The Wedding Banquet* he helped me with rewrites and expanding the English portion of the screenplay, especially the first and last quarter of the film regarding the development of Simon's character. *Eat Drink Man Woman* was entirely in Chinese, but he helped me in revising and rewriting the script. When we began work on *Sense and Sensibility*, I brought him along because I didn't know anybody in England, and he became the producer. Back then, I felt very insecure about the white world, and James was a very liberal and knowledgeable person—and a very hip person. He is really like a walking dictionary. He could help me with everything, from public speaking to writing letters, checking out facts, and selling films. He always gave me all kinds of advice, telling me that I'd be doomed if I did this, or it would be great if I did that. So I developed the habit of checking with him on all kinds of fronts. . . . Gradually James extended his services to write almost all of my screenplays from *The Ice Storm* on. I never treat him quite like a writer, but he provides me with the kinds of textures that I need. I have tried working with different writers, but it always seems very difficult. It is hard for them to understand me and really know what I need, and provide me with what I am looking for. James seems to be the closest.[36]

It is clear from Schamus' work on screenplays that he is an extraordinary writer. His solo adaptation of *The Ice Storm* garnered him the Best Screenplay prize at the 1997 Cannes Film Festival. Despite speaking no Mandarin, he also took on the challenging role of working with Chinese cowriters for Lee's early trilogy films, *Crouching Tiger, Hidden Dragon*, and *Lust/Caution*. For *Crouching Tiger, Hidden Dragon*, he was nominated for Academy Awards for Best Music (Song) for composing lyrics to the title song, "A Love Before Time," and Best Adapted Screenplay (along with his cowriters). The importance of Schamus' contributions to both the writing and the shaping of the screenplays cannot be overstated, for it was Schamus who brought New York sensibilities to the American characters in Lee's two earliest screenplays, as well as grim 1970s realism to the screenplay for *The Ice Storm* (like the adolescents in the film, Schamus grew up in the 1970s). His screenplay for *Ride with the Devil* is simply gorgeous English prose. It is also clear that Schamus was largely responsible for making the martial arts epic *Crouching Tiger* not only comprehensible but palatable to a Western audience. The same is true of *Eat Drink Man Woman*, for which Schamus not only suggested key plot points but which he shaped for Western tastes, accounting for its phenomenal international success.

In addition to the writing credits, Schamus must be recognized for the ingenious marketing of Lee's films, from the very earliest days, when fortune cookies were handed out in movie-house foyers as a promotion for *The Wedding Banquet*, to the limited and staggered release of *Brokeback Mountain* (first, to strategically-selected cities and later, after successful word-of-mouth advertising, to the American heartland). In addition to the almost surgical precision used in the targeting of cities and venues for *Brokeback Mountain*'s initial run (an understanding of New York's micro-climates helped Schamus immensely), another strategy used in marketing *Brokeback Mountain* was to sell it as a romance for women rather than a controversial gay-bashing tale. (Focus Features also marketed the film to the gay community, with press junkets to gay venues and articles in gay magazines like *Out*.) Schamus demonstrated remarkably strategic expertise in writing articles and editorials for New York newspapers and magazines to stir up interest in *Crouching Tiger, Hidden Dragon, Hulk*, and *Brokeback Mountain*. He has served as official apologist for the films, writing lengthy public treatises to defend them; no doubt his skill with public debate is aided by his academic background. For example, Schamus publicly addressed accusations that the marketing strategy for *Brokeback Mountain* had made a conscious effort to "de-gay" and play up the heterosexual aspects of the movie. In the *New York Review of Books*, Schamus responded to this claim:

> Daniel Mendelsohn, in his finely observed review of *Brokeback Mountain* ["An Affair to Remember," *NYRB*, February 23], sets up a false dichotomy between the essentially "gay" nature of the film and the erasure of this gay identity through the marketing and reception of the film as a "universal" love story. . . . Mendelsohn is rightly nervous about what happens when a gay text is so widely and enthusiastically embraced by a mainstream hetero-dominated culture; and it is true that many reviewers contextualize their investment in the gay aspects of the romance by claiming that the characters' homosexuality is incidental to the film's achievements. . . . To begin with, there is a very real sense in which the film is, or at least aspires to be, "universal" in just the way Mendelsohn describes it, as a "distinctively gay story that happens to be so well told that any feeling person can be moved by it." One thing this means is that we solicit every audience member's *identification with* the film's central gay characters; the film succeeds if it, albeit initially within the realm of the aesthetic, *queers* its audience. But in doing so, it paradoxically figures its gayness not just as a concretely situated identity, but also as a profound and emotionally expansive experience, understandable by all.[37]

One of the most striking characteristics of James Schamus is his willingness to give the limelight to Ang Lee, whose name is the far better known of the two. James Schamus has stood behind Lee and supported him from the early days, when Lee was just another risky proposition as an independent filmmaker, and has played a critical role in helping to fashion Lee's reception in the international arena.[38]

Miscellaneous Projects of Ang Lee

In 1995, the same year he made *Sense and Sensibility*, Lee cowrote and coproduced a movie called *Siao Yu* (*Shaonü xiaoyu*). For this film, he collaborated with the influential Taiwanese film star Sylvia Chang (who had appeared as Jin-Rong, the father's love interest and mother to Shan-Shan in *Eat Drink Man Woman*). He and Sylvia Chang worked together on the screenplay, based on a novel by Geling Yan. The story contained some of the East/West elements Ang Lee was already known for from *The*

Wedding Banquet and *Pushing Hands*. A poor Chinese girl, Siao Yu (Rene Liu), working in a New York sweatshop, needs a Green Card to stay in the United States. She and her boyfriend (an illegal Chinese immigrant) make a deal with an elderly American man, Mario Moretti (Daniel J. Travanti), a former political activist and writer who, aging into his sixties, urgently needs some money to pay off a gambling debt. Her boyfriend borrows some money from his friends to pay the old man so he and Siao Yu can fake a marriage as husband and wife. While Immigration and Naturalization Service (INS) agents check on them repeatedly to make sure it is a legitimate marriage, the story takes some moving turns before the Green Card is finally granted. Rene Liu, whose prodigious talents as a young actress were showcased for the first time in this film, has become a well-known actress in both China and Taiwan. *Siao Yu* is one of her earliest movies.

This film shows some of the familiar themes of other Ang Lee films, including the East/West dialectic, the deceit to keep peace which leads to chaotic comedy—with Rita (Marj Dusay), Mario's first wife, arriving suddenly in his apartment—a focus on the harmonizing influence of food, and the touching scene with a sweatshop worker singing along with an old Chinese song on the radio about how her life could have been different. There are light jokes about language, as Mario gently chides Siao Yu over her habit of saying "I'm sorry" all the time. As they gaze at the moon on an evening walk, Mario tells her, "Don't say you're sorry." It also has a quiet ending, with Siao Yu in tears, having made an important decision that will change her life.

In 2001, Ang Lee shot *The Hire: Chosen*, a short film for the automobile manufacturer BMW. BMW had asked a series of directors (including John Woo, John Frankenheimer, Ridley Scott, and Alejandro González Iñárritu) to make promotional films in their distinctive styles. Clive Owen plays the Driver, and Lee's son, Mason, appears in the film as a passenger. The film is six-and-a-half minutes long and was formerly available on the manufacturer's website. The plot is as follows: The Driver collects a Tibetan child who has just arrived in America on a ship. He must drive him through a dark night in the city to get to a monk's house, while eluding several would-be kidnappers driving American cars. Because of the BMW's superior maneuverability, they are able to evade the kidnappers. At the end of the film, Clive Owen sticks a bandage on his ear, and on the bandage is the image of "the Hulk," an inside reference to Lee's future release in 2003. This inside joke was prescient as this film was also made at the level that could be enjoyable for both adults and children.

Finally, Lee is the first Taiwanese screenwriter to have one of his films rewritten in English and produced as a Hollywood movie. *Tortilla Soup* (2001), the American remake of *Eat Drink Man Woman*, was directed by María Ripoll and released in 2001. Using the basic plot of *Eat Drink Man Woman*, this film recast the story in Hispanic/American culture, with Hector Elizondo as the father of three rebellious daughters who share their love through food. As in Lee's film, the plot turned on the device of the father losing his sense of taste. This is an unprecedented case of a Taiwanese film remade outside the island.

In 2003, Lee was credited as executive producer for the film *One Last Ride*, about a man's descent into gambling addiction. This endeavor reunited him with actor Pat Cupo, who had starred in his award-winning graduate thesis film *A Fine Line* in 1984.

While still in the planning stages, Lee has announced that he will executive produce a film directed by Yuen Wo Ping, the action choreographer for *Crouching Tiger, Hidden Dragon*, for future release. The film, entitled *The Hands of Shang-Chi*, is based on the Marvel Comics kung fu hero who learns that his father is the world's worst criminal.

In addition, it has been announced that Lee is to follow up his Academy Award–winning *Life of Pi* with a very different kind of 3D film, this time focusing on the legendary boxers of the 1960s and 1970s. Joe Frazier and Muhammad Ali's classic 1975 "Thrilla in Manila" fight will be one of the movie's climactic centerpieces, with Lee hoping to advance visual special-effects techniques into new territory—the 3D depiction of some of the greatest fights in boxing history. There are few further details available, but the screenplay is by a highly-celebrated screenwriter, Britain's two-time Academy Award–nominee Peter Morgan, nominated for both *The Queen* (2006) and *Frost/Nixon* (2008).

While it surprised some U.S. viewers that Lee beat Steven Spielberg (*Lincoln*, 2012) in the best director category at the 2013 Academy Awards ceremony, *Life of Pi* was unquestionably one of the most well-received award-winners with global audiences, having claimed a hugely impressive US$609 million in worldwide box office sales. With this new film, Lee's decision to venture further into visual special-effects comes at a time when 3D revenues are falling in the U.S., the world's largest box office, though the medium remains popular elsewhere around the globe.

Ang Lee: In the Midst of the Tide

Ang Lee has said in interviews that he feels he in some ways embodies the rapidly deepening relationship between American and Asian cinema, and that Hollywood has been a few years behind the curve. "I'm in the midst of this tide," he has said.[39] From making small international films like *The Wedding Banquet* and *Eat Drink Man Woman*, to making "quality English movies" like *Sense and Sensibility*, and finally to becoming accepted as a mainstream Hollywood director, with *Brokeback Mountain* and *Life of Pi*, Lee's career has been a pioneering experience. "By the time I made *Crouching Tiger, Hidden Dragon*, everything seems to have come together. . . . On the receiving side, I think the whole world is more ready, with the Internet, with film festivals and DVDs. It used to be a one way street from West to East: we were receiving and the West was producing. I think we're getting closer and closer. The gap between the cultures is getting erased every day. . . . The world's getting smaller."[40] Lee's films, from his earliest Chinese-language trilogy to *Crouching Tiger, Hidden Dragon* and *Life of Pi*, not only anticipated but also facilitated current trends in globalization and cultural exchange that are becoming an increasingly common part of the twenty-first century worldview.

THREE

Confucian Values and Cultural Displacement
in Pushing Hands

I don't know where I am, but I never know where I am. [My family originated] in China, then my parents moved to Taiwan, where we were outsiders, then [I moved] to the States, then back to China, then back here. I trust the elusive world created by movies more than anything else. I live on the other side of the screen.

    —Ang Lee (no date)

ANG LEE'S THREE earliest films, *Pushing Hands* and his two phenomenal early international successes, *The Wedding Banquet* and *Eat Drink Man Woman*, explore the topic of cultural identity using the English language as a tool for both communication and miscommunication. The medium of English is used for comic effect and to indicate a cultural barrier. In illustrating the capabilities and limitations of the use of English as a second language, Lee casts a discerning eye on the cultural landscape that exists in the blending and metamorphosis of Chinese and Western thinking. In this way, he is a filmic pioneer into the interrelationships of cultural identities created by the modern phenomenon of globalization of the English language. The early films of Ang Lee chart a course into the dense and treacherous territory of the Chinese speaker approaching Western culture through English as a second language. One example is the miscommunication between the non-English-speaking Taiwanese father-in-law and the Western daughter-in-law in *Pushing Hands*. This film clearly delineates the dehumanizing effects of hi-tech modernization and globalization on the second-language speaker facing an English-only culture. Lee's unselfconscious portrait of the difficulties faced by Chinese speakers of English as a second language presents a useful perspective for both Chinese and English speakers as they face the "other."

The narratives of all three films, but particularly *Pushing Hands* and *The Wedding Banquet*, are also concerned with cultural hybridity and diversity arising from issues of Chinese diasporic identity. Ang Lee is the child of two "mainlanders" who moved from China to Taiwan, displaced by the outcome of the Chinese civil war in 1949. While the Hokkien-speaking majority of Han Chinese in Taiwan were also "mainlanders" at some point, centuries of living on the island, which has gone through a series of foreign conquests including occupation by Japan, has given rise to strong separatist sentiments. Thus the offspring of 1949 mainlanders living in Taiwan would necessarily face uncertainties of identity. Ang Lee's identity confusion was compounded by his move abroad to the United States to pursue higher education in 1978. Thus, Lee characterizes himself as follows:

> To me, I'm a mixture of many things and a confusion of many things . . . I'm not a native Taiwanese, so we're alien in Taiwan today, with the native Taiwanese pushing for independence. But when we go back to China, we're Taiwanese. Then, I live in the States; I'm sort of a foreigner everywhere. It's hard to find a real identity.[1]

Recent scholarship on diaspora experience and the resultant cultural hybridity and shifting identity has focused on the changing cultural conditions of far-flung immigrant communities in the era of globalization. The complexity, fluidity, and diversity of cultural identity among diasporic immigrants have been explored by a number of scholars including James Clifford (1997), John Tomlinson (1999), and Stuart Hall (2003). *Pushing Hands* is an intimate study of the cultural tensions of the diaspora that at its essence deals with the confrontation between Chinese and Western culture. (Sheng-mei Ma has placed Ang Lee's early trilogy films in the tradition of "overseas student literature" (*liuxuesheng wenxue*), a genre of Chinese literature dealing with the "overseas student-immigrant" experience.)[2]

In their representation of Lee's view of the traditional Chinese patriarchy, his first three films should be taken as a set. In their prescient 1997 article "Breaking the Soy Sauce Jar," Wei Ming Dariotis and Eileen Fung recognize the unique vision of these three films—it is in this groundbreaking article that the term "Father-Knows-Best trilogy" is first used in an academic context to apply to this early series in Lee's oeuvre.[3] The title "Father-Knows-Best," taken from the late 1950s television situation comedy and now considered to be an ultraconservative cultural reference, is used ironically because indeed, in Lee's trilogy, it is not the patriarch's traditional view that is considered "best." However, the argument can be made that, although patriarchal control is initially subverted, it is ultimately recognized and reaffirmed/reoriented with a self-reflexive twist in all three films: the patriarchal position is threatened but ultimately reestablished, revealing and paralleling Lee's own personal struggle with the issue of paternal control.

The idea that all three films reinforce traditional patriarchy is explored by Shu-mei Shih (2000), who argues that the patriarchy is made "flexible" by accommodating challenge and difference, while it maintains power by negotiation and what is meant to seem "well-intentioned" duplicity.[4] In the first film, the father's traditional tai chi skill, which is at first set in opposition to the "modern" West, ultimately brings him honor, recognition, new employment, and respect as a teacher. In the second film, the father, more than the mother, is aware of the reality of his son's homosexual lifestyle choice, and ultimately affirms it while still maintaining an external appearance of patriarchal control (he will have a grandson, the family line will be continued). In *The Wedding Banquet*, traditional values are subverted but ultimately allowed to remain intact through an overly-contrived "happy ending." In the third film, *Eat Drink Man Woman*, the patriarchal position at first appears rigid, for example through the father's insistence on the weekly Sunday family dinner ritual. However, the ending of the film proves that he is not the rigid conservative he appears, when he makes a marriage proposal that shocks everyone. Thus, the father figure in each of these films emerges as triumphant; traditional patriarchy is reestablished.

A Discussion of Pushing Hands

The use of English as a second language and the effects of globalization feature prominently in Lee's three earliest films: *Pushing Hands*, *The Wedding Banquet*, and *Eat Drink Man Woman*. In addition, as noted above, these three films have come to be known as the "Father-Knows-Best" trilogy because they each explore the changing role of the Chinese father in the late twentieth century. Moreover, these films share a unifying strand in that they all feature the actor Sihung Lung in the central role of the father. In Lee's feature-length directorial debut, *Pushing Hands*, the father's alienation and loneliness are brought on by his lack of communication with his American daughter-in-law; in this situation, language forms a daunting cultural barrier. Lee has said that he based the film on the loneliness and isolation he felt after he first moved to the United States; the atmosphere of the film vividly reflects the struggles and difficulties of the second-language speaker facing an English-only culture in an increasingly impersonal world of hi-tech modernization and globalization.

Pushing Hands is a sensitive portrait of a traditional Chinese father faced with change in a fast-paced, English-speaking world. The plot and the central conflicts of this film are simple to outline because of its small cast. Master Chu, a retired Chinese tai chi master, moves to Westchester, New York, to live out his final years under the care of his son, Alex, his American daughter-in-law, Martha, and their young son, Jeremy (Haan Lee). Predictably, the cultural differences cause misunderstandings and animosity between the father and daughter-in-law, who suffers writer's block as she works at home on her second novel. The aging and traditional Chinese father tries to get along with his Westernized family while simultaneously adjusting to a new place and culture, where even the ringing of the telephone startles him.

During the first fifteen minutes of the film, there is almost no dialogue—only visual action to establish these glaring cultural differences. This absence of dialogue is conspicuous and helps to establish the slow, gentle pace and attention to domestic detail which have become the hallmark of Ang Lee's films. Some examples of the diversity in cultural identity between the Chinese father and his American daughter-in-law include the following: the opening shot of hands pushing away into the air, which the viewer comes to realize are the hands of an elderly Chinese man performing tai chi; this can be contrasted with the tension of Martha typing the beginning of her novel on the computer in the room behind him. The camera focuses on the paragraph on the screen with the cursor blinking, and the viewer can make out the words "children," "white linen," and "homestead"—a traditional American pioneer narrative reminiscent of Laura Ingalls Wilder's *Little House on the Prairie* (1935) and another marked contrast with Chinese culture. Master Chu quietly washes his face and silently meditates on a pillow on the floor; this is contrasted with Martha's compulsive staring into the refrigerator and seeking to soothe herself with a fingerful of frosting she swipes off the top of some leftover cake.

When Master Chu begins to heat up something in the kitchen microwave, he mistakenly covers it with aluminum foil. Predictably, this causes the oven to flame and spark, after which Martha runs in and scolds, "No *metal* in the *microwave!*" This is the first spoken line in the movie. There is no eye contact between the two as they begin preparing and eating their lunches; here again is a contrast: she eats cold salad and dry wheat crackers while he eats a hearty, mouthwatering stir-fry. After lunch, more contrasts: he practices calligraphy with a writing-brush while she again types at the computer. Finally, he chuckles looking at her through the window as she runs by in a tight jogging outfit, punching the air with her fists.

Over the course of the film, Martha's overstressed attitude and resistance to her father-in-law take their toll on her physical health—she develops a serious stomach ulcer. Master Chu tries to help her, first by saying, "Tell her not to get all worked up—years from now, we'll all be underground." Second, he gently and silently places a mug of freshly brewed Chinese herbal medicine beside her computer while she is working. She leaves it untouched. Finally, he attempts to help her using massage and tai chi therapy but she screams with fear and ends up in the hospital with a bleeding ulcer. The climax of the movie is brought on when Master Chu moves out of the house and leaves a note to his son, Alex, containing the following words: "In China we lived together happily through so many bitter times . . . but here in America, surrounded by so many fine material things, it seems there's no place in your home for me." Alex counters this statement with his own painfully honest admission: "I came to America to raise money to bring you here to have a good life." Master Chu's loneliness and desolation (he is fired from his job and lands in jail) are a testimony to how devastatingly his son's plans have failed.

Language is a very important aspect of this multilingual film, adding an important dimension of shaded meaning. For example, the American daughter-in-law has only learned one word in Chinese, "Xie-xie" ("Thank you"), which she mispronounces, in a toneless American accent, as "Shay-shay." At one point, she says, "Your father has not learned any English in the month since he arrived [in the U.S.]." Her husband counters, "How much have you tried to understand him?" The answer is implied by Martha's unwillingness to meet her father-in-law halfway; instead, she refers to herself as his "babysitter," and criticizes him for becoming "more and more like a child." When he asks her to accompany him on a walk, she fails to understand his fear of becoming lost. They begin to yell at each other in two different languages, and the daughter-in-law finally shouts "Don't you understand what I'm telling you?" This line points out the ultimate irony—that because of the language difference neither can understand the other at all, no matter how loudly they yell.

The troubles associated with growing up in a bilingual family are also highlighted by Master Chu's presence in the household. Conversations across the dinner table occur in two languages, switching back and forth between English and Chinese, with the monolingual members of the family asking "What?" or "What did he just say?" The young son, Jeremy, has "Chinese time," in which he practices calligraphy and memorizes Chinese poems with his grandfather. On weekends, the family goes to the local community center, where Jeremy takes Chinese classes with the American-born Chinese children. As the film goes on, there is even more comic confusion over language. There is a scene in which a man speaking standard Mandarin Chinese and a woman with a strong Taiwanese accent cannot communicate clearly. When the woman pronounces "you fan" as "you han" (translated in the subtitles as "oily ice" rather than "oily rice"), comic confusion ensues, and the difference even among different Chinese-speaking peoples is underscored.

Pushing Hands anticipates Lee's highly-crafted future films in several signature ways. First of all, this comedy/drama contains the essential elements of intimate domestic detail the viewer has come to associate with Ang Lee: details of eating, sleeping, disagreement and reconciliation, sexual behavior, exercise, etc. One scene that especially presupposes his future work on the male/female dialectic is the simple and wordless scene where Martha turns away from her husband in bed, rejecting his sexual overture. This scene is very painful and carries the punch of Lee's forthcoming work in its intimacy and fearless honesty. In addition, the cultural divide between Asian and American lifestyles is highlighted, as it will be much more succinctly in his next film, *The Wedding Banquet*. Here, for example, the calming techniques of tai chi exercise are contrasted with the violent and tension-filled striving of the American jogger. Finally, the sweet, elegiac ending is an intimate portrait, lingering on with gentle grace into the final fadeout.

Pushing Hands is still little known in the West; on the whole, very few people have seen it, even those highly familiar with Lee's work. There are several reasons for this. First, the limited budget for this film is evident and affects the quality and overall feel of the movie. For example, special-effects sequences are executed rapidly, in order to hide the comparatively low budget; a scene of a speeding car was made from several shots edited in a sequence to make the car appear to be driving very quickly, and lighting suffers in some scenes. The sound quality is not always dependable—the sound in the picnic scene (filmed near a super-highway) is distracting because the roar of traffic overwhelms the spoken lines. The final product appears grainy and more cheaply made than Lee's subsequent films. The second difficulty for the Western viewer is related to the emotional arc of the story, which comes through as melodrama. Certain scenes require a deeper knowledge of Taiwanese social interaction and unspoken behavioral codes; otherwise, for the Western viewer these scenes seem maudlin or slightly over-the-top. One example is a scene in which a large student, "Fatty," appears to challenge the teacher but instead is shot across the room and into a table of dumplings being prepared by a Chinese women's cooking class. This gives the tai chi students a chance to enthusiastically pitch in to help the women clean up the mess and to roll new dumplings—a type of bonding that is natural in Taiwanese social intercourse but seemingly far-fetched to Western thinking. Another moment of disconnection for the Western viewer is when the father, after being fired from his job, stubbornly resists the efforts of the boss and other employees to remove him from the restaurant (he stands rooted in place, summoning energy from tai chi). The viewer is supplied with signifiers to imply that this is indeed a heroic action; however, a Western viewer is tempted to wonder what kind of legal case the father has warding off the employer who has fired him and ordered him to leave the premises. The film asks the viewer to sympathize with the father's actions although they are indefensible from a legal standpoint (indeed, he is subsequently arrested). The viewer is given to understand that the father's display of strength is ennobling in a Chinese context. However, this again requires a distracting cultural shift for the Western viewer.

Finally, the American female character is portrayed unsympathetically. Her character is flat and one-dimensional; the role is deliberately set up as an oppositional force, which makes her unlikeable. Although Lee refrains from dooming her to the role of caricature, she still holds attitudes that seem overly ignorant and closed-minded toward Chinese culture. For example, when the father-in-law suggests that the cartoons his grandson watches on American television are too violent, Martha snaps back with the criticism that Chinese tai chi is more violent than the cartoons (although throughout the film the healing and holistic properties of tai chi are emphasized). The character of the husband is pretty much a blank; he is not given much to do except look anxious and work on his laptop computer—besides this, he must serve as translator between his father and wife (although he is absent for most of the day due to his work). One wonders why Martha, with her lack of interest or tolerance for Chinese culture, would have been drawn to marry her Chinese husband. At the end of the film, Martha's character has undergone a transformation: she is cooking Chinese food (egg rolls) and thinking about a new topic for her novel: the history of Chinese railway workers in America.[5] This shift in cultural signifiers for her character is intended to illustrate her new openness to her family's ethnic background, but there seems to be little to lead up to this too-tidy and oversimplified change.

Sihung Lung was retired by the time Ang Lee began casting for *Pushing Hands*, but the director, who had childhood memories of seeing Lung acting in films, asked him to play the father. Before working with Lee, Sihung Lung had been known primarily in his later years for playing toughs and gang bosses. However, due to Lee's talent for spotting potential in his actors, the director brought out some of Lung's best screen performances; under Lee's direction, Lung played the lead in all three early films with stately charm and grace (in 2000, he also had a small role as Sir Te in *Crouching Tiger, Hidden Dragon*). Interestingly, although Sihung Lung was required to speak significant English lines in *The Wedding Banquet*, the actor never actually learned to speak English at all; his English lines for the film had to be memorized phonetically. Lee elaborated on his casting of the actor, who died in May 2002 at the age of 72, in a special featurette on the DVD of *The Wedding Banquet*, when he called Sihung Lung the "all-Chinese father figure . . . playing his part in modern society." He continued: "[Sihung Lung] has a very fatherly look; you look at his face and it's like five thousand years of suffering and responsibility is all in his face. And yet inside he's a humorous person."[6] This combination of warmth and toughness was the critical integration of the personality Lee sought for his quintessential Chinese father figure. He has said that had it not been for the face and acting skill of Sihung Lung, he might never have been able to express his vision of the traditional Chinese father.[7]

A son's American lifestyle alienates his traditionally-minded father: Ang Lee's intensely personal vision of filial piety.

Ultimately, the tai chi concept of "Pushing Hands" is used as a very effective metaphor in the film. On the one hand, it represents the clash between husband and wife. As the husband, Alex, explains in the film, "['Pushing Hands'] is like tai chi for two—a way of keeping your balance while you're unbalancing your opponent." ("Like marriage," Martha replies.) Alex further explains: "If you try to unbalance me, I simply avoid your energy and turn it back on you." Martha falls on the bed, toppled by her own force, laughing. The final shot of the husband and wife is of their hands alone, slowly and carefully moving in an intertwined dance. This is the "Pushing Hands" exercise, which has been described as "a rhythmical, non-competitive exercise between two people, keeping constant contact with [ones's] partner."[8] The more technical description of the tai chi maneuver known as "Pushing Hands" is as follows: "The exercise teaches a student to be submissive (invest in loss). To 'invest in loss' means to lose balance in order to acquire it—to be prepared to yield."[9] In this final shot of the husband and wife doing the "Pushing Hands" exercise together as partners, Alex says to his wife, "Relax, don't resist, and don't break contact." There is a close-up of their hands, almost blurry. "Feel it?" he asks. As Alex explains and translates his father's tai chi philosophy to his wife, the two find healing and wisdom from this bicultural synthesis.

The "Pushing Hands" metaphor could also be applied to the forces of two cultures—American and Chinese—clashing in the film. In the "Pushing Hands" exercise, the first person offers no resistance at all to the pressure or push the other person is exerting and keeps borrowing this strength until the two feel they have fused into one and thus have achieved harmony. This is what happens to Master Chu when Martha keeps misunderstanding him. At first he tries to resist or challenge her, but ultimately, he chooses to walk away gracefully. In the end, the daughter-in-law learns to accept the father, symbolized by her decorating the guestroom for him and asking if he will ever visit; likewise, the father achieves the balance he seeks in tai chi.

The ending of *Pushing Hands* is a sweet and understated scene that anticipates the director's gentle and intuitive future work, especially in his third film *Eat Drink Man Woman*. Master Chu has finally found a companion in Mrs. Chen (Lai Wang), a lonely, single friend he meets at the community center. However, he seems paralyzed in his pursuit of her. At the end of the film, when she suggests, "You should come by sometime and visit," he suddenly breaks his paralysis and boldly asks, "What are you doing this afternoon?" "Um, nothing," she replies shyly. "Nothing . . . nothing," he repeats equally shyly. There is an atmosphere of sweet expectation as the two grin at each other and the screen slowly fades to black. It is a truly charming scene, sensitive and full of nuance in Lee's style.

In understanding *Pushing Hands*, it is important to keep in mind Lee's own claims that the feelings of loneliness he records are semiautobiographical[10]—that in the father's loneliness and isolation one can see a reflection of Lee's own six-year period of loneliness and alienation as a foreigner cast adrift in American suburbia, speaking too slowly in heavily-accented English, unable to achieve his dreams as a filmmaker.[11] Likewise, it may be inferred that the American woman's haughty and dismissive treatment of her Chinese father-in-law reflects some of the treatment Ang Lee himself received—Martha and her best friend discuss in English what a burden "grandpa" is, within the hearing of Master Chu. It is also reflected by Master Chu's line to his son: "Let me tell you," he says, who was persecuted by Mao's Red Guards during the Chinese Cultural Revolution, "compared to loneliness, persecution is nothing." This film shows that in the fast-paced, modern lifestyle of American society, there is little respect accorded to traditional Chinese customs or lifestyle. This is epitomized by the sad spectacle of Master Chu watching martial arts and Peking Opera on dated and grainy videotapes—Martha makes him wear headphones because she is bothered by the high-pitched singing in Chinese opera. *Pushing Hands* shows Lee's vision of Chinese culture as it exists in a shadowy form in American suburbia: marginalized, kept on the periphery, preserved only in a rapidly deteriorating form by first-generation immigrants in the process of assimilation, their memories of the "real China" becoming grainy and blurred.

Other aspects of this film also reinforce the idea that *Pushing Hands* is one of Lee's most personal and autobiographically revealing films. For example, the backyard used as a setting in the film is actually the yard of Lee's own home in the New York suburbs. In using his own "space" for this film, Ang Lee was signifying that the experiences of the family patriarch—a foreigner stranded in American suburbia—were in some cases self-referential. As noted, since he did not have a regular job for six years, he was quite familiar with the inactive, silent daytime experience of suburbia and its bone-crunchingly slow rhythms. Nowhere is this made clearer than in the heavy slap of the thick *New York Times* on the doorstep of the house, an image which, for the American viewer, is almost unnoticeable in its ordinariness. However, for the non-English speaker, the thud signifying the arrival of the thick American newspaper represents just another impenetrable wall barring him from truly entering into the new society. This daily delivery of the newspaper would be a source of burden and alienation for the non-English speaker; each day another thick newspaper full of information in English is dropped on the doorstep as a ritual reinforcement of his status as an outsider.

Another personal detail is the presence in the film of Lee's son, Haan, playing a child growing up within a family of two conflicting cultures. Although his own son was not pulled between his mother's and father's culture because his parents are both Chinese, inevitably there is tension for the child of a first-generation immigrant to the U.S. Thus, the film portrays the struggle to have regular "Chinese time" in the home, the participation in Chinese language classes and the relegation of the traditional arts of Chinese tai chi and cooking classes to community center activities. There is pathos in the director's presentation of yellowing hallways in the dilapidated public building where Chinese activities are preserved by the lonely and aging immigrant community portrayed in the film. The scene in which Haan, after receiving Chinese tutoring from his grandfather, lies half-asleep in a stupor on the bed reciting a Chinese poem from memory in a weary monotone, shows the pressure on Chinese children growing up in a different culture. Ang Lee's script also aptly deals with the tension between child-rearing methods in both American and Chinese cultures: while Chinese culture trains children to respect authority, the American mother in the film makes agreements with her son; if he finishes his milk from dinner, then he may watch television. The Chinese grandfather points this out, insightfully asking if this style of parenting is too much like American democracy, where everyone's rights must be respected.

What comes through utterly clearly is that for a non-English speaker in America, time passes slowly, and one can feel useless and trapped. This is demonstrated when the grandfather moves out of his son's home, and the only work he can find is a demeaning position as a dishwasher in a restaurant in New York's Chinatown. It is a job he cannot even do quickly enough, causing him to rely on some of the younger workers to help him finish on time. His dignity is all but stripped away when he is fired from even this menial position, but summoning the energy of tai chi, he performs a remarkable demonstration of strength which gets him arrested and broadcast on the evening news. Although this part of the story is the most far-fetched—would a Chinese tai chi expert's feat of strength and subsequent arrest really make it onto the evening news in New York?—it does restore to him a measure of dignity and even heroism.

In the earliest draft of *Pushing Hands* submitted by Lee to win the Taiwan film-making contest in 1990, there is a line which no longer exists in the movie, spoken to Martha by a dentist (who also no longer exists in the movie). This line expresses Lee's latent desire to share Eastern thought with the West, demonstrating the filmmaker's tenacity and boldness despite the frustration of his six-year period of waiting in limbo:

> Dentist: A very good Indian friend of mine gives yoga and meditation classes twice a week. He teaches you how to relax and soft movements and all that kind of stuff. I can't tell you how much I've benefited from it. I'm not joking—*it's time to look to the East.*[12]

This line demonstrates Lee's fundamental vision in setting up the cultural dichotomy between Chinese and American cultural traditions in *Pushing Hands*. Above all, *Pushing Hands* seeks to explore the topic of cultural identity, through language, cultural diversity, lifestyle contrasts, etc., to illuminate unique yet misunderstood aspects of Chinese culture. Deliberately or not, in *Pushing Hands*, Lee casts a more positive slant on Chinese culture than on American culture. In such scenes as the martial arts sequences and the final resolution of the "Pushing Hands" exercise and what it teaches the American daughter-in-law, Ang Lee offers Chinese culture as a positive alternative to the tension-filled, junk food–saturated, ulcer-ridden society of the U.S.; he presents an alternative worth knowing. This is Lee's offering of the finest arts of Chinese culture: tai chi in *Pushing Hands*, Chinese cooking in *Eat Drink Man Woman*, and later, with *Crouching Tiger, Hidden Dragon*, the most exquisite presentation of Chinese martial arts. Lee has been enormously successful at using his films to bridge the gap between Chinese and Western cultures, and best of all, at translating Chinese culture into a language that is not only comprehensible but also enjoyable and intriguing for the Western viewer.

In addition, *Pushing Hands*, with its focus on Confucian filial piety, reflects Chinese films' historically long engagement with the problem of filial piety in changing times. *Pushing Hands* is an echo of key Chinese films and themes from the past, updated to the global, multilingual, and diasporic level. The film appropriates the theme of filial piety but interrogates and updates it. Michael Berry (2005) notes that all three films in Ang Lee's early trilogy highlight the strained relationship between the younger generation and the older generation, tradition and modernity, Confucian and Western values; this is a theme directors were exploring in the earliest Chinese films, such as *Two Stars* (*Yinhan shuangxing*, 1931). Lee comments, "That was one of the reasons I initially did not want to make *Pushing Hands*, because that is 'the oldest movie in the book,' the kind that people had already stopped making when I was little—those old movies that explore whether or not a person is loyal and expresses filial piety toward his parents. But somehow those themes still hit home and speak to us today."[13] *Pushing Hands* revisits the ethical conundrums of family and modernity and examines the impact of globalization on traditional Chinese cultural and behavioral norms.

FOUR

Transgressing Boundaries of Gender and Culture in The Wedding Banquet

WHILE *Pushing Hands* was a hit in Taiwan and popular in Asian markets, *The Wedding Banquet* was Ang Lee's breakout film for the American general public. Although the film dealt with less-than-mainstream subject matter, according to coproducer James Schamus, the storyline followed the arc of a typical 1930s Hollywood screwball comedy—"except that it was gay and Chinese."[1] The film's plot is perhaps by now familiar—a Chinese son, Wai-Tung (Winston Chao), with a gay American lover, Simon (Mitchell Lichtenstein), wishes to get his parents to stop badgering him to marry; he is unwilling to tell them the truth about his homosexuality for fear of breaking their hearts. Simon comes up with the suggestion of a sham marriage between Wai-Tung and their Shanghainese artist friend Wei Wei (May Chin). Wei Wei moves into the basement and everything is fine until Wai-Tung's parents, Mr. and Mrs. Gao (Sihung Lung and Ah-Leh Gua) decide to make the trip from Taiwan to attend the wedding. The young couple's plans for a small civil ceremony at City Hall are thwarted when an old friend of Wai-Tung's father offers his posh restaurant for a huge traditional Chinese wedding banquet. The plans go further awry when Wei Wei and Wai-Tung spend a drunken wedding night together, and Wei Wei becomes pregnant from that single encounter.

The construction of this film, in which the five main characters are trying to conceal things from one another, is complex and poignant. Ultimately, although Wai-Tung wishes to keep his homosexual identity a secret, his father sees through the pretense. The father does not let his son know that he knows, however; instead he shares the secret with his son's gay lover, by offering him a red envelope to welcome him as a kind of "son-in-law." The father and the son are both keeping secrets from each other and living under the pretense of normality—both are playing along by pretending the wedding is real and the son is not gay. This unresolved tension fuels the movie's somewhat madcap hijinks; even at the end of the film, this tension remains unresolved, as the father departs without revealing to his son what he knows—in experiencing *The Wedding Banquet*, only the viewer is allowed a universal, privileged viewpoint.

Wedding Banquet's structure is unique in its balance of its five principal roles. It opens with a scene of Wai-Tung going through an elaborate exercise routine with weights and weight machines. The calm and meticulous manner in which he works combined with his expressionless face suggest a meditative state, while the greenish lighting and shiny, metallic glitter of the machines contributes to a sense of institutional aseptic cleanliness. The voice-over is an older woman whom the viewer comes to realize is the man's mother who has recorded a letter to him (which he listens to on headphones as he mechanically completes his exercise routines). There is an interesting contrast, too, between his attractively muscular, sweating body on the one hand, and his passive, expressionless face as he listens to the letter. He does not react with warmth or any other emotion in those inhuman surroundings, so the viewer is uncertain what to make of it.

At the beginning of the film, as Chris Berry (2003) observes, the opening sequence appears to suggest this will be Wai-Tung's story. However, as the film goes on, the other characters are given screen time and backstory in almost equal amounts. The viewer is treated to a scene of Simon at work in his job as a physical therapist, and Wei Wei's background as an artist and rugged individualist from China is also fleshed out. When the parents arrive in New York, their history and personalities are also revealed through their intimate conversations not only with their son, but with Simon, and especially in the conversations between Wai-Tung's mother and Wei Wei. Berry notes that the group must thus be observed as a unit, and that the narrative reflects how powerfully decisions made in the film impact the five-member family unit as a whole. There are many scenes to back this up: the final scene at the airport when they all look at the photo album; the group eating despondently together after the courthouse wedding; and the many "family" dinners at home and discussions around the dinner table. There is an especially funny moment when all

An elaborate ruse: Wei Wei and Wai-Tung pay respect to Wai-Tung's parents while real lover Simon stands by.

five are asked to join in a wedding ritual together and Simon takes a running leap over the long train of Wei Wei's wedding dress; this indecorous behavior shocks the visiting parents.

Latin-inflected music, such as salsa and tango, is used throughout the film, adding both a comic and high-energy touch to the narrative, and serving a structural purpose. The salsa and tango are intense and sexually provocative dances, and this film provides an elaborate dance among its leads. In addition, in tango and salsa, the focus is on one's partner and one's connection with the other, listening to the other's "body language" and imagining what he/she might be experiencing. The tango's intensity is created by the flow of creativity that comes from the unusual freedom in tango to improvise. Thus, the high art of tango dancing serves as a good metaphor for this film in which characters must keep a connection with each other while responding to unexpected improvisation and the complex maneuvers of the dance, which include swapping partners. This elaborate switching of partners in the film includes Wai-Tung with Simon, Wai-Tung with Wei Wei, Wei Wei with Wai-Tung's mother, and Wai-Tung with his own father. In the final, unexpected maneuver, Wai-Tung's father "dances" with Simon, as he reveals his true heart. Two standard Latin numbers in the soundtrack include "Quisiera Ser" and "Virgenes del Sol."[2]

The Use of Language in The Wedding Banquet

Language plays a humorous role in this film as the language barrier enables the five main characters to gossip around the dinner table in their respective languages. Wei Wei's pregnancy is discussed in English by the younger characters, while Wai-Tung's mother wonders aloud in Chinese what the argument is about, asking, "Didn't Wai-Tung pay his rent?" Another hilarious scene in the film is the civil wedding ceremony at City Hall, which details the truncated and comical wedding vows pronounced by the judge and the Chinese couple—Lee has said he based this scene on his own nuptials—where the judge calls the bride "Wee-wee," and the bride takes the vow "in sickness and death," rather than "in sickness and health."

The climactic scene in *The Wedding Banquet* is one in which the language barrier between the Chinese-speaking father and the English-speaking Simon is broken. They have not communicated directly throughout the movie; instead, the language barrier between them has prevented them from being able to have any honest communication at all. In one scene, the father mutters complaints in Chinese as Simon helps him do physical therapy. The father expresses his frustration about the pain of the physical exercises and yearns for a cigarette. Simon reacts without comprehension or care; he simply says, "Yes . . . right." In another scene, Simon shouts and rages in front of Wai-Tung's parents about Wei Wei's pregnancy. When asked by Wai-Tung to be quiet, Simon shouts out that Wai-Tung's parents do not even understand English so they cannot possibly know what he is saying. He also shouts out the telling line, "I will speak my own language in my own house!"

Because the father and mother have spoken nothing but Chinese throughout the movie, the final climax comes as a palpable shock, when the father speaks several sentences of clear English to Simon. "Happy Birthday, Simon," he says, offering him the red envelope as a gift. Simon is clearly stunned that the language barrier has been broken; Mr. Gao's English is fluent and smooth, thus revealing that his knowledge of the English language far surpasses what everyone (including the viewer) has been led to believe. This is a great moment in the film, signaled by the switch of language by one of the main characters. Simon expresses further surprise when he opens the envelope of crisp bills and understands the implications of the father's gift. "Ba," he stammers, "You know . . . you've known." The father replies in English: "I watch, I hear, I learn. Wai-Tung is my son, so you are my son, also." The process of watching, listening, and learning is also that undergone by a non-English speaker in the process of adapting to a new culture; this underscores the twice-over "adaptation" of the father—first in breaking through the language barrier between Chinese and English, and second in his shattering of cultural taboos through tenuous acceptance of his son's homosexuality.

The quiet slow-motion final scene as the father raises his arms over his head for a security check and the screen slowly fades to black can be read in a variety of ways. Most commonly, this ending is viewed with relation to *qigong* martial arts, where the father strikes a pose (resembling a graceful crane with wings aloft) in the physical art of *qigong*. This dignified movement of *qigong* reiterates the Chinese narrative and implies that the patriarch of the family has come to terms with his son's situation; his smooth and confident movement, like a bird taking flight, demonstrates that he is at peace with his son's decision. Interestingly, like many of Ang Lee's endings, it can also be interpreted as ambiguous and inconclusive—this duality of interpretation is a fascinating dimension in Lee's work. For example, the pose of the father raising his hands at the bidding of the customs official also (to the Western eye) looks very much like a position of surrender. In this interpretation, the father is read to have been overwhelmed by the dynamics of change caused by modernizing global influences which force him to release his once-rigid ideology and embrace his son's choice. The two interpretations demonstrate how this film can be read differently through different cultural lenses, and yet still be understood as a coherent narrative with basically—but not quite—the same meaning.

Personal Reflection and Autobiographical Detail

Ang Lee's confronting of his own emotions about his father played an important role in the film. He says: "For me, all of my first three movies up until *Eat Drink Man Woman* (which I didn't understand until I made the third one) are actually a trilogy about my father . . . and the need for the releasing [letting go] of the Chinese tradition, so to speak. . . . The thing that used to be [the backbone of Chinese society] and provide us security is now drifting away."[3] There is a poignant scene in *The Wedding Banquet* in which the father proudly insists on washing the dishes after the meal—an inversion of the traditional male/female roles. The father says in Chinese, "Simon cooked, so [Dad] will wash the dishes." It is as if he is trying to learn to live in a new way, and make sense of this new modern world where traditional male/female roles can be called into question. In the process of the washing, however, he drops a dish, which shatters on the floor, suggesting the difficulty of his learning and accepting a new way of life. This signifies Lee's conflict with his own father, a highly traditional man who had difficulty accepting his son's choice to be a mere "entertainer"—a walk of life that does not command respect in traditional Chinese culture. Because Lee was the firstborn son in his family, he felt guilty not honoring his father's expectations with his career choice. Referring to the making of *The Wedding Banquet*, he explains, "It's a tremendous guilt on my part . . . I ended up an entertainer . . . It's a tremendous guilt I felt toward my father. I had to work it out of my system."[4]

Lee describes the film in autobiographical terms:

> A lot of the scenes in *The Wedding Banquet* [are taken directly from] my personal story (although I don't live a gay life), but the way I talk to my parents, the parents' dialogue, is pretty much strictly from my parents. And things like the City Hall marriage is pretty much a documentary of mine [laughs]. . . . It was just a mess. My mother just kept crying, "It was shabby, it was such a disgrace," and my father [he makes a grimace]. . . . I carried that guilt for a long time.[5]

These lines from the screenplay reflect this autobiographical nature of the writing:

> Mr. Gao: Wai-Tung, you're getting married. I have to tell you something. Do you know why I joined the military?
>
> Wai-Tung: You responded to General Chiang's call to join the army during the Sino-Japanese War.
>
> Mr. Gao: No. I wanted to run away from home. So I joined the army. Your grandpa had arranged a marriage for me. I got mad and just took off. After the war, we fought the Communists. A relative escaped to Taiwan and brought me a letter from your grandpa. He told me that there was no longer a Gao family and that I should start my own family outside the mainland, to continue the family name. Son, imagine how I feel to be able to attend your wedding.[6]

What makes this scene especially moving is that the Gao family history in this film—the grandparents killed when Communist rule began in China, the father escaping alone to Taiwan—reflects Ang Lee's own family history. Similarly, as the firstborn son, he was obligated to carry the mantle of the Lee family. Disappointing his own father with his career choice (as a movie director) parallels Wai-Tung disappointing his father with his lifestyle choice (as a homosexual).

Politics and Homosexuality in The Wedding Banquet

A striking aspect of this film is the controversial line "Wo yao jiefang ni" ("I'm going to liberate you"). This line is uttered as the newly-married Wai-Tung and Wei Wei enjoy their first moments of solitude in their wedding suite, and the drunken

Wei Wei begins physically seducing her new husband. Wei Wei has always harbored a deep affection for Wai-Tung (she expresses jealousy when she sees him "dating" another girl), and her infatuation grows as the film progresses to their wedding night. As she prepares for the wedding, at points she seems to hold out the hope that the marriage will become a true one. The viewer has become sympathetic to Wei Wei's plight as she has had to play-act intimacy with her pretend groom, and genuine intimacy grows between her and Wai-Tung's family. Here it is emphasized that although the conspiracy of the sham marriage was designed not to hurt anybody, there is indeed a price to be paid for this web of deceit. Wei Wei's loneliness is underscored by a tearful long-distance phone call to her family in Shanghai as she is getting ready on the morning of her wedding. She does not tell them she is getting married, which illustrates again how alone she is in the situation. At the wedding banquet itself, when the couple is goaded by the crowd to kiss ("Put some passion into it!"), Wei Wei becomes visibly aroused and can barely keep her balance. On the wedding night, in the half-asleep predawn drunken state that Wei Wei and Wai-Tung find themselves in, they lie on the bed with their eyes closed. Suddenly Wai-Tung's eyes fly open; he asks Wei Wei what she is doing with her hand. Wei Wei responds seductively that Wai-Tung had lied when he said he had no attraction to women. He asks her to stop, but then she pronounces the fateful line, "I'm going to liberate you." This line demonstrates her desire to "normalize" her gay husband—she wants him to enjoy a heterosexual relationship with her, so that her dreams of a real marriage can be realized. Dariotis and Fung's polemic is that, because of Wai-Tung's refusal and because of Wei Wei's agression and dominant physical posture, this qualifies as a "rape"—however, in their view, this aggressive act results in her (re)location to a position of domesticity as Wai-Tung's pregnant wife.[7]

At the same time, in Wei Wei's pronunciation of the line "Wo yao jiefang ni," she uses the language of political liberation. Several critics have commented on the union created by a Taiwanese man and a mainland Chinese woman; therefore, the line "I am going to liberate you" would have political significance. Gina Marchetti (2000) analyzes this allegorically: "The nature of this 'liberation' remains uncertain: Is Taiwan, the wayward province, returned to the motherland, or is Taiwan, the bourgeois, decadent (homosexual) spawn of intercourse with America, returned to a 'true,' 'Chinese' (heterosexual) path? Or is Wai-Tung, ironically, really liberating Wei Wei from communism?"[8] Even more overt and unambiguous is the film's satiric treatment of a "sham marriage" between a Taiwanese man and a mainland Chinese woman—the idea is that the "unity" between Taiwan and China is also a sham. Marchetti notes that the political allegory concerning relations between Taiwan and the mainland is highlighted for Mandarin speakers, particularly in the scene in which Mr. Gao blesses the union of Wai-Tung and Wei Wei as a coming together of Taiwan and China. Continuing the allegory, Marchetti observes:

> In any intercourse between the two Chinas (embodied by Wai-Tung and Wei Wei) America (Simon) plays a critical role. America ambivalently brings the Chinas together (i.e., Simon suggests the marriage of convenience to Wai-Tung as a way to solve both his and Wei Wei's problems) and pushes them apart (i.e., Simon threatens to leave Wai-Tung

when he learns that his lover has had sex with Wei Wei, which, in turn, pushes a lovelorn Wai-Tung to distance himself from Wei Wei, the cause of the problem.[9]

Ultimately, however, Wai-Tung reconciles with Simon, and Wei Wei invites Simon to be the second father to her baby. Therefore, at the end of the film, the allegorical relationship between the three characters continues to mirror this political situation. Marchetti notes: "America may not be to everyone's liking, but allegorically it is accepted, in this case, as a bedfellow."[10]

Chinese critics have noted the different reception of *The Wedding Banquet* among Chinese and Western audiences; the cultural bias of the audience determines what they will "see" in the film. Eileen Chow (1997) has noted this divergence of details during the frenetic scene in which the two men frantically attempt to "redecorate" their home as a heterosexual environment, in preparation for the arrival of Wai-Tung's parents. The homosexual signifiers, such as the scantily clad "Ken" doll, are removed and replaced with Chinese calligraphy scrolls, the representation of classical Chinese moral rectitude. The scrolls include a poem by Tang poet Bai Juyi (Po Chü-yi, 772–846), who, like the renowned Tang poet Du Fu, was deeply concerned with the social problems of his time. While the Chinese viewer is unaware of the humorous significance of a "Ken" doll as an American homosexual signifier, the Western viewer is unable to read the Chinese calligraphy on the scrolls; thus, both the Chinese and Western viewer are not "seeing" vital cultural clues in the film. Chow describes attending a cinema screening of *The Wedding Banquet* where Chinese and American audience members laughed aloud at different times and at different images and jokes. This dichotomy is underscored by the reception of the film in other countries as well. For example, in France, the promotional campaign for the film brought Simon's character to the forefront; the film's French title was *Garçon d'Honneur* (*The Best Man*). The film's advertising showed Simon and Wei Wei in the foreground with intimacy suggested between them, while Wai-Tung's character hovered more in the background; Mitchell Lichtenstein's name was also listed first in the caption. Dariotis and Fung have commented that this not only brings to mind David Henry Hwang's *M. Butterfly*, but that it demonstrates a privileging of the Western viewpoint over the Chinese, referring principally to the Caucasian man's struggle with sexual identity.[11]

The screenplay published by Neil Peng in Taiwan (Lee and Peng 1993) is different from the final cut of the film; Peng wanted to publish the original award-winning screenplay that had won second prize in the Taiwan government's screenwriting contest. This version had Wai-Tung working at an advertising agency designing advertisements for products for left-handed people. Wai-Tung's company presentation is thus an object-lesson about conventional treatment of homosexuality in Taiwan:

> Wai-Tung: The problem as I see it then is this: In Taiwan most left handers
> are made over to be right-handed, "converted" if you will, to the
> recognized majority, so our challenge would be to encourage the
> Chinese lefties to use your product. Now, the way to do that might
> be to [attract] right-handed customers to buy your merchandise

as a gift for their left-handed friends and relatives. For example, children might buy a present for their mothers on Mother's Day or a lover for his sweetheart on Valentine's Day; this might be the ideal means to promote your merchandise. . . . We must recognize that the people who will buy your product are not necessarily the same people who will use it. To buy such merchandise will show the customer to be a very considerate individual, one who thinks of the needs of others.[12]

In addition, in the initial screenplay, Wai-Tung and Simon originally lived in suburban Connecticut, rather than in a trendy brownstone in Greenwich Village. It was James Schamus who was able to add a credible New York flavor to the script. Simon's character was expanded by Schamus and made more likeable. Moreover, lines from the marriage scene at City Hall (one of the funniest examples of English dialogue in the final version) did not appear in the original screenplay. The conflict between Wei Wei and Simon is spelled out clearly when, after the wedding night, they confront each other in a heated argument over Wai-Tung's sexuality; although this dischord and jealousy between Simon and Wei Wei seems very believable under the circumstances, the scene was excised from the final version of the screenplay to preserve a tone of comic levity. Finally, the ending of the film is different. There is no evidence of the trenchant final image of Mr. Gao raising his arms for the security check; instead, when the Gao parents leave the younger generation and walk through the airport hall to their plane, Mrs. Gao begins to cry inconsolably. The ending of the original screenplay had Wai-Tung and Wei Wei discuss legal details of "joint custody" of the child, and the film ended with the line, "Have you thought of a name yet?"

In locating the film's viewpoint toward homosexuality, Dariotis and Fung examine the screenplay's ambivalence about the topic, noting that in the original screenplay, Wei Wei calls the two men "vampires" during an argument. The film's denouement also deals uneasily with the subject of homosexuality from the Chinese point of view, without answering the complex questions it raises. With his father in the hospital and his condition uncertain, Wai-Tung breaks down and shares his life's biggest secret with his mother. At first, Mrs. Gao innocently thinks he is talking about Wei Wei's pregnancy. This scene makes it very clear that this secret is a shameful one in Chinese culture; Wai-Tung and his mother agree to spare his father from knowing the truth. Meanwhile, Mrs. Gao's response to Wai-Tung's revelation is both naïve and telling. Mrs. Gao wonders aloud if perhaps Wai-Tung has been "made" gay since arriving in the U.S., citing past girlfriends he had in Taiwan. She asks Wai-Tung "Did Simon lead you astray?" This very truthful scene demonstrates a further dimension of the situation—that of foreignness and alienation "causing" homosexuality. This is rightly observed by Dariotis and Fung, whose lengthy argument about the film's ambivalent stance toward homosexuality can be found in their 1997 article on the film.[13] The argument is echoed by Gina Marchetti: "Avowedly homosexual, [Wai-Tung] falls for a woman and impregnates her. He upholds a Chinese tradition of filial piety and duty and still manages to keep his male lover. Is he gay? Is he heterosexual?"[14]

The treatment of the film's homosexual theme is dealt with at length in screen-writer Neil Peng's preface and postface to the published screenplay of *The Wedding Banquet*. In his preface, Peng relates the personal story of his childhood friend from Taiwan (identified only by the initial "A") "coming out" to him in America, and the dilemma "A" experienced in keeping the truth from his parents (like Wai-Tung, "A" was the only male child in his family). This is where the core of the story developed. Peng relates how his friend said "*Wo shi* gay" or "I am gay" (using the adjective in English), pointing to a tendency to look at gay life as "Western" or "foreign." In his preface to *The Wedding Banquet* screenplay, Peng describes how he and "A" were friends in middle school and high school in Taiwan; by coincidence, Ang Lee also met "A" when they served in Taiwan's compulsory military service together. Going abroad for graduate school, "A" experienced true freedom for the first time as a gay man in the American gay community, whereupon he decided to make his home permanently in the U.S. after finishing his studies.[15] In the closing credits of *The Wedding Banquet*, the film is dedicated to "N. Yu and his longtime companion B. Geyer"—most likely the true identity of "A" and his Western companion. In his preface and postface, Neil Peng also details the history of the American gay liberation movement and states the hope that the film will reduce Chinese stigmatization of homosexuality. The book contains a photograph of Ang Lee with May Chin and Winston Chao attending a Gay Pride demonstration in New York City to research their roles. Peng writes that Lee's attitude toward homosexuals matured over the years as he lived in America; he came to strongly believe that the screenplay should not treat them as "different"—this is reinforced not only by *The Wedding Banquet* screenplay but by Lee's stance in the making of *Brokeback Mountain*. Interestingly, *The Wedding Banquet* is the only film of Lee's in which the director himself appears. It is curious that he made the decision to appear as a wedding guest and to utter the comic line, in response to an American guest's surprise at the over-the-top wedding antics: "You're witnessing the result of five thousand years of sexual repression."[16] This demonstrates the filmmaker's strong criticism of this repressive aspect of Chinese culture.

Intimate Revelation

Written in 1987, *The Wedding Banquet* was not made until six years later. When it came to raising money to make the film, the idea proved too Chinese to raise money in the United States, while at the same time too gay for China. As noted previously, Ang Lee entered a film contest held by the Taiwanese government, in which his main submission was *Pushing Hands*; he submitted *The Wedding Banquet* almost as an afterthought. *Pushing Hands* was released only in Taiwan, where it was well received. *The Wedding Banquet* was made for under US$1 million and took fewer than six weeks to complete. As noted, this film earned more than US$23 million interna-tionally and enjoyed phenomenal success, making it the most financially lucrative return on investment for a movie in 1993. Although the problems with financing demonstrated that the subject matter was difficult, Lee felt that it was essential to ensure that the important issues that the film discusses were able to make it to the screen. For him, the encouragement of honest debate amongst a wider audience was paramount. As he says:

> I have both theatrical and cinema backgrounds; the bottom line is you have to be willing to open up to your viewer, expose yourself—although you open yourself up to criticism and all that—you have to take that step. You have to be moved by your material at a gut level. [I have to] constantly judge if I'm being honest with how I feel, and what I put on the screen. I think people respond to that . . . Honesty is the best policy. It's just the best way I've found to live my life and go about my career, and hopefully be able to sleep at night.[17]

In the film's closing credits, Ang Lee offers special thanks to his father, Lee Sheng, his mother (Su-Tsung Yung), and his wife (Jane Lin). In certain respects, this film is the most personal of all of Lee's works, in its heartwrenching yearning for parental acceptance. Lee has also said that he had great fun making this film, both because of the celebratory atmosphere among the Taiwanese cast and crew as they filmed typical Chinese wedding customs (the raucous partying in the bridal suite; the late-night game of mahjong, etc.) and the similarities with his own wedding (at which he confesses he drank too much, just as Wai-Tung did). Ang Lee's younger son, Mason, makes his first appearance in *The Wedding Banquet*, jumping on the bridal bed in a prewedding ritual and kissing the blindfolded bride in a game at the banquet itself. Jane Lin (carrying Mason in her arms) and Haan also appear in the wedding festivities. With the appearance of each of his own family members onscreen and a cameo of the director himself, as well as the screenplay's nearly word-for-word recording of conversations between Ang Lee and his own father, *The Wedding Banquet* intimately reveals the heart of its director.

FIVE

Globalization and Cultural Identity in Eat Drink Man Woman

NO DIRECTOR OF modern film seems to contribute more to the debate on globalization, in the sense of blurring the distinctions between cultural identities and plumbing their interrelationships, than does Ang Lee. His own path to worldwide recognition has been a crossing of boundaries. As was detailed in this volume's introduction, Lee left Taiwan in 1978 and relocated to the United States, where he completed a Masters of Fine Arts in Directing at New York University. His directorial focus shifted back and forth between his homeland and his adopted home in his earliest films, as he directed a series of critically-acclaimed independent dramas—these include two films shot in America (*Pushing Hands* and *The Wedding Banquet*), and one Taiwan-made coproduction, *Eat Drink Man Woman*. He followed this success with three English-language literary adaptations, *Sense and Sensibility*, *The Ice Storm*, and *Ride with the Devil*. Having completed a "trilogy" of Chinese-language films, and a "trilogy" of English-language films, he then completed the pan-Chinese epic *Crouching Tiger, Hidden Dragon* before returning to English-language adaptations *Hulk* and *Brokeback Mountain*. Most recently, he returned to China with *Lust/Caution*, and then to English-language cinema again (America, Canada, and India) with his latest works, *Taking Woodstock* and *Life of Pi*. Within this multinational and multilingual career achievement, Lee's *Eat Drink Man Woman* is his work that most reflects the forces of globalization. In the imagination of the artist, however, the cultural entities of the West and the East have been metamorphosed and blurred, and traditional attitudes called into question. As such images of a young male student pondering Dostoevsky and female college students working at fast-food restaurants in cosmopolitan Taipei indicate, globalization is a trend that cannot be resisted. And yet, through this dialectic of shifting interrelationships of cultural identities, an opportunity arises for Ang Lee to uniquely display Chinese culture (or a hybridization of Chinese culture) in a way which in many respects serves as an enlightenment. While his work appeals to consumer culture, it also signals the more traditional grand narrative, demonstrating that people living in the new millennium have developed a unique sensibility to deal with the contradictions of their age.

The most striking example of the transference of symbols between East and West is in *Eat Drink Man Woman*, whose title alone impresses "otherness" for the native English speaker. A direct translation of a common Chinese idiom, the title in English conjures up pidgin grammar, thus suggesting a whole history of Asian "otherness" in a Western setting. (The English words from the roughly translated Chinese proverb "eat drink man woman" served as a working title for the script, penciled in for the crew and actors to work with—the problem of setting up a formal title was left until after the filming, when it was suggested that the working title be left as is.)[1] The suggestion of binary opposition in the title also calls to mind the East/West dialectic. The title implies larger themes that the narrative of the movie will explore, e.g., the difference between male and female, yet it suggests an interdependence, such as that between eating and drinking. In the two pairs of the four-word idiom, "Eat Drink Man Woman," the larger motifs of food and sex, the fundamental components of all human life, are implied in a neat shorthand of translated Chinese, and are universally recognized to be transcendent of any cultural boundary or border. Thus, the title of the film itself is a sign of the globalized, territorially nonspecific themes within. A final twist on the meaning of the title is given when the proverb—"Eat drink man woman" (or in Chinese "yinshi nannü")—usually employed to describe the bare necessities of sustaining life, is given an ironic reading when pronounced by the main character in the film to illustrate that even life's simplest elements have a way of becoming complicated.

As the film opens, the viewer is treated to the sights and sounds of all manner of traditional Chinese gourmet cooking, which presumably involves the use of certain tools, cooking techniques, and animal organs not found in the Western kitchen. This may provide a shock or at least pleasurable voyeurism for the Western viewer. However, this is set against later semiotic signals that suggest the power and the reach of globalization—specifically, the appearance of the Western fast-food chain in which the two teenage friends work in Taipei with all of its Western accoutrements such as the uniforms, burgers, shakes, fries, etc. This may also prove to be a shock for some Western viewers unused to seeing Asian faces in the uniforms of American franchises. Food in the film is emblematic, infused with significance, and an intergenerational means of communication. "We communicate through food," is a line spoken by the middle daughter of the family, Jia-Chien (Chien-Lien Wu) and in the film food truly serves as a linguistic signifier. This is further emphasized by the father's, Mr. Chu's, disability in the film—although a gourmand and master chef, he loses his sense of taste, and this becomes a major theme in the narrative. When this sense of taste is restored at the end of the film—while he shares a meal cooked by his middle daughter—it serves as a fitting denouement to demonstrate that communication and understanding has been restored. "Daughter," he says; "Father," she replies to him.

As a semiotic discourse, in this film there are signs of cultures and influences colliding and synthesizing which demonstrate the true nature of globalization. For example, with the roles of three sisters in the family, each has a juxtaposition of contradictions. The eldest, Jia-Jen (Kuei-Mei Yang), brings Christianity into her closed, loveless existence—the presence of the Christian church in Asia, often a signal of

"I can taste it": While eating his daughter's soup, Mr. Chu regains his sense of taste.

Western colonialism, is here simply presented on its own terms, in the form of the unsteady faith of the Christian sister. The middle daughter is an executive for a Taiwanese airline which is expanding into new countries by acquiring new airline routes in the international market. The youngest sister, Jia-Ning (Yu-Wen Wang), works at a Wendy's burger outlet, although as a contrast to that, when she gets off work she enjoys a bowl of noodles at a traditional roadside food stall. International influences abound—globalization is demonstrated by franchise infringement in modern Taipei, a boyfriend's petulant perusal of Dostoevsky, Jia-Ning studying French in a college course, etc. The film's structure itself suggests a Western stage play. The tried-and-true formula of family drama—three very different sisters, under the tutelage of a hapless father whose generational separation from his daughters renders him incapable of true understanding—is instantly recognizable to a Western audience raised on Shakespeare's *King Lear* and the plays of Anton Chekhov. As Ang Lee undoubtedly supposed, this placement of unfamiliar food/city/language within a well-traveled plot would help the film reach audiences versed in Western literature. The drama is a keenly-observed character vehicle, especially the quiet ending which serves as delightful theater—a tableau of father-and-daughter bonding.

The familiar plot calls to mind the intertextuality the film shares with other classics of the genre, not only from Taiwan, Hong Kong, and Japan but also from America and Europe. Emilie Yueh-yu Yeh and Darrell W. Davis (2005) list possible source films from the Chinese and Japanese traditions, including the classic Hong Kong urban comedy *Our Sister Hedy* (*Si qianjin*, literally "four thousand gold," 1957), about four rival sisters and their widowed father, directed by Tao Qin. Other influences include the Shaw Brothers' *Hong Kong Nocturne* (1967), a film directed by Inoue Umetsugu that was a remake of two of his earlier Japanese films, *Odoritai yoru* (*Tonight We'll Dance*, 1963) and *Odoru taiyo* (*Dancing Sun*, 1957), about three rival sisters. Another Japanese forerunner of the "food film" is *Tampopo* (1985), a popular art-house film that attracted a large audience in the U.S. in the mid-1980s and in which food is also paired with sex. The most obvious influence is the Taiwan television series *Four Daughters* (also entitled *Si qianjin*, like the 1957 film), about a widowed father and his daughters. Central Motion Pictures Corporation production manager Xu Ligong, who had launched the popular television series in Taiwan, asked writer Wang Huiling to do a screenplay based on both *Our Sister Hedy* and *Four Daughters* for Lee's film.[2] *Eat Drink Man Woman* rode the popular wave of Chinese art-house films, noted by Steve Fore as "*the* hot ticket on the international festival circuit in the late 1980s and early 1990s."[3] This trend includes the last Hong Kong films of John Woo, much of the work of Wong Karwai, Zhang Yimou's three early masterpieces *Judou* (1990), *Raise the Red Lantern* (1991), and *The Story of Qiuju* (1992), Chen Kaige's *Farewell My Concubine* (1993), and Tsai Ming-liang's *Vive L'Amour* (1994). Yeh and Davis believe *Eat Drink Man Woman* was "deliberately designed to capitalize on the burgeoning popularity of Chinese-language art film."[4]

Eat Drink Man Woman shares striking similarities with European and American film classics as well. For example, the Franco-Italian coproduction by noted auteur Marco Ferreri, *La Grande Bouffe* (*Blow-Out*, 1973), a satire of Western decadence, shares similarities with *Eat Drink Man Woman* in the usage of food and sex, as well as art-house filming techniques. Confined to the single set of a decaying town mansion, this film treats the theme of Western excess—food, sex, self-pity—while alluding to the high arts of philosophy, art history, and literature. The filming technique pairs long takes of darkly-lit static shots that are dense with detail alongside extreme close-ups that are pitilessly revealing. *La Grande Bouffe* was a milestone in Western cinema at the time of its release because of its depiction of debauched sex and gluttonous eating, which scandalized American viewers. On a milder scale, *Eat Drink Man Woman* raised eyebrows in the highly conservative atmosphere of Taiwan when it was first released in the early 1990s. Other Western "food films" comparable to *Eat Drink Man Woman* include Denmark's *Babettes gjestebud* (*Babette's Feast*, 1987) and Mexico's *Como agua para chocolate* (*Like Water for Chocolate*, 1992), which both artfully use food to raise the level of sensuality and depict the art of seduction by gastronomical pleasures.

Critical Reception of Eat Drink Man Woman

It is interesting to consider that the criticism leveled against *Eat Drink Man Woman* in the United States centered on how the film was not easily classified as a comedy or a drama. Andrew Tudor notes: "The crucial factors which distinguish a genre are not only characteristics inherent in the films themselves; they also depend on the particular culture within which we are operating."[5] However, criticism of the film from its home country, Taiwan, centered on how the drama itself was too "Westernized" and that such "exaggerated" events could never take place in the conservative Chinese cultural environment of early 1990s Taiwan. Clearly, this made the film less popular with its Chinese audience in Taiwan. Ti Wei compares the revenues in the United States and Taiwan and finds that while the success of *Eat Drink Man Woman* surpassed *The Wedding Banquet* in America, in Taipei, *Eat Drink Man Woman* earned only NT$50 million, less than half of the NT$120 million earned by *The Wedding Banquet*. Taiwanese viewers also criticized the film's unrealistic depiction of contemporary Taipei.[6] Ang Lee expressed his own cultural confusion over the film as he received criticism for its portrayal of Taiwan culture. "I was confused. I did not know how the film would look . . . I couldn't taste it. . . . I couldn't even smell it."[7] Sheng-mei Ma has recognized this film's penchant for making Chinese culture an object of Western gaze, an observation he applies to the entire Father-Knows-Best trilogy: "The trilogy reveals an increasing propensity toward exotic travel in search of the Other rather than nostalgic lamentation over loss of the Self."[8]

This criticism reflects the argument of James Clifford (1992) in confronting global identity. Clifford puts emphasis on the dislocation of culture, that culture has become deterritorialized and diasporic. Arjun Appadurai builds on Clifford's view by demonstrating that deterritorialization "creates new markets for film companies, art impresarios, and travel agencies, which thrive on the need of the deterritorialized population for contact with its homeland."[9] The members of diasporas thus may imagine or fashion new post-national identities, making and remaking themselves in response to new localities, social and political pressures, and transnational cultural discourses.[10]

Slavoj Žižek writes:

It is because the Real itself offers no support for a direct symbolization of it—because every symbolization is in the last resort contingent—that the only way the experience of a given historic reality can achieve its unity is through the agency of a signifier, through reference to a "pure" signifier. It is not the real object which guarantees as the point of reference the unity and identity of a certain ideological experience—on the contrary, it is the reference to a "pure" signifier which gives unity and identity to our experience of historical reality itself. Historical reality is of course always symbolized; the way we experience it is always mediated through different modes of symbolization: all Lacan adds to this phenomenological common wisdom is the fact that the unity of a given "experience of meaning," itself the horizon of an ideological field of meaning, is supported by some "pure," meaningless, "signifier without the signified."[11]

Conflict Between the Traditional and the Modern

Eat Drink Man Woman takes as its premise the intergenerational conflict and alienation caused by the forces of globalization and Westernization in the modernizing capital city, Taipei. Semiotic shorthand is used to contrast Chinese traditional conceptualization and thought: neat rows of utensils, endless jars of sauces, the dimly-lit interior of the home, the sounds of chopping, frying, fileting. These are put in blunt contrast with the impersonal high-rises that fill the city; the encroachment of contemporary steel-and-glass architecture upon the sprawling Japanese-style traditional homes (the home owned by the father in the film, although located within a congested area of the city, includes a yard to raise chickens).¹² The father has lost his taste—possibly because he cannot find flavor or pleasure in the conflict between traditional and modern. What is valued by him does not seem to be valued by the younger generation, and as he goes through the Sunday-night dinner ritual week after week, he has lost his taste for it. At the end of the film the father has moved from the old family home into a new place, and the camera framing his new wife Jin-Rong's (Sylvia Chang) enlarged belly promises a second start for him. The apartment where he has relocated has a modern and up-to-date feel—decorated in a cool, minimalist aesthetic—which seems to show he has adapted and come to terms with modernizing his lifestyle. The evidence of Jia-Chien's attempt to purchase one of the newly-developed properties in the city, and its subsequent condemnation for being on a polluted site—causing her to lose her savings in the investment—points to the necessity for her to adapt as well. This plot development points Jia-Chien toward her destiny: she will continue to live in her father's home, and give up her position in the airline. She trades wealth, status, and power lunches for her own cherished desire—cooking, like her father. The irony is that although Jia-Chien pushed herself to join the globalized society in order to please and support her family, ultimately she finds that she must let all of that go and be true to herself. She must do what comes naturally for her, which is to enjoy her skill in traditional Chinese cooking.

The film is thus brought to the most conventional of conclusions, that of returning to roots or basic nature. For only when Jia-Chien is living this new lifestyle does her father's "sense of taste" return. He had pushed her to move beyond her roots, to escape the limitations of the kitchen. He had wanted her to have a better lifestyle than he had; she simply wanted the lifestyle they were already living. The hint of this need for reevaluation and a return to roots comes during an earlier conversation with her ex-lover Raymond (Lester Chit-Man Chan), in which Jia-Chien tries to share her heart and tell him about the true happiness she experienced in the kitchen as a child. She describes her father's tradition of baking her bracelets made from dough and letting her play after school in his restaurant's big kitchen. She says the telling line, "I don't have any childhood memories unless I cook them into existence." Raymond responds, "I can't remember a thing from my childhood," signifying his lack of emotional depth and lack of a significant connection with food; he then unwittingly crushes Jia-Chien's enthusiasm by picking up a ring of calamari from the dish and slipping it on her finger in a teasing manner. When she quickly pulls her hand away, horrified that he has not taken her seriously, he then holds the squid ring up to his ear, and says suggestively, "How about nibbling on my earring?" Jia-Chien is offended; she takes the ring from him and puts it back in the dish. Raymond looks on, confused and slightly annoyed. The use of food as a dramatic device comes through clearly in this scene where Jia-Chien, nostalgic for the past, feels connected to it through food. The shifty and uncomprehending response from Raymond reveals his inappropriateness as a guest at her table, and highlights the need for Jia-Chien to sever ties with him and return to her roots.

Metaphorical Implications of Food and Sex

The use of food as an element of semiotic discourse is one of the most striking elements in this deeply-layered film. Throughout the story, food is used in different locations and settings, and at different levels of formality and casualness, to demonstrate through visual shorthand the relationships being explored onscreen. Hundreds of dishes appear in the film, including soups, all manner of fish and fowl, bean curd, and elaborately carved fruit; many of these dishes are not even eaten because of the other action on the screen. One example of this visual shorthand is the simple tea shared by Jia-Chien and Li Kai when they have agreed not to have a sexual relationship, but instead to shake hands and be friends. This marks a turning point in Jia-Chien's lifestyle. Another example is the elaborate feast for the grand hotel wedding banquet in which Mr. Chu is called out of retirement to come and save the day. As he sets the place in order and makes split-second decisions with an almost military precision, while legions of sub-waiters, sous-chefs, and other helpers stand at the ready, the entire process is amazing visual shorthand to inform the viewer of Mr. Chu's status in the kitchen. The opening sequence in the film, too, sets the tone for what will follow: this four-minute, dialogue-free sequence of Mr. Chu preparing Sunday dinner for his family, shows a pair of hands working with food with skill and precision and a balletic beauty—some of which took three days to film correctly. This opening, during which the viewer only experiences the sights and sounds of food preparation, the slicing and gutting of fish, the chopping of vegetables, the frying and steaming of various meats, sets up food as a commanding presence in the film. Ang Lee's intention was to make people's mouths water by arousing their appetites, and to achieve this level of skill and speed in slicing, preparing, and handling the food, he employed three of the top chefs in Taiwan as hand doubles—Yeh and Davis have pointed out that hand doubles are commonly used making porn films, drawing yet another connection between this filming of food preparation and sexual seduction.[13] The experience is exciting as well because of the violence—the slaughter of chickens, the slicing of red meat, the unrecognizability of certain vegetables, cuts of meat, and other ingredients. This film invites the viewer into a hidden and unknown world—a world of unfathomable mystery with the promise of truly appetite-whetting results.

The combination of this kind of stimulation of the physical appetite in juxtaposition with the other vibrant element of the story—sexuality—is truly potent. This being an early 1990s Taiwanese film, the sexuality portrayed on the screen will be conservative by Western standards, and artfully hidden instead of thrust in the limelight. However, the contrast of the liberality and excess of the food preparation becomes sensually fulfilling in its stead. One of the amusing aspects of the English-language advertising for this film is that the promotional material seems to promise a "sexy" movie; the cover design shows three young women lying on their backs next to plates filled with appetizing food, while a line from *New York Newsday* promises: "It's hard to tell where sex stops and food begins . . . Electric!"[14] However, in the film itself the lovers all remain completely clothed onscreen, and no sex is shown. All five of the couplings that take place during the film are presented with an absolute minimum of actual physical contact. In the conservative Taiwan of the early 1990s, this is true to behavioral codes where men and women do not hold hands or kiss in public; with no homoerotic overtones, men frequently put their arms around other men in public, or girls hold hands/link arms with other girls. The scene in which the oldest sister vamps herself up after thinking she has received a love letter from an admirer is perhaps the most smoldering image in the movie, and even then she is wearing a turtleneck sweater. Another potentially erotic scene, where Li Kai and Jia-Chien begin to kiss in the office, is made less sexy by Jia-Chien's high-necked office blouse. These conservative treatments of sexuality can be contrasted with the searing sensuality of Zhang Ziyi in *Crouching Tiger, Hidden Dragon*, when she is a prisoner of the bandit/lover in the desert cave and must take a bath in front of him, or in the scene where she approaches Mu Bai (Chow Yun-Fat) in a wet costume with the come-hither line: "Is it the sword you want, or me?" This unusual line, unorthodox to common Chinese patriarchal codes of authority and sexuality, will be discussed in depth in the chapter on *Crouching Tiger, Hidden Dragon*.

The conservatism of sexual display in *Eat Drink Man Woman* can be compared to the lack of eroticism in *The Wedding Banquet*, which despite the highly-charged sexual subject matter (gay love, a marriage and wedding night sexual coupling) did not contain any overtly sexual scenes. The two physical encounters between the male characters were a quiet and tender kiss, and an unconsummated playful romp while running up a stairway. On the other hand, the scene with May Chin, as Wei Wei, in the overheating apartment where she mops the sweat off her neck with a damp rag is one of the most voyeuristic in the movie, as is the later scene in the bedroom where she uses a fan to dry herself as she stands in a sheer nightgown talking to her husband (in addition, she emerges naked from the shower in a short previous scene); the irony is that because he is homosexual, these very erotic sights are meaningless to him; he has no response to heterosexual signifiers.

On the issue of sexuality, *Brokeback Mountain* is an important example. The film's so-called inflammatory subject matter attracted many audiences interested in seeing how far the director would cross the boundary of conservative values by showing homosexual sex in a mainstream movie. It is reasonably safe to say that a large majority of the audience knew about and expected the coupling that occurred within the first twenty minutes of the film. This was due to the promotional campaign, the parodies of the film that got widespread play on television (on shows such as *Saturday Night Live* and *The Late Show with David Letterman*) and the internet, and the labeling of the film as a "gay cowboy movie." There was even a sort of suspense experienced while awaiting the beginning of the two men's physical relationship. When the inevitable coupling occurred, it was in semidarkness with the actors' faces nearly unreadable. In addition, the scene where Ennis and Jack's sexual horseplay turns into a physical brawl that ends up with Jack getting punched in the face is much more realistic on the page than when brought to the screen. This scene, while poignant in the short story, did not seem to make much sense when played out on the screen in the film. It was calculated that the film contained 37 seconds of sexual activity. Gay activists claimed that *Brokeback Mountain* did not go far enough, that it should have been more graphic in its depiction of homosexual sex. One viewer commented in response, "What did you expect—gay porn?"[15] Meanwhile makers of the film countered with the idea that the tender scenes of the men holding each other in their arms were what were truly groundbreaking about the film.

Another significant aspect of *Eat Drink Man Woman* is that so much of the narrative takes place in or around a school environment; this resonates with Ang Lee's personal experience growing up under the strict training of his father with the Confucian emphasis on education. Because so much of Ang Lee's childhood was spent at school, it was easy for him to recapture the familiar atmosphere. The school where the eldest sister teaches is a typical all-male high school in Taipei. This film clearly challenges the ideal Chinese image of education—that of young men devoting themselves to Confucian classics and to advanced learning. Instead, the realistic view of school life in *Eat Drink Man Woman* demonstrates that school, for the average Chinese male student, is just a prison to be tolerated and endured; the few pleasures it affords are writing notes and tossing paper airplanes—the rest is just a bleak existence. The reality hits hard that schools all over the world face the battle of wills between teachers and sullen teenagers who would like to be just about anywhere else but in a classroom. In presenting the drab colors of the school uniform, the institutionalized greenish hue of fluorescent lighting, the aging teachers in the faculty lounge drinking tea and reading newspapers, and the sweaty teenage angst-filled existence, Ang Lee documents the stagnation and torpor of this environment that corresponds with his personal experience.

The Impact of Globalization on Traditional Chinese Culture

The scene where Jia-Chien and Li Kai, who have begun a flirtatious relationship at work, go shopping together at a large, brightly-lit "Toys R Us"-style department store, is a good example of the challenges posed by postmodern, globalized culture. Li Kai has asked Jia-Chien to help him choose a toy to send to his young son, who lives in America with his mother. He specifically would like to find "something Chinese"—a toy that will represent traditional Chinese culture rather than the mass-produced plastic items that line the shelves. As they wend their way through the aisles, the items all seem to look more and more identical and soulless. The exported Western iconic figures and Disney toys that fill the shelves in such abundance cannot satisfy Li Kai, who longs for a toy that carries actual cultural significance. The whole effect is extremely alienating, as the two have this conversation:

Li Kai: I always wanted to find something Chinese for him. He has plenty of these already.

Jia-Chien: He's interested in Chinese culture?

Li Kai: I wish. I can't believe that in a few [short] years, my son is growing up to be an American. Sometimes I look at him and wonder if he's actually my son. He was raised in America, and his mother doesn't mind.

Jia-Chien: His mother? How does she feel about you being away all the time?

Li Kai: She's glad I'm not around. I think the only reason we're not divorced is that we're both too busy. That sounds so cynical, doesn't it?

Jia-Chien: I'm just as cynical when it comes to my personal life.

Li Kai begins to discuss his university life with Jia-Chien. This is a key plot point and she becomes troubled by his revelations. Toward the end of their conversation, Jia-Chien hastily grabs a "Barney" lookalike doll off the shelf (the "Barney" doll is called "Harvey" in the film).

Jia-Chien: This looks Chinese.
Li Kai: That's [Barney]. You have no idea how much I suffered from those [TV] shows. Wanna hear the theme? "I love you, you love me . . ."
Jia-Chien: Please don't [sing it].
Li Kai: What the hell. I'll just buy this one. He'll like it.

The sentence "This looks Chinese" to describe the "Barney" doll is heavily ironic—it implies that the label of "Chinese-ness" can be tacked on to any Western icon and refashioned as an item of cultural significance. Li Kai's singing of the "Barney" theme song is just as troubling; although he complains to Jia-Chien that hearing the theme on the television show every day drove him crazy, he now mindlessly repeats it, showing how successful the "brainwashing" that comes with mass export of culture can be. Jia-Chien asks him not to sing it, calling a stop to the powerful infiltration of Western culture. In the scene's final troubling conclusion, Li Kai abandons his original plan to expose his son to traditional Chinese culture—he hastily dismisses the idea with the words, "What the hell. I'll just buy this one. He'll like it." Both Li Kai's fruitless quest for a traditional Chinese toy and Jia-Chien's misidentification of "Barney" as "Chinese" underscore the bleak prospects of passing on Chinese traditional values in a world of globalized consumer culture.

Another good example of the damaging effects of globalization on traditional Chinese culture is the scene in which, late in the film, the hotel restaurant manager (Man-Sheng Tu) asks the retired Mr. Chu to return to work as a chef. He calls Mr. Chu an expert chef, and also the only remaining specialist in the major Chinese styles of cuisine—the classic, authentic tastes of Beijing, Sichuan, Yangzhou, Chaozhou, Zhejiang (Shanghainese), etc. Mr. Chu replies that being a specialist no longer has significance, because after forty years all the different regions are now jumbled and adulterated. Thus, Mr. Chu is an archive from the past; his cooking represents "a lost world, not only in Taiwan but also on the mainland."[16] Yeh and Davis claim that this "carelessness of culinary preservation" underscores the destructive force and high cost of globalization.[17]

The end of *Eat Drink Man Woman* is traditional, both from a dramatic standpoint and according to conservative cultural values. As in traditional Western drama, the gentle exchange between the father and daughter with the screen fading to black provides the traditional denouement of classical Western melodrama. Meanwhile, the film is also an elegy to the honoring of tradition and continuity; it reiterates that tradition must not be lost in the face of lightning-fast modernization and the race into the future. There are several elements in the film to support this notion. For example, when the young boyfriend, Guo-Lun (Chao-jung Chen), brings the youngest daughter, Jia-Ning, to his home, he shows her his evocative black-and-white photographs of his grandmother; they are bonded over an experience of his childhood nostalgia. In addition, one of the most affecting scenes in *Eat Drink Man Woman* is when Jia-Chien and her ex-lover Raymond eat in a restaurant together "just like old times." Raymond, engaged to be married to another woman, proposes a continuing tryst with Jia-Chien, telling her he has a room in the back just for that purpose. Jia-Chien, shocked, leaves the restaurant shortly thereafter. Without getting more than a few steps outside, she is overcome with nausea and vomits in the restaurant's front garden. The humiliation and degradation of this scene are overwhelming. It is clear that Raymond's modern "free love" view of male/female sexuality, that coupling can come at random according to the desires of the moment, is shown to be ultimately unacceptable to her. Thus, Jia-Chien, although previously enjoying her freedom as Raymond's lover, returns instead to traditional cultural values—she trades sexual "freedom" for self-respect.

Criticism of *Eat Drink Man Woman* by its Chinese audience was that it was unrealistically Western in the arc of its story, that the actors were acting like liberal Americans, although they were speaking Chinese. This is due both to Ang Lee's attempt to balance the "global" with the "local" and to James Schamus' work on the script—in his own words, he tried to make it as "Jewish" as possible, and when struggling to present the conceptualization of traditional Chinese thinking, he was urged with each new draft to make it "more Jewish." Schamus tells the full story in the introduction to *Eat Drink Man Woman and The Wedding Banquet, Two Films by Ang Lee*:

> Writing screenplays in such a cultural stew is no easy feat. For each of the scripts . . . first drafts were written in Chinese, then translated into English, re-written in English, translated back into Chinese, and eventually subtitled in Chinese and English and a dozen other languages. . . . There was many a time when I, working with my American assumptions, would be re-working a scene and finding myself frustrated by Ang's insistence that the psychology of the characters I was sketching was not naturally Chinese. My initial inclination was to study even harder the Chinese poems, stories, and histories I had been accumulating as research, usually to no avail. Finally, in frustration, I'd simply give up and write the scenes as "Jewish" as I could make them. "Ah-ha," Ang would respond on reading the new draft. "Very Chinese!"[18]

The screenplay for *Eat Drink Man Woman* is credited to Ang Lee, Wang Huiling, and James Schamus. Ang Lee has pointed out that Schamus was responsible for several key plot elements and narrative twists, including the critical device of the father's loss and regaining of his "sense of taste," which was entirely Schamus' idea. In addition, Schamus suggested that since in the first two films of the trilogy the children disappointed the father, in *Eat Drink Man Woman*, the father should disappoint the children. Therefore, the father figure in *Eat Drink Man Woman* is stripped of much of his patriarchal reserve and becomes a weaker figure with a more human side, i.e., giving weight to his own desires and pursuing a romantic relationship.[19]

The most common criticism was that Ang Lee's film was "un-Chinese" in its libertine portrayal of sex and "overly Westernized" in its treatment of the interactions between characters. This over-the-top lack of realism is part of the element of "screwball comedy" that felt distinctly Western, as when the college-age daughter,

Jia-Ning, announces at the dinner table that she is pregnant with her boyfriend's baby, or when the father does not pursue a relationship with the woman his own age, Mrs. Liang (Ah-Leh Gua), but instead marries her daughter, Jin-Rong. Both of these events would be a matter of "shame" in Chinese culture, and would not be accepted and not propel the film toward a happy ending, as they do in the film. The Westernized atmosphere in this film is one which insists on a happy ending, of loose ends neatly tied up. This is not as common in Chinese films and for the audience it comes across as absurdly unrealistic, the "put-a-band-aid-on-it," "happy-go-luckyism" of the West. Emilie Yueh-yu Yeh and Darrell W. Davis have noted that this raises issues of "exoticism, commodification, and complicity . . . leading to charges of pandering to Western tastes."[20] They also note that these are "premonitions of controversies that dogged the success of *Crouching Tiger, Hidden Dragon*."[21] However, Yeh and Davis defend Lee's work, calling his visions of China (and Taiwan) "highly idealized, romantic, even mythical."[22] Other features shared by *Crouching Tiger, Hidden Dragon* and *Eat Drink Man Woman* are a four-character idiomatic Chinese title, a Chinese-language script, a Chinese setting, focus on traditional arts (martial arts and cooking), and a revisiting of classic literary-cinematic themes from forerunning Chinese films.

In Ang Lee's three earliest films, *Pushing Hands*, *The Wedding Banquet*, and *Eat Drink Man Woman,* the themes of globalization and cultural identity are explored with depth and humor. The language barrier acts as a palpable force of conflict in *Pushing Hands*, while in *The Wedding Banquet*, each character is forced to grow and change when facing a new, disorienting worldview. In *Eat Drink Man Woman*, Ang Lee's ideas on the impact of globalization are expressed with a new level of subtlety and sophistication. Each of his early films challenges the viewer to examine the effects of globalization and the daunting difficulties imposed by language barriers; they underscore the significance of the simple things in life (i.e., "eat" "drink" "man" and "woman") in an increasingly impersonal and globalized world.

SIX

Opposition and Resolution in Sense and Sensibility

I want this film to break people's hearts so badly they'll still be recovering from it two months later.[1]

THOUGH JANE AUSTEN'S *Sense and Sensibility*, published in 1811, seems a work wholly restricted to the English countryside, the 1995 film rendition by Ang Lee illuminates the global and universal implications revealed by the dialectical struggle of this narrative. In addition to the titular dichotomy of "sense" and "sensibility," an artistic divide in English literature was developing during the two most prolific decades of Austen's writing career (1798–1818); the rationalism of the eighteenth century was gradually yielding to the nineteenth-century romantic emphasis on the psychology of the individual. In recent years, with the advancement of critical studies, Austen's work has been held up to scrutiny for the way in which it responds to these two opposite sets of impulses. According to Meenakshi Mukherjee, "In terms of narrative mode and structure, her work takes elements of the conventional novel and quietly subverts them, without revealing any crack on the surface."[2] The fundamental motifs of Austen's novel also have resonance with the previous work of Ang Lee (in particular, *Eat Drink Man Woman*), whose films already proved a familiarity with the universal issues of family ritual and social duty. In addition, both the original Austen novel and Lee's film of *Sense and Sensibility* point outward through references to the larger global community.

Historically, the work of Jane Austen has seemed to critics to be nonpolemical and nonchallenging to eighteenth-century orthodoxy (Duckworth 1971), and yet recent criticism, including feminist criticism (Monaghan 1980; Armstrong 1987; Clark 1994) and postcolonial criticism (Mukhergee 1991), brings to light original interpretations of the text which offer new possibilities and insights into its narrative meaning. These help the reader understand the economics, politics, geography, and social conventions of Austen's world. The novels of Jane Austen, such as *Pride and Prejudice* (1813), *Emma* (1816), *Persuasion* (1818), and *Sense and Sensibility*, cannot be read as a microcosm of British society, a realistic and indisputable historical record—such a reading is unfair to Austen, whose work has a complexity and tension that will be elucidated by examining *Sense and Sensibility* in detail. Some of the dialectical aspects of Austen's work include parody versus mimesis, private (emotion, personal feeling) versus public (propriety, duty), the individual's need for self-actualization versus society's dictate that one should conform to gender and occupational roles, space versus enclosure, movement versus stasis.

The Conceptualization of "Sense" and "Sensibility"

The themes of family ritual and social duty are the main cultural motifs of Jane Austen's *Sense and Sensibility*. In this narrative, the British cultural emphasis on dignity and duty is in full display. *Sense and Sensibility* tells the story of the Dashwood sisters, Elinor and Marianne, who struggle to find suitable marriages to insure their social position after the death of their father leaves their financial prospects uncertain. Elinor forms an attachment with Edward Ferrars, the brother of her sister-in-law and heir to a large estate, while Marianne becomes infatuated with John Willoughby, the cousin of a neighbor. Both relationships encounter difficulties. It is revealed that Edward is previously engaged to Miss Lucy Steele, and he feels bound to honor that engagement. Meanwhile, Willoughby abruptly leaves Marianne and is later discovered to have married a wealthy heiress. Marianne becomes desperately ill over her failed love affair. However, things work out in the end with happy marriages for both Elinor (after Miss Steele breaks her engagement to Edward), and Marianne (who marries the doting, much older Colonel Brandon). Representing "sense" in the form of strict adherence to duty and social custom is Elinor, who is very proper and guarded in affairs of the heart, while Marianne's romantic sensibility guides her heart and her impetuous actions through a painful process of self-discovery. By the end of the narrative, each sister finds a balance within herself—Elinor opens up and becomes vulnerable to her romantic sensibility, while Marianne gains a new guiding sense which grounds her without compromising her zeal to live life to the fullest.

Elinor and Marianne are introduced at the end of the first chapter. Elinor, at 19, is two years older than her sister, and considerably more mature. She is described in the first chapter as follows:

> [Elinor] possessed a strength of understanding and coolness of judgement which qualified her . . . to be the counselor of her mother, and enabled her frequently to counteract . . . that eagerness of mind in Mrs. Dashwood which must generally have led to imprudence. She had an excellent heart; her disposition was affectionate, and her feelings were strong; but she knew how to govern them. . . .[3]

Marianne is described in the first chapter after the description of Elinor. She is given abilities

> . . . in many respects quite equal to Elinor's. She was sensible and clever but eager in everything; her sorrows, her joys, could have no moderation. She was generous, amiable, interesting: she was everything but prudent.[4]

The above description of the Dashwood sisters focuses on their "sense" and "sensibility"—key elements to the reader's understanding of their characters. The *Oxford English Dictionary* demonstrates that the definitions of the words "sense," "sensible," and "sensibility" have shifted and changed between the eighteenth and twenty-first centuries, but these key terms are delineated by the capacity for and control over feelings. Various key words applied to Elinor's character include her *understanding* and *judgement*—"her feelings were strong, but she knew how to *govern* them." In Marianne's character, her feelings lack "*moderation . . .* she was everything but *prudent*" and "Elinor saw, with concern, the excess of her sister's *sensibility*."[5] Although Austen goes to great lengths at the end of the first chapter to imply that the two major characters will represent the opposition suggested in the title *Sense and Sensibility*, the dichotomy is not nearly as clear-cut as the reader may expect. For example, Austen does not find disadvantage in sensibility itself, but in an "excess" of sensibility. Moreover, while Elinor is clearly assigned the role of the representative "sensible" one, Marianne too is described in the first chapter as "*sensible* and clever." By the same token, Elinor is described as having "feelings" characterized as "strong."

This attention to the terms "sense" and "sensibility" illuminates the quite complex way Austen employs these dichotomous notions in the novel's plot and characters. This opposition is important to Austen's work. As Edward Neill (1999) has stated:

> Here the initial point seems to be that Elinor is Augustan humanism and Johnsonian control, Marianne incipient Romanticism and emotional open-ness, or display, Elinor "hide" Marianne "reveal"–and thus Elinor "right," Marianne "wrong". . . . *Sense and Sensibility*, then, is rather trickier than it looks. If it evokes, it also refuses the smartly diagrammatic oppositions it appears to ground itself on . . . both words are highly ambivalent, and not merely positive and negative vectors respectively.[6]

Another opposition implicitly stated by the novel is that between self-interest and social duty, or between the service of *self* and *society*. The narrator's allegiance seems to lie with Elinor, who is lauded for her ability to subvert her own emotions in the interest of good manners. The character of Elinor demonstrates the narrator's opinion that to behave in a socially acceptable and duty-bound manner is as important as being true to one's own feelings. In the opposition between self and society, from a didactic point of view, Elinor is on the side of society. Thus, the novel also concerns itself with the demands of self and others.

The Global and the Local: The Universality of Cultural Influence

The struggle faced by the Dashwood sisters, while localized to a British setting, has universal implications. The rigorous moral, intellectual, and religious structures of nineteenth-century British society—family rituals, social customs, codes of decent behavior, adherence to duty—are the rich comic territory of Jane Austen's Britain. These themes take on a universal significance in the hands of Ang Lee. Social duty, the chief cultural principle in evidence in this film, is central to Victorian

England and to Lee's previous works. Although the story is two hundred years old and from a remote setting and period, it has a timelessness and universality which Lee brings to the screen, proving the director an apt observer of global cultural codes of behavior. The central cultural principle of social duty also calls to mind Lee's previous works, especially *The Wedding Banquet* and *Eat Drink Man Woman*. Even the title, *Sense and Sensibility*, reduces the plot to basic elements that express the essence of life itself—*Sense and Sensibility* is indeed stylistically similar to the condensed, summarizing effect of Lee's own *Eat Drink Man Woman* title. The challenge of bringing the nineteenth-century pastoral world of Jane Austen to the screen would have proved daunting even to those well-versed in British tradition; however, beneath the unfamiliar customs (curtsying, social dancing) and costumes (topcoats, corsets, etc.), the fundamental motifs of the story—family ritual and social duty—were already familiar territory to Lee. The story has an enduring humanity and global appeal which Lee, although previously known as a maker of Chinese films only, was uniquely suited for. Furthermore, as mentioned in the introduction to this volume, the films have another striking similarity: the producer, Lindsay Doran, and screenwriter, Emma Thompson, became convinced Ang Lee was the best choice as a director after discovering the same line in both *Eat Drink Man Woman* and *Sense and Sensibility*, when one sister says to the other, "What do you know of my heart?"[7]

Nevertheless, it took a great leap of faith to put the classic British narrative of Jane Austen's *Sense and Sensibility* into the hand of a Taiwanese director whose previous work was in Chinese films exclusively. It was a synthesis of the producer's and screenwriter's growing appreciation of Lee's *The Wedding Banquet* and *Eat Drink Man Woman* as films which combined both satirical and romantic elements.

Ang Lee takes on British period drama in his first all-English film.

These opposites called to mind the suggestion of binary opposition in the title *Eat Drink Man Woman*, as well as the East/West dialectic of Ang Lee's previous films. As in *Eat Drink Man Woman*, the title implies larger themes that the narrative of the movie will explore. The title *Eat Drink Man Woman* underscores the difference between male and female, yet it suggests an interdependence, such as that between eating and drinking. In the two pairs of the four-word idiom, "Eat drink man woman," the larger motifs of food and sex, the fundamental components of all human life, are implied in the tidy shorthand of this Chinese proverb, and are universally recognized to be transcendent of any cultural boundary or border. Thus, the title of the film itself is a sign of the globalized, territorially nonspecific themes within. In an early meeting to discuss the making of *Sense and Sensibility*, Ang Lee noted the universality of Jane Austen's narrative; "sense" and "sensibility" were "two elements that represent the core of life itself."[8]

The conception of globalization is not only realized as the synthesis and transcendence of opposites but also as the representation of geographic localities and notions of territory—including nationalism, identity, narrative, and ethnicity. Ang Lee's films complement the current focus on cultural identity and globalization in literary studies. The implications of globalization must be considered in light of the relationship between commodity and economic exchange and symbolic and cultural exchange—globalization studies are a continued rethinking of the relation among nations, economies, cultures, social practices, etc. Globalization theorists are divided on whether to view globalization historically or from a strictly postmodern perspective. Writers such as Roland Robertson (1992) and Edward Said (1994) argue that the globalization process has a long history and must be worked through key historical periods—beginning with the development of maps, maritime travel, and global exploration. This paradigm stands at odds with that of postmodern theorists Anthony Giddens (1990) and David Harvey (1990), who argue that globalization is linked much more directly to modernity and postmodernity. According to Giddens, the "'lifting out' of social relations from local contexts of interaction and their restructuring across time and space" is made possible by the cohesion and strength of twentieth-century nation-states.[9] Meanwhile, Harvey takes his position on globalization from the point of view of recent developments in mechanization and technology—such as the internet—causing the shrinking and contracting of time and space worldwide; thus globalization is a thoroughly modern or even postmodern phenomenon.

Globalization—according to Giddens—leads to the "intensification of worldwide social relations which link distant localities in such a way that local happenings are shaped by events occurring many miles away and vice versa."[10] The implications of this theoretical paradigm are striking and provide fertile ground for comparative literary study, itself a field caught up with influences and relationships. Though scholars of globalization focus largely on the fundamental impetus of capitalism and the spread of economic and commodity exchange, Malcolm Waters does not agree that "the driving force for global integration is restless capitalist expansionism."[11] Instead he feels that globalization has been fueled by symbolic exchanges, i.e., television, advertising, films, novels, music, fast food—cultural entities that are circulated and recycled simultaneously in many locations throughout the globe. This is based on the understanding that "symbols can be produced anywhere and at any time and there are relatively few resource constraints on their production and reproduction."[12]

In keeping with this, Ang Lee's portrayal of the world of Jane Austen in *Sense and Sensibility* hints at global and multicultural influences just beginning to be felt. Although the world of Jane Austen seems restricted to the territory of Britain, and particularly the English countryside—manor homes, cottages, and stables set among tidy green meadows—Meenakshi Mukherjee points out that: "It must be recognized that in the late eighteenth century, when Jane Austen was growing up, England's economy was already inextricably tied up with territories overseas."[13] Mukherjee, whose own postcolonial, non-Western reading of Jane Austen is brought to bear on the social conventions of Austen's world, highlights repeated examples in which the English colonies and the global world beyond England are discussed in Austen's novels, and proves that Austen herself was informed of the importance of England's colonies on a global scale.

In one scene from *Sense and Sensibility*, Mukherjee demonstrates that a broad knowledge of the world, including the colonies, is worthy of Elinor's—and hence the author's—esteem. Elinor, speaking of Colonel Brandon's service in the East Indies, praises him, saying, "He has seen a great deal of the world; has been abroad, has read and has a thinking mind. I have found him capable of giving me much information on various subjects." Marianne, in her usual self-absorbed fashion, makes light of this, replying, "That is to say, he has told you that in the East Indies the climate is hot and the mosquitoes were troublesome." Elinor counters, "He would have told me so, I doubt not, had I made any such inquiries, but they happened to be points on which I had been previously informed." To which Willoughby replies, "Perhaps . . . his observations may have extended to the existence of nabobs, gold mohurs and palanquins."[14] Mukherjee points out the following:

> It is to be noted that Marianne and Willoughby, the two self-obsessed romantics, seize upon the twin clichés associated with the East—heat and discomfort on the one hand, pomp and splendor on the other—whereas Elinor . . . is genuinely curious about things outside her own experience and immediate concerns."[15]

Clearly then, this scene demonstrates the limiting narrow-mindedness of the self-involved Marianne and Willoughby, who can only relate to the "other" through prejudice and cliché, while Elinor and Colonel Brandon are upheld for their multicultural understanding and broader perspective.

This is demonstrated even further by the filmic interpretation of Jane Austen, which elevates the character of the youngest sister, 11-year-old Margaret, to bring evidence of global influences to the foreground. In the film, Margaret's (Emilie François) favorite possession is a world atlas, which she plays with day and night, often disappearing under tables and into her treehouse to pore over its pages. Presumably, Margaret has a deeper desire to know the globe beyond the barriers of her limited scope. The importance of Margaret's atlas to her is underscored by a brief exchange as the Dashwoods prepare to move out of Norland, leaving behind the home's furnishings (including Margaret's atlas) to their brother, John (James Fleet), and his wife, Fanny (Harriet Walter):

Elinor: If you come inside, we could play with your atlas.
Margaret: It's not my atlas any more. It's their atlas.
(*CLOSE on ELINOR as she ponders the truth of this statement.*)[16]

In a later scene, the atlas is used by Edward (Hugh Grant) to draw out a hidden, unwilling Margaret. Elinor (Emma Thompson) and Edward joke in a deliberate way about world geography, which exasperates Margaret into emerging from her hiding place. The joking between Elinor and Edward as a semiotic discourse creates a sense of cultures and influences colliding and synthesizing, which demonstrate the true nature of globalization.

(*INT. NORLAND PARK. LIBRARY. DAY. EDWARD walks in loudly.*)
Edward: Oh, Miss Dashwood! Excuse me I was wondering do you by any chance have such a thing as a reliable atlas?
Elinor: I believe so.
Edward: Excellent. I wish to check the position of the Nile.
(*EDWARD appears to be utterly sincere.*)
Edward: My sister says it is in South America.
(*From under the table we hear a snort. ELINOR looks at him in realization.*)
Elinor: Oh! No, no indeed. She is quite wrong. For I believe it is in—in Belgium.
Edward: Belgium? Surely not. You must be thinking of the Volga.
Margaret: (*from under the table*) The Volga?
Elinor: Of course. The Volga, which, as you know, starts in . . .
Edward: Vladivostok, and ends in . . .
Elinor: St Albans.
Edward: Indeed. Where the coffee beans come from.
(*They are having such a good time that it is rather a pity the game is stopped by the appearance from under the table of MARGARET who reveals herself to be a disheveled girl of eleven. She hauls the atlas up and plonks it in front of EDWARD.*)
Margaret: The source of the Nile is in Abyssinia.
Edward: Is it? Good heavens. How do you do. Edward Ferrars.[17]

Another interesting feature to the character of Margaret in the film is that she plans, upon growing up, to become a pirate. Margaret's "piracy" has interesting implications, both from a global and a feminist perspective. On the one hand, Margaret is studying the atlas so that she may travel the world as a pirate. Edward encourages Margaret in this fantasy by agreeing to go with her on a voyage to China.

Elinor: Margaret has always wanted to travel.

Edward: I know. She is heading an expedition to China shortly. I am to go as her servant but only on the understanding that I will be very badly treated.

Elinor: What will your duties be?

Edward: Sword-fighting, administering rum and swabbing.

Elinor: Ah.[18]

This idea—the fantasy of piracy—is explored and elucidated in a further conversation between Edward and Elinor:

(*EXT. FIELDS NEAR NORLAND. DAY. EDWARD and ELINOR are on horseback. The atmosphere is intimate, the quality of the conversation rooted now in their affections.*)

Elinor: You talk of feeling idle and useless—imagine how that is compounded when one has no choice and no hope whatsoever of any occupation. (*EDWARD nods and smiles at the irony of it.*)

Edward: Our circumstances are therefore precisely the same.

Elinor: Except that you will inherit your fortune. (*He looks at her slightly shocked but enjoying her boldness.*)

Elinor: (*cont.*) We cannot even earn ours.

Edward: Perhaps Margaret is right.

Elinor: Right?

Edward: Piracy is our only option.[19]

The idea of "piracy" is developed as a solution to the enduring trouble faced by eighteenth-century women who are allowed no employment and no means of self-support. Because eighteenth-century inheritance laws favored male heirs, females were left with no option but to seek social advancement through marriage. Although the idea of Margaret becoming a pirate is intended to be humorous, the plight of women in the eighteenth century is underscored nonetheless when Elinor points out to Edward that although he will one day inherit his family's fortune, she, on the other hand, has no control over her financial destiny. Thus, as Edward points out significantly, "piracy" is the eighteenth-century woman's only option for self-support.

By the middle of the narrative, Margaret, and Austen, have been allowed to make their point through this speech where Margaret has particular compliments for Mrs. Jennings (Elizabeth Spriggs) and Colonel Brandon (Alan Rickman):

Margaret: I like her! She talks about things. We never talk about things.

Mrs Dashwood: Hush, please, now that is enough, Margaret. If you cannot think of anything appropriate to say, you will please restrict your remarks to the weather. (*A heated pause.*)

Margaret: I like Colonel Brandon too. He's been to places.[20]

"He's been to places" is the key phrase here, indicating an appreciation for travel, an acceptance and admiration for things new and different. In considering the global perspective of Jane Austen and what Ang Lee brings to it, "He's been to places," seems an apt remark. Critics of Austen's work agree that her genius was informed by an active and well-read intellect, which is revealed by the narrative complexity of her novels. Although Austen's world often appears to have a remote, restricted, and static nature, there are hints in the book and film that the writer is looking outward to the world at large and absorbing what she sees.

There have been a number of excellent adaptations of Jane Austen's work in recent years; *Sense and Sensibility* is one of at least seven film adaptations made of Austen's novels in the 1990s. These films include *Pride and Prejudice* (1995), *Persuasion* (1995), *Emma* (made as *Clueless* in 1995, two versions in 1996), *Sense and Sensibility* (1995), and *Mansfield Park* (1999).[21] (A new version of *Pride and Prejudice* was made in 2005.) The abundant variance among these adaptations demonstrates the extraordinary versatility of Austen's work that came into play at the same time that Ang Lee was interpreting Austen's world. Each of the film adaptations of Austen's novels uses different combinations of elements (and excludes different elements) to bring the story to the screen, including variations in plot, characterization, setting, and acting style. For example, Amy Heckerling's *Clueless* uses the cliques and peer rivalries in contemporary California high-school culture to provide a modern-day scenario in which the dynamics of Austen's fiction become just as relevant as they were in Austen's time, while Patricia Rozema's *Mansfield Park* represents a more extreme departure from Austen's worldview, adding a strident antislavery message, gratuitous nudity, and hints of lesbianism. On a lesser scale, Lee's vision (with Thompson's screenplay) for *Sense and Sensibility* also experiments with Austen's work; in Austen's novel, the male characters of Edward and Colonel Brandon are painted realistically without passion or attractiveness—Edward is unappealingly awkward and Colonel Brandon is lifelessly dull. Thompson's screenplay adds scenes and dialogue to make these characters decidedly more attractive than they appeared in Austen's original text. In addition, as M. Casey Diana points out in her 1998 study, the central characters of Elinor and Marianne Dashwood are fleshed out more fully by a viewing of the film. Finally, as discussed previously, the film provides a comment on the novel by evoking much more resonantly the character of young Margaret, emphasizing further a feminist dimension of Austen's work.[22] These changes provide a valuable perspective; all of these adaptations bring Austen's works to life and read into her fiction in unexpected ways, enabling a deeper appreciation for Jane Austen's timeless prose.

Cultural Collaboration/Cultural Clash

When executives at Mirage and Columbia began the search for a possible director for Emma Thompson's adaptation of *Sense and Sensibility*, it was generally assumed the studio would limit their search to English directors, women directors, or English women directors. Thus, when Ang Lee first received the studio's offer to direct, he was shocked when he saw Jane Austen's name on the script; even Lee himself thought it was a risk to ask a Taiwanese director to do a British classic.[23] His first-ever English-language film was also an iconic work in the English literary canon, his first period film, and his first time directing major stars. The many existing adaptations of Austen's work had set an almost expected style and tone, and it seemed impossible to do anything new with the form; therefore, at the outset, the director faced enormous odds. Ang Lee, responding to a question about scouting locations and designing sets, props, and costumes for *Sense and Sensibility*, illustrates the enormity of the learning experience:

> There was [a period of] about six months of research prior to shooting when I just learned whatever I could from literature, museums, visiting houses, landscape scouting, looking at costumes, checking the animals—the dogs and horses, pigs and sheep—everything. It was a long learning process. And I was also privileged to work with Emma Thompson, who was very helpful, as was the production designer. She was very generous about taking me to museums to go through paintings from that particular time so I could see the spirit of romanticism coming up, the rise of metropolitanism, and the industrial revolution. She introduced the whole deal to me: landscape design, drawing, painting. It took a long time.[24]

Emma Thompson's descriptions of working with Lee on this first foray into English filmmaking are recorded in a near-daily diary kept during the making of the film which represents possibly the most personal account and most detailed record of the experience of working with Ang Lee. The candid diary entries expertly portray various discomforts and misunderstandings brought on by culture shock. For example, a particularly trying moment happened just at the start of filming, when the actors (Thompson and Hugh Grant) made a good-natured suggestion to the director concerning a long shot. Ang Lee, unused to such a forthright relationship between actors and directors, clearly felt disrespected and threatened and had difficulty adjusting to the cultural experience of working within a British setting:

> I've learned that Hugh and I caused Ang great suffering the other day. He has never had any actor question anything before. In Taiwan the director holds complete sway. He speaks and everyone obeys. Here, actors always ask questions and make suggestions. In this instance he'd designed a particular shot where Elinor and Edward walk through the gardens at Norland talking. Hugh and I were concerned about shooting (or "covering") their expressions as there's so little time in which to see these people fall in love and the shot seemed too far off to capture them. In the event his idea was much better than ours, but that we should have had an idea at all came as a genuine shock and he was deeply hurt and confused. Better today, after Lindsay and James explained that these were perfectly normal working methods. We talked and I think he feels easier. I feel terrible—as though I've ruined Ang's first day by not being sensitive enough to his situation. It must have been terrifying—new actors, new crew, new country and then us sticking our oars in.[25]

The culture shock experience was heightened because Lee had just been filming in Taiwan, where the director's authority is unquestioned. Taiwanese casts and crew yield to the director in every decision and are not expected to have any creative input. The director in Taiwan is treated akin to an "emperor"—Lee's own wording—and followed around with chairs, ashtrays, wet towels, and tea. Coming off of filming *Eat Drink Man Woman* in Taipei, Lee was still in that mindset when he arrived in England. Notoriously, he simply thought the crew was joking when they asked him repeatedly to extinguish his cigarette while filming a barn scene with horses—he was not familiar with the emphasis on animals' rights over the director's.[26]

The different expectations of directing style provided a slight feeling of culture shock for the British actors as well as the film's director. As Thompson describes: "This culture shock thing works both ways, it seems."[27] Thompson records Alan Rickman's reaction:

Alan [is] in slight state of shock about working methods but I have assured him it works. We seem to feel our way into the shots. Ang's style of leadership is somehow to draw us all to him silently and wait for things to happen. He has the shape of shots in his head always and will stand silent for minutes on end thinking through the flow of the scenes to see if what we're doing will fit his vision. I find it very inspiring but it's quite different from being told what to do. More collaborative. I think he's enjoying our ideas more now he knows they don't present a threat or a lack of respect.[28]

The comments, or notes, given to the actors throughout production reveal the cultural divide in working methods. The actors were often hurt or distressed by the short "director's notes" Lee provided them, the most blunt of which was to Emma Thompson: "Don't look so old." Lee famously required written homework from his actors; when Kate Winslet turned in a 20-page analysis of her character, Marianne Dashwood, he pronounced it "Wrong—all wrong." Looking back, Emma Thompson found these notes humorous because of the misunderstandings brought on by cultural differences. A sampling of Ang Lee's "director's notes" to the cast include the following:

First note to Kate Winslet [Marianne]: "You'll get better."
To Emma Thompson [Elinor]: "Very dull."
To Alan Rickman [Colonel Brandon]: "More subtle: do more."
To Greg Wise [Willoughby]: "Great acting. I think."[29]

Thompson also records this conversation between Lee and Hugh Grant prior to shooting the film's important love scene:

Ang to Hugh: "This is your big moment. I want to see your insides."
Hugh: "Ah. Right-o. No pressure then."[30]

Thompson describes some of the high points of working with Lee as well:

Arrived for the opening "Big Luck" ceremony—a Buddhist ritual Ang observes at the beginning of every film. He had set up a trestle table with large bowls of rice, two gongs, incense sticks, oranges (for luck and happiness), apples (for safe, smooth shooting), a bouquet of large red-petalled flowers (for success), and an incongruous pineapple (for prosperity). Everyone lit a stick of incense, bowed in unison to the four corners of the compass and offered a prayer to the god of their choice. The camera was brought in . . . for a blessing, and a few feet of film were rolled. Ang struck the gongs; we all cheered and planted incense in the rice bowls. I cried. Al Watson, one of the electricians . . . passed Ang and said, "Is this going to happen every day, guv?"[31]

Thompson also details the dialectical elements of filmmaking with Ang Lee. She notes, for example, the behavioral contradictions that characterize him: he does tai chi but has poor posture with slumped shoulders; he is both spiritual (he meditates) and earthbound (he smokes); he is not overweight, but he eats enormous amounts. In addition, she observes the contradictions of Lee's worldview—his sensibility is very unsentimental, like Jane Austen's. For example, he cut a pair of swans out of a love scene, considering the presence of swans to be overkill. While filming the scene where the hero enters on a white horse—Willoughby riding to the rescue of the beleaguered Marianne—Lee pronounced the idea "ridiculous," while the producer and Thompson insisted to him "It's a girl thing." Despite the complications of working with live animals, Lee requested sheep in every exterior shot and dogs in every interior shot. As the actors worked through their performances, a consistent suggestion from the director was for something subtler, with less emotion. He was particularly interested in the flow of energy in a film—its qi (breath, or spirit)—taking everything as a whole, in its widest possible context. In the scene where Willoughby first enters the women's cottage, Lee reflected back on his experience of directing the scene: "Later, Ang said that he wanted the camera to watch the room, sense the change in it that a man, that sex, had brought. For Ang, the house is as important a character as the women."[32]

Thompson notes that Lee "loves the unspoken undercurrents everywhere." He finds particular emotional nuance in the natural world, sometimes holding back a shot while waiting for the wind to blow, expressing that the look of the wind-blown clothing has "something nostalgic, lonely about it."[33] She also notes Lee's pleasure at filming scenes in which there is no dialogue at all: "Ang is in heaven. There is no dialogue. 'This is pure cinema,' he says, pleased." She continues:

Ang is thrilled with all the topiary in the gardens. He had Marianne walking by this extraordinary wiggly hedge. Apparently it snowed one year and the snow froze the hedge. When the thaw came, they cut away the dead bits and continued to grow the hedge— in the shape of a wild snowdrift. It looks like a brain. "Sensibility," said Ang, pointing to it triumphantly. "And sense," he continued, pointing in the other direction towards a very neat line of carefully trimmed flowerpot-shaped bushes. The stone and lines of Montacute—grand, almost too grand though they are—give this part of the story a Gothic and mysterious flavor.[34]

The tall, misshapen hedge provided the ideal backdrop for filming Marianne's physical and emotional collapse. In the filming of the interior scene of the bedroom where

Marianne is confined for her illness, there is a Chinese vase on the mantel above the fireplace. On this vase is the Chinese character "xi" in calligraphy; this detail was no doubt intentionally added by the director. The character "xi" ("happiness, great joy") is associated with weddings and used to bless marriages, so it presents a sad irony in the dark room where Marianne, devastated by her failed dreams of a union with Willoughby, is wasting away. Yet another detail related to this scene is the exterior shot of Montecute House at dawn, where a shimmer of light appears on the horizon to herald the happy news that Marianne's fever has broken. The criss-cross of the path in the yard suggests the empty cross of the Resurrection, just before Marianne awakens lucid from her life-threatening fever in a similar "rebirth."

Ang Lee and Jane Austen: Dissecting Traditional/Global Family Identity

Ultimately, Jane Austen and Ang Lee are both consummate at painting family rituals and social customs. Underneath the strange, otherworldly costumes and strict eighteenth-century codes of behavior, the world of Jane Austen and the worldview of Ang Lee represented in his early trilogy films are closely connected by tradition—in both societies, there is a life-enhancing emphasis on harmony and on achieving a careful balance of opposites. The simplicity and grace of Jane Austen's eighteenth-century world, the confidence in God and the monarchy, the determination to do one's duty, and the lack of archness in human communication, are all similar in tone to the conservative and patriarchal traditional Chinese society Ang Lee had clearly portrayed in the "Father-Knows-Best" trilogy. Lee shares with Austen a keen sense of the tension between human behavior and the social restrictions and taboos that are meant to keep it in check. "Elinor's sense of duty may prevent her from reaching emotional fulfillment, and Marianne's romantic sensibility makes her very vulnerable to false promises. But you cannot really see them as black and white opposites. Each sister learns from the other by finding a quality that is already in herself—Elinor becomes brave enough to be seen as vulnerable and express her sensibility, while Marianne grows into sense without sacrificing her sensibility. Both find the proper balance within themselves."[35] This, too, reflects the nature of the sibling relationships in *Eat Drink Man Woman*. Lee notes: "Austen describes the sad feeling of growing up, and how we must go through so much hurt to learn about true love and integrity. This kind of struggle shapes all of our lives in one way or another—it's universal."[36] The exploration of common family relationships and the revelation of deep emotional ties are a unifying link between Austen's world and Ang Lee's work.

SEVEN

Fragmentary Narratives/Fragmented Identities in The Ice Storm

ANG LEE'S FILMIC voice indicates the paradigm of globalized fragmentation in the contemporary era—that ours is no longer a world of totality—that the world has become more and more fragmentary. One of the most harrowing examples of this fragmentation in the work of Ang Lee is *The Ice Storm*. In this film, Lee challenges the viewer with a new level of deconstruction and fragmentation of the family. This choice is an interesting one for the director, who had already negated and subverted the traditional Confucian patriarchal Chinese family structure in *The Wedding Banquet*. In that film, the homosexuality and individualism of the protagonist challenged and transgressed traditional Chinese cultural norms. Now, in the *The Ice Storm*, Lee had come to a new challenge of representing on film the deconstruction of the American family in the 1970s. It is quite an achievement that he was able to deeply penetrate and appropriate the spiritual and moral emptiness of 1970s American suburbia. In doing so, he strikes a balance between the postmodern fragmentation of meaning and signifiers, and the true humanity of searching for meaning. And once again, as he did in his previous Chinese films, he explores intergenerational conflict by focusing on the younger generation, bringing their indiscriminate longings to the forefront. The pivotal roles in *The Ice Storm* all belong to teenagers, especially the high-school age brother, Paul Hood (Tobey Maguire), who humiliatingly struggles through experiences with drugs and sex, his 14-year-old sister, Wendy (Christina Ricci), whose mysterious and perverse sexual journey dominates the film, and her boyfriend Mikey (Elijah Wood), whose search for transcendence has a fatal outcome.

In this film, set in the 1970s glasshouse suburban world of New Canaan, Connecticut, Ang Lee creates a stark, alienating, gray microcosm for his players—difficult to watch, but oddly compelling. The Connecticut winter is at its most harsh and unforgiving, and the scenes leading up to the famous storm are filled with bare trees, dead leaves, and bitter cold air. This paints an apt picture for the tone of the film, which is about sexual detachment and alienation within the family. The film is a masterpiece of irony and bitterness. One can go so far as to say there is practically no communication—that is, the transference of understanding and coherent exchange of ideas between the characters—in the film. Each scene is fairly short, and if conversation takes place, it is usually brief or interrupted. Characters speak with their backs to each other, from under bedclothes, from behind closed doors, from within a Nixon mask, without meeting each other's eyes. Characters do not listen to each other. Silence is an actual medium in the movie—the film is all about what is unsaid—and the unexpressed thoughts fill the movie like a picture highlighted in relief. Kevin Kline and Joan Allen play a married couple, Ben and Elena Hood, for whom an upcoming weekend of Thanksgiving vacation could provide a chance to reconnect with each other and with their two teenage children, Paul and Wendy. Instead, however, Ben Hood is distracted by his own affair with a neighbor, Janey Carver (Sigourney Weaver), while his children are engaged in their own precocious sexual pursuits. Children mimic parents in their meaningless and labyrinthine chase.

Some of the most unforgettable scenes in the film regarding miscommunication and the search for true intimacy include Ben Hood and his daughter Wendy's silent walk through a wet and muddy woods, as he carries the chastened teenage child home in his arms (her feet are cold). The final scene is also a masterfully delicate moment, as Ben weeps, penitent, bent over the steering wheel of the family car, while in the backseat, his son looks on quizzically, watching the rear view of his tortured father's head. Other haunting scenes include the kiss, in a winterized, drained swimming pool filled with dead leaves, between Wendy and her adolescent boyfriend—he first takes chewing gum out of his mouth in a gesture that seems both sexually charged and boyishly innocent. Lines from the film which linger in memory include Janey's scathing line to Ben, postcoital: "You're boring me. I already have a husband." Her husband, Jim (Jamey Sheridan), returns from a business trip to Houston and says to their two boys, "Hey, guys, I'm back." The older son Mikey replies, "You were gone?" There is also the angelic cherub-like son, Sandy (Adam Hann-Byrd), who tells Wendy, "I love you." In response, she asks, "Are you drunk?" In addition, there is an early scene where Paul recommends to a girl on whom he has a crush to read *The Idiot* by Dostoevsky, as he stands on a staircase feeling like one. "I think you'd really like it"—he says—"*The Idiot.*"

Ang Lee's familiarity with 1970s Connecticut life is formidable—even more so considering *The Ice Storm* was his first feature film on an entirely American subject. The movie was filmed on location in New Canaan, Connecticut, including the town's main street, train station, drugstore, library, and Waveny Park. This town is the epicenter of white upper-middle-class Anglo-Saxon Protestant culture, and the accoutrements of the movie—stereo phonographs playing "Montego Bay," rainbow-colored toe socks, polyester fashions of the ugliest nature including long lapels and gaudy leisure suits, hairspray-hardened hairstyles, waterbeds, the hardcover volume of *Watership Down*, etc.—are all products well-remembered by those who came of age in those years. The modernist houses used in the set—shag carpets, wall-sized windows, flat interior design, gray paneling, unattractive box TV sets, etc.—are all exact replicas of the 1970s community. Even the television commercials (i.e., the weeping Indian, Iron Eyes Cody, in an advertisement for environmental protection) and programs in the background are authentic television footage that clearly evoke the era. The use of both drugs and sex as escape routes in the movie accurately mirror the American social scene as it unfolded in 1973. The human dramas in the film are made all the more convoluted, murky, dreamlike, and detached by the emotionally-numbing involvement of drugs, sex, and alcohol. Alcohol is served at every party and gathering among the adults in the film—there is never an adult without a drink or a cigarette, usually both. The sexual relationships include those between Wendy and the two sons of a friend's family, Paul and his love interest, plus the adulterous relationships of both parents. This culminates in the notorious "key party" in which everyone exchanges car keys and goes off with everyone else—including, until his early exit, the town's preacher ("Sometimes the shepherd needs the company of the sheep," he says to Elena; "I'm going to try hard not to understand the implications of that," she replies).

The date of 1973 is pinpointed by the footage of Richard Nixon on the television set; Thanksgiving week in 1973, in which Nixon is about to be relieved from office over the Watergate scandal, the war in Vietnam is an ongoing political disaster, and disillusionment pervades the atmosphere. This was the accurate historical date of the famous ice storm which hit Connecticut and a large swath of New England in 1973, in which the air over the eastern seaboard suddenly turned to a freezing temperature, and in a single night a rain storm coated every exposed surface with a glaze of ice. The storm was dangerous, and entire communities and neighborhoods were immobilized and isolated for days. Trees cracked under the weight of the ice, and the falling of these huge trunks crushed houses, buildings, and automobiles. The storm in both the movie, and in reality, highlighted the distance and alienation felt at that time. This is

After the storm, the "embarrassment of forgiveness"—Paul's family awaits him at the train station in the final moments of the film.

captured in Lee's film by the sights and sounds so clearly etched in one's memory—the clinking and cracking of the ice as the wind blew through ice-encrusted trees, the squeaking cracks of falling branches, the impassible roads, the loss of electricity. The "ice" metaphor is given further weight by the close-ups of a metal ice tray appearing in the film. Metaphors are further suggested by the short, cold days accentuated by the gray skies and the bleakness of the approaching winter. Those from the New England area recognize Thanksgiving as the beginning of a long winter season, incessant and relentless until April. The ice is even given a role in the film, as husbands and wives gingerly make their way across slippery, unfamiliar terrain.

Challenges in the Making of The Ice Storm

The Ice Storm is a remarkable achievement on the part of Ang Lee because it demonstrates, just as *Sense and Sensibility* did, the director's amazing versatility, proving definitively that his directorial range cannot be confined to a single culture or genre. Indeed, the film demonstrates a phenomenal grasp of the 1970s American suburban experience it depicts. In addition, the book itself, which became a best-seller in the United States, was written by Rick Moody, who grew up in the environment he describes, and for whom the experiences related are semiautobiographical. While Moody's fiction shows a confidence with his material, the film in some ways surpasses the fictional experience—how often can it be said that the book was not as good as the movie? And yet in this case, the book can be judged due to its appeal as a type of "pulp fiction"—it contains far more explicit sex than the film—almost needing to entice the reader through its softly pornographic writing on nearly every page. The movie transcends this sexual obsession, presenting the sexual material more obliquely, or even omitting it, in favor of more sophisticated portraits of its characters. The book, for example, opens with a scene in which Ben Hood is wandering around in his neighbor's house, and he takes a pair of her underwear and masturbates into it, and then throws it into her son's room. The film omits this graphic scene. Another specific example is the teenage son's crush on his Manhattan classmate—in the book, a detailed scene of masturbation is described as the boy takes advantage of the girl's drugged stupor. The movie treats this situation more tenderly and comically—more skillfully in general—the girl passes out in the boy's lap; the expression on the boy's face is one of stunned gratitude. However, he does not take advantage of the situation in such a prurient way. Instead, trapped under her body, he uncertainly and clumsily moves her, clunking her head against the ground in one of the most bittersweet and believable scenes in the movie. Then he has to leave, running for his train that will carry him into the freeze of the ice storm. The subtlety of Lee's presentation trumps the graphic sexuality of Moody's fiction. James Schamus has also commented on his "censoring" what he called "Paul's horrifically endearing bout of masturbation at Libbets' apartment."[1] According to Schamus, "[Reading about it is one thing, but] seeing it would have been something else altogether, in particular if the image were stripped of the help the book's narrator gives us in appreciating the moment in all its pathos and humor."[2]

The ice storm itself is one of the key elements of the film and perhaps plays its largest role, at least for the director, who clearly enjoyed lingering on its otherworldly sights and sounds. Lee obviously relished filming a true period in history in which "The entire world becomes covered in transparent crackling glass."[3] The making of *The Ice Storm*, with its heavy metaphorical imagery, was perhaps most closely related to *Eat Drink Man Woman* with its emphasis on food—slicing, stewing, stuffing, and frying. In both *Eat Drink Man Woman* and *The Ice Storm*, the director freely and extravagantly experimented with rich visual imagery, taking large amounts of dialogue-free screen time to do so. Lee's signature technique came through clearly in both films as he used visual metaphor to tell his story, independent of dialogue. In discussing the making of *The Ice Storm*, Lee wrote in the preface to the shooting script:

When I think of *The Ice Storm*, I think first of water and rain, of how it falls everywhere, seeps into everything, forms underground rivers, and helps to shape a landscape. And also, when calm, of how it forms a reflective surface, like glass, in which the world reappears. Then, as the temperature drops, what was only water freezes. Its structure can crush concrete and push iron away, it is so strong. Its pattern overthrows everything. This is the structure I have hoped to create in my movie, *The Ice Storm*. Whatever the surface patterns you might see reflected there, the customs and morals, and hopes, and loves of the characters are infused, and overturned, and reestablished by the force of nature that the storm represents.[4]

Not all critics agree that Ang Lee was successful in his adaptation of Moody's work. Charles Taylor represents one dissenting opinion:

Everything about "The Ice Storm," from the cool green titles that seem to smoke and shift (as if seen through ice) to Mychael Danna's score of lonely, Asian-sounding wind instruments, is tasteful and distant. . . . Moody was writing from the inside; Lee doesn't get beyond displaying artifacts from a lost civilization . . . the movie does call up the early 1970s. But being an anthropologist isn't the same thing as being a dramatist, and I'm not convinced Lee understands the period. How could he? Lee's being Taiwanese didn't matter in his last picture, *Sense and Sensibility*, because the early 1800s are distant to everyone, but the calamity of American life in 1973 is still fresh in the minds of anyone who lived through it. The exhausting, one-damn-thing-after-another tenor of American life, with the outrage of Watergate striking before the hangover from Vietnam wore off, was far removed from the cool, ascetic portentousness on display here.[5]

The biggest challenge for the film was to make a coherent narrative out of a book that presents a fragmentary one. The story is not linear, but rather patchy series of events described without chronological order in a chapter-by-chapter exposition each told from a different character's point of view. Only in the final chapter is it revealed that the story has been told from the point of view of an omniscient narrator, the teenage son Paul Hood. Because the narrator could not have had access to each character's private thoughts and stream of consciousness, as he did by the skillful literary device in the book, the story had to be told in an entirely different format in the film. James Schamus' screenplay filled in backstory that was only hinted at in the book—the first half of the movie does not occur in Moody's novel at all. Dialogue was created from the parts of the book that were inner musings in characters' heads. Thus, part of the postmodern, splintered feeling of this film comes from its source material—the filmmakers had to create a narrative from what is essentially a cubist and fragmented piece of work. In an interview published in 2005, Lee explores this idea further:

> The Ice Storm represents the natural evolution of the ideas I began exploring in Eat Drink Man Woman. I think that beginning with Eat Drink Man Woman I started departing from what I had done in the first two films. I was beginning to experiment with cinema and was thinking mostly of cubism. Instead of a linear structure, I was looking at a different way to hold the movie. So I was trying to develop one incident or one character and look at it from all sides. But when you want to watch from all sides, you also have to shoot in a way that reflects that. It is funny, when I went back to Taipei to shoot Eat Drink Man Woman, I felt like the whole city—it is kind of an ugly city—looked like a painting by Braque or Picasso. I didn't go all the way with [cubism] at that time, but I couldn't wait to develop it further with The Ice Storm.[6]

The nature of the film is part satire, part psychological drama, and part tragedy. It is also a period piece, requiring the director to address accurately a time period in which he was not physically located in the United States, and also an era that is very recent in people's minds.

> I basically made the movie from the crew's suggestions. For one scene, I wanted some kids' toys against the wall in Mikey's room, to give the scene texture, and we tried a field hockey stick. It looked really good to me, until someone had to say that in America, field hockey is more of a girl's game. Gradually I got tuned into the world—that happens on every movie. I did a women's movie, and I'm not a woman. I did a gay movie, and I'm not gay. I learned as I went along. What hit me the most was when Wendy says, "Mom, are you all right?" And I couldn't understand when Ben tells the kids to go to bed by 10, and they don't do it—I couldn't relate to that. I had to learn from the crew, who explained to me that this was a time when the kids were really raising their parents. The parents were so self-absorbed that the kids had to take responsibility for their own upbringing.[7]

Fragmentary Dialogue and the Use of Silence

One outstanding element in the screenplay for The Ice Storm is its dialogue, which reflects the repressed communication style of families steeped in unhappiness, a lack of communication, and unfinished conversations. Although Rick Moody's novel is a lengthy narrative told from the point of view of an omniscient narrator, the screenplay by James Schamus develops Moody's ideas through broken sentences, unfinished thoughts, and interrupted communications.[8] This creates a marvelous sense of abstraction and fragmentation; at the same time, the viewer is able to piece together the bits of dialogue to come to a more complete understanding of the characters. As has been mentioned, this fragmented effect is similar to cubist art, where small segments of the picture can be observed from different angles. Most of the lines spoken by the actors are only one or two phrases, or incomplete sentences. Conversations overlap, weave together, and are interrupted. A speech longer than two or three sentences, or sometimes two or three words, is rare in this film.

In one example of charged dialogue, the characters use simple words flooded with meaning in emotion and tone to set up the primary conflict between them. In this scene, Elena and Ben Hood are attending a dinner party at their neighbors' home. All has gone smoothly, and the conversation has remained superficially polite, but the spilling of some wine onto Ben's trousers results in Janey Carver wiping the stain absentmindedly with a napkin. This action is ambiguous; however, there is a slight charge in the atmosphere as Elena, Ben's wife, notices the casual exchange between her neighbor and her husband. Soon after it is indeed revealed that the two are having an affair. However, at this early stage, the only hint of Janey's guilt appears as she sharply refuses to let Elena help with the dishes. The two maintain the utmost in propriety in etiquette while their true feelings are not at all hidden.

> (*The dinner party has moved to the living room for after dinner drinks. Elena remains behind to help Janey pick up the table. She stacks a plate on top of another.*)
>
> Janey: Please don't.
> Elena: It's not a bother.
> Janey: I insist.
>   (*beat*)
>   Don't touch them.
>   (*Elena realizes that there's an edge to Janey's voice.*)
> Elena: Oh.
> Janey: (*realizing she's gone too far*) It's really quite all right.
> Elena: Of course.[9]

In a second example, the two characters, Elena and Philip (Michael Cumpsty), are engaged in a conversation at a used-book sale. Philip is trying to charm Elena and flirt with her, but Elena abruptly changes the topic when she sees her daughter riding past them on her bicycle. This shift in conversation makes the self-important minister change tack; however, he is unable to see what Elena is thinking. Elena herself becomes confused, lost in thought, and transfixed by the distant memories of childhood. In an interesting twist, Elena forgets what the topic is and it is Philip himself who reminds her; she then agrees with him as if he were the one to bring it up. The conflict is perfectly transparent to the viewer in the following exchange:

> Philip: Well, I of course flatter myself that our church is not exactly
>   what most people would call organized religion—at times it's the

disorganization that's liberating—and of course I've begun to minister much more in what one might call therapeutic environments, in small groups, and one on one, couples . . .

(Elena looks outside the window, and sees Wendy speed past on her bicycle.)

Elena: *(cutting him off)* My daughter. I haven't been on a bike for years.
(still not really looking at him)
When was the last time you rode a bike?

Philip: *(a bit taken aback by the abrupt topic change)* They say you never forget.

Elena: *(jarred back to his presence)* Forget what?

Philip: Forget how to ride a bike.
(Silence.)

Elena: No, of course you don't, you're right.[10]

A third example of dialogue is that of an intimate conversation between a husband and wife, Ben and Elena. These two are very familiar with each other, having been married nearly twenty years, and can finish each other's sentences. This has become a habit of communication with them, so that they do not even clearly articulate what they mean, and in fact, may not even be certain of exactly what they are trying to say.

Ben: Elena. I need some help here if this thing's gonna defrost by tomorrow.
(She comes up and together they tug and pull until they succeed in extracting a large, frozen turkey. As they pull it out, it slips from their hands and, after a dull thump, slides along the floor. They smile. Elena bends over to pick it up. Ben observes her. She notices his look.)

Ben: Here.
(He goes over and picks up the turkey, placing it in the sink. He looks back at her and notices her vaguely distraught look.)

Ben: You all right there?

Elena: Oh. Sure, I—Did you remember to pick up the cranberry sauce?

Ben: Um, yes.
(They stand together, his concern and her vulnerability forming an awkward attraction between them.)

Elena: Because you like it on your turkey sandwiches.

Ben: I do . . . I'm—are you . . . ?

Elena: I . . . I think I . . .

Ben: *(pause)* You know Elena, I've been thinking . . .

Elena: Ben, maybe no talking right now? If you start talking, you're going to . . .
(She kisses him as if she needs him.

INT. HOOD HALLWAY. DAY.
Ben and Elena enter their bedroom. Elena closes the door quietly behind her.

INT. HOOD BEDROOM. DAY.

    Ben and Elena undress shyly. They make love. Elena's face is almost fearful.

INT. HOOD BEDROOM. LATER.

    Elena and Ben lie in bed side by side in the pale afternoon light.)

Ben: Wow. You kind of forget what you're missing . . .
    (He gets up and starts to get dressed.)

Ben: I should probably be getting going, to get Paul.
    (He smells the armpits of the shirt he's putting on.)

Ben: Yikes—I was hoping to wear this thing to the Halford's Friday.
    (He looks at Elena, and realizes she's started to cry.)

Ben: Hey. Elena?

Elena: It's nothing.

Ben: What? What is it?

Elena: That shirt?

Ben: What?

Elena: Leave it—I'll wash it for you.
    (He looks at her ruefully.)[11]

This dialogue is presented very realistically, with the two uttering fragmented sentences in their most intimate exchange, as they discuss their momentary physical attraction: "I do. I'm—are you?" The other replies: "I . . . I think I . . . " Here, meaning is exchanged without being explicitly stated, while Elena's hesitancy reflects her feeling of ambivalence. When Ben asks Elena twice how she is feeling, the first time she changes the subject: "Oh. Sure, I—Did you remember to pick up the cranberry sauce?" and the second time she denies her feelings: "It's nothing." At the end of this short series of scenes, the conversation comes to a heartbreaking conclusion over the subject of Ben's dirty shirt. In promising to wash the shirt for him, Elena promises to continue to stay in her marriage despite her deep dissatisfaction. She will go on repressing her true feelings; this is the decision she must make to preserve her family.

In another example, a soliloquy from the adulterous wife character, Janey, has a special poignancy as she has caught her lover's teenage daughter acting inappropriately with her own preteen son. As she attempts to upbraid the girl, her efforts falter and she sputters in futility. She fulminates on quasi-biblical notions, perhaps half-remembered truths from a Catholic-school education: "A person's body is his temple," and "This body is your first and last possession." When misquoting scripture does not help her, she turns to a more anthropological argument:

Janey: A person's body is his temple, Wendy. This body is your first and last possession. Now as your own parents have probably told you, in adolescence our bodies tend to betray us. That's why, in Samoa and in other developing nations, adolescents are sent out into the woods, unarmed, and they don't come back until they've learned a thing or two.[12]

Clearly, this lecture from Janey Carver to Wendy Hood is misplaced parenting—how does the cheating Janey Carver have any integrity to model for the sex-obsessed young girl? In addition, Janey is furious and full of righteous indignation over Wendy's promiscuous behavior, but from this speech we can see her moral impotence. She cannot even reprimand the girl directly, for she herself offers no better a role model. This is echoed in the conversations between Ben Hood and his son Paul, as the father wishes to take the proper opportunity to tell his son about "the birds and the bees." This excruciating conversation is a classic moment in the "sexual education" of every post-1960s American teenager. The representation in *The Ice Storm* is acerbic and true. In this case, the conversation takes place on the drive home from the train station after Paul has been picked up at the beginning of Thanksgiving vacation:

Ben: You know Paul, I've been thinking, maybe this is as good a time as any to have a little talk, you know, about—well—
(He makes a sharp turn. Paul puts his arms up on the dashboard to steady himself.)

Paul: *(nervous)* About?

Ben: Well, the whole gamut. Facts of life and all. Some fatherly advice, because, I tell you, there's things happening that you're probably old enough to . . . digest.

Paul: Uh . . . things?

Ben: Well . . . things that happen between a . . . For example, on the self-abuse front—and this is important—it's not advisable to do it in the shower—it wastes water and electricity and because we all expect you to be doing it there in any case—and, um, not onto the linen, and not on your sister's underwear or any clothing belonging to your mother . . .
(He pauses to gauge the effect of his monologue on his son, then continues.)

Paul: Uh, Dad—
(Just then Ben runs a stop sign and almost slams into another car.)

Ben: Holy! Well. If you're worried about anything, just feel free to ask, and, uh, we can look it up.

Paul: Uh, Dad, you know I'm 16.

Ben: All the more reason for this little heart-to-heart . . . great.
(They drive up to the house.)

Ben: Um, Paul. On second thought . . . I was thinking, can you do me a favor and pretend I never said any of that.

Paul: Sure, Dad.

Ben: Thanks.[13]

The fact that at the end of the conversation Ben Hood asks his son to ignore his own "fatherly advice" and to actually cancel out his words is doubly subversive, once again pointing to the pivotal role of the father figure in Lee's films. In the first place, as a cheating spouse, Ben Hood is a poor role model (as Janey is to Wendy in the previous example), and does not have the moral integrity to parent his son. Ben is an antihero in the narrative; he lacks authority over his household. Other father figures also provide examples of weakness and absence: the Carver father is frequently away on business trips, the town preacher (also a type of father figure) demonstrates moral weakness by his seductive behavior toward the married Elena, and Libbets' (Katie Holmes) father is also vacationing in Switzerland, leaving his daughter to spend the school holiday alone in their New York apartment. Finally, in the film as in the novel, at the symbolic center of narrative are Richard Nixon's televised addresses to the nation and the Watergate Hearings, which offer an ongoing demonstration of crumbling integrity by reiterating that the nation's ultimate father figure has, in fact, been lying. In the second place, the above exchange offers yet another example of *The Ice Storm*'s truncated or aborted attempts at communication. Ben's telling his son "Can you do me a favor and pretend I never said any of that," is a particularly clear example.

The Comic Genre: The Fantastic Four

Finally, both the beginning and ending of *The Ice Storm* focus on comic book imagery. Paul Hood is reading issue number 141 of *The Fantastic Four* when his train from Manhattan to New Canaan gets caught in the ice storm, preventing the train from continuing its journey. The carriage is in predawn shadow with only dim light, perhaps emergency lights on the train, for Paul to see the comic book page. The camera focuses on the comic book, on a page where Reed Richards (also known as Stretch) has just shot his young son with a cosmic ray gun to neutralize the destructive energy that the enemy, Annihilus, has implanted in him. The Thing, Medusa, Flame, and Richards' wife, Sue Storm, are shocked into silence, stunned by the callousness of the father's action. The comic book reads: "THEN YOU'VE TURNED HIM INTO A VEGETABLE. YOUR OWN SON." In the comic panel, Richards replies: "DON'T YOU SEE, SUE? HE WAS TOO POWERFUL . . . IF HIS ENERGY HAD CON-TINUED TO BUILD, HE WOULD HAVE DESTROYED THE WORLD!" Paul mulls this over as the train sits immobilized on the track.

This reference to the Fantastic Four as a metaphor could relate to either the Hoods or the Carvers, whose nuclear family members both come to a total of four. The original Fantastic Four, as is commonly known, were permanently altered at the molecular level when a rocket in which they were traveling passed through a storm of cosmic rays. Reed Richards, in the original comic book, was a ponderous and stuffy scientist who acquired the somewhat contrasting super-power to stretch his body into any conceivable shape. His wife, Sue Storm, could transform herself into The Invisible Girl (and later the more matronly Invisible Woman), and also had the ability to project a force field as a defensive weapon. Both of these roles seem to fit Ben and Elena Hood, especially Elena's meek demeanor which renders her nearly invisible, as well as her powerful defensive force field. The third member of the Fantastic Four in the original comic was Johnny Storm, Sue's younger brother, who was given human torch capabilities and seemed more interested in showing off than using his super-power to fight crime. Finally, the last member of the group was The Thing, a test pilot with a rough sense of humor, who is transformed into a hideous craggy monster. The key character in the *Fantastic Four* issue read by Paul on the train is the young son of Richards and Sue Storm, Franklin, who is a stand-in for Mikey Carver. The son is a threat to human existence and is basically neutralized by his father to stop the destructive energy implanted in him ("If his energy had continued to build, he would have destroyed the world"). The odd electric humming heard repeatedly by Mikey in the film (and imperceptible to anyone else) identifies him definitely with the doomed Franklin. Mikey repeatedly says, "Can you hear that?" referring to what can only be described as electrical buzzing. This foreshadows Mikey's fate during the night of the ice storm; the sobering fact of Mikey's death is what brings clarity and balance to the off-kilter world of the adult generation.

As the film opens, the *Fantastic Four* comic book takes a prominent role, and the very first voice-over relates the narrative of the Fantastic Four to the four-member families that will be presented in the film.

> In issue number 141 of *The Fantastic Four*, published in November 1973, Reed Richards has to use his anti-matter weapon on his own son, who Annihilus has turned into a human atom bomb. The problem is that the cosmic rays that infused Richards and the rest of the Fantastic Four on their aborted moon mission have made young Franklin a volatile mixture of matter and anti-matter.
> (*The train moves slowly through a suburban, semi-forested landscape.*)
> And that's what it is to come from a family, if you analyze it closely. Your family is kind of like your own personal negative matter. And that's what dying is—dying is when your family takes you back, thus hurling you back into negative space . . .
> (*On Paul, as the sun breaks over the horizon. His face glows warmly in the yellow light. He looks down idly at the comic book.*)
> So it's a paradox—the closer you're drawn back in, the further into the void you're thrown.[14]

The juxtaposition of the comic book narrative with Paul and his family is significant. In the opening scene with Paul on the train, the final panel of the comic book reads: " . . . AFTER WHAT YOU JUST DID, THERE CAN'T BE A TEAM ANY-MORE. . . . THIS IS THE END. . . . THE END OF THE FANTASTIC FOUR!" This foreshadows the threat of Paul's father's adultery against the family—at times, the Hood family's resiliency is in doubt, but the emotionally-charged reunion at the train station hints that the Hood family will endure the hurt and stay intact. "Perhaps the finest moments of the Marvel Age occurred in the pages of *The Fantastic Four*, where a group of humanized superheroes squabbled with each other, but rose above their conflicts to confront the vast gulfs of an overwhelming universe. The comic book took on mystical and cosmic overtones, which no one suspected the medium could achieve."[15] This theme of rising above the family's own conflicts to confront the world at large is reflected in the opening and closing scenes of *The Ice Storm*. The idea that the hurts inflicted upon the family by individual members must be overcome is demonstrated by the solidarity shown by the Hood family as they await Paul's arrival on the train. In the preface to the shooting script, Ang Lee talks about his film being made of "small details and particular moments. . . . In this case, it was the moment when Paul is joined at the train station by his family."[16] Elsewhere Lee has remarked how this climactic moment helped convince him to make the film; he visualized the entire film around Paul's frightening and yet deeply moving experience of seeing his own father in tears. This truly transcendent moment in the film is also described in the script by screenwriter James Schamus: "At the end of the film, it is Paul's face on which we finally hold. It is his vision of his father's tears through which he, and we hope, the film as a whole achieves a troubled but still liberating epiphany, a kind of embarrassment of forgiveness."[17] Lee adds:

My producers and I often joked that 1973 was America's most "embarrassing" year; with Nixon, polyester, the admitting of defeat in Vietnam, stagflation, the energy crisis. In researching for the film, my production team and I read many of the novels and the self-help books of the period, and watched many movies made in the early 1970s. Rather than approach the period as one of "kitsch," this process led us to a tremendous respect and humility. It turned out that there were many truths buried inside the pop psychology and sometimes painfully naive self-help philosophies of the day, and that we, two decades later, have much to learn from the "embarrassing" past.[18]

In an interview given when the film was made, Lee especially brings attention to the advantages he had making the film as an outsider and a director from a different cultural background.

I tried to keep the emotional core of the tragedy—that's what prompted me to make the movie. . . . I think [the tone] is a lot softer. Less angry. I didn't grow up there. I wasn't pissed off. That distance helped me to make it art—it wasn't so personal. But I think if the movie moves people, it's because it has a subtext that's universal, that anyone, from any culture, can relate to. [19]

In the last sentence of this statement, Ang Lee himself points to the global nature of the story of the dissolution of marriage and family that is a common theme in his work. The universality of Lee's filmic voice transcends cultural boundaries. Lee himself has stated "Quite honestly, I don't know what's what anymore. I wanted to make a Chinese film [*Crouching Tiger, Hidden Dragon*] so that I could be different from Hollywood, but actually my Hollywood films are more Chinese in vision than the Chinese films I made before. My first three films were just made for the mainstream Taiwanese audience. I wasn't thinking about being Chinese or not Chinese."[20] In considering the work of Ang Lee, questions must be raised about the relation between parts and whole, between local and general, between individual and global. For Lee, the filmic voice he has created reflects a multifaceted approach which symbolizes globalization and informs it with a process of enlightenment and liberation.

EIGHT

Race, Gender, Class, and Social Identity
in Ride with the Devil

ANG LEE HAS continued to surprise audiences with his versatility, and many were interested to learn of his initial foray into the genre of Civil War epic with *Ride with the Devil*.[1] As a study of the psychological subtleties and conflict of war, this film has much to recommend it. This is a period piece, and, as such, can bring to life the remote era of conflicted North-South relations, racial and class issues, social struggle, etc., which were in high relief during the American Civil War. Set in the border states of Kansas and Missouri, the film explores the nature of lawlessness and violence of war fought on the periphery through the eyes and thoughts of 16-year-old Jake Roedel. During the winter of 1861 Roedel grows up quickly, choosing to defend the South with a group of young cohorts and experiencing a brutal, lawless parody of war without standards or mercy. The film is based on Daniel Woodrell's novel *Woe to Live On* (1987); the author himself is a direct descendant of Ozarker ancestors who fought in the Civil War. How Ang Lee became involved is explained by Woodrell in Liz Rowlinson's interview with him for the *Richmond Review*:

> The film came about in a series of happy accidents. The book came and went, wrapped in lavish silence from reviewers and readers, but a woman named Anne Carey read it in 1987 while working for another producer and liked it. Years later she was working for the production company associated with Ang Lee. He said he'd like to make a film that wasn't all domestic drama, she gave him the book, he read it in one night and they bought it. The book was scarcely known, so Ms. Carey was the conduit of my good fortune.[2]

In bringing this historical drama to the screen, Ang Lee provides a rare glimpse into this period as both a literary landmark and a dramatic narrative. Moreover, he stays true to the period by working with a script rife with the metaphors and allusions of Civil War America, creating a film with daring poetic style (which could partially explain its commercial failure). Viewers of this drama are offered an exposure to metaphorical conundrums as well as florid and expressive language—a challenge greater than that usually offered at the multiplex.

Ride with the Devil deals with a number of ideas typical of an Ang Lee project, such as racial tension, intolerance, class issues, love and marriage, as well as gender and sexuality, the fragmentary nature of the narrative, globalization/cultural identity, etc. The film assumes a high level of knowledge about the Civil War, from a time when the world was technologically and mechanically less advanced and when human codes of behavior differed markedly from modern times. This film deals with human behavior from a time period more than one hundred years ago; the conservative behavior of the period, especially among men and women, seems quite alien to modern sensibilities. The different concerns of the period are illustrated by codes of honor which no longer have contemporary importance; these include a marriage that takes place to legitimize an illegitimate child. In addition, the film deals with racism and the changes that take place in the relationship between the young black man and the young white protagonist. In a letter-reading scene, the film suggests that only one of the boys in the group could read; this rate of illiteracy among a group of young men in their twenties seems surprising to modern audiences. Furthermore, the music used in the film has a strong Celtic and bluegrass flavor, adding to its historically-distant and wistful atmosphere.

The Genre of the Western

Ang Lee avoids the clichés of a typical gunpowder-and-uniform Civil War movie, and dispels preconceptions of what the "western" as a genre should be. In the place of a standard Hollywood war movie, he offers an "intimate epic"—a slow-moving world of human relationships that is alternately fragile and violent. The film has been criticized by followers of Civil War history as "inauthentic" because the story focuses almost exclusively on fictitious characters rather than the real-life heroes and villains of the Civil War. However, *Ride with the Devil* does not try to bring a documentary view to the Civil War, but instead creates a tender and thoughtful portrait of the true emotional and psychological struggles within war itself: idealism, loyalty, affection, betrayal, hardship, compromise, and love. Lee stages massive battle scenes with competence, but the film's focus is on the emotional journey of its single main character, Jake Roedel (Tobey Maguire).

While at the outset Roedel appears to merely drift along with the tide of events, his story becomes the film's central story: a narrative of misguided loyalty in a longing for acceptance and a place to call "home." Jake Roedel and his black counterpart, Daniel Holt (Jeffrey Wright), are examples of loyalty stretched to the limits. Roedel is a German immigrant seeking to gain acceptance into the world of Southern civility, and Daniel Holt is a freed Southern slave who travels with his former owner and childhood friend George Clyde (Simon Baker), who also purchased his freedom. Within the tension of war and the constant threat of violence, Roedel and Holt are tested in a crucible of conflicting loyalties. When they are pushed too far and the tension finally snaps, these two characters suddenly find themselves "free"—new men with a stronger identity are brought to birth. This film does its finest work as it

Among a sleep-deprived band of ragtag soldiers, Jake Roedel and Daniel Holt begin to doubt their allegiance to the Southern cause prior to the raid on Lawrence, Kansas, in Ang Lee's penetrating look at the American Civil War.

illustrates the emotional growth that human beings experience as they mature—as old ties are broken and they are forced to face who they really are and what they will become. Over the course of the film, Jake Roedel is transformed very realistically from naïve boy to emotionally mature man. In addition, both Jake Roedel and Daniel Holt exhibit traits of mercy, gratitude, and civility which make them stand apart from the other characters. Daniel Holt is silent through many of the initial scenes, still indicative of the bondage from which he only recently escaped. However, as the film goes on, and he and Roedel strike up an unlikely friendship; the two stand out from the crowd as the true vestige of decency and integrity in a world turned upside down by war and conflicting loyalties.

Language Used in Ride with the Devil

One of the most compelling aspects of *Ride with the Devil* for the viewer is its intricate use of language. The script, adapted from Daniel Woodrell's novel *Woe to Live On* by James Schamus, is a compilation of authentic-sounding nineteenth-century speech. With its rolling, poetic lines, it comes across like the prose of Herman Melville or Mark Twain. Certainly Shamus and Woodrell must have been intimately familiar with great nineteenth-century American writers to be able to imitate the rhythms of their texts in so grand a fashion. Only someone immersed in the literature of the period would have been able to successfully re-create the actual atmosphere and feeling of nineteenth-century American English.

The effect of this authentic detail—language of the period—is remarkable. Actors Tobey Maguire and Jewel Kilcher (playing Sue Lee Shelley) actually seem to be transported back in time—and not by clothing and setting alone. The elegance of nineteenth-century English at the time of the American Civil War is given life again, as if in the letters of soldiers of the period, or in the prose of fledgling Southern regionalism. It is a treat for the ear to listen to the delightful cadences and lengthy sentences of nineteenth-century speech. Even seemingly simple statements become long-winded, meandering, and poetic; jokes become funnier, seemingly more clever and sophisticated when couched in these terms. Vocabulary used is more elegant than that of a modern-set film, thus affording many opportunities for exposure to gracious and eloquent speech with beautiful idioms and lyrical grammar.

The young Southerners in the film are from Lafayette County in western Missouri, and they join a band of Confederate guerillas early in the war. Most of them are the sons of plantation owners or farmers and have seen their fathers or elder brothers killed by Northerners in raids, or had their own homes burned to the ground. These men constantly refer to themselves as "Southern men," or "sons of Missouri." One of the most interesting characters is Jake Roedel (also known as "Dutchy"—a racially-motivated nickname), the son of a German immigrant. Some of the Southerners have trouble accepting a German into their gang, but when his father asks him to relocate to St. Louis to wait out the war in the safety of the big city, he refuses sharply, with an attitude of similar prejudice, "I'm not going to go to St. Louis to live with the Lincoln-loving Germans."

The movie tells its story slowly (nearly three hours in length). It lingers in the pleasure of casual conversations between friends and, typically of Ang Lee, leaves silence for the viewer to digest the subtext of what is being said. There is little use of profanity, and only between men, accurately reflecting the moral standards of the period. A typical example of the lazy, "down-home" dialect from *Ride with the Devil* comes during a scene where the two main protagonists, Jake Roedel and Jack Bull Chiles (Skeet Ulrich), are camping out under the stars:

Jack: What is it, Jake? I hear you ruminating louder than a cow chewing in my ear and it's keeping me from my sleep.

An opening exchange in the film also introduces this conversational style, as the two friends observe the final moments of a wedding and the departure of the bride and groom:

Jake: I've been thinking, Jack Bull. A wedding is a peculiar thing.
Jack: It's no more peculiar, Jake, than slavery.
Jake: Well, that's certain. That's why I've often wondered for what cause those Northerners are so anxious to change our Southern

institutions. For in both North and South, men are every day enslaved at the altar regardless of their state or color.

Jack: That is a type of subjugation. We shall avoid it, Jake.

What seems unusual here to modern-day sensibilities is the use of such erudite vocabulary between teenagers: "subjugation," "institutions," and "peculiar." This conversation takes place at a casual, joking moment in the film to indicate that the two friends regularly speak to each other in this florid style. Another example is the following lightly humorous conversation between two best friends in the film:

(*Camping out, Jack Bull Chiles and Jake Roedel discuss Jake's finger, which was shot off in a skirmish.*)

Jack: My father's under the dirt to stay. Like that's gone to stay, too.

Jake: My finger?

Jack: Mmm-hmm.

Jake: Well, so it is. And it makes me notable by the loss.

Jack: You sound pleased . . . as if that finger'd been pesterin' you for rings.

Jake: No. It was a fine finger and I'd rather have it still, but . . . it was took from me and it's been et by chickens for sure. And I say, what is the good side to this amputation? And there is one.

Jack: Name it, Jake.

Jake: Well, you say one day some Federals catch up to me in a thicket. They would riddle me and hang me and no Southern man would find me for weeks or months and when they did I'd be bad meat pretty well rotted to a glob.

Jack: That's scientifically accurate, I'm afraid. I've seen it.

Jake: I'd be a mysterious gob of rot. And people would say, "Who was that?" Then surely someone would look up and say, "Why it's nub-bin' fingered Jake Roedel." Then you could go and tell my father that I was clearly murdered and he wouldn't be tortured by uncertain wonders.

Jack: And that's the good of it?

Jake: Yes sir, that's the good.

The ear of the writer is perfectly attuned to the dialect of his subjects, much like Mark Twain's attention to dialect in *The Adventures of Huckleberry Finn*. In its slowness of pace, it challenges the modern audience's concept of time, and hearkens back to a more civilized era.

Another example is this conversation between Sue Lee Shelley and Roedel as they are discussing rumors of their engagement:

Sue Lee: So do you wanna marry me?

Jake: No, not too bad.

Sue Lee: Good. That's good news, 'cause I wouldn't marry you for a wagon-load full of gold.

Another example is this formal conversation between Mackeson (Jonathan Rhys Meyers) and Roedel as they face off against one another, where Roedel gives an almost polite response to Mackeson's threat:

Mackeson: Why you little Dutch son of a bitch. You do what I tell you or I'll kill you.

Jake: (*pulls his gun a few inches from Pitt's face*) And when do you figure to do this mean thing to me Mackeson? Is this very moment convenient for you? It is for me.

The language in *Ride with the Devil* accurately reflects how the people of the time spoke, according to the letters and written narratives from that period. The dialogue of *Ride with the Devil* has been criticized because the actors in the film speak slowly and repeat themselves often. However, this is true not only of the time but also of southern dialects of the present day. The ornate style of the language reflects the way the people of Jake and Jack Bull's class thought, and in this way the film accurately captures the atmosphere and nuance of the American South. The scene where Jake and Jack are eating with their host family in the winter holds some of the most stirring and realistic Civil War movie dialogue. The host makes the statement that the Northern side will most likely win the war because they use education ("the schoolhouse") to indoctrinate the children to "think and talk the same free-thinkin' way they do with no regard to station, custom, propriety."

Mr. Evans: You ever been to Lawrence, Kansas, young man?

Jack: (*scoffs*) No, I reckon not Mr. Evans. I don't believe I'd be too welcome in Lawrence.

Mr. Evans: I didn't think so. Before this war began, my business took me there often. As I saw those Northerners build that town, I witnessed the seeds of our destruction being sown.

Jack: The foundin' of that town was truly the beginnin' of the Yankee invasion.

Mr. Evans: I'm not speakin' of numbers, nor even abolitionist trouble makin'. It was the schoolhouse. Before they built their church, even, they built that schoolhouse. And they let in every tailor's son . . . and every farmer's daughter in that country.

Jack: Spellin' won't help you hold a plow any firmer. Or a gun either.

Mr. Evans: No, it won't Mr. Chiles. But my point is merely that they rounded every pup up into that schoolhouse because they fancied that everyone should think and talk the same free-thinkin' way they do with no regard to station, custom, propriety. And that is why they will win. Because they believe everyone should live and think just like them.

This dialogue is a distillation of the philosophical differences between the Northerners and the Southerners in the Civil War, and presents a fair-minded view of why the war was fought.

The Historical Background and Plot

The storyline of *Ride with the Devil* represents in some ways a departure for Ang Lee from the more accessible topics he had previously chosen to direct—yet in other ways, it is a continuity. The typical Ang Lee film is in no way typical—he has covered everything from 1970s post-Vietnam, post-Watergate American suburbia to the conservative, subtle Chinese world of Qing dynasty martial artists. The subject matter of the film *Ride with the Devil* proved in many ways too remote to win a popular following in Hollywood. The world of the American Civil War is far removed from the average person's daily experience—this film upped the ante by placing its focus on a period even less accessible, a topic even less familiar, a subject that was clouded in controversy for historians and completely unknown to the average moviegoer. The plot concerns a band of Southerners in the Confederacy, neighbors along the Missouri/Kansas border, who fight a bloody feud to defend themselves against the aggressions of the North. These young guerilla fighters, also known as Southern Bushwhackers, draw together as they experience the violence of war, and the loneliness and longing for love and companionship. Of course, one of the most compelling aspects of the film is its focus on the issue of racial discrimination. Interestingly, it is none other than the first-generation American Jake Roedel who begins to see the light on this issue. It is in the relationship between Roedel and the black servant Daniel Holt that the poignancy of the film is realized. And, indeed, this was the focal point for Ang Lee and James Schamus, who wished to explore the topic of racial discrimination from a fresh angle.

Such a topic does not lend itself readily to promotion; the film was badly advertised and it can be argued that the publicity team for Universal Pictures did, in fact, misunderstand the film themselves. In Taiwan, the film was first advertised at Warner Village in Taipei, a multiplex that normally runs only films that meet the qualifications of a blockbuster. A large, attractive poster advertised a film called *Ride with the Devil* by Ang Lee. The mysterious title seemed to suggest something new and altogether scandalous. What kind of story would this be? Would it be a ghost story? A horror movie? Would it be a love story, like *Gone With the Wind*? Certainly it dealt with the same historical period, and the large image of a man and woman passionately embracing—the woman's breastbone heaving with desire, her wispy dress falling away dangerously—superimposed over an image of desperate figures of soldiers on galloping horses, seemed to suggest none other than a *Gone With the Wind* remake. So what was Ang Lee up to now? It was confusing, it was mystifying, it was exciting, it was certain not to disappoint.

For the average moviegoer, the film itself seems to renege on some of the poster's promises. For example, the pace of the film is remarkably slow and has drawn the film's heaviest criticism. The film runs for three hours, and much of this is meandering, quiet screen-time. For the contemporary youthful audience, this might seem an eternity. As James Gleick points out in *Faster: The Acceleration of Just About Everything*, "Our computers, our movies, our sex lives, our prayers—they all run faster now than ever before . . . and the more we fill our lives with time-saving devices and time-saving strategies, the more rushed we feel."[3] Those who understand the technique of Ang Lee will realize that he aims to do a convincing job of portraying the unhurried nature of time in the nineteenth century, as well as the intolerable and mind-numbing boredom of war. Scenes around the periphery of the soldier's camp show how similar these small-scale skirmishes were to contemporary gang street-fights. The film slows almost to a halt as the original little band of friends hides out in a cave for the winter. The slowing of time is, for Ang Lee, a touch of nineteenth-century realism. He takes his time with the pacing, even giving the viewer glimpses that border on the poetic. In one scene, Jake steps out onto the porch on a frosty winter night and gazes up at the moon. Under Lee's lyrical direction, the camera holds Jake's view of the moon in its lens for a full minute. It is a deeply moving scene—a young teenager in a no-win situation wondering if he will ever find peace and security again in his life. But, of course, that is Ang Lee's territory—displaying heartrending beauty in the midst of cold pain. Lee chose to film on location in the western territory of the state of Missouri, and to schedule shooting during each of the four seasons for an authentic look. Missourians cannot fail to notice the hardwoods, rolling hills, and tall grasses of the authentic American central states.

While many critics take *Ride with the Devil*'s three-hour running time as the cause of its commercial failure, there was clearly no effort on the part of Universal Pictures to promote the film, which nearly guaranteed its quick demise. One critic summarized the situation as follows: "After an early release in mid-December to sixty theatres nationwide, Universal Pictures in early January cancelled the main release of *Ride with the Devil* and sent it straight to video production. Studios rarely do this unless attendance at the film is very low and/or the critics savage the movie, neither of which was the case with Lee's film. Universal Pictures would not give a reason for their decision."[4] A brief explanation from Ang Lee in a later interview was "[October Films] dumped the movie";[5] he indicated it was because of poor test screenings. As a result of this experience, Lee no longer allows his films to be test screened.[6] James Schamus also noted the studio's mishandling of the film, commenting that the DVD version of *Ride with the Devil* was released without African-American actor Jeffrey Wright, one of the main protagonists of the film and central to the story, appearing on the cover. Internet sites also mistakenly listed *Ride with the Devil* as a "porno film." When Schamus and Lee contacted Universal to have this categorization of the film corrected, the studio did nothing.[7] Ultimately, Schamus commiserated with Lee over a scotch in a New York bar, saying with light humor: "*The Wedding Banquet* was the most proportionately profitable movie of 1993, and this one is the most proportionately unprofitable movie of 1999."[8] The film was more popular in England where it enjoyed a big launch prior to the U.S. release. The film played in 300 theaters and was overwhelmingly praised by British critics.[9]

The title of this film, *Ride with the Devil*, is an interesting phrase to reflect the demonization of the Southern/Confederate side in Civil War history—the viewer of this film is asked to sympathize with the "wrong" side. The question often posed of the Southern side is "How could they have been fighting to preserve slavery?" However, the Civil War, as this film shows, was not only about slavery and abolitionism (such as that depicted in the 1982 miniseries *The Blue and the Gray*). Such a simplistic definition of the two opposing sides and their motivation for fighting could not capture the complex ambiguities of the war. Rather, *Ride with the Devil* demonstrates how many were caught up in the maelstrom of the Civil War: neighbor taking up arms against neighbor simply because an army had invaded their home and forced the inhabitants to take sides. Civil War movies also tend to gloss over the history of the war in the West, where many of the men who fought in the war had no particular loyalty to the side on which they served. Historically, it is known that many people in the West switched sides at necessary intervals to preserve their lives or protect their families. The character of Jake Roedel accurately displays this ambiguity; he openly demonstrates his motivations for fighting. On the one hand, he is merely trying to stay alive; on the other, he yearns to enhance his status in the eyes of his neighbors who have discriminated against his ethnic background (German) as an outsider. However, the film does not "side" with its characters—instead it presents them with the struggles and ambiguities of real life and does not attempt to persuade the viewer to believe one side is "right" and the other "wrong."

The title *Ride with the Devil* also reflects the horror and violence of the Civil War. This film does not skimp on violence; on the contrary, it is by far the most violent of any of the films of Ang Lee. The violence is not typical of an action movie, however, because it is not at all gratuitous. It is violence that is at once vicious and deeply affecting, which makes sense because the Civil War—as was made plain by the later film *Cold Mountain* (2003)—was one of the most horrifically violent wars in human history. However, while the violence of *Cold Mountain* seems designed for shock value and manipulative of the audience's emotions, the battles and skirmishes in *Ride with the Devil* seem very real and personal, necessary to reveal the psychological development of Roedel's character. The pace of the film—with its sudden action sequences followed by long stretches of little or no action—is also an accurate refection of combat situations, especially in guerilla warfare. In any war, the pace will follow a version of this general pattern: moments of intense violence alternating with weeks or months of extreme boredom and repetitive training in relative calm. *Ride with the Devil* accurately depicts not only the psychological detail but the costumes/uniforms, weaponry, fighting tactics, and living conditions of the Civil War, especially in the West. One outstanding historical detail was the upturned "US" belt buckle in the scene where Jake and Jack Bull take revenge for the massacre of the latter's family. In addition, a great amount of historical research had gone into the scene involving the raid on Lawrence, Kansas, when the Southern Bushwhackers are ordered by their general, Quantrill (John Ales), that no lives should be spared. This scene in the film is based on the authentic speech given to the Bushwhackers to convince them to carry out this horrific attack.

The Cast

Ride with the Devil has a far more sprawling setting than Ang Lee's earlier dramas *Sense and Sensibility* and *The Ice Storm*, but this movie's characters are no less finely drawn and the director imbues each with color and depth. In this film, Lee again returns to using his stalwart male lead, Tobey Maguire. Already Maguire had proved himself, while still a young teenager, in Lee's earlier film, *The Ice Storm*, where he played the lead and central core of the film. Here, Maguire takes on an even greater challenge, operating within a distant and remote context of nineteenth-century history. His performance is again superb. The cast also includes a startlingly good Skeet Ulrich as Jack Bull Chiles. In another surprising turn, Ang Lee cast a recently acclaimed pop singer, Jewel Kilcher, as the young female lead, the widow Sue Lee. While it is uncertain what factors led to her being cast, her presence in the movie was no doubt thought to raise its appeal especially for young people following the trends of pop music. (Casting pop stars in films is certainly more common practice in Asia; examples are Hong Kong's Anita Mui and *The Wedding Banquet*'s May Chin, megastars with pop music careers as well as film leads.) Kilcher's performance has been widely praised by critics, who considered her amazingly intuitive as an actress; her open face and childlike beauty perfectly suited the role.

Jeffrey Wright takes another main role as Daniel Holt, a black man caught up in the fighting for the South—this controversial position becomes a central contradiction in the film. Wright turns in the best performance as a freed slave who takes up the cause of the South in loyalty to fight alongside the man who freed him. As time goes on and the war becomes more bloody and brutal, this quiet, sensitive man begins to realize that even loyalty has its limits in the face of overwhelming wrongdoing. For Lee, Jeffrey Wright's role was a pivotal one for the film; it provided him with the opportunity to explore the familiar topic of the outsider caught in circumstances through no fault of his own that alienate and distance him from society. Wright gives a nuanced and delicate performance (in his early appearances in the film, his hat is drawn down deeply over his forehead and his eyes are lowered in a world-weary deference to social mores). Only as time goes on does Wright slowly add a guarded warmth and humanity to his character, demonstrating the ingrained and implacable social barriers faced by a man in his circumstances.

Ang Lee's knack for selecting up-and-coming actors is clearly apparent in this film; for example, Mark Ruffalo appears in a bit part as the traitorous Alf Bowden. The cast further includes a viciously brooding Jim Caviezel, in one of the best and most intense supporting roles, as Black John. Jonathan Rhys Meyers is also supremely petulant and abhorrent as Mackeson. The director's selection of Ruffalo, Caviezel, and Rhys Meyers predates many of these actors' larger roles and successes: *Ride with the Devil* is populated with young male actors who later went on to take leading roles in subsequent films.

The Denouement

The ending of the film provides a challenge for the audience—a satisfying image that is also a conundrum. The friendship between the young white soldier and the older black man has grown into a true, brotherly love. With no further sign of discrimination, the two are equals. And yet, this is an impossibility at that time and in that place. Thus, the film is forced to make an odd choice at the end, leaving the viewer with an unresolved sense of ambivalence. The final scene is one of farewell between the two men, and the last image is one of the freed black man, riding quickly away through a beautiful open prairie to an uncertain future. One is supposed to be left with a sense of hope—and it is indeed a hopeful and optimistic image of American freedom—but perhaps not a realistic one. Left with no companions, black or white, the man is most certainly free to enjoy his independence. However, when he is again in the company of men, what kind of future will he face? This scene can be compared, in its complexity, with the closing scene from *Crouching Tiger, Hidden Dragon*. In that film, the closing image was of the young, brilliant martial artist hurling herself off a bridge to atone for past wrongs, and, simultaneously, to make her unspoken wishes come true. The conundrum was that the audience was never allowed to know what happened when she hit the ground. After showing the beautiful, liberated image of a woman flying through the air, the film faded to black. Whether the girl miraculously lived and was granted the desires of her heart, or whether her death was a tragic sacrifice to atone for her mistakes, the audience could never be certain; instead, Lee leaves his audience with a titillating question.

Conclusion

Ride with the Devil is delightfully satisfying, with its slow and pleasant pace, its rich and evocative setting, and its historical and cultural significance. The film is very compelling, and the band of young protagonists continues to hold its appeal. It is a finely-crafted movie that reminds the viewer of the power of film to bring the truth to life when it is made with the care and skill it deserves. The film brings to the audience a fascinating chapter of North/South history in the United States during the Civil War era, and it presents the Southern side of the war with greater sympathy and comprehension than has been attempted in the past. Ang Lee and James Schamus raise fascinating questions—about race, class, and cultural values—with this film. In addition, Lee once again displays the knack for presenting peaceful and pastoral scenes that serve as a background for the turmoil that his characters are experiencing. It is this sense of internal peace that they are striving for, and as the movie develops, the viewer yearns to see the characters attain it.

The genre of the western is often associated with the conflicts of civilization and progress, of the making of masculinity, of the lure and freedom of the West, the myth of leaving one's past. Ang Lee invokes this myth, but, using race, subverts it. Daniel Holt starts the film a minor, unreadable figure, head bowed and silent, demonstrating the shadow cast by his former enslavement. But as the violence increases and the Southern/western codes are found wanting, he stands up straight and grows in dignity as his role increases in importance. At the end of the film, all the dreams of the western—of freedom, progress, and journeying alone into the great unknown—are given to Holt; conversely Roedel's character, like the Easterners in old westerns, is stuck with a wife and child, reduced in his independence and his "manhood." Holt rides off into the distance, the wide-open spaces representing the hope and possibility of a better future, heroic and truly "free." And yet, even this is given an ironic twist in the film: his quest is his disrupted past—he looks for his mother, another quest that reveals deeper levels of meaning obscured by the traditional western.

NINE

Wuxia *Narrative and Transnational Chinese Identity in* Crouching Tiger, Hidden Dragon

[In *Crouching Tiger, Hidden Dragon*] my team and I chose the most populist, if not popular, genre in film history—the Hong Kong martial arts film—to tell our story, and we used this pop genre almost as a kind of instrument to explore the legacy of classical Chinese culture. We embraced the most mass of art forms and mixed it with the highest—the secret martial arts as passed down over time in the great Taoist schools of training and thought.[1]

IN 2001, ANG LEE'S astonishing film, *Crouching Tiger, Hidden Dragon*, the prototype of the new global swordfighting martial arts genre, gained major success in awards ceremonies in the United States, including, most notably, the Academy Awards. Best Music (Score) winner Tan Dun described *Crouching Tiger, Hidden Dragon* as crossing boundaries—of film genres, musical traditions, and national cultures. This description of the film succinctly suggests the exciting trend toward globalization reflected by mainstream acceptance of a subtitled motion picture in Mandarin. This conception of globalization is not only realized as the synthesis and transcendence of opposites but also as the representation of geographic localities and notions of territory—including nationalism, identity, narrative, and ethnicity. Lee's films represent not only the international crossing of boundaries but the repackaging and reappropriation of Chinese cultural identity. *Crouching Tiger, Hidden Dragon*, as well as three of Lee's earlier works, *Eat Drink Man Woman*, *The Wedding Banquet*, and *Pushing Hands*, are particularly clear examples of this phenomenon.

Crouching Tiger, Hidden Dragon proved to be his most globally recognized work yet. It was the highest-grossing foreign-language film ever to open in Britain, and the first Chinese-language film in history to become a mainstream American hit. Although Ang Lee had anticipated a fairly limited art-house response to the film, *Crouching Tiger, Hidden Dragon* was widely acclaimed by critics, as well as receiving overwhelmingly positive word-of-mouth reviews. By March 2001, a few months after its U.S. release, *Crouching Tiger, Hidden Dragon* continued its successful reception by becoming the highest-grossing foreign-language film in American history. Its earnings stand at close to US$127 million, easily surpassing the record-breaking success of Roberto Benigni's Academy Award–winning film, *Life Is Beautiful* (1997). At Cannes, it garnered four of the top awards, while at the British Academy Awards (BAFTA) in 2001, it won the David Lean Award for Best Director, Best Score, Best Costume Design, and Best Film in a Foreign Language. At the Golden Globes, the film won Best Foreign Film and Ang Lee won Best Director. The film received ten Academy Award nominations, the greatest number of any foreign-language film in history. As noted earlier, the film received four awards, but not the coveted Best Director award, nor Best Film, as Lee had been hoping. Moreover, Taiwan neglected to honor Ang Lee as best director at the Golden Horse Awards that year. However, in Hong Kong, a month after the Academy Awards ceremony, the film won eight awards, including Best Director and Best Film.

The director adapted the screenplay from a five-part martial arts series written by Wang Dulu in the early twentieth century.[2] The movie is mostly from the fourth book, set in Qing-dynasty China, about the *wuxia* expert Li Mu Bai, who plans to retire and spend the rest of his life with the widowed warrior Yu Shu Lien, when the theft of his sword "Green Destiny" interrupts his plans. Mu Bai and Shu Lien track the theft to the young daughter of an aristocrat, Jen, a wonderfully complex character who hides both her martial arts expertise and a secret lover. *Crouching Tiger, Hidden Dragon* is a story of repression in the face of the Chinese virtues of loyalty and chastity—repression represented by the unspoken love between Mu Bai and Shu Lien, as well as the young Jen's repressed desire to break free from the social constrictions of family and conventions. Again, the timeless, universal qualities that are the larger themes of Lee's works are present in full force. On the surface is daily life, the structured social codes and conventions that dictate people's behavior. Underneath the restrictive social mores are found the repressed desires—the hidden dragon. The social restrictions common to Chinese culture are at times inverted in the film—loyalty is opposed by betrayal, and chastity is supplanted by sexual transgression.

Wang Dulu, Qing China, and China of the Imagination

The story presented by Ang Lee is condensed and adapted from Wang Dulu's original narrative in the five-part series. Some of the major changes include the following: Li Mu Bai does not die in the fourth book; instead, he outlives the three other principal characters and is still alive twenty-one years later at the conclusion of the five-part saga. Jennifer Jay (2003) notes that Li Mu Bai's screen death is a much more stirring depiction of the lovers' tragedy: that the unspoken love between Li Mu Bai and Yu Shu Lien can never be consummated. Jade Fox is killed earlier in the series, not by Mu Bai but by Shu Lien. In addition, while the ending remains ambiguous in the movie, Jen's leap in Wang Dulu's book clearly does not end in death; she survives and has a final encounter with her lover Lo before disappearing to Xinjiang, where she gives birth to their baby.[3] Emilie Yueh-yu Yeh and Darrell W. Davis quote Wang Dulu's expository coda for the novel, which explains that Jen, out of duty to her parents and in keeping with her highborn status, could never marry the bandit, Lo. After returning to him for a single night of sexual intimacy (as in the film), Jen leaves

Jen's astonishing leap displays unusual artistry and creates a memorably haunting and ethereal atmosphere at the end of the film.

Lo the following day. The novel reads: "She left him the next day, without hesitation, like the tail of a celestial dragon slipping away, always 'hidden,' never to be found."[4] This prose hints through writing at the "hiddenness" of Jen expressed visually by Lee in the breathtaking ending of *Crouching Tiger, Hidden Dragon*.

This film represents Qing dynasty (1644–1911) Chinese society, but does not specify an exact time period—and with good reason. Lee did not seek to present a historically accurate vision of China, but instead, the "China of the imagination," an image of China that is felt deeply in the heart. Thus, the film's most stunning scenes—an airborne battle among wispy bamboo plants; a final, suicidal leap to earth in reference to an ancient legend—are images displaying uncommon artistry for the average martial arts film. While making the film, Ang Lee had to shoot for a balance between Eastern and Western aesthetics, and a balance between drama and action. For example, the pacing of the film broke away from traditional *wuxia* martial arts films because the first fight did not occur until nearly fifteen minutes into the movie—an eternity for Lee's Chinese audience. In addition, actors in traditional martial arts films are not usually expected to both perform stunts and, simultaneously, produce real dramatic emotion; in this film, the actors had to do both at the same time. Because *Crouching Tiger, Hidden Dragon* garnered greater public acclaim in the West than in Chinese-speaking markets, some of Lee's critics have accused him of making a Hollywood version of a Chinese martial arts film—an orientalist version of kung fu, set adrift from its Chinese roots. However, it must be kept in mind that Lee fought to retain the Mandarin dialogue for the film's release in the United States, a choice which normally would restrict the marketability of the film to a limited art-house audience. Lee has memorably said, "[Making] a martial arts film in English to me is the same as . . . John Wayne speaking Chinese in a western."[5]

Crouching Tiger, Hidden Dragon mixes romance, feminism, martial arts, and high-art aesthetics. As a female lead, Jen's character has mysterious powers which only gradually become clear. At her first appearance, living a cloistered existence as the daughter of a wealthy aristocrat, she may be easily underestimated by the viewer, seeming to be trained only in the arts of brush calligraphy and pouring tea. However, it is soon revealed that this young woman has been given advanced training in high-level martial arts. Nothing is what it seems. Not even when Jen, riding through the desert in a caravan, has her comb stolen by the rough and swashbuckling Lo (Chang Chen), does the viewer see passion on her face. The heat generated onscreen while Jen is held captive in the bandit's lair is intense. The sexuality in this film is unsurpassed because it is eroticism with both Western and Chinese sensibilities. Chinese films, on the whole, are not normally so frank and explicit—especially surprising is the attention given to the bathing/sleeping that goes on in the bandit's cave; these bluntly physical matters are usually unexplored by the more restrained Chinese filmmakers. This section of the film seems to have the gleeful and revelatory tone of *It Happened One Night* (1934), in the scenes between Claudette Colbert and Clark Gable. Later on, when Mu Bai watches the drugged, and dripping wet, Jen in the otherworldly scene in the abandoned factory, there is again a very Western-style electricity and spark between them. She says, "Is it the sword you want . . . or me?" Chinese critics of this film have observed that such a blunt come-on is shocking from a Chinese woman, and have explained that she may be excused because she was drugged.

China in Ang Lee's imagination also has a deep emotional resonance. The China mainland, where this film was made, is the homeland of his parents, from which they were forced to flee during the Communist takeover of China. Both of his parents were from the mainland and moved to Taiwan following the Nationalists' defeat in the Chinese Civil War in 1949. His grandparents and the rest of his father's family were slaughtered during the struggle for Communist/Nationalist dominance of China. Lee's father, a native of Jiangxi Province in southern China, escaped to Taiwan as the family's sole survivor. Some of the ineffable longing and sadness in this film is surely attributable to the depth of loss experienced by Lee's parents when they had to leave China. Although Lee grew up in Taiwan, the nostalgia for old China and the glories of its past is still a strong pull among the older generation of Chinese in Taiwan, especially the generation of Nationalist soldiers who retreated to Taiwan in 1949. It is important to realize that the film was not intended to be faithful to a historically-accurate China as much as it was intended to be faithful to the image of China in Ang Lee's mind.

Cowriter James Schamus explained the difficulty of trying to work on the screenplay with two Chinese coauthors Wang Huiling and Cai Guorong (Tsai Kuo-jung). He originally wrote it in English, but upon receiving back his revised draft, he saw how far off he had been from telling the story correctly. Not speaking the Mandarin language in which the film was produced, or in which the original novel was written, Schamus describes the experience of writing the film as both rewarding and nerve-wracking. "It was weird because on the one hand, I was writing an original screenplay because I didn't know the novel. . . . And on the other hand, I knew that I had to maintain fidelity to something I didn't know."[6] Schamus described the process of writing the film in what he called "International Subtitle Style":

> It was really rewriting the script so many times, translating back to English, back to Chinese, writing it and, of course, finally rewriting the film one last time in the form

of the subtitles and at that moment, through discussion . . . realizing how little of the movie I understood. [The film's] meanings remain embedded in the Chinese language and culture.[7]

Ang Lee adds: "I grew up in Taiwan and this was the kind of film that captured public fantasy back then—the storytelling, the melodrama and the morality. That was what I was aiming at, the nostalgic feeling."[8]

Criticism of Crouching Tiger, Hidden Dragon

One of the criticisms of this film is that it is "not Chinese enough," or that it presents a hybridized version of Chinese culture. The cast is transnational and represents all the "Chinas." The actors and crew were selected from all Chinese diaspora cultural zones (including overseas Chinese in America): Chow Yun-fat (playing Li Mu Bai), Yuen Wo Ping (martial arts director), Peter Pao (cinematographer), and Tim Yip (art director) all hailed from Hong Kong; actor Chang Chen (Lo) and director Ang Lee from Taiwan; and overseas "Chinese-Americans" included Chinese-American Tan Dun (composer of the musical score), Taiwanese-American Yo-Yo Ma (cellist), and Hong Kong–American Coco Lee (performer of title song). In addition, James Schamus' work on the screenplay brought a heavily non-Chinese element to the narrative.

Another discrepancy is that the pinyin system used in the subtitles is inconsistent. Li Mu Bai is romanized in mainland Chinese pinyin, while Shu Lien is romanized in Taiwan's Wade-Giles, creating an appearance of uniformity to the Western viewer, while in reality simply mixing unrelated pinyin systems without explanation or comment. In a third example, the experience for the Chinese viewer is admittedly different from the Western viewer—the Western viewer sees a subtitled Chinese movie, while for Mandarin speakers, the actors' language skills were uneven and distracting. Chow Yun-fat and Michelle Yeoh both had to learn Mandarin to make the film; Yeoh could not even read Chinese and had to learn her part line-by-line in pinyin. Chinese audiences heard distinct differences in the Chinese accents of the four leads: only Zhang Ziyi spoke with a standard Beijing accent; Chang Chen spoke with a Taiwanese accent; Chow Yun-fat, a Cantonese accent, and Michelle Yeoh, a Malaysian-English accent. Ang Lee defends his choice against the Shaw Brothers/Golden Harvest practice of dubbing actors with standard Mandarin voices:

> From the start . . . I made up my mind to make an all-Mandarin-speaking film, knowing full well that Chow and Yeoh can speak only Cantonese Mandarin. Honestly speaking, the Mandarin spoken by Chow in the film is better than that of Chen Shui-bian . . . and even Jiang Zemin. I think ninety percent of it is no problem at all. There are problems though, with Michelle Yeoh's pronunciation and intonation. But I think the quality of the voice which is capable of carrying emotions is more touching than listening to dubbed standard Mandarin. Therefore I kept their voices.[9]

In addition, some of the lines from the screenplay could not be translated directly between the two languages, resulting in further blurring, repackaging, and hybridization. The climactic line in which Li Mu Bai finally swears his love to Shu Lien as he is dying is rendered in the English subtitle as follows:

I would rather be a ghost drifting by your side as a condemned soul than to enter heaven without you. Because of your love, I will never be a lonely spirit.

A literal translation of the same line would be:

I would rather wander at your side, following you, and be a ghost in the wilderness for seven days; and even as I drift into the darkest place, my love will not let me be an eternally lonely spirit.

Jennifer Jay rightly points out that:

A literal translation would be too cumbersome for the Western audience, not familiar with the Taoist and Buddhist concepts of ghosts and the dead. But bringing in the Western notions of the condemned soul and entering heaven without a loved one is too foreign to traditional Chinese thought. This translation appeals to the Western audience, providing an obvious example of Westernized hybridity in the film.[10]

The problem inherent in translation is pinpointed by Rey Chow (1995) when she writes: "Genuine cultural translation is possible only when we move beyond the seemingly infinite but actually reductive permutation of the two terms—East and West, original and translation—and instead see both as full, materialist, and most likely equally corrupt, equally decadent participants in contemporary world culture."[11] Felicia Chan (2003) also examines the different reception the film was given in Asia and the West, examining how the different cultural backgrounds brought to the film by the viewer not only shape their understanding of the film but may also hinder the film's translatability. Chris Berry and Mary Farquhar (2006) add that the film "projects a mythic, cultural version of Chineseness for Chinese and non-Chinese audiences,"[12] with a contemporary comment: first, the mix of accents and origins in the film represents the ethnic diversity of the diaspora itself, and second, the film displays "a Chinese cultural nation in which Western-style individualism is celebrated by younger generations to the dismay of older generations. . . . Youthful rebellion and female liberation are central to the storyline, to the combat scenes, and to the generational tussle between Chinese and Western lifestyles that is part of the diasporic Chinese experience."[13]

Ang Lee himself admits to the blurring and metamorphosis brought on by his blending of Eastern and Western filmmaking techniques in this movie:

The *wuxia* operates in a realm under the surface of society and the rule of law, called *Giang hu* [*jianghu*]. This is a world made up of individuals and their relationships. . . . For example, the *wuxia* can be a member of an underground, Mafia-type organization, but loyalty and honor are still the main values. In serving a master, the *wuxia* keeps his or her word, even to the point of death. [Today, the term *jianghu* has a broader meaning, referring to the entanglements of life and relationships in a society.] . . . In Chinese philosophy as a whole—and not just martial arts—inner and outer strength are both integral parts of every living being. Just as everyone [according to Chinese Buddhist thought] has the Buddha within themselves, they also have a tremendous power—the crouching tiger, ready to leap out. The key is to achieve a balance, to see harmony and reduce conflicts. . . . Coming from this kind of culture, stories like *Crouching Tiger* have been generally filmed in a particularly Eastern cinematic style. I have also worked in the very different Western cinematic tradition. Rather than choose between these two, I let the creative tension between these two styles become an important part of the making of *Crouching Tiger*.[14]

The success of *Crouching Tiger, Hidden Dragon* raises issues of cultural power, differentiation, and subordination, bringing accusations of Ang Lee catering to the West, of perpetuating Orientalism, of packaging Chinese materials with Hollywood wrapping. This is a hot topic in scholarship on the film; citing financial investment as an indicator, Kwai-Cheung Lo (2005) notes the difficulty of categorizing Lee's *Crouching Tiger, Hidden Dragon* as a Chinese or Hollywood film, since the financing of it was based on advance sales of the international distribution rights to various American, Japanese, and European companies. These companies included Tokyo-based Sony, Sony Pictures Classics in New York, Columbia Pictures in Hollywood (for the rights to Latin American and several Asian markets), Columbia Pictures Asia (based in Hong Kong), and Sony Classical Music. Lo notes the actual cash for the film was provided by a bank in Paris.[15] Yeh and Davis refute the argument that *Crouching Tiger, Hidden Dragon* makes narrative concessions by following Hollywood patterns of pacing for international action films. To them, the film does not follow these patterns at all; instead, the film "starts and closes very quietly."[16] This subdued pacing defies the typical action film, in which the action normally begins immediately with an explosive force. Chris Berry and Mary Farquhar further refute the notion that *Crouching Tiger, Hidden Dragon* was made for a primarily non-Chinese audience; instead, they find in the film concrete details relating to what they refer to as the "Chinese nation" and the diasporic Chinese experience.[17]

The Chinese Genre of Wuxia

The *wuxia* tradition can be translated as "martial arts chivalry." A "*xia*" is a "knight-errant," except that he can be from any social class; the *wuxia* heroes are "outlaws" or "bandits" who live on the edge, outside of government regulation—the most similar parallel in Western culture is Robin Hood and his band of Merry Men. While the Western literary concept of "knight-errant" begins in the late fourteenth century, where the term first appears in the romance *Sir Gawain and the Green Knight* (c. 1350), the Chinese concept of the *xia* is found as early as the fourth century B.C. However, not until the Tang dynasty, around the ninth century A.D., do the stories begin to resemble the *wuxia* genre of today with its tales of chivalric derring-do. The literature of the *wuxia* genre hit its highest peak of development in the fiction of China; one of China's most famous novels, *Shuihu zhuan* (*The Water Margin*, or *Outlaws of the Marsh*, compiled from legends in the fourteenth century by Shi Nai'an) details the exploits of the outlaw *Jianghu* clan, a chivalrous gang that lives in marshes at the edge of Liangshan. These men are characterized by brave deeds, honor, loyalty to the clan, and extraordinary fighting skills, with the relationship between teacher and student bordering on master/servant. A person highly skilled in martial arts attains an esoteric knowledge of fighting techniques and an intense concentration of almost mystical powers. Many trained and gifted warriors excel in acts of physical prowess magnified beyond human power—flying, jumping impossible heights, hurling balls of fire, or becoming invisible. To fully enter into the experience of the *wuxia* world, a reader must take these impossible feats as a matter of course.

For the Western viewer experiencing *wuxia* for the first time, the fact that these clan members can run up walls and take off into flight (as the masked robber of the Green Destiny sword does in an early scene), ignoring normal laws of gravity, or can stand on bamboo stalks and sway around dangerously, lightly jumping from one bamboo stalk to another (as Mu Bai and Jen do), without any branches breaking, is initially startling. For Chinese viewers familiar with the *wuxia* genre, these tropes are well known; Chinese readers have pored over these novels and imagined the scenes of flying warriors in their heads for years—however, the advent of Lee's film *Crouching Tiger, Hidden Dragon* marked the first time a director actually risked attempting to portray these fanciful visual images onscreen. The aforementioned "bamboo grove" fight sequence is one example of a common trope for the genre— King Hu's masterpiece *wuxia* film, *A Touch of Zen* (*Xianü*, 1969), also had a bamboo grove fight scene, but his warriors had to stay at ground level because of the limitations of special effects at that time. In Lee's world, *wuxia* warriors magically float at the tips of the trees, and for the uninitiated Western viewer, images like this were entirely new and unexpected, leading to a sense of childlike wonder and exhilaration. Western audience members may have spent a few seconds wondering about these strange occurrences, but ultimately decided that they just did not mind, even if it did not make "sense." The flight choreographer for these otherworldly scenes was Yuen Wo Ping, who had already come to the attention of mainstream cinemagoers for his work in *The Matrix* (1999), another visually startling film. (One can only imagine how much more powerful these images would have been had one not already seen the astonishing special effects of the twirling slow-motion flight choreography of *The Matrix*.)

A second example of a familiar trope from *wuxia* literature is the inn scene, in which Jen, cross-dressing as a young male fighter, defeats legions of challengers while triumphantly reciting classical Chinese poetry. This blending of martial arts and high drama results in an exultant scene, recalling both martial arts norms and the cinematic grandiosity of traditional Chinese opera films such as *Love Eterne* (which also employs the operatic convention of cross-dressing). Jen repels one man with the poke of her finger on a sensitive pressure point; another she drives out for sharing the surname "Gou" with her husband from the arranged marriage. When one of her enemies asks in fear, "Who are you?" she replies with this high-energy speech:

> Jen: Who am I? I am . . .
> I am the Invincible Sword Goddess.
> Armed with the incredible Green Destiny.
> Be you Li or Southern Crane
> Lower your head
> And ask for mercy.
> I am the desert dragon.
> I leave no trace.
> Today . . . I fly over Eu-mei.
> Tomorrow . . . I'll kick over Wudan Mountain![18]

The film even uses self-reflexive language to explain conventions of the genre of the *wuxia* tradition. Early in the film, Jen expresses her secret longing for the *wuxia* lifestyle, set against the harsh reality expressed by Shu Lien. In this scene, Jen keeps up her appearance as a naïve young aristocrat, while Shu Lien explains that the *wuxia* lifestyle is not as glamorous as it appears in books, while pointing out the conservatism of friendship and trust in the *wuxia* chivalric code.

> Jen: (*longingly*) It must be exciting to be a fighter, to be totally free.
> Shu Lien: Fighters have rules too: friendship, trust, integrity . . . Without rules, we wouldn't survive for long.
> Jen: I've read all about people like you. Roaming wild, beating up anyone who gets in your way!
> Shu Lien: Writers wouldn't sell many books if they told how it really is.
> Jen: But you're just like the characters in the stories.
> Shu Lien: Sure. No place to bathe for days, sleeping in flea-infested beds. . . . They tell you all about that in the books?[19]

The title *Crouching Tiger, Hidden Dragon* has multilayered meanings. On the most obvious level, the Chinese characters in the title connect to the narrative since Jen's Chinese name contains the character for "dragon" and her lover Lo's given name in Chinese means "tiger."[20] Thus the film's title, to those familiar with Chinese characters, is as obvious a reference as "Romeo and Juliet," or, in a related example, the famous Chinese lovers that Ang Lee admits inspired this film, Liang Shanbo and Zhu Yingtai. On another level, the Chinese idiomatic phrase "wohu canglong" (crouching tiger hidden dragon) is a common expression referring to the undercurrents of emotion, passion, and secret desires that lie beneath the surface of polite society and civil behavior. These subverted desires, although hidden, are very potent and mysterious, and can emerge unexpectedly, or powerfully change the course of people's lives. For example, Jen and Lo express their desires in sudden and unpredictable ways—as they do in the desert cave—because they are young, wild, and headstrong. Jen's unrestrained desires lead to trouble for the others—she steals the Green Destiny sword as a prank to see if she can get away with it; she runs away and dresses as a man so that she can enjoy the excitement of the *wuxia* lifestyle instead of docile acceptance of the marriage her parents have arranged. In addition, her rash actions inadvertently put Li Mu Bai in danger and lead to his death. And finally, the film ends with Jen's impulsive leap from the mountain bridge.

In contrast to this are the repressed desires of the older characters Li Mu Bai and Shu Lien, who honor their code of duty above their own feelings. This code of honor has shaped their lives, and Shu Lien's early engagement to one of Li Mu Bai's brothers-in-arms (who was later killed) prevents the two from being able to act on their own feelings—if they choose to do so, they would be dishonoring the dead man's memory and abandoning the code of honor that has shaped their lives. However, in their pursuit of the foolhardy and impetuous Jen, their own "dragons," or hidden desires, are awakened. Jen's youth, energy, and passion remind them both of the romance and freedom that they have traded in pursuit of duty. This stirs the dragons of their longings and suppressed desires—most importantly, their love for each other which, although always lurking right beneath the surface, has never been openly expressed. It is Li Mu Bai's fascination with the youthful Jen and his desire to teach her that, in a subliminal way, ignites his long-repressed passion:

Li: You need practice. I can teach you to fight with the Green Destiny, but first you must learn to hold it in stillness.
Jen: Why do you want to teach me?
Li: I've always wanted a disciple worthy of Wudan's secrets.
Jen: And if I use them to kill you?
Li: That's a risk I'm willing to take. Deep down, you're good. Even Jade Fox couldn't corrupt you.
           (*The figure's eyes cloud with tears.*)[21]

In turn, this rouses Shu Lien's jealousy, and stirs her repressed feelings for Li Mu Bai:

Li: But, this girl . . . I saw her last night.
Shu Lien: I knew she would intrigue you.
Li: She needs direction . . . and training.
Shu Lien: She's an aristocrat's daughter. She's not one of us. In any case, it will all be over soon. You'll kill Fox, and she'll marry.
Li: That's not for her. She should come to Wudan and become a disciple.
Shu Lien: But Wudan does not accept women.
Li: For her, they might make an exception. If not, I'm afraid she'll become a poisoned dragon.
Shu Lien: It's not our affair. Even if Wudan accepts her, her husband might object.
Li: I thought by giving away the sword, I could escape the [*jianghu*] world. But the cycle of bloodshed continues.

Shu Lien: I wish there were something more I could do to help you.

Li: Just be patient with me, Shu Lien.[22]

An important later scene displays the growing boldness between the two duty-bound friends:

Shu Lien: Have some tea.

(As Shu Lien passes the cup to Li, their fingers touch. Embarrassed, Li pulls back.)

Li: Shu Lien . . . The things we touch have no permanence. My master would say . . . there is nothing we can hold on to in this world. Only by letting go can we truly possess what is real.

Shu Lien: Not everything is an illusion. My hand . . . wasn't that real?

Li: Your hand, rough and callused from machete practice . . . All this time, I've never had the courage to touch it.

(Li takes Shu Lien's hand and presses it to his face.)

Li: [*Jianghu*] is a world of tigers and dragons, full of corruption . . . I tried sincerely to give it up but I have brought us only trouble.

Shu Lien: To repress one's feelings only makes them stronger.

Li: You're right, but I don't know what to do. I want to be with you . . . just like this. It gives me a sense of peace.[23]

The relationship between Jen and her governess is very complicated. The vengeful Jade Fox (Cheng Pei Pei), posing as a governess, has secretly taught Jen martial arts since she was a child. Formerly, Jade Fox was a part of the *jianghu* clan, but the leader of the clan refused to teach her, preferring to use her as a sexual partner. In revenge, she killed him and stole a manual of martial arts. She needed the child Jen to read it to her because she was illiterate; thus Jen's apprehension of the martial arts quickly grew beyond that of Jade Fox. In one of her most introspective moments in the film, Jen expresses her fear and ambivalence about the situation:

Jen: Master . . . I started learning from you in secret when I was ten. You enchanted me with the world of [*jianghu*]. But once I realized I could surpass you, I became so frightened! Everything fell apart. I had no one to guide me, no one to learn from.[24]

Jade Fox views the *jianghu* world as liberating; she welcomes Jen to join her in living in this state of nonconformity and nonallegiance with the rest of society:

Fox: Come with me. You don't want to waste your life as the wife of some bureaucrat. Denied your talent. . . . As a master and disciple we will rule.

Jen: I'll never live as a thief!

Fox: You're already a thief.

Jen:	[Stealing the sword] was just for fun. How can I leave? Where would I go?
Fox:	Wherever we want. We'll get rid of anyone in our way. Even your father.
Jen:	Shut up!
Fox:	It's the [*jianghu*] fighter lifestyle . . . kill or be killed. Exciting, isn't it?
Jen:	I owe you nothing.
Fox:	Yes, you do. You are still my disciple.
	(*Jen lunges at the governess, and the two exchange a few blows. Jen presses her finger against one of the Governess's pressure points, disabling her. Jen pushes her across the room.*)[25]

Jen's bullheaded rejection of the *jianghu* chivalric code puts everyone in jeopardy, including herself. First, in stealing the Green Destiny sword, she ignores the code, but steals the sword "just for fun." This frivolous act causes the untimely death of one of the night guards. More significantly, Jen's rejection of Jade Fox subverts the *jianghu* code of loyalty to one's teacher. By betraying her own master, Jen breaks the code, which leads to Jade Fox's attempt to poison her. However, Jade Fox's act of revenge is also tempered by her own personal sense of rejection by the "only family" she had ever known. This complicated psychological twist is expressed in Jade Fox's final monologue as she dies:

Fox:	(*To Li Mu Bai*) You deserve to die, but the life I was hoping to take . . . was Jen's.
	(*To Jen*) Ten years I devoted to you. But you deceived me! You hid the manual's true meaning. I never improved . . . but your progress was limitless! You know what poison is? An eight-year-old girl, full of deceit. That's poison! Jen! My only family . . . my only enemy . . . [26]

Finally, in the abandoned factory, when Jen asks the sexually transgressive question in which the forbidden wish is articulated, "Is it the sword you want, or me?" Li Mu Bai does not answer. He has become more expressive toward Shu Lien through his repressed passion for Jen. Jen, in the meantime, has grown more like a true Wudan disciple from her time spent with Shu Lien and Li Mu Bai; in the end she selflessly rushes to find an antidote for Li Mu Bai's poison, and her final leap could also be interpreted as an attempt to resurrect him. As the director himself has pointed out, this film's use of *wuxia* is not simply to provide gratuitous action sequences—the *wuxia* displays also serve a narrative function. Because the martial arts form externalizes the hidden passions and emotions, these scenes also help tell the story. The violence, restraint, and exhilaration in the fighting sequences are, in Ang Lee's mind, equivalent to verbal altercations in domestic dramas. Thus, when Jen and Shu Lien clash in a fight, the fight's root source is indicated by Shu Lien's furious and possessive remark: "Don't touch it. That's Li Mu Bai's sword."[27] This remark displays the hidden passion of Shu Lien in a subtext that is almost Freudian.

The Ending/Homage of Crouching Tiger, Hidden Dragon

The ambiguous ending of the film is a challenge to the viewer. There are two ways to view Jen's death-defying leap from the mountain bridge and flight through the air, which goes into gorgeous slow motion as Jen flies downward. The first way to view it is of Jen's wish coming true, that indeed she will fly and land safely because of her "leap of faith." This is the ending steeped in magical realism—not too far-fetched, since Jen already displayed capabilities of flight at different points throughout the movie. Further developing this allegory, Fran Martin (2005) reads Jen's flight as signifying the "rebel girl" of global pop-feminism, much in the same tradition as the final death-defying drive off the cliff at the conclusion of Ridley Scott's *Thelma and Louise* (1991)—that film also "refuses visually to imply the deaths of its heroines, who seem to remain forever suspended in their ultimate trajectory."[28]

A second way to view the ending is with the finality of tragedy. As in a Shakespearean tragedy when the principal characters' corpses litter the stage at the drama's denouement, the killing of Jade Fox and the sorrowful death of Li Mu Bai followed by Jen's suicide leap take a heavy toll on the viewer, with this unexpected turn of gravity in the plot. This is one reason the film was so well-received worldwide; it was classical tragedy in the best sense, a genre that has become a rare treat for modern audiences. This is perhaps because heavy-handed tragedy of this type is overwhelming to modern sensibilities, just as the fate of Laius, Jocasta, and Oedipus seems overwrought in Sophocles' tragedy; Greek tragedies are often performed on the modern stage by adding some attractive, modernizing gimmick. As the example of *Crouching Tiger, Hidden Dragon* has shown, this type of drama was best attempted by an outsider presenting a foreign culture. The emotion-laden lines were spoken in Mandarin and read visually as subtitles—in this way the emotional power came to the English-speaker in a muted and lyrical form. This also explains why the film's English-dubbed version was not popularly received.

"Green Destiny," the name of the sword in the story, was a metaphor for the movie, and one from which Ang Lee took his inspiration. "It's exquisite, sharp and flexible. It's mysterious and overpowers you, and that became very fascinating to me, and I decided to make sight and sound out of it."[29] The magical 400-year-old weapon issues a startling metallic whoosh from the soundtrack whenever it appears, to demonstrate at the auditory level the sword's tingling, magical energy. "I even take the color of green and make it a motif: jade, onyx, green bamboo. Mercury green, as they say in Chinese Taoist theory, is the most remote and mysterious place of the ultimate yin, where all existence comes from."[30] The Taoist element plays into Li Mu Bai's final decision to remain a lonely ghost with the woman he has secretly loved: "So this male . . . makes [the decision] before he dies to be a wondrous ghost with the company of another lonely ghost who transcends through eternity. He finally makes a commitment. To me, that is what a romantic relationship is about, a man is ultimately trying to find someone, a yin is finding a yang."[31]

Many viewers are unaware of the homage to King Hu in the bamboo forest scene. In King Hu's film the bamboo grove battle was played out at ground level, under the

Taking flight—Li Mu Bai and Jen fight over the Green Destiny sword in the unforgettable martial arts sequence at the top of the bamboo forest.

trees in dim light. Here the battle takes flight to the tips of the trees, as it does in the original source material. Ang Lee describes King Hu's influence on him:

> The first time I met [King] Hu was in 1984. That was a long time ago, when I graduated from film school and I wanted to go back to Taiwan to look for opportunities to make films. . . . I drove 17 hours up there [in New York] to see him. I really worshipped him, because he was the first Chinese director to be known internationally, because of the "swordsman" movies, a really special theme with unique visual effects. For this reason, I thought that maybe I could work for him, get to know him, hear him speak. People like me who grew up in Taiwan, receiving Chinese education, have lost touch with the mainland, because I was brought up as a Chinese, but I haven't really been to mainland China. That's why I sometimes feel strange about my Chinese identity. This identity was obtained from Mr. Hu's movies and Li Hanxiang's movies, from TV and textbooks. It was very abstract, not because of blood relationship or land but rather an ambiguous cultural concept. It was like a dream. You couldn't make sense of everything, but it was a holistic Chinese influence and it is in my blood. I think his martial arts films are different from modern kung fu action pictures. It was swordsman, not action and fighting. In his time, his style was relevant to Chinese history. He used the world of the swordsman to present the abstract part of Chinese culture. He guides you into Chinese landscape paintings, a legendary atmosphere which was very special. His cinema skills were very modern. He used quick editing techniques to all action, all visual effect . . . very Chinese, yet very modern. He was an amazing and unique director.[32]

Kwai-Cheung Lo points out Ang Lee's Chinese, yet modern, stylistic features, which the director seems to have taken from his source. Many Chinese film critics have also pointed out similarities with King Hu's filmmaking, placing the film squarely within the tradition of King Hu's intellectual and spiritual swordplay (*wuxia*) films—such as *A Touch of Zen*—with their deep philosophical seriousness. The presence of actress Cheng Pei Pei (as Jade Fox) also indicates this homage, because in the 1960s, Cheng was one of the biggest martial arts actresses and widely known to be King Hu's favorite actress. David Bordwell calls *Crouching Tiger, Hidden Dragon* "a millennial synthesis of the great *wuxia* tradition."[33] Bordwell cites examples to demonstrate how *Crouching Tiger, Hidden Dragon* references, recapitulates, and pays homage to the greatest elements of Chinese swordplay films. He outlines some of these references:

> The serene self-possession of Li Mu Bai is reminiscent of King Hu's fighters. . . . Shu Lien's rooftop pursuit of the mysterious thief echoes 1960s' adventures, and her unfussy prowess puts her in the line of women warriors played by Wu Lizhen, Josephine Siao Fong-fong, and Cheng Pei Pei. Cheng herself is on hand as a witness to the golden age, playing Jade Fox, the vengeance-mad swords-woman. The young couple, Jen and Lo, recall the combative couples of *Shaolin vs. Ninja* [1983]; by the end, however, their love affair, told through sumptuous desert flashbacks, acquires a sweeping poetic anguish akin to that of *Ashes of Time* [1994]. Behind the scenes is choreographer Yuen Wo Ping, a living encyclopedia of Peking Opera, martial arts techniques, and cinematic fireworks. . . . Blending everything is Ang Lee, fully aware of the landmarks of the genre he's working in, and like his predecessors he at once pays homage to them and reworks them to new effect.[34]

The cumulative effect of these references leads Bordwell to praise the film's continuity with the great *wuxia* tradition while carrying it into the twenty-first century—Lee's film sets the bar higher than ever.

Resuscitative Force in Cinema

When *Crouching Tiger, Hidden Dragon* was released in 2000, critics began to consider Ang Lee as a director with a very unique vision. Not only had he done a marvelous job re-creating an ancient and now nonexistent China—"the China that is fading away in our heads," as Lee has called it—but he was bringing a breath of fresh air into a cynical, inbred, and inward-looking Hollywood.[35] In recent years, Hollywood films, especially comedies, have sunk to a new level of tired self-referencing and referencing of other recent, unfunny comedies; at the same time, the topics of mainstream dramas and serious films are often formulaic and dictated by box office receipts. The answer, at least for the *New Yorker*'s film critic Anthony Lane, is the freshness brought in by foreign filmmakers like Ang Lee. Writing in 2000, Lane sees similarities between Lee and old Hollywood filmmaker Michael Curtiz, the maker of such films as *The Adventures of Robin Hood* (1938, to which *Crouching Tiger, Hidden Dragon* offers the best comparison) and *Casablanca* (1942). Born Mihály Kertész in Budapest, the director changed his name to conform to American standards, but retained the old-world sophistication of his directing vision. Lee can be compared to Curtiz in that they are both "civilized craftsmen with honor and humor."[36] Lane calls Ang Lee a "Curtiz for our times; the uncondescending outsider," and claims that: "China and the Pacific Rim are delivering the liveliest and least cynical filmmaking in the world, and also the most uncowed."[37] This point is certainly true, as Lee bravely takes on not only homosexuality in his own culture in *The Wedding Banquet*, but then further dares to take on homosexuality in the United States with *Brokeback Mountain*, or sheds a glaring light on the Vietnam era in *The Ice Storm*, or presents the Confederate side in *Ride with the Devil*. Lane poses this question:

> Is it too fanciful to suggest that the generation of [Ang] Lee, Chen Kaige, Wong Kar-wai, Zhang Yimou, and Hou Hsiao-hsien, or perhaps the generation that follows them, might ride to the rescue—or, at any rate, resuscitation—of American movies with some of the panache that marked the great Mitteleuropa immigration of the 1930s and 1940s, itself an escape into the entertainment industry from a world of threat? Would Ernst Lubitsch, watching *The Wedding Banquet*, not have recognized the stirrings of a kindred spirit?[38]

These observations about the power of foreign and international influences to "resuscitate" American film are prescient and anticipate Ang Lee's dominance of awards ceremonies in 2005 and 2006—the point that Ang Lee makes "uncowed" cinema seems to anticipate the daring social commentary in *Brokeback Mountain*—and again, in 2013, Lee's second Academy Award for Best Director for the innovative use of 3D technology in the similarly "wondrous" and "magical" *Life of Pi*. With the making of *Crouching Tiger, Hidden Dragon*, Ang Lee not only dares to refashion a classic Chinese genre with his own expansive vision, he also successfully brings the *wuxia* world to global popularity to enliven international cinema.

TEN

The Ultimate Outsider: Hulk

Moviemaking is never as good as what you imagine. Any good idea that's floating in the air—that's the best.[1]

THE CHARACTER OF Spiderman was created by Marvel Comics editor Stan Lee in 1962 as a "modern" hero who would break the comic book formula by losing as many battles as he won. He was a more human superhero, riddled with angst, who would interact with the real world and experience self-doubt and failure. Similarly, Dr. Robert Bruce Banner, as the Hulk, is an antihero, a figure who in times of stress finds himself transformed into the dark (green) personification of his subconsciously repressed rage and anger. In the early 2000s, both Spiderman and the Hulk were the first of the Marvel superheroes to have internationally-acclaimed studio films made of their comic strip personas. Sam Raimi's *Spider-Man* (2002) led to sequels in 2004 and 2007, and has been credited with reigniting the comic book genre and making "superhero-ism" fashionable again, leading to increasing forays into the comic book universe (more recently with the Iron Man franchise, the Avengers, and Captain America, etc.). Lee's $150 million blockbuster *Hulk* (2003) was an early anticipator of this trend, coming just a year after Raimi's film, and seemed set to capitalize on the new popularity of the superhero film.[2] The ubiquitous presence of these comic book heroes in the media since they were created by Stan Lee and Jack Kirby in the early 1960s, including the *Spiderman* animated cartoon series (1967–1970) and *The Incredible Hulk* television series (1977–1982, with Bill Bixby and Lou Ferrigno), established them as international icons. (In 1978, a Spider-Man *tokusatsu* animated series was produced for Japanese television by Toei Company Ltd; apart from Spider-Man's costume it was not based on the original source, but despite its differing storyline, this animation helped push Spiderman to the status of worldwide iconography.) And yet, what was the draw of the comic superhero Hulk for a filmmaker of the stature of Ang Lee, coming as he did off the success of *Crouching Tiger, Hidden Dragon*?

No doubt Lee was drawn to the subject because comics are treated as a serious art form in Asia; "man hua" or "comics" in Taiwan have a devoted following.

Young people in Lee's home country of Taiwan are thoroughly acquainted with the comic book medium—more so than young readers in America or Europe. Taiwanese young people are very involved with comic strips, comic books, and comic art in the form of cartoon images and characters. Beginning with "Hello Kitty" and "Snoopy," most Taiwanese students from a young age are enamored with comic books and characters. As they grow into their teenage years, Taiwanese students spend a great deal of time poring over comic books produced in Taiwan and also "manga" imported from Japan—comics are an art form that they already have appreciated with considerable sophistication. Young Taiwanese also admire the heroic qualities of present-day cartoon icons such as Doraemon, Yu-Gi-Oh, or various Pokémon figures such as Pikachu, and these characters take on a profound and well-loved cultural significance. Students at the university level continue to enjoy renditions of ancient Chinese legends and elaborate martial arts series. In a related example, it can be observed that the popularity of animation from Asia has been taken more seriously in the West in recent years, particularly Hayao Miyazaki's *My Neighbor Totoro* (*Tonari no Totoro*, 1988), *Spirited Away* (*Sen to Chihiro no Kamikakushi*, 2001), which won the Best Animated Feature at the Academy Awards in 2002, and *Howl's Moving Castle* (*Hauru no Ugoku Shiro*, 2004), which was nominated for Best Animated Feature in 2005.

The comic strip and comic book art forms are also very fresh and exciting media for exploration by a filmmaker. Joe Kubert (1999) dates the appearance of the first superheroes in comics to the mid-1930s.[3] The unique nature of comic book and comic strip conventions can be explored on film: the vocabulary, the characters, the frame-by-frame narration, the humor, and speech versus thought bubbles, for example. The characters are generally static from week to week—a reader may become familiar with the characters and the nature of the comic strip, and then be fairly confident about what to expect in terms of characters, vocabulary, setting, style of humor, etc. Comic strips such as *The Hulk* or *Spiderman* also have their unchanging protagonists; in addition, these superhero comic strips are of a serial nature, telling a continuous narrative story from week to week. *Spiderman* and *The Hulk* have both also been serialized in comic books devoted to these characters alone. These characteristics of the medium build up loyalty and familiarity within the comic book subculture. In addition, these comic book heroes and their films provide the student with a simple narrative plot, the story of good versus evil played out by basic archetypes. There is much room for culturally relevant inquiry concerning "good guys" and "bad guys," justice and redemption. Moreover, comic books and films are an offshoot of the fertile genre of science fiction, with its traditional laboratory elements such as experiments gone awry, Cold War sensibilities, suspicion of the government and secrecy of scientific inquiry, the introduction of nuclear power and radiation/mutation (in the case of the character of Spiderman, who is bitten by a radioactive spider, and the Hulk, who is injected with mutating cells touched off by a laboratory accident dealing with nuclear fusion). Finally, a third interesting feature of these comics/films is the wide range of cutting-edge language and modern English pop-art idioms; some examples included the comic book sound of a fist hitting someone's face ("Pow!"), a shriek of terror ("Eek!"), or Doonesbury's use of slang.

In a discussion on comic heroes, several topics may be explored in greater depth, such as the origins of comic heroes, the meaning behind comic narratives, or the filmmakers' objectives in bringing their narratives to the screen. For example, Ang Lee's motivation for making *Hulk* is a curious question. Why would a filmmaker thus far devoted to telling sentimental tales aim to make a summer blockbuster with a budget in the many millions of dollars? Had Lee finally "sold out," shamelessly devoting himself to this ill-fitting format of megawatt advertising and market tie-ins? Was this—the superhero action genre—how Lee now sought to have his name imprinted in the consciousness of the international filmmaking world? In all probability, the film *Hulk* became larger and more unwieldy than the one Lee had originally set out to make. His trademark themes—of family and deep, personal character study—were no doubt foremost in his mind as he envisioned *Hulk's* screenplay. The film retains much of the small-family focus. Intimate moments abound—between Bruce (Eric Bana) and his father (Nick Nolte), Bruce and Betty (Jennifer Connelly), Betty and Bruce's father, Betty and her own father (Sam Elliott). Stripped of its over-the top, comic book antics, this film is a small family drama of the kind at which Lee excels. The scene in which Bruce and his father (in chains) face off on a large, brightly-lit stage is nearly Shakespearean in the force of its tragedy and drama. The set is even lit like a stage—with tortured soliloquies performed under spotlights. It is in scenes like this that the viewer is treated to Ang Lee's true greatness of interpretation in the drama of the family.

In addition, the element of *Hulk's* narrative which most likely attracted Lee's interest is his dislocation from society—his alienation caused by his maniacal father. The Hulk longs to be normal—and to have a happy romance with his love, Betty— but he cannot fit in. He will never fit in. Betty tries to accept him, but she cannot. He is too strange, too different, doomed to walk through the world as an outsider. This theme of alienation, of being a cultural misfit, is a common theme in Lee's work. His three earliest films—the Chinese trilogy consisting of *Pushing Hands*, *The Wedding Banquet*, and *Eat Drink Man Woman*—all deal with the dislocation between Western and Eastern cultures. The figure of the Hulk, who longs to be loved and accepted, embracing his girlfriend Betty tenderly after going on a wild, untamed rampage, is a pathetic one, as is the image of the Hulk plummeting forlornly back to earth after hanging onto the fuselage of an airplane. No one wants him—he is completely rejected by humanity. He is the ultimate antihero.

Perhaps Lee was facing an impossible task as he attempted to win the audience's sympathy, understanding, or affection for the disenchanting Hulk. The Hulk, as he was first drawn in the early comic book series, is not a superhero but an antihero. His abnormal powers do not lead to glory and honor, but to alienation and isolation. Dr. Robert Bruce Banner is a Jekyll-and-Hyde figure who cannot control his anger. Instead of keeping his negative emotions inside, he becomes overwhelmed by them and is transformed into a hideous green monster acting out his repressed rage.[4] The source of this rage, in Lee's film, is his father's accidental murder of his mother, but in modern psychological terms he demonstrates the externalization of his dysfunctional childhood; this is to gain sympathy for his character and his plight. Lee's treatment of him reflects a sympathy with this unmanageable pain and anger. The film was a plaintive cry, asking the audience to show compassion for this terrible, flawed hero. But were the hearts of the audience soft enough to love this character?

Spiderman as a hero is a different story. The character is an "everyman" superhero, a very human superhero who experiences angst, self-doubt, and failure. Peter Parker is a scrawny nerd who faces inevitable mediocrity and unrequited love until a bite from a radioactive spider infuses him with supernatural powers. As Spiderman, he carries on a battle for justice—the triumph of the little guy—but at great personal sacrifice. Thus, Spiderman offers a more likeable and audience-friendly hero than the Hulk. Interestingly, both the *Hulk* (debut May 1962) and *Spiderman* (debut August 1962) were among Stan Lee's most famous comic book creations, which also include *The Fantastic Four* (debut November 1961). The difference is that the audience cheers for Spiderman and pities the Hulk. Stan Lee outlines the formula for his superhero comics' success in the introduction to a book on Marvel Comics: "The trick . . . is to create a fantastic premise and then envelope it with as much credibility as possible."[5] He explains how *Spiderman* endows a man with the supernatural abilities to spin webs and fly through the air, but then makes him as familiar and human as a next-door neighbor. "Despite his super powers, he still has money troubles, dandruff, domestic problems, allergy attacks, self-doubts, and unexpected defeats."[6] He also highlights Marvel's strict requirements for natural-sounding dialogue between the characters, as well as the element of humor essential to even the most somber of stories.

In understanding Stan Lee's achievement as the creator of the superheroes Spiderman and the Hulk, it is illuminating to review the literary origins that served as a source of inspiration to him. He had a considerable literary background and anticipated that he would only be in the comic business for a short time before going on to become a serious writer. In publishing his comic book creations, Lee changed his name from Stanley Martin Lieberman because "I felt someday I'd be writing the Great American Novel and I didn't want to use my real name on these silly little comics."[7] Some of his literary influences include Edgar Rice Burroughs, Arthur Conan Doyle, and Robert Louis Stevenson, and he admired the sonority of Shakespeare and the Bible.[8] His creation of the original *Hulk* series (*The Incredible Hulk*) was drawn from two distinct literary and cultural sources. Boris Karloff's filmic portrayal of the monster in *Frankenstein* (1931) was an inspiration because, in the film narrative, the monster is "basically good at heart," but he is "hunted and hounded" by society;[9] these twin characteristics are shared by the Hulk. The second influence is Robert Louis Stevenson's *The Strange Case of Dr. Jekyll and Mr. Hyde*—Lee was interested in a character that would transform from normal to monstrous and back again at random. In the Hulk, he sought to create a character with a tortured soul on the scale of Greek tragedy. His description of the Hulk is that of a character who would "never know a moment's peace, never have the chance to have a normal life or dare to wed the girl he loved."[10] In summing up the complexity of his comic creations, Lee concludes, "We're proud that Marvel was largely responsible for transforming comic books into a form of entertainment which today appeals to readers of all ages."[11] Stan Lee was given a positive sign that the comic book heroes he had created were having a social impact when a contingent of Columbia University students came to his office to announce the Hulk was their new mascot; Ivy League students could obviously sympathize with an intellect-driven scientist who was periodically pushed over the edge into an emotional rampage:

> Marvel's revolutionary style of storytelling was still in its embyonic stages, but already it was attracting an older and more sophisticated audience than comic books were conventionally expected to reach. . . . Despite condescending conventional wisdom, the imaginative world of comic books has always attracted the most intelligent kids: the introverted readers and dreamers who have fantasies of acquiring brawn to match their brains. And the Marvel heroes, with their sudden physical transformations and endless personal problems, spoke to the hopes and fears of troubled adolescents everywhere. Hordes of readers who had not looked at a comic book in years were suddenly being drawn back into the fold by Marvel's new approach. . . . Marvel had fortuitously tapped into a demographic gold mine: the gigantic generation of baby boom children and teenagers who had been born in the years following World War Two. This group [was] one of the largest, best-educated and most affluent generations in American history.[12]

For the sophisticated *Hulk* reader, this film also affords its pleasures, in the form of subtle parallels with the original comic series. There are numerous self-referential plotlines that conjure up references to former *Hulk* stories. For example, when Betty first meets David Banner, they discuss a man named "Benny." This is a reference to a soldier named Benny from the *Hulk* comics' "Dogs of War" story arc, which introduced the concept of Hulk dogs used in this film. Another example is the scene in which General Ross heads toward San Francisco to intercept the Hulk, and his helicopter is codenamed "T-Bolt"; this is in homage to the nickname by which he is usually referred to in the *Hulk* comics, General "Thunderbolt" Ross, because of his short temper. In addition, the actor playing Ross in the film, Sam Elliott, had his doubts about wearing a mustache as the army does not encourage facial hair, but he agreed to Ang Lee's wishes as General Ross sports a mustache in the comic books. Other corresponding details between the comics and the film include the following: David Banner works as a janitor in the film; this is a reference to the comic book character Samuel Sterns, a janitor who would eventually become the Hulk's arch-enemy, "The Leader." When Banner first bombards himself with gamma rays, the "mimic" powers he displays are a homage to "The Absorbing Man," a villain from the *Hulk* comics. Finally, Banner's transformation into the giant electrical being near the end of the movie is a homage to the classic *Hulk* villain "Zzzax."[13]

Stylistic Features of the Hulk and Spider-Man

The success of comic book films like *Hulk* and *Spider-Man* was largely dependent upon the film technology of computer-generated imaging (CGI), a relatively new technology at the time. Creating the CGI Hulk was the most complex task ever undertaken by Industrial Light & Magic (ILM) to date; ILM employees logged over 2.5 million computer hours in the one-and-a-half years it took for *Hulk* to come to life. The computer model of the Hulk created by ILM used 12,996 texture maps and required 1,165 muscle movements. ILM designers studied human subjects performing the actions Hulk does in order to create his movements; initially they used bodybuilders but found them to be too cumbersome so eventually they settled on personal trainers. The amount of CGI involved in the scene where Hulk battles the three mutant dogs was one of the hardest, most complicated scenes ILM had ever done. Ultimately what ended up on screen was only a third of what was originally storyboarded; to have filmed the entire storyboarded version would have been simply too expensive. According to Ang Lee's DVD commentary, the dogfight scene in the woods was originally envisioned with the Hulk fighting the monster dogs while naked. However, this was thought to be too difficult for a PG-13 movie, and so the Hulk does not appear naked until the very end of the fight. It was a deliberate decision to withhold showing Hulk in daylight until much later into the film, giving the audience the chance to get used to seeing him. When the first Hulk-out (transformation of Banner into Hulk) occurs, the color of the Hulk is either gray or greenish-gray; this is in homage to the original appearance of Hulk when he was actually gray in his first comic book appearance (*Hulk* #1, May 1962). From the second Hulk-out he maintains his prominent green hue. Moreover, there are three distinct Hulks in the movie; as Hulk gets angrier he gets bigger. The first (angry) Hulk is nine feet tall, the second (angrier) Hulk is 12 feet, and the third (angriest) Hulk is 15 feet tall. The Hulk had to move at a top speed of 300 miles per hour and be able to leap 3–4 miles in a single bound. According to ILM, the Hulk would be able to exert 14 tons of pressure per square inch and thus smash through almost anything in his path.

How successful, then, were the filmmakers (in the early days of CGI) at bringing these superheroes and their narratives to life? The original 2002 film *Spider-Man* greatly condensed the story of Peter Parker and his physical/psychological transformation, but still presented a stirring and complex story of one man's struggle to do the right thing with the limited choices he is given. *Spider-Man* garnered critic accolades and high box office grosses. What of the *Hulk*? Touted as an even larger blockbuster than *Spider-Man*, and costing US$137 million to make, the *Hulk* achieved only moderate returns at the box office. A preview advertisement run several months in advance of the film's opening seemed to draw only negative reactions from audiences, who criticized the film's CGI graphics as being less sophisticated than *Donkey Kong*, a reference to the look of outdated video-game technology. A 2003 *New Yorker* article described the desperation of the studio in reaction to this news as Ang Lee himself climbed into the motion capture technology suit in an effort to improve the work of the graphic designers and give the Hulk a more realistic bearing.[14] In a nuanced performance, Lee tried to capture with his own body and facial expressions the anger and agony of the character of the Hulk. Ultimately, due to the limits of the technology, however, the complexities of human emotion could not be captured effectively in a computer-generated image. Rather than depicting the sweaty, tearful, grief-stricken expression of a human being, the computer image seemed limited and puppet-like, without nuance or pathos. The computer-generated Hulk lacked the eyes and expressiveness of a real actor/person, so that the human element the audience needed to identify with the character was missing. Looking into a computer-generated character's eyes, all the viewer sees is computer art; looking into a person's eyes, the viewer sees into a soul, a life. While the audience was sometimes allowed to sympathize and identify with Hulk when he was in the form of Bruce Banner, more often the viewer was called upon to sympathize with Hulk as a CGI figure. Meanwhile, *Spider-Man* fared better, because when the audience was called to sympathize closely with the protagonist, he was not suited up as Spiderman but instead maintained intimacy as the real, human face of Peter Parker.

In some ways it can be argued, however, that the *Hulk* film is rendered more imaginatively and takes more daring risks. For example, the structure of the plot in *Spider-Man* is a straightforward hero-versus-nemesis theme, while *Hulk* explores family drama in several different directions: Bruce versus his own father, Bruce's mother versus his father (in flashback), Betty versus her father, and finally, Betty versus Bruce. In addition, the presentation of the *Hulk* is unique in its use of comic book conventions from the written page. For example, in the opening of the film, the Green Marvel font of the main titles pays cultural homage to the original comic books. In addition, during certain action sequences Lee splits the screen into multiple comic book panels that dramatize the original comic strip format of the *Hulk* narrative. Moreover, Lee comments that the film has a complex philosophical subtext involving change and transformation embodied by lichen growing on rocks and mutation at a cellular and molecular level; images representing this idea occur throughout the movie. In preparation for filming *Hulk*, Lee studied "molecular growth, blood cells, galaxies, and [according to] Dennis Muren, ILM's senior visual-effects supervisor, 'how there's some connection in the universe that makes everything work: a kind of yin-yang thing he wanted to get into the story.' Lee also collected twenty-four boxes of rocks—'their texture shows the flow of time, they remind you that the universe is kind of a big pot of soup,'—as well as lichen, starfish, and jellyfish, whose shapes were intended to help his collaborators imagine the Hulk's dissonant interior."[15] There is no such imaginative subtext in *Spider-Man*.

The films' taglines can be compared as well. "With great power, there must also come great responsibility" is the tagline in *Spider-Man*, a line spoken repeatedly by Peter's uncle to remind him of his obligation to serve justice. This obligation comes at great personal sacrifice to Peter, who must give up his love interest, Mary Jane Watson, to serve society at large. This idea is noble and heroic in comparison to the *Hulk's* tagline: "The inner beast will be released." Other taglines used to advertise the film include: "Rage. Power. Freedom," "On the 20th of June, let it all out," and "Unleash the hero within."[16] These lines are evidence of the mixed message of the film; the release of rage is considered, on the one hand, heroic, and on the other, destructive. Even the taglines reflect that the makers of the *Hulk* weren't entirely agreed on the message they wanted to promote, demonstrating a fundamental lack of unity in the film's vision.[17]

The Challenge of Hulk

Ultimately, Ang Lee's *Hulk* is about taking risks and attempting to transform the genre of hero-action movies in the same way the director has experimented with the conventions of "genre" in his past films. In stretching to create a unique vision, the filmmakers worked hard to bring a depth to the film that is surprising in its sophistication. John Lahr notes in the *New Yorker* interview that Ang Lee's office walls revealed the esoteric inspirations for his cinematic imagery: "de Chirico for the colors and shapes of the Southwest, where part of the movie is set; Maxfield Parrish for sky tones, Rousseau and the Hudson River School Painters for the sense of scale; Picasso's Dora for the montage of tension; and Cezanne for everything else. On the other side, interspersed with moody comic-strip panels, were the swirling patterns of William Morris and Jackson Pollock."[18] It is difficult to imagine that the makers of the *Spiderman* franchise put such lofty erudition into the filming of *Spiderman* and *Spiderman 2*.

The complexity of the *Hulk* plot mirrors this sophisticated thematic vision. The narrative is a challenging parable about modern science being a double-edged sword—both the threat of out-of-control experimentation and the promise of a better future. Marvel Comics heroes from the 1950s, 1960s, and 1970s historically reflected twentieth-century anxiety over the inexorable forward momentum of scientific discovery. Specifically, radiophobia, the fear of radiation and radioactive materials brought on by extensive atomic weapons' testing and experimentation (in Hiroshima and Nagasaki), played a large role in the comic book narratives of this era.

> The fear of radiation was a theme that recurred throughout the early 1960s, and again, radiation was the gimmick that provided the protagonist with his uncanny powers. Overt anxiety about the unleashed atom had diminished somewhat since the 1950s, even if only due to familiarity with the idea. However, a strong undercurrent of concern remained, and many of the superheroes of The Marvel Age owed their existence to the dreaded new technology. For Jack Kirby, the concept was more than just an easy way to set a story line in motion: "As long as we're experimenting with radioactivity . . . there's no telling what may happen, or how much our advancements may cost us." The Hulk became Marvel's most disturbing embodiment of the perils inherent in the atomic age.[19]

This inherent danger in radiation experiments is illustrated in the *Hulk* film, capturing the contradictory nature of these scientific advancements. Experiments in the film's research facility are designed to help heal wounded animals by injection with gamma rays. However, in one scene, a bullfrog receives too much gamma radiation and literally explodes—a shocking and graphic demonstration of how wrong scientific experimentation can go.

These same complexities of theme run through the *Hulk* narrative. Berkeley scientist Bruce Banner does biomedical research, and struggles with his absence of memories from his early childhood. He has flashbacks and dreams which obliquely refer to a terrible early-childhood trauma. Bruce believes himself to be an orphan until his father David Banner appears as a janitor in the lab. David Banner is truly the "mad scientist" and villain of the story, whose tampering with biomedical research and experimentation with his own DNA has caused a genetic flaw to be passed on to his son. When Bruce's genetic structure receives accidental exposure to strong radioactivity, it sets off a terrifying reaction which turns him into a gigantic, raging monster.

Bruce's on-again, off-again girlfriend, Betty Ross, struggles with her own past and her father, General Ross, in a way that parallels Bruce.

Betty:	How are you feeling?
Bruce:	OK, I guess.
Betty:	I think that somehow the anger you felt last night is triggering the nanomeds.
Bruce:	How could it? We designed them to respond to physical damage.
Betty:	Emotional damage can manifest physically.
Bruce:	Like what?
Betty:	A serious trauma . . . a suppressed memory.
Bruce:	Your father grilled me about something I was supposed to remember from early childhood.
Betty:	He did?
Bruce:	Yeah. It sounded bad. But I honestly don't remember.
Betty:	What worries me is that a physical wound is finite, but with emotions, what's to stop it from going on and on, and starting a chain reaction?
Bruce:	Maybe next time, it'll just keep going. You know what scares me the most though? When it happens, when it comes over me—when I totally lose control—*I like it*.[20]

Bruce's past haunts him in dreams, but his memory has been cauterized by the terror he experienced as a child. Thus, his memory is repressed—he is unaware of the terrible childhood memories that afflict his psyche. The discussion relates physical damage with emotional damage, referring to the common idea in psychoanalysis that subconscious emotions and memories can have physical manifestations, and that the doer may not be aware of these subconscious motivations. This dialogue displays the key statement: "You know what scares me the most though? When it happens, when it comes over me—when I totally lose control—*I like it*." This line from Bruce Banner underscores how the dark and mysterious forces inside the human heart can be pleasurable to express. It explores the question of whether or not humans should control their animal instincts, and to what degree the expression of this rage and anger is acceptable, normal, or healthy. Lines such as the following suggest that expressing uncontrollable anger is bestial, or something other than human:

Betty:	How long are you gonna keep Bruce sedated?
Ross:	The rest of his natural life, if I have to.
Betty:	You said I could trust you.
Ross:	I'm your father. You can trust me to do what I think is right, not what you think you want.
Betty:	He's a human being.
Ross:	He's also something else.[21]

This is a conversation between Betty and her father General Ross. Betty and her father also have issues—he has wanted to capture Bruce as a weapon to be used by the U.S. government. Rather than viewing him as the inhuman result of a scientific experiment gone awry, Betty expresses a desire to protect and nurture him—she is torn between her fear of his raging, uncontrollable anger and her loyalty to the Bruce she has known as a tender human being. Betty says to her father:

Betty: Look, I know the government thinks they have a weapon on their hands or he'd be dead already. They can probe and prod all they want, but in the meanwhile, you have to let me help him. Nobody knows him better than I do.[22]

In the above dialogue from the screenplay, Betty reveals her fierce loyalty to the Bruce Banner she knew as an intimate friend, and the memories of their shared past ("Nobody knows him better than I do"). Betty refuses to give in to the pressure to view Bruce Banner as something different, something inhuman.

David Banner's motives are mixed, perhaps reflecting his mental instability as he slowly becomes more and more deranged. At first, his actions seem to simply reflect the conventional Greek-tragedy storyline of the sins of the fathers visited on their own sons. At certain moments, he actually seems regretful and contrite toward his son. However, he has other darker motives for reestablishing contact with Bruce. Throughout the film, but especially toward the ending, David Banner's major desire is for achieving an infinitely powerful state of existence in which he will be able to become immortal by cheating death. To do so, he must harness his son's power. It is a classic father/son conflict: the father loves his son, but his love becomes clouded by his lust for power.

Father: And what did I do to [my son], Miss Ross? Nothing! I tried to overcome the limits in myself—myself, not him. Can you understand? To improve on nature, my nature. Knowledge of oneself, that is the only path to the truth that gives men the power to defy God's boundaries.[23]

This aspiration for absolute power is set in contrast with the Oedipal notion that men must kill their fathers if they want to grow up:

(*David Banner walks toward his son, reaches out with his manacled hands.*)
Bruce: No. Please don't touch me. Maybe, once, you were my father. But you're not now—you never will be.
Father: (*Beat.*) Is that so? Well, I have news for you. I didn't come here to see you. I came for my son.
          (*Bruce looks up at him, confused.*)
Father: (*Cont'd.*) My real son—the one inside of you. You are merely a superficial shell, a husk of flimsy consciousness, surrounding him, ready to be torn off at a moment's notice.

Bruce: Think whatever you like. I don't care. Just go now.
           (*The Father smiles, laughs.*)
Father: But Bruce—I have found a cure—for me. (*beat—now more menacing*) You see, my cells too can transform—absorb enormous amounts of energy, but unlike you, they're unstable. Bruce, I need your strength. I gave you life, now you must give it back to me—only a million times more radiant, more powerful.
Bruce: Stop.
Father: Think of it—all those men out there, in their uniforms, barking and swallowing orders, inflicting their petty rule over the globe, think of all the harm they've done, to you, to me—and know we can make them and their flags and anthems and governments disappear in a flash. You—in me.
Bruce: I'd rather die.
Father: And indeed you shall. And be reborn a hero of the kind that walked the earth long before the pale religions of civilization infected humanity's soul.[24]

The final climactic battle between father and son is ambiguous, and this confusion has led many critics to condemn the film. This dramatic confrontation can be understood in various ways. As James Schamus has explained the complexity of the drama in the *New Yorker*: "The Hulk sacrifices himself to defeat his enemy, which is, in the

Ang Lee's interest in the father-son conflict is brought into high relief as Bruce Banner clashes with his mad-scientist father.

person of his father, really himself."[25] A deleted scene from the DVD has Bruce the scientist offering the following explanation:

Bruce: Life is both the ability to retrieve and to act on memory . . . Part
          of life is death, is forgetting, and unchecked, it's mutateous, it's
          monstrous . . . Basically to stay in balance and alive we must forget
          as much as we remember.

The intensity of the repressed memories has caused Bruce severe emotional damage. However, in the end, he may have been able to forget or to give out his memory/power and transfer it/relinquish it to his father (who is given the powers of Absorbing Man, an obscure Marvel villain). Special effects render the father's astounding mutation into a humongous, tortured, and bloated creature. In the end, the father has absorbed too much of his son; the power is out of control. "Take it back!" he screams, "It's not stopping—TAKE IT BACK!" This is the chilling ending to the classic conflict.

The last moments of the film show us that Bruce Banner has not only survived the battle, but is using his skills as a physician in South America. His alter ego the Hulk has survived as well, ready to smash evil and defend innocent people. The last line of the film comes when Bruce, confronting a soldier, says in Spanish: "You're making me angry. You wouldn't like me when I'm angry." This is a reference to the line made famous in the pilot and opening sequence of *The Incredible Hulk* (1977). It also leaves the plot open-ended, to set up a possible sequel. The line about "anger" displays one of the central questions in the story: how to control, or alternately, how to express, anger. The film deals with how sorrow, anger, and all the other related emotions can build up within a man and can manifest physically. The anger caused by the familial conflict within *Hulk*, as the father and son wrestle over the son's power and potential, is of course reminiscent of the troubled relationship Ang Lee had with his own father as he yearned to break free of parental control to pursue his artistic vision. "I gave you life," the father David Banner tells his son, implying obligation and service to the creator's will. In reality, Lee never dared to respond to his own father's pressure with the type of anger Bruce displays in *Hulk*; however, one can ascertain in this film a certain subconscious Oedipal aggression.

In another complicated plot twist the fathers (Banner and Ross) are enemies because of some terrible event in the past involving Banner setting off a radioactive bomb that turns the army base into a wasteland—General Ross bans him permanently from the U.S. army. Ross makes reference to this:

Betty: I want you to help him! Why isn't that simple? Why is he such a
          threat to you?
Ross: Because I know what he comes from! He's his father's son, every last
          molecule of him. He says he doesn't know his father—he's working
          in the exact same goddamn field his father did. So either he's lying,
          or it's far worse than that, and he's . . .
Betty: What? Predestined? To follow in his father's footsteps?
Ross: I was gonna say "damned."[26]

Thus, the Greek tragic theory of the sons being punished by the sins of the fathers comes full circle—Betty as well is under a curse from her family lineage. The *Hulk* is both an intricate psychological drama with a modern-day Achilles as a hero, and a love story of doomed lovers who can never have a happy ending to their love story (in this way, it prefigures the themes of *Brokeback Mountain*). The question is, can the audience sympathize with the Hulk's predicament; to take Betty Ross's position, is it possible to accept the Hulk as he is, fatally flawed? Critical response to the film showed that the audience did not have its sympathy won over by the sensitive portrait of the antihero. The thinking man's action movie about Man's inner demons did not hold broad appeal. While some critics praised Lee's daring departure from the conventional treatment of the comic book drama, the film was pummeled by most viewers who criticized the effort to turn Hulk into Hamlet with art-house visual effects. According to the IMDb website, while the film's first weekend gross was $62,128,420, its second weekend gross was $18,847,620, a mere 30 percent of the first weekend. *Hulk* holds the record for largest second weekend box office drop for a film that opened at number one, with a −69.7 percent drop.

Historically, Bruce Banner became one of the first comic book protagonists to hate his constant transformation into a superhero. What comes through most clearly in the *Hulk* film is that Banner himself has conflicting views of his own abilities, and that he knows he presents a real danger to himself and others. The threat of this danger provides a tension throughout the film. Aware that his destructive emotions lead to unpleasant consequences, the Hulk must necessarily become antisocial: "Have to get away—to hide."[27] This condition makes him a sympathetic menace. The Hulk is cursed with a weakness of character (which he battles with the strength of his will) who throughout the film is trying in vain to hold his rage in check and not be transformed into the alter ego he despises—a brutish, out-of-control monster. Thus *Hulk* is not a story of anger, destruction, and hatred, but a parable about triumph of the will, courage, and hope. It is this compelling, hope-against-all-hope desire to see Bruce learn to control his rampaging emotions that provides the dramatic tension of the narrative.

While the *Hulk* was not the best comic book film, and not the most successful of Ang Lee's movies, the shadow of what Lee is looking for appears in the film—the continued desire to invite the outsider in, to render acceptable what is unacceptable. This is what Lee calls the "juice" of the film, "The thing that moves people, the thing that is untranslatable by words."[28] It is this underlying theme of longing for a kind of redemption—for acceptance—that *Hulk* shares with all of Lee's films.

ELEVEN

Transcending Gender in Brokeback Mountain

After making *Hulk*, I wasn't sure if I wanted to continue making movies.
—Ang Lee, introducing *Brokeback Mountain* at the Toronto
International Film Festival in September 2005

ANG LEE'S FILM *Brokeback Mountain*, a romance between two uneducated farm-hands based on the 1997 short story by Annie Proulx, has been described as exploring the "last frontier" in mainstream film.[1] From the time of the film's release in 2005, producer James Schamus, director Ang Lee, and screenwriters Larry McMurtry and Diana Ossana continued to receive numerous awards and accolades for making a film that revolutionizes the idea of love, obliterates gay stereotypes, and subverts traditional "macho" cowboy iconography. Instead, the film conjures bittersweet yearning for lost love and lost opportunity, transcending any narrow issues of sexuality or gender, and as a result, becoming a more universal love story between two men. Throughout 2006, the "gay cowboy story" was both hailed as a vehicle for gay activism and vilified by American conservatives. An initial reading of the narrative through the lens of modern gender theory demonstrates, however, that the story is not overtly political, but rather seeks universality in the experience of human longing for affection and acceptance.

Gender Studies and Queer Studies are concerned with the interactions between people that constitute power, gender, and sexual relations. There are processes of interaction between identity markers such as gender and sexuality and axes of difference such as race (Stoler 1995), ethnicity, and class. "Queer theory" is largely a discourse about the logocentric interdependency of gay and straight, and the centrality of queerness to "normalcy" (see Warner 1993; Messner 1997). The resulting research ranges across a wide spectrum, from a more personal, journalistic literature on self-help to castigating social critiques (Connell 1987; Kimmel 1992). Other work in the field includes examinations of homosexuality in the study of racialization, transnationalism, and globalization. Examples include Martin Manalansan's (2003) studies on Filipino gay males, Gayatri Gopinath's (1995) work on gender in South

Asian diasporic music/culture, and Roderick A. Ferguson's (2004) research on the projection of homosexuality as deviance onto African-Americans.

Eve Sedgwick's research presents a cogent analysis of the connection between early homosexual experiences and their impact on the future identity of a gay male: "If queer is a politically potent term, which it is, that's because, far from being capable of being detached from the childhood scene of shame, it cleaves to that scene as a near-inexhaustible source of transformational energy."[2] Sedgwick and others in the field of Queer Studies, including Michael Warner's assessments of "normal" (2000) and Leo Bersani's research on "homos" (1996), have posited "an early childhood experience of sexual shame that has to be reclaimed, reinterpreted, and resituated by a queer adult who, armed with a theoretical knowledge about his or her sexuality, can transform past experiences with abjection, isolation, and rejection into legibility, community, and love."[3] Similar to this, in *Brokeback Mountain*, the early experiences of the two male lovers (not yet twenty years old) cement their future bond and provide a reference point from which their lives develop, and to which they are permanently tied. In addition, an early exposure to vicious prejudice leaves one traumatized by fear and shame, while social intolerance of homosexuality dominates and directs both of their futures.

Annie Proulx's "Brokeback Mountain"

Annie Proulx's short story "Brokeback Mountain" was published in the *New Yorker* in the October 13, 1997, issue to great acclaim, and not a small amount of controversy.[4] Already renowned for her Pulitzer Prize–winning novel *The Shipping News* (1993), Proulx created a sensation with the haunting language and heartbreaking conflict of "Brokeback Mountain." In this story, she compressed the twenty-year love story of two loner ranch hands into thirty tight pages, full of raw masculinity and spare, realistic dialogue. In the film version of *Brokeback Mountain*, Ang Lee captured the essence of Annie Proulx's narrative with his faithful rendition (working with McMurtry and Ossana's screenplay, which reproduced the story's existing dialogue almost verbatim). Both Proulx and Lee aimed to create a very compelling love story transcending gender or prejudice. The focus is not on sexuality, but on love—sexuality is actually downplayed in the story. References to physical contact are spare, rather than exceptionally explicit. What is highlighted is not the sexual theme, but the emphasis on human affection, human attraction, and love. The story and the film represent a universal take on humanity. Below the surface story, an undercurrent of commonality regarding what human beings feel—isolation, regret, longing, fear, connection—transcends gender, race, culture, social, or even political identities.

The short story "Brokeback Mountain" is a tragedy of doomed love, and for this reason, perhaps, Lee has called it "the great American love story." Jack Twist (Jake Gyllenhaal) and Ennis Del Mar (Heath Ledger) are barely educated, itinerant ranch hands who first meet in Signal, Wyoming, in the summer of 1963, when they are hired at the same time for a sheepherding job on Brokeback Mountain. They are nineteen

"I'm not no queer." "Me neither."—The taut, repressed lives of the young ranch hands Jack and Ennis on Brokeback Mountain.

at the time, but these events will stay with them for the rest of their lives. In both the story and the film, the narrative is not "told" to the viewer, but instead unfolds with slow grace. The friendless pair find themselves bonding over chopping wood, cooking beans over a campfire, and simple conversation. The spare beauty of their exchanges helps make this a quintessential Ang Lee vehicle. At last, one night after the two have been drinking whiskey, they turn to each other for physical intimacy. Both deny their homosexual activity after the fact, "I'm not no queer." "Me neither."[5] However, the two share a passionate affection that neither man can erase nor forget for the rest of his life.

After their initial summer together, the two men's lives take them in different directions. They both become husbands, to wives whose suspicions are only raised gradually over time, and each has children. The conformist society of their families and neighbors forces them to keep their true feelings a secret. Within these strict confines, neither can imagine or define a lifestyle that would keep them together. The homophobia of American society in the 1960s and 1970s—especially in the American heartland and Midwest—changes too slowly for them to truly make a life together. A reunion four years after they first meet—which ends up as a tryst at a roadside motel near the Grand Tetons—brings these issues to a head, as Jack asks Ennis to set up a ranch with him, but Ennis refuses. Over the years, the men continue to see each other on rare camping trips, trying to hold on to the innocence and beauty of their first connection on Brokeback Mountain. In an argument many years into their relationship, Jack berates Ennis for refusing his offer for a more permanent relationship with the now iconic line: "I wish I knew how to quit you."[6]

The setting of the story, in Wyoming, is crucial to the narrative's poignancy. In the mountains and the wilderness, where the men are isolated geographically and emotionally from the rest of society, they are free to behave how they wish without moral or social restriction. They are away from the probing eyes of an unforgiving society which would normally keep their behavior in check. The story is essentially about two very poor young men who have nothing but the raw beauty of rural Wyoming and their emotions toward each other to bring them comfort in an otherwise bleak and colorless existence. The tragedy lies in the fact that although they can bring each other happiness, the strict conventions, mores, and taboos of the period keep them apart. Only away from those restrictions, on Brokeback Mountain, are they free. The story plays out over the cruel passage of time as the men age. Only when Jack dies does Ennis discover the true depth of his devotion, visiting his childhood home and finding his own shirt tucked inside Jack's in an endless embrace.

Controversy Regarding Brokeback Mountain

Because of the vast amount of innuendo and preconception facing the film, Focus Features used a very strategic marketing campaign, releasing the film in limited areas around the Christmas blockbuster season and relying on word-of-mouth to spread the film's popularity. Schamus' aggressive campaigning comes through in these quotes:

> We have never made an apology from the beginning for making this movie, which we believe will deliver an emotional experience to a larger audience than the art house. The movie gives us the tools to create that appeal. We're saying, "Here's the movie, here's what it looks like, come join us."[7]

In an early discussion of how to market the film, when Ang Lee assumed it might appeal most to a gay audience, Schamus insisted instead that the film would also appeal to women. Consequentially, when Schamus and his team selected the poster design, they did not turn to the designs of famous westerns, but to a choice of what were considered the "fifty most romantic movies ever made. If you look at our poster," Schamus says, "you can see traces of our inspiration, *Titanic*."[8] The final poster resembles *Titanic*'s placement of the two main actors with lowered eyelids, one face nestled in another's shoulder, with Heath Ledger's massive arm replacing the position occupied by the ship's hull in the former design.

The short story "Brokeback Mountain" was published almost exactly a year before the October 7, 1998, killing of the 21-year-old gay man Matthew Shepard, a student at the University of Wyoming, who was beaten to death by two men on his way home from a bar. Pistol-whipped and lashed to a fence, Shepard died of massive brain injuries. On trial, his killers confessed to the murder being due to "gay panic." *Brokeback Mountain* touches close to this territory when Ennis tells Jack about two cowboys who lived with each other on a ranch, sparking disapproval in the nearby community. Ennis explains that one of the cowboys was taken out and beaten to death, his genitals removed with a tire iron. This story overlaps one of the film's few flashbacks of a man lying dead, a victim of violent physical abuse. Ennis remembers this event because his father actually took him to view the mutilated corpse to demonstrate his (the father's) intolerance of the gay lifestyle.

Throughout 2005–2006, the controversial nature of the film brought it both good press and bad. On the one hand, the film received criticism for its subversive subject matter, polarizing American audiences already sharply divided on the issue of same-sex marriage. For example, when the film first opened, the influential Conference of Catholic Bishops gave it an "O" rating, classifying it as morally "offensive."[9] In addition, cinemas in two states, Utah and Washington, refused to show the film. The screening was cancelled just two hours before it was due to start at the Megaplex at Jordan Commons in Sandy, a suburb of Salt Lake City. Towns in the state of West Virginia also threatened to ban the film. Others welcomed it with great humor, calling it a "gay western," "the first mainstream gay cowboy movie," and "a gay man's *Gone with the Wind*."[10] In any case, Ang Lee and James Schamus obviously walked into the fray with their eyes open. Schamus' marketing strategies presented the film with a mission to reach sympathetic viewers, particularly women and gays. Meanwhile, for Lee, the challenge seems to have come from simply daring to normalize and conventionalize people who are routinely considered outsiders and unacceptable, as he does in many of his films (for example, Wai-Tung in *The Wedding Banquet*, and, of course, the Hulk). The casting of actors Jake Gyllenhaal and Heath Ledger added a further surprising dimension, because in the recent past Hollywood actors feared the career scourge brought on by homosexual roles, while in *Brokeback Mountain* the young, popular actors were proud to take on the challenge.[11] Jake Gyllenhaal said in the *New York Times*, "When I read it, it moved me so much that I couldn't not do it."[12]

Homosexuality in Mainstream Film

Looking back at the history of the representation of homosexuality in mainstream American film, it is impressive to recall how significant the making of *Brokeback Mountain* was as a cultural watershed in 2005, venturing into territory never before given wide play in the mainstream American film industry. While independent films at the time had their share of gay romances given limited play in art-house cinemas, a view of the history of homosexuality in mainstream film productions demonstrates the remarkable risk that was taken to turn *Brokeback Mountain* into a mainstream movie. In the 1970s, the homosexual act was displayed as an act of sodomistic humiliation in the film *Deliverance* (1972); in that film homosexuality was portrayed as the deviant behavior of uneducated hillbillies, a combination of sadism and bestiality. In 1982, the first mainstream sympathetic gay romance, *Making Love*, bombed at the box office and was widely blamed for derailing the career of (straight) actor Harry Hamlin. A single onscreen kiss between the two male leads in the film caused audible gasps in the theaters and widespread audience walkouts. Possibly due to this, the Jonathan Demme film *Philadephia* (1993), for which Tom Hanks won an Academy Award for his portrayal of Andrew Beckett, an AIDS patient fighting for his rights, steered a wide berth around gay romance—Hanks and his onscreen partner (Antonio Banderas) did not film any sexual scenes, nor did they kiss onscreen. With its full-blooded sex scenes and passionate couplings (Ledger reportedly nearly broke Gyllenhaal's nose while filming a kissing scene), *Brokeback Mountain* breaks both of these former taboos. Far from the deviant cruelty of gay sexuality in *Deliverance*, in *Brokeback Mountain*, backwoods love is treated with compassion and respect.

The making of the film took a circuitous route since no major Hollywood studio would back it (in this way, the film's production resembles Ang Lee's earlier experience with gay subject matter in *The Wedding Banquet*). Director Gus Van Sant and producer Scott Rudin originally tried to make *Brokeback Mountain* at Columbia Pictures, but they were unable to get any actors to commit; the actors and their agents both feared the taboo subject matter. Ossana and McMurtry's screenplay languished; it became notorious in the industry as one of the great unproduced screenplays. New York veteran independent film producers James Schamus and David Linde eventually took over the project, and when they were promoted to head Universal's Focus Features, a studio specialty division, in 2002, they brought along the script, which they had already been trying to make for several years. Finally, Ang Lee, who had read the script a few years before and found it extremely moving, agreed to direct the movie, and began filming near Calgary, Alberta, in 2004. Social critics like Frank Rich have noted the perfect timing of *Brokeback Mountain*—the shifting social and political climate in the United States helped prepare audiences for a mainstream homosexual romance.

> *Brokeback Mountain*, a movie that is all the more subversive for having no overt politics, is a rebuke and antidote to [the proposed same-sex marriage ban]. Whether it proves a movie for the ages or as transient as *Love Story*, it is a landmark in the troubled history of America's relationship to homosexuality. It brings something different to the pop culture marketplace at just the pivotal moment to catch a wave.[13]

His article predicts that heartland America is ready for this film—that the film represents a cultural shift in the American consciousness:

> The history of *Brokeback Mountain* as a film project in itself crystallizes how fast the climate has shifted. Mr. McMurtry and Ms. Ossana bought the screen rights to the Proulx story after it was published in the *New Yorker* in 1997. That was the same year the religious right declared a fatwa on Disney because Ellen DeGeneres came out of the closet in her ABC prime-time sitcom. In the eight years it took *Brokeback Mountain* to overcome Hollywood's shilly-shallying and at last be made, the Disney boycott collapsed and Ms. DeGeneres's star rose. . . . No one has forgotten she's a lesbian. No one cares.[14]

Rich also notes that most conservative groups made a conscious decision not to protest the movie, but to ignore it rather than drawing more attention to it through a culture war. Nevertheless, in the years since *Brokeback Mountain* was released, the topic has become a subject of increasingly polarized debate in America—the film is thus notable as a cultural milestone in the continuing debate in American politics over the acceptance of homosexuality in mainstream American culture.

Language in Brokeback Mountain

This story is put together using the true-to-life language and idioms of less-educated farmhands who, because of the restrictions of the times and their lack of education, have no words to express their feelings. What is most painful is the characters' inability to deal with, or even to define, their relationship. They know what they feel, but societal norms, their upbringing, and all they have experienced thus far in life has taught them that "this thing" cannot exist. They are both high-school dropouts and come from broken homes and they simply do not have the frame of reference to acknowledge what is going on. Instead they are rough-mannered and rough-spoken, describing their feelings in unadorned language, without romantic cliches—when Jack writes asking to see Ennis, he responds with two words, "You bet." At the end of the story, Ennis expresses the devotion he has kept pent up for his entire life in the whispered line to his dead lover, "Jack, I swear . . . "[15] Because of their stoic characters, the story has much to do with what is unspoken, with the shame and guilt that fills them. In this way, the story is similar to Lee's *The Ice Storm*, which also had very little direct communication—most of the emotions were repressed. In fact, the whole language of *Brokeback Mountain* lies in circuitous words, and dialogue that creates an artful and poetic, though simple and roughhewn, code. Jack and Ennis are men of few words, and the two never mention their feelings, nor do they utter words such as "sex," "love," or "relationship." Instead, they constantly refer to their relationship as "this thing." On the other hand, through their actions and body language it is impossible to be mistaken about their true feelings.

> "That summer," said Ennis. "When we split up after we got paid out I had gut cramps so bad I pulled over and tried to puke, thought I ate somethin' bad at that place in Dubois. Took me about a year a figure out it was that I shouldn't a let you out a my sights. Too late then by a long, long while."[16]

In the quotation above, which is one of the longest speeches made by Ennis in the course of the narrative, Ennis uses a visceral and earthy illustration (vomiting) to articulate his discovery of his deep affection for Jack. He also employs a hunting metaphor, "I shouldn't a let you out a my sights," which ties together the two men's common background of hunting while herding in the mountains. In response, Jack is equally unable to name or define their mutual affection; instead he calls their relationship a "situation." Other examples include the following:

> "You know, friend, this is a goddamn bitch of a unsatisfactory situation. You used a come away easy. It's like seein' the pope now."[17]

A conversation between Ennis and Jack's ex-wife Lureen demonstrates the truncated and emotionless communication style, as the two discuss Jack's death and burial:

> The little Texas voice came slip-sliding down the wire. "We put a stone up. He use to say he wanted to be cremated, ashes scattered on Brokeback Mountain. I didn't know where that was. So he was cremated, like he wanted, and like I say, half his ashes was interred here, and the rest I sent up to his folks. I thought Brokeback Mountain was around where he grew up. But knowing Jack, it might be some pretend place where the bluebirds sing and there's a whiskey spring."
>
> "We herded sheep on Brokeback one summer," said Ennis. He could hardly speak.[18]

The spare language used by Proulx beautifully captures the rhythm of the western setting, like poetry offering respite from bleakness, as in the paragraph in which she describes the places Ennis and Jack worked over the years. In this paragraph, the names of mountain ranges provide a bleak, rhythmic litany, beautiful and heartbreaking. Again, it is the sound of names like "Medicine Bow" and "Owl Creek" that conjure up poetry in an otherwise featureless expanse, names full of vivid life in a place that provided little respite from dullness:

> Years on years they worked their way through the high meadows and mountain drainages, horse-packing into the Big Horns, Medicine Bows, south end of the Gallatins, Absarokas, Granites, Owl Creeks, the Bridger-Teton Range, the Freezeouts and the Shirleys, Ferrises and the Rattlesnakes, Salt River Range, into the Wind Rivers over and again, the Sierra Madres, Gros Ventres, the Washakies, Laramies, but never returning to Brokeback.[19]

This narrative detail is echoed by Ang Lee cinematically. The beauty and purity of the emotions is matched by the rustic majesty of the landscape; in reducing the story to a universe of simplicity of scenery and emotion, Lee was trying to create a new depth for a love story. His filming of the scenery is so meticulous and studied, and so attentive to detail, that it seems to approach nature with scientific accuracy and rediscover it through close observation. In addition, the film brings out the innate properties of the natural world on such a visceral level that a viewer can practically smell the air. This reflects Proulx's narrative: "Jack, the same eagle feather in his old hat, lifting his head in the heated noon to take the air scented with resinous lodgepole, the dry needle duff and hot rock, bitter juniper crushed beneath the horses' hooves."[20]

Ennis does not want to accept his homosexual urges and continues throughout the story to lie to himself, to protect himself from reality. This is demonstrated by the last line in the story: "There was some open space between what he knew and what he tried to believe, but nothing could be done about it, and if you can't fix it you've got to stand it."[21] This "space" between what Ennis knows and what he tries to believe is the interesting space with which Lee is so familiar and so skillfully presents in his films. The depth of the tragedy seems wrought here; that Ennis can never run away to make a life with Jack (even though Jack does propose this early on), because he is never fully willing to admit that he is gay. Lee has compared the self-denial, guilt, and twisted psychology of Ennis to the Hulk. The character of Ennis, like Hulk, has an irresolvable tension, a tragic flaw, which carries bottomless grief and a sense of anguish and loss. "You know, I was sittin up here all that time tryin' to figure out if I was—? I know I ain't. I mean here we both got wives and kids, right?"[22]

Jack, however, is the more courageous one who comes to accept the romance:

What Jack remembered and craved in a way he could neither help nor understand was the time that distant summer on Brokeback when Ennis had come up behind him and pulled him close, the silent embrace satisfying some shared and sexless hunger.

They had stood that way for a long time in front of the fire, its burning tossing ruddy chunks of light, the shadow of their bodies a single column against the rock. The minutes ticked by from the round watch in Ennis's pocket, from the sticks in the fire settling into coals. Stars bit through the wavy heat layers above the fire. Ennis's breath came slow and quiet, he hummed, rocked a little in the sparklight and Jack leaned against the steady heartbeat, the vibrations of the humming like faint electricity and, standing, he fell into sleep that was not sleep but something else drowsy and tranced until Ennis, dredging up a rusty but still useable phrase from the childhood time before his mother died, said, "Time to hit the hay, cowboy. I got a go. Come on, you're sleepin' on your feet like a horse," and gave Jack a shake, a push, and went off in the darkness. Jack heard his spurs tremble as he mounted, the words "see you tomorrow," and the horse's shuddering snort, grind of hoof on stone.

Later, that dozy embrace solidified in his memory as the single moment of artless, charmed happiness in their separate and difficult lives. Nothing marred it, even the knowledge that Ennis would not then embrace him face to face because he did not want to see nor feel that it was Jack he held. And maybe, he thought, they'd never got much farther than that. Let be, let be.[23]

In a 2005 interview with Carlo Cavagna, Ang Lee discussed the difficulty of bringing Annie Proulx's spare prose to film:

Not only did I want to be loyal to [Proulx's] writing, but I needed to do additional scenes to confirm her writing, because we don't have the internal depictions which she did most brilliantly. We don't have that benefit; we are photography. So, that tent scene for example—I needed to add another tent scene, to confirm that they commit to the love, so it's reasonable for the next twenty years they want to keep going back. I don't even know if she liked it. I always had this theory that she would hate it. I think in movies, in cinema language, you have to see them committed. In a book, it's in the writing and you don't [have to] see it. She's very good in terms of [being] hands-off. Once you make the movie, it's your work. I told her, "Your prose is very hard to translate into cinema." She just smiled and said, "That's your problem."[24]

It comes as no surprise that Ang Lee is willing to characterize a story of two cowboys falling in love as "the great American love story."[25] This is because Lee's previous work on *The Wedding Banquet* already presented a sympathetic and stereotype-free vision of a gay relationship. Viewers of *The Wedding Banquet* have been treated once before to Lee's tender portraits of gay men in love. Lee is also familiar with the difficulties of this topic since he had to wait six years for help from Taiwan to produce his first gay feature. In addition, he had to cast an unknown actor in the lead role of *The Wedding Banquet* because no established Asian actor was willing to play a gay male lead. As previously noted, Winston Chao was a former flight attendant who had never before acted in a film. Ang Lee selected him from photographs and flew him to the United States to read for the part. In making the film, Lee was able to direct Chao so that the fact he had never before appeared in a film was imperceptible. However, Chao was unable to realistically portray his physical engagement with the other male lead in *The Wedding Banquet*, to the point that his face is turned away from the camera in a scene of a kiss.

As discussed earlier, *The Ice Storm* deals similarly with sexual detachment and alienation within the family, this time in 1970s suburbia. Like *Brokeback Mountain*, *The Ice Storm* is a masterpiece of silence. The screenplay reflects how the characters do not listen to each other; instead they talk at each other without resolution. This technique, the use of silence, is similarly employed in *Brokeback Mountain*. Here, however, the dialogue is never superfluous; every spoken word is loaded with significance. The silence, the imagery of the Wyoming landscape, and the sparse musical score all work together to convey the unfathomable loneliness of these two men. However, although much of the movie is austere and quiet, like *The Ice Storm*, it is full of emotional tension. One example of how this silence provides for the pure cinematic experience of visual storytelling is the quiet scene where Jack, having experienced a rebuff from Ennis, drives across the border from Texas to Mexico, ending up in a dead-end border town. In a daze of quiet despair, he leaves the bustle of an outdoor market and enters a wide alleyway where on one side there is a row of men. One of the men steps away from the wall, approaches Jack, and softly addresses him: "Señor?"[26] Jack says nothing, but with a short nod gives his consent and the two men walk down the alley past the other men. The end of the alley is illuminated by a single source of light glaring down, with only a void-like darkness ahead. Jack Twist and his new acquaintance pass through this illuminated area and walk onwards into the darkness—they are virtually swallowed up by the blackness of the night. With its spare dialogue and limited cuts, this scene is pictorially told, relying almost exclusively on images. The use of Mexico in the side story also brings an undercurrent of foreignness and cultural difference adding to the mystique of this encounter. This is also significant in the original short story, for Mexico becomes the point of contention between Ennis and Jack in their most volatile argument toward the end of the story, and in the film: "Count the damn few times we been together in twenty years . . . then ask me about Mexico and then tell me you'll kill me for needin' it and not hardly never gettin' it."[27]

Lee has stated: "People say I bend or twist genres. I think I'm twisted. It's a tricky thing for foreigners. You're not molded to cultural convention. You can do it as authentic as you want. That's the advantage of the outsider."[28] In preparation for the filming of *Brokeback Mountain*, Lee steeped himself in the iconography of the American West. He gained a familiarity with and a deep respect for western film heroes (Gene Autry, John Wayne, and more recently, Clint Eastwood), the photography of Richard Avedon, and the westerns based on McMurtry's books (*Hud* [1963] and *The Last Picture Show* [1971]). He realized it was challenging the "sanctified" image of the ultra-masculine western man, yet as an outsider he felt the freedom to make an honest film about a taboo subject considered the "last frontier." Some of the scenes in *Brokeback Mountain* have the visual depth and panoramic imagery of westerns by John Ford and Raoul Walsh. Even the smaller, more intimate scenes set in apartments and houses loom large—despite cramped space, the depth of narrative is astonishing.

Brokeback Mountain is about longing for lost love, for lost opportunity, and a bittersweet yearning for that impossible, unfinished love the two men shared. Ennis blames his lover, for he could never move on with his life and failed in his marriage, while Jack blames himself for never quitting this love. Moments between the two men, comprised of nothing more than subtle glances, brief facial expressions, and the slightest of body language, discharge their energy so intensely that a hint of truth is suddenly illuminated. Lee was especially pleased by the depth of emotion revealed in the performances by his two main actors. He said: "There's a private feeling to the movie, an intimate feeling . . . I think eventually everybody has a *Brokeback Mountain* in them. Someone you want to come back to. And of course, some people don't come back."[29] In whatever medium, short story or film, *Brokeback Mountain* tells a powerful and visceral love story. The story's power lies in its breaking of stereotypes, in that the men's affection for each other defies classification and categorization. The narrative involves family, children, prejudice, and anger, but it also deals quintessentially with the truth and mystery of a love relationship. The story is reduced to elemental experiences of the natural world, and human love.

TWELVE

Eroticism and Performance in Lust/Caution

ANG LEE'S *Lust/Caution* is a powerful meditation on the topic of obsession and sexual desire played out against the epic backdrop of the Japanese occupation of Shanghai in World War II. The multilayered narrative of *Lust/Caution* offers a penetrating glimpse into the interplay between fantasy/performance and reality/truth. While the female protagonist Wang Chia-chih appears on the surface to be aiding the Chinese war effort in seducing the traitorous Mr. Yee, the intensity of their erotic bond causes her to lose hold of the original plan of the student conspirators, leading to an unexpected betrayal. The question, "Why did she do it?" is discussed at length in the introduction to the *Lust/Caution* screenplay by the film's coscreenwriter James Schamus, who writes that "only behind the mask of the character Mai Tai-tai can Chia-chih truly desire"[1]—in other words, Wang Chia-chih can discover her true desire only through performance. Schamus also elaborates on Mr. Yee's complicated psychology: "Yee doesn't simply desire Mai Tai-tai while suspecting she is not who she says she is; it is precisely *because* he suspects her that he desires her"[2]—implying that Mr. Yee's desire springs from mystery and intrigue, a transgression of trust. In other words, fear itself imbues the transgression with great value; the narrative of *Lust/Caution* bears out in great detail how the experience of fear gives value to the transgressive act. The actions of Mr. Yee and Wang Chia-chih display the uncontrollable force of their obsessive desire which leads them both into danger, and provides a commentary on the interplay between social restrictions and taboos and the inability to control obsession.

Lee's Chinese historical drama *Lust/Caution* is the first film he chose to direct after winning the Academy Award for *Brokeback Mountain* in 2006, and his first Chinese film since directing *Crouching Tiger, Hidden Dragon* seven years earlier. Having his status as world-class director secured by his Academy Award win, it is noteworthy that Lee would choose, for his next project, to return to a Chinese-themed film. Perhaps predictably, outside of Asia, worldwide critical response to Lee's China-related topic was less than enthusiastic; the film's NC-17 rating almost certainly reduced its accessibility, but despite the film's early win of the Golden Lion, the top prize of the Venice International Film Festival, critical response to this World War II–era espionage film was only lukewarm.³ This may be because the film is a complicated and politically charged treatment of early twentieth-century Chinese history and culture. The film also presupposes a fairly advanced understanding of the conflicts and divided loyalties within China during World War II; notably, the film lacks any explanatory text in the opening frames that is a common feature of historical dramas.⁴ While being centered on a historically Chinese topic, the film also references the pervasive influence of globalization on traditional Chinese culture.

The film depicts a tale of espionage involving a young student, Wang Chia-chih (Tang Wei), who goes undercover to entrap a married man, known only as Mr. Yee (Tony Leung), who is collaborating with the Japanese in occupied Shanghai during the Second World War. In trying to snare the wealthy and powerful Mr. Yee, Wang Chia-chih takes on the identity of the married Mai Tai-tai, entering into a world of luxury and conspicuous consumption dominated by the powerful Mrs. Yee (Joan Chen). In the Yee family circle, Wang Chia-chih must adapt to playing the role of an elite and sophisticated woman who knows the finer points of wealth and status in upper-class Chinese society—ironically, this requires her to be fluent in English and familiar with the styles and tastes of the Western world. The Westernized elements incorporated into haute Chinese culture serve to both highlight the intense danger of Wang Chia-chih's ruse and give her a sense of otherness or distance from her own identity. This globalized identity drives the movie deeper into psychological intricacies as Wang struggles to keep her mask from slipping when she begins to fall in love with Mr. Yee. The final events in the film take place on a ring-shopping trip in a jewelry store run by an Indian shop owner, when after Mr. Yee has presented Wang Chia-chih with a large diamond ring as a gift (symbolizing a commitment), Wang is unable to hide her emotions any longer and tips off Mr. Yee to the subterfuge, allowing him to escape.

In attempting to grasp the complexities of the character of Wang Chia-chih, her experience of obsessive desire in the film can be read in juxtaposition with Georges Bataille's theories of taboo and transgression. Bataille posits that the pursuit of a forbidden action is increased by the presence of social taboos; while taboos help to create an orderly society, they also open up the possibility of transgression. Bataille sees the act of erotic fusion as similar to religious sacrifice, in which the subject seeks to be "loosed from its relatedness to the I"—in other words, the subject experiences a discontinuity with that which is subjective and rational. Bataille sees this as a way to reach a lost "continuity of Being," a primordial force that could close the gap between the world of disciplined rationality and the outlawed "other of reason." This may explain why Wang Chia-chih can find her true self only through performance: in the elite social circle she finds herself in, dominated by Mrs. Yee, everything around her is pretense, obfuscating the truth. However, through Wang Chia-chih's performance of her role as Mai Tai-tai, submitting to transgressive sexual acts with a Japanese collaborator—only through this performance is she able to arrive at the truth. In exercising her sexual power and the force of her acting, she finds her true self. Ultimately, however, in trying to be two people at once, Wang Chia-chih's duplicity causes her acute psychological strain, to the point where she loses hold of reality (or the certainty of which reality is "real" to her). Faced with the overwhelming inner contradiction between truth and performance, Wang Chia-chih must subvert one role, casting off her original selfhood, and leaping into the "other of reason" as Mai Tai-tai. This is one explanation for the startling decision that she ultimately makes in the film and story.

Bataille—Eroticism and the Allure of Transgression

The relationship between Wang Chia-chih and Mr. Yee in *Lust/Caution* neatly expresses this interplay between taboo and transgression; reading *Lust/Caution* through Bataille's theories on taboo and transgression helps to articulate this symbiotic relationship. Bataille described transgression in terms of Cold War history and grounded his theories in historical concerns in a way quite applicable to the wartime political psychology of the Japanese occupation. The complex international politics of the Cold War between the United States' Central Intelligence Agency and the vast espionage network of Russia shares similarities with Chinese and Japanese political history, in that the transgressive individual became equated with the enemy. This enemy status of the transgressor created intense intrigue as well as highly-charged emotion due to its threat to the national security of the beleaguered nation. In addition, in Bataille's works, transgression is a desire created by the taboo itself: "the object of the prohibition was first marked out for coveting by the prohibition itself: If the prohibition was essentially of a sexual nature it must have drawn attention to the sexual value of the object (or rather, its erotic value)."[5]

Bataille's statement elucidates how the prohibition itself gives value to the transgressive behavior. For Bataille, it is fear itself that imbues the transgression with great value: "The forbidden action takes on a significance it lacks before fear widens the gap between us and it and invests it with an aura of excitement."[6] The idea of fear giving value to the transgressive act is demonstrated clearly by the relationship between Wang Chia-chih and Mr. Yee; *Lust/Caution* demonstrates how erotic excitement can be generated by fear. In addition, Bataille's notion of the sacred and the profane also complements his ideas on taboo and transgression. In Bataille's description, the profane world is constituted by work and reason, the world of taboos. However, in the sacred world, according to the author, the human seeks a lost unity, a continuity found only in death. Bataille theorizes that this totality that one finds in the sacred, which is unachievable and remains out of reach, can be sought "only at the price of great sacrifice."[7] Thus, Wang Chia-chih gives her life as a sacrifice for this lost unity that must by its very definition remain out of reach.

For Bataille: "The final aim of eroticism is fusion, all barriers gone."[8] The transgressive value of eroticism helps to displace the experience of subjectivity and achieve unity with the sacred world. This unity with the sacred, as in religious sacrifice, would result in the obliteration of the personality, an obliteration connected with death. Bataille reiterates: "If the union of two lovers comes about through love, it involves the idea of death. . . . This aura of death is what denotes passion."[9] Bataille further explores eroticism's connection to expenditure/sacrifice, indicating that the drive toward transgressive eroticism requires a great expenditure of energy as well as a risk of death. He writes: "Erotic activity can be disgusting: it can also be noble, ethereal, excluding sexual content, but it illustrates a principle of human behavior in the clearest way: what we want is what uses up our strength and our resources, and, if necessary, places our lives in danger."[10]

In connection with Batille's theory on transgression, one of the taboos dealt with in *Lust/Caution* is premarital sexuality/loss of virginity: for the sexually conservative China of the 1930s–1940s, the activity of premarital sex being prohibited and taboo thus imbues it with an aura of excitement, danger, and fear. Premarital sex is considered wrong; consequently, only one of the student conspirators is not a virgin. This lack of sexual experience leads to the awkward scene in the film in which Wang Chia-chih must be taught to perform sexually by Liang Jun-sheng (Ko Yu-luen), whose only sexual experiences have come from visiting prostitutes. Wang offers up her body—her virginity—as a "sacrifice" to the cause. However, the virginity of the young male and female students causes them to treat Wang Chia-chih differently after she has shared her body with Liang Jun-sheng; they distance themselves from her and no one dares to speak with her. Wang Chia-chih is tainted because of her taboo behavior; she has lost her virginity, her innocence, and the wholeness of her identity.

Even more significant is the connection between the taboo of the illicit sexual relationship combined with the espionage effort. Wang states how she will finish the sexual act and end up with Yee's "blood and brains" covering her. This can be juxtaposed with Bataille's notion of love as "sacrifice," a quasi-spiritual notion. Does Wang feel that she will be redeemed by Yee's death and her act of patriotism? The image of his blood covering her body seems to evoke a religious sacrifice—this can be juxtaposed with the idea of her being "cleansed" by being with Mr. Yee in a way that evokes Bataille's notion of sacrifice and death. She says to the cell group leader Old Wu (Tou Chung-hua):

> That's why I torture him until he can't take it any longer, and I will keep going until I can't go anymore. . . . Every time when he finally collapses on me, I think, maybe this is it, maybe this is the moment you'll come, and shoot him, right in the back of the head, and his blood and brains will cover me.[11]

Also evoking Bataille's notion of eroticism and death, in the screenplay both the character of Mr. Yee and the character of Wang Chia-chih share the implication that they are already dead. Mr. Yee knows he is already a dead man, living the monstrous, alienated existence of the betrayer who can trust no one. When the war ends, Mr. Yee has no future—he cannot be accepted by the Japanese (with whom he is siding) nor by the Chinese (who will punish him for his betrayal). He is already a non-person, with no country and no lasting allegiance. Likewise, Wang Chia-chih is dead. This is alluded to when Wang Chia-chih's life is given little value by the group leader, Old Wu, who burns her final letter to her father to destroy proof of her existence. This action demonstrates that Old Wu expects Wang Chia-chih to die, and his burning of her letter seems to already signify this coming extinguishment—in his eyes, she is already dead. He also speaks offhandedly of two female spies who died in the mission before her—in the business of war, Old Wu views the female spies as a necessary sacrifice to the cause.

When she first takes on the spy mission, Wang Chia-chih naively believes she can emotionally bear the strain of living a double life. However, as the playacting becomes more serious, she sacrifices more and more of her personhood, her self-hood. This becomes apparent as Wang Chia-chih begins to adapt the mannerisms and tastes of Mai Tai-tai—for example, choosing to have a cigarette after a long day, and no longer enjoying the carefree identity of a young student, as her friends still do in the scene where they try out the latest fashionable dance steps. As she becomes more and more comfortable in the "dress-up" clothing of Mai Tai-tai, Wang Chia-chih is slowly subsumed by the character she is playing, becoming more mature, graceful, and elegant in her bearing. The "death" of Wang the student innocent is revealed most clearly after her young friends commit murder and she runs off into the night, disappearing into blackness, without uttering a single word to anyone. When next she appears onscreen, her face is pale, drained of life and emotion: she is a living cadaver.

Throughout the story, Chang's fiction reflects Bataille's connection between love and sacrifice, between sex and death. There are textual references to this idea of sacrifice: "she had already determined to make a sacrifice of herself,"[12] and "In truth, every time she was with Yee she felt cleansed, as if by a scalding hot bath . . . "[13] In addition, the idea of taboo and transgression is reflected in Chang's writing by the reaction of Wang Chia-chih's friends as the scheme collapses and the Yee family returns to Shanghai. She feels alienated from her former group of friends, no longer accepted by the orthodoxy, the status quo: "All the time she was with them, she felt they were eyeing her curiously—as if she were some kind of freak, or grotesque."[14]

Even more markedly, it is Ang Lee's unflinchingly graphic sex scenes between Wang Chia-chih and Mr. Yee that bear out Bataille's notion of erotic fusion and the connection between eroticism and death. Although these controversial scenes earned the film an NC-17 rating and thus made it less commercially marketable, and although Eileen Chang's original short story made only oblique references to the sexual intercourse between the two characters, Lee and producer James Schamus continued to defend the scenes as pivotal to explain the complexity of the relationship between Mr. Yee and Wang Chia-chih (Lee has stated that he made the sexual choreography up in his own head, choreographed as carefully as he did the fight scenes in *Crouching Tiger, Hidden Dragon*). Altogether there are three sex scenes in *Lust/Caution*, amounting to approximately ten minutes in total, which occur comparatively late in the film's 157-minute running time. In each scene, the explicit sex metaphorically represents a different stage in the relationship between Mr. Yee and Wang Chia-chih, a growing intimacy between the two characters demonstrating Mr. Yee's gradual acceptance of Wang and the tenuous bond of "trust" between them.

The first sex scene reveals the sadomasochism and violence of Mr. Yee which are crucial in illustrating his character: it is one of dominance and, strangely, vulnerability due to the bitter times that he lives in. He has to create pain in her in order to "feel alive"—and Wang Chia-chih intuitively understands this. His lack of trust, due to the harsh reality of his traitorous political identity as a Japanese collaborator, leads him to suppress his emotions and to place his trust in no one. Thus, in the first sex scene, Mr. Yee expresses his distrust by keeping Wang's face turned away from him, not allowing her to face him. The sex in the first scene is like a rape, violent and carnal; he tears her clothes and treats her brutally, as a pimp would treat a prostitute. Yet the end of the scene show's Wang's eroticization of this dominance as she smiles to herself nearly imperceptibly, feeling herself drawn to the man who just used her. In the second sex scene, the tables have begun to turn: with Wang Chia-chih's threat to leave, Mr. Yee is in a weaker position. His change of attitude is reflected by more revealing of his physical body, as if he has begun to let his guard down. At the same time, Wang is able to use her sexuality to powerfully attract him and gain more control over him. Wang's growing confidence is apparent in this scene; nevertheless there is still an underlying tension.

Finally, the third scene is the most crucial in revealing the changing nature of their relationship: in this scene, the suspicion of both characters is revealed. With the close proximity of Mr. Yee's gun near the bed, Wang has an opportunity to shoot Mr. Yee. However, even with the conditions ideal for her mission, she chooses not to shoot him, but instead continues with their lovemaking. At that moment, she has finally gained Mr. Yee's total trust. His vulnerability to her is subsequently revealed when he allows her to cover his eyes with a pillow although he had previously confessed to a fear of the dark. In addition, in this third scene, there is a palpable tenderness completely unlike the violence of the previous two scenes. Finally, Mr. Yee is no longer dominant; instead it is Wang who remains on top throughout most of the scene, a visual metaphor for her taking the lead and gaining the advantage in their relationship. This scene is anchored most fully in emotion, exposing the deep bond between the characters, and demonstrating that the boundaries between "occupier" and "occupied" have become blurred.

While these three scenes have been a focus of much debate and have been criticized for being borderline pornographic, the inclusion of such explicit sex scenes in the film was a decision made to bring more clarity to the narrative—telling the story and revealing the characters' inner psychology through the display of their physical actions. Because the word "lust" is used in the film's title,[15] it is unsurprising that Lee as a director felt that the graphic display of lust was necessary for the film, and although these scenes may be difficult for some viewers to watch, they viscerally express the urgency and violence that necessarily accompany the notion of lust.

Eileen Chang and the Original Story of "Lust, Caution"

"Lust, Caution" is a relatively short piece among Chang's works, and it is considered unusual in her oeuvre due to its controversial subject matter and unconventional narrative technique. Chang ostensibly based her narrative on the true story of Zheng Pingru (1918–1940), a 22-year-old female spy who failed in the assassination attempt of Wang Jingwei's security chief, Ding Mocun (1903–1947) and was later executed. Chang was apparently captivated by this subject matter and started writing the story while living in Hong Kong in the 1950s; a surviving manuscript from the period shows that the story was originally written in English and entitled "The Spy-ring." However, Chang obsessively revised the story for a period of more than twenty years before it was finally published in Taiwan in 1977 in Chinese as "Se, Jie" ("Lust, Caution"). The famed author's obsession with the story is noteworthy because the emotions in the story seem to be at least partly autobiographical. For example, both Chang and her protagonist Wang Chia-chih were students in Hong Kong when the city fell to the Japanese in 1942, both made their way to Shanghai, and, most noto-riously, both fell in love with pro-Japanese collaborators—members of the Wang Jingwei government controlled by the Japanese. Eileen Chang's first husband was Hu Lancheng, who was still married to his third wife when they met in 1943. In 1945, a year after the two were married, the Japanese surrendered and Hu was forced to go into hiding in a nearby city. Throughout this tense period, Chang remained loyal to Hu and supported him financially, but she later discovered his continuing infidelities and the two parted bitterly. She finally divorced him in 1947.

Chang's writing is known for its psychological intricacy. The short story is written in the third person, with lengthy sections of dialogue. However, with the complex-ity of William Faulkner, to whom Chang is sometimes compared, the narrator will at times suddenly voice the inner thoughts of the characters, often without first identifying to which character the thoughts belong, through a style that mixes inte-rior monologues with third-person narration that is a triumph of fictive modern-ism. Chang also masterfully transitions from general explanations of plot and vague, slightly disorienting flashbacks, to vivid dialogues and meticulously-recorded details from Wang Chia-chih's present-day experiences. (Similarly, the film has a highly complex timeline of flashbacks, which make it seem like many years have passed—and yet the main events of the film all happen over the course of a single after-noon.) The sensitivity and technical skill with which Chang re-creates the variance of human temporal memory—distant memories are more hazy, while recent ones are vivid with adjectival detail—can be understood as a commentary upon the unreli-ability of human memory and the subjectivity of historical judgment. Another dis-tinctive aspect of Chang's style is her ability to contrast the banality and minutiae of the upper-class bourgeois world with the calculated brutality of wartime Shanghai. The triviality of the conversation among the wealthy *tai-tais*, whose long exchanges serve as bookends opening and closing the narrative, is contrasted with the life-and-death undercurrents of the main story.

The psychological complexity of "Lust, Caution" also includes a father/daughter conflict, in that Wang Chia-chih's father's abandonment of her is also a driving force behind her warped search for love. This emphasis on the father/daughter conflict is given a very detailed backstory in the film, much more so than in Chang's original story; this is in keeping with Lee's particular fascination with the generation gap, and the relationship between parent and child, a frequent topic explored in his films, especially in *Pushing Hands* and *Eat Drink Man Woman*. In *Lust/Caution*, screen-writers Wang Huiling and James Schamus have fleshed out details regarding Wang's father's divorce, his remarriage in England, and his refusal to send for his daughter to join him in his new family. Thus, in Lee's film, Wang Chia-chih is completely rejected by her father in ways that shatter her and complicate her identity; this is not unlike the struggles of Bruce Banner and Ennis Del Mar as two further examples of negative paternal influence. Similarly, this reflects Eileen Chang's own background, coming as she did from an unhappy childhood in a wealthy but highly dysfunctional family in which her much-absent father sided with her stepmother against her and, in a well-known incident from her teen years, locked her up and savagely beat her. Chang's own marriages, first to Hu Lancheng, when she was 24 and he was 37, and later to Ferdinand Reyer, an American screenwriter thirty years her senior, suggest a hunger for paternal love that is reflected in the relationship between Wang Chia-chih and Mr. Yee.

Chinese High Society, Western Cultural Influences, and Performance/Truth

The short story "Lust, Caution" begins at the mahjong table, with a description of the hot lamps blazing down on the white table-cloth and the clicking of tiles. The opening lines of Chang's story draw attention to these details:

> Though it was still daylight, the hot lamp was shining full-beam over the mahjong table. Diamond rings flashed under its glare as their wearers clacked and reshuffled their tiles.[16]

Lee begins the film with this same image: the film opens with complicated and multiangled filming of a scene of mahjong, technically very exacting and involving, using four cameras. Through this scene, the viewer is plunged into a world with signifiers of high-society China, manners, taste, and wealth, with ladies making small talk around a mahjong table—nothing is spelled out clearly. The clothing of the participants sitting around the mahjong table is highlighted in Chang's description—this echoes Chang's characteristic emphasis on ornament and high-society elegance, the fashions dominant in Shanghai in the 1940's "Golden Age." Chang also focuses her attention on the detailed and ornate patterns in tasteful, upper-class furnishings. These period details add a great authenticity to Chang's descriptions as well as providing a rich collection of visual details for Lee to accentuate in the film. At the same time, these signifiers highlight the artifice of high-society Shanghai because they are props in an elite social drama.

The mahjong itself is only one of the "games" being played: the mahjong scene sets the tone as an artifice, as the *tai-tais* at the mahjong table are competing, not only at the game of tiles on the table, but in their dress and jewelry, financial background, and social status. They each want to show off their wealth and status to prove that they are in a superior position to anyone else at the table. This opening scene reveals the entire plot of Eileen Chang's narrative in a microcosm—everyone at the table has secrets, and no one can trust anyone else in the room. Their relationships are based on intricate connections of business and social obligation, so they cannot speak of real feelings. Instead, they must communicate in a sort of double-talk, jockeying for position though light-hearted chatter that uses cloaked humor to hide more nefarious purposes. They discuss whose turn it is to treat the group to dinner, in which restaurant they plan to dine, and the prices of high-society articles in the inflationary economy of Shanghai. The scene encapsulates Wang Chia-chih's alienation from the high-class, fashionable world she has entered. For example, Wang Chiah-chih is ashamed of her simple ring, which does not compare to the glittering display of wealth on the fingers of the other players in the mahjong game: "She should have left her jadeite ring back in its box, she realized; to spare herself all those sneering glances."[17] The important elements of the scene, such as the outfits and accessories worn by the wealthy *tai-tais*, point out their social class, and Wang Chia-chih's lack of a diamond ring makes her stand out as an outsider, unable to fully assimilate.

This upper-class world of posturing and deceit is skillfully evoked by Eileen Chang's fictive description in this first scene. Chang's writing is known for its focus on the clothing, accoutrements, the furnishings and curtains, the ornaments and decorations, the lighting and the subtle sensitivity to detail which her highly-attuned sense of fashion and taste could give her, as a member of the wealthy class in Shanghai of the period. She adds minute details through short sentences, and tends to use words to describe sizes, shapes, colors, and patterns—the throwaway details that only someone of her wealthy background and privileged social class could have observed so keenly. At the same time, careful dissection of these visual metaphors shows that Chang ironizes their vulgarity with abject disdain. She talks about the women's clothing as if they were wearing uniforms, or costumes. A great deal of care is taken in describing the outfit worn by Wang Chia-chih with its "shallow, rounded collar standing only half an inch tall, in the Western style."[18] Chang also records "her makeup was understated, except for the glossily rouged arcs of her lips."[19] Special focus is also given to the drapes, which were cut in broad swaths to match the intricate pattern, which, Chang notes deliberately, allowed for "extra wastage," exhibiting the ostentatious display of wealth in the Yee household:

> The wall behind him was swathed in heavy yellowish-brown wool curtains printed with a brick-red phoenix-tail fern design, each blade almost six feet long. . . . False french windows, and enormous drapes to cover them, were all the rage just then. Because of the war, fabrics were in short supply; floor-length curtains such as those hanging behind Mr. Yee—using up an entire bolt of cloth, with extra wastage from pattern matching—were a conspicuous extravagance.[20]

The passage further notes that the Yee family had this particular pattern for their curtains because a prominent official in the Wang Jingwei government had a pair—thus the Yees were obligated to follow suit in extravagant decorating. This "wastage" during wartime was a luxury unimaginable to more than the select few who enjoyed this privileged status.

In the film, Lee puts particular emphasis on the dichotomy and disconnection that Wang Chia-chih feels as she takes on the identity of the married Mai Tai-tai, entering into a cosmopolitan world of luxury and conspicuous consumption that is outside of her usual character and experience. In the elite cosmopolitan atmosphere of 1940s Shanghai, the connotation of status involves a complex interplay between the traditional and the modern, as well as the Chinese and Western. The six languages used in the film—Mandarin, Japanese, English, Hindi, Shanghainese, and Cantonese—are an early twentieth-century example of the effect of globalization. The high-end jewelry shopkeeper and the manager of the jewelry shop are Indian and communicate with each other in Hindi, but the language of luxury in Shanghai is English—when Wang Chia-chih first enters the shop, she conducts all of her business in English. Later, when Wang Chia-chih finally receives the ring from the Indian shopkeeper, the Indian man breaks into the Chinese conversation between Wang and her lover, using English to say "Congratulations, Miss!" This English phrase—congratulations on an engagement—adds an unexpected emotional element to the scene. English is also the language used at the Keissling Café in Shanghai where Wang Chia-chih sets the trap for Mr. Yee; she uses English to address the waiter and to ask to use the phone in the restaurant. These multilingual abilities are a common trope in espionage films—a world-class spy must be fluent in several languages—moreover, the seamless shift among languages highlights Wang Chia-chih's sophistication. Many of the major street names and shop names are in English; for example, as Wang Chia-chih flees from the assassination scene, she gives the address "Ferguson Road" to the pedicab driver. This use of English gives the scenes of post-Qing Shanghai and the stylistic elegance of colonial Hong Kong an extra air of pedigree and intrigue.

Western styles of clothing, which were in vogue in Shanghai during the period, also play a significant role in the film. Western materials, especially English wool, are in demand, and men like Mr. Yee wear custom-tailored Western suits. But by far the most significant statement is made through the clothing of Wang Chia-chih. In earlier scenes in Hong Kong where Wang attends class as a student, she wears a simple, unadorned blue *qipao* worn by all the female students, and dressed like this, with no makeup, she appears young and innocent. However, later, in the scenes at the Keissling Café, waiting to entrap Mr. Yee, she wears the garb of a classic spy with her trench coat, red-rouged lips, and a black hat tipped down over her eyes. This clothing is an archetypal signifier for a classic Western spy—while telling a shorthand version of the espionage story and helping propel the narrative forward, the Western clothing demonstrates in strong visual terms that Wang Chia-chih is far removed from her original character.

Moreover, Lee takes care to demonstrate how Wang Chia-chih was significantly influenced by Western film culture, especially film noir, through references to five different Western films. First, she is shown on two separate occasions watching Western films in a movie theater; these are *Intermezzo: A Love Story* (1939), and *Penny Serenade* (1941). *Intermezzo* is the story of a love affair between a married man (Leslie Howard) and his young daughter's piano teacher (Ingrid Bergman)—the victimized seven-year-old daughter is caught between the heartbreak of the betrayed mother and her own devotion to the adulterous father. Wang Chia-chih's face is covered with tears as she watches the film. This reaction reveals Wang's own loneliness due to the abandonment by her own father, who left China for England, remarried, and began a new life in a new country, abandoning his daughter. It is notable that this Western film is a catalyst for unlocking Wang Chia-chih's deeply buried emotions concerning betrayal. In addition, posters for specific films are seen outside of the cinema: *The Thief of Bagdad* (1940), which Wang Chia-chih contemplates briefly, *Destry Rides Again* (1939), and *Suspicion* (1941), a poster seen inside a cinema Wang

In war-torn Shanghai, Wang Chia-chih (*right*) gazes at a movie poster of Hitchcock's *Suspicion* (1941) as she contemplates her own choice to seduce and murder the traitorous Mr. Yee.

visits. *Suspicion*, in which a shy young Englishwoman (Joan Fontaine) begins to suspect her new husband (Cary Grant) of trying to kill her, is replete with the film noir characteristics of shadowy darkness and claustrophobic intensity which echo the elemental composition of *Lust/Caution* itself.

Before Wang Chia-chih falls in love with Mr. Yee, she first falls in love with performance, as a young leading actress in a Hong Kong student theatrical troupe. Early in the film, the viewer sees Wang Chia-chih after her own first performance onstage—she is breathless, exuberant, and the euphoria carries her late into the rainy night; she can't sleep for all the excitement she feels. This theatrical bearing is what first attracts Wang to performance: she enjoys the power she feels over her audience. A day later she is drawn back to the stage on which she had performed so successfully, and she wanders, musing among the false trees of the fictional scene until Kuang Yumin (Wang Leehom) and his friends call her from the audience seats in the balcony to join their meeting. Metaphorically, they are calling her "back to reality," where they request her aid in an actual assassination. Kuang's lines in the film underscore the dichotomy between reality and performance when he says that it is more valuable to kill a real flesh-and-blood traitor than to wrench tears from an audience. She agrees to join the plot, naïvely and innocently, intrigued by the challenge of her new performance.

While her passion for performance is what seems to drive Wang Chia-chih, her own emotion plays a significant role. This is metaphorically suggested by the cyanide pill that Wang is instructed to take if she is ever caught. The pill appears twice in the film: the first time, when Wang defines herself as Mr. Yee's false lover (as performer, when she agrees to be a spy and is given the pill by her group leader), and the second time, just after she defines herself as Mr. Yee's real lover (after she admits to herself that she truly loves him). After the conspiracy plot is compromised, Wang Chia-chih does not take the pill as she was instructed. This refusal to commit suicide in service to her country is the metaphorical conclusion of the story: Wang becomes her true self only when she gives up playing the role of agent. She stops performing and allows herself to be true to her actual emotion. As if to confirm this, immediately following there is a flashback to the scene in Hong Kong University where Kuang Yumin first calls her off the stage. It is as if she is bidding goodbye to performance a second time, this time from the other side of the stage, from her performance of her role as agent, and back to the freedom of her own real self.

At the end of the film, after Wang Chia-chih reveals her true feelings to Mr. Yee, she is left spent and empty, and stumbles out of the jewelry store in a daze. From there, she wanders along the sidewalk, pausing briefly to gaze at the display window of an expensive department store. The mannequins in the windows are all dressed in high-society blouses, wraps, and gowns, resembling the styles of fashion icons from European haute couture. The scene underscores Wang's helplessness and loneliness, as the accoutrements of high fashion can no longer help her or offer any meaning to her life. The expressionless, phantom-like mannequins underscore the emptiness and falseness of Wang Chia-chih's position—she has been stripped of her high-class identity, and her life will soon be extinguished; however, the false status of Western fashion, with which she had carefully constructed her identity, now offers her no help or refuge.

Intriguingly, Lee has said that the actor he identified most with at the shoot was not Tony Leung as Mr. Yee (male), but Tang Wei as Wang Chia-chih (female). Asked how he selected Tang Wei to play the role, he described this unexpected symbiosis:

> She's very close in disposition to how Wang Chia-chih is described in the story—she's like one of my parents' generation, which is pretty rare these days. She didn't seem strikingly beautiful but she did the best reading and there was something about her. Most of all, she's like the female version of me—I identify with her so closely that, by pretending, I found my true self. So the theme of the story has a personal identification for me.[21]

In an article by Moira Macdonald entitled "Ang Lee and the Power of Performance," Lee also speaks about the inspiration he drew from the character of Wang Chia-chih, and how it became a motive for making *Lust/Caution*. In the article, Lee referred to the scene early in the film where Wang Chia-chih is euphoric after her first stage performance, in high spirits and breathless on a rainy night. In the interview, Lee recalled his own first performance at the Taiwan Academy of Arts, his personal account of a rainy night when he experienced the transcendence of acting on stage, of moving the audience, and how his life was changed unexpectedly and permanently by performance. He linked his own experience with that of Wang Chia-chih, saying:

> *I'm like that girl* [Wang Chia-chih], basically. *She's awakening. She feels the power.* There's something funny about acting—you become empowered . . . [I was] a repressed kid, never allowed to touch art, only academic work. I flunked the college examinations, and I went to art school to prepare for the next year. By chance, I was on stage. I realized the rest of my life. So, when I read that in the short story, I decided to do it.[22]

Lee draws a connection between himself and Wang Chia-chih, revealing that his motivation for doing the film had to do with Wang Chia-chih's moment of transformation as she fell in love with the power of performance. Lee emphasizes the awakening power of performance, and how though pretending, one may discover the truth. This is similar to Bataille's notion of seeking the primordial "continuity of Being" through the transgressive power of the breaking of taboos and the surrender of one's own subjectivity. Lee's films have often contained autobiographical elements—for example, the treatment of the loneliness and alienation in *Pushing Hands* or the father/son conflict in *The Wedding Banquet*. Similarly, there is an element of autobiography in the narrative of *Lust/Caution* regarding the power of performance for discovering truth. The encoded message is that Lee is still discovering truth through storytelling, drama, and filmmaking.

The question "Why did she do it?" is still unanswered at the end of both the film and story. Wang Chia-chih's character is trapped between performance and reality, between her commitment to her cause and her unexpected love for her victim. Cowriter James Schamus compares the unveiling of Wang Chia-chih's character to a game of mirrors: "Wang Chia-chih . . . is a woman caught up in a game of cinematic and literary mirrors, a game that has now ensnared Ang Lee as he reflects his own cinematic mirror onto [Eileen Chang's] remarkable work."[23] The confusion is caused by an actress playing a role within a film of an actress playing a role—a labyrinthine puzzle that Lee willingly takes on in *Lust/Caution*. In the process, Lee unearths complex emotions toward identity and truth, as revealed in only the most intimate moments between illicit lovers in times of extreme duress.

THIRTEEN

Memory, Narrative, and Transformation in Taking Woodstock

ANG LEE'S FILM *Taking Woodstock* deals with memory, narrative, identity, and the reproduction of history and nostalgia vis-à-vis digital saturation in the media age. While the event of the Woodstock concert has been previously experienced as a product of memory, preserved through scattered recollections of the people present and grainy film images, the event has a powerful sense of nostalgia, a key element in Lee's work. To further illustrate this nostalgic element, Lee shot the movie using an older type of film so that the film experience would not have the cutting-edge feel of digital film, but instead a slightly yellow-brown tinge associated with the films of the late 1960s/early 1970s. *Taking Woodstock* has the appeal of an inside story told from an especially intimate perspective. But beyond that, the film is a celebration of the way this event has gone into memory and of the meaning it has acquired. Lee acknowledges this—that he is filming the memory, not the reality—by borrowing cinematic techniques directly from Michael Wadleigh's *Woodstock* (1970) documentary, such as the use of split screen and the predominant position of Crosby, Stills and Nash on the soundtrack. Also to echo Wadleigh's work, at different points in the film Lee makes use of a grainy film stock to give shots a rough-edged documentary feel, and at one point he shows the *Woodstock* cameramen filming the iconic shot of young nuns flashing peace signs while walking to the concert. Referencing Wadleigh's work and the notion of shared historical memory, Lee re-creates the famous, almost indelible images of the Woodstock stage, the inclement weather which forced concertgoers to take refuge under makeshift tents and blankets, the young people bathing nude in a lake and bodysurfing in the mud. In the process, he turns something that previously may have appeared sloppy and drug-induced into something fresh and joyous. Throughout the film, Lee aims for a feeling—that piercing sense of yearning nostalgia that at times overwhelms the human heart—of moving through a golden moment and knowing it. *Taking Woodstock* tells the story of the concert's conception and execution from the perspective of Elliot Tiber, who played an arguably significant role in bringing the concert into existence (he suggested its now-mythic location), while, at the same time, struggling internally with his own personal issues of identity. This narrative, based on Tiber's eponymous book, deals with issues of public versus private, and the global reach of media versus internal discovery.

The film *Taking Woodstock* premiered on the fortieth anniversary of the epoch-defining concert in August 1969. As the saying goes, "If you remember Woodstock, you probably weren't there," referring to the prolific drug use that characterized the event and indeed much of the 1960s. This search for meaning among the disaffected youth in the 1960s is captured in Joni Mitchell's 1969 folk-rock anthem "Woodstock," written a month after the concert. The song, which begins with a single individual on his way to Woodstock who is joined by others until he finds himself at the center of a crowd of half a million, captures the simplicity of mood and spirit embraced by this generation of young people. Joni Mitchell's famous refrain, "We are stardust, we are golden,"[1] celebrates the history-making event which epitomized a young generation's ideals of free love, social harmony, nonviolence, organic food, love for nature, psychedelic drugs, and rock music. Even more important than the music itself was the identity-defining experience of the youth of America, who felt themselves as "stardust" and "golden"—this was their moment. Nearly half a million people attended the Woodstock concert on August 15–18, 1969, advertised as "An Aquarian Exposition: 3 Days of Peace and Music in White Lake," which was a culmination of 1960s hippie style and subsequently became a celebrated cultural milestone. The multiband concert, including Jefferson Airplane, The Who, Country Joe and the Fish, Janis Joplin, Richie Havens, Joan Baez, Joe Cocker, Jimi Hendrix, and two dozen more acts, was gloriously disorganized and humorously sloppy due to the venue being changed just a few weeks prior to the event. A young man named Elliot Tiber (née Eliyahu Teichberg)[2] stepped in to rescue his parents' failing hotel in upstate New York by convincing the organizers to change the venue to the dairy farm of his neighbor, Max Yasgur. This is the topic of the film, and yet the story Ang Lee tells is the true story of the sixties: a celebration of uncharted cultural waters as young people sought to break away from the restrictions of the older generation, at a time when it was still disreputable to be "different," when to be an artist (as Elliot is portrayed in the film) wasn't respectable, and when parents wanted their children to be exceptional only academically. *Taking Woodstock* is a story of nonconformity, experimentation with identity, and ultimately acceptance and love. Clearly Lee was drawn to this topic because of these themes of the search for identity, and acceptance, both prominent themes in his work.

This experimentation and rebelliousness of the sixties grew out of the rigidity and social constraints of the 1950s in America, a time of uniformity and mass production, and of maintaining the status quo. It was an era of social and sexual restriction, and of following prescribed roles in the family and in the American nation, marked by sameness and convention. This was captured in Lee's earlier film *Brokeback Mountain*, which vividly depicted the social restrictions placed on Ennis and Jack in early 1960s Wyoming. While Jack and Ennis faced the tragic consequences of their unorthodox love—Jack paid for it with his life—what was demonstrated was just how menacing the atmosphere could be, and how dangerous it was to be different, or to fall outside the social norm. During the 1960s, many young people began experimenting with breaking the mold, and finding freedom from convention. As Joni

Elliot, Tisha, Michael Lang, Max Yasgur, and Miriam Yasgur survey the sloping fields of Yasgur's farm as a possible venue for the Woodstock music festival.

Mitchell's "Woodstock" suggests, young people desperately believed that humans were to take care of the earth as Eden, to live off the land, and to be in touch with nature. This grassroots folk movement also had its origins in antiwar protests against the Vietnam War. Antiwar sentiment in the song "Wooden Ships" (used at length in the film's soundtrack) expresses the breaking down of cultural barriers between warring sides—the hippie battle cry of the period sums this up with the catchphrase: "Make Love, Not War." This same sentiment is reflected in epochal photographs from the period showing peaceful demonstrators placing flowers into the barrels of soldiers' rifles, or the image (again from the film) of young men in the Woodstock crowd encouraging one another to tear up their draft cards and become conscientious objectors. Because nearly 500,000 people came together (planners' estimates had been too low at 50,000–100,000, and TV news stations showed footage of the cars turning the New York Thruway into a parking lot), Woodstock proved to be a highly visible, well-publicized confirmation of the number of people who felt similarly and were apparently on the same "side" (hippies, antiwar protesters, nonconformists, rebellious students). Woodstock served to illustrate that collectively this community was much larger in terms of numbers than they had ever imagined.

Taking Woodstock is a natural choice for Ang Lee as a topic because it delves into the psychology of the human heart at a crucial moment of change in American history. As noted, through the astonishing diversity of his earlier films, Lee has dealt repeatedly with topics that displayed keen cultural and historical insight. For example, Lee's early works such as *Pushing Hands, The Wedding Banquet,* and *Eat Drink Man Woman* helped to demonstrate the effects of globalization and culture clash; these themes in Lee's work from the early 1990s seemed to predict and foreshadow the rapid changes and need for adaptation to the twenty-first-century globalized world. Following his Chinese trilogy, Lee continued to make films that dealt with important periods in history: an early nineteenth-century British classic, a 1970s period piece, an American Civil War film, a Qing dynasty martial arts epic, a film dealing with societal restrictions in early-1960s Wyoming, and finally, *Lust/Caution*, a challenging World War II epic that demonstrated all of Lee's strengths in filming morality, patriotism, repression, performance, and political choice at a very complicated historical moment. In much the same way, *Taking Woodstock* details the outcome of a personal journey toward self-identity undertaken against a vivid historical backdrop. As outlined in this book's chapter on *Brokeback Mountain*, Eve Sedgwick, Judith Halberstam, and others in the field of Queer Studies have discussed the transformative power of early homosexual experiences and their impact on the future identity of the gay male subject, while in the pioneering LGBT volume *Gay Shame* (2009), David Halperin and Valerie Traub seek to reclaim emotion, embarrassment, and dissidence as central elements of queer practice.

> Ever since the Stonewall Riots of 1969 and the era of gay liberation they inaugurated, gay pride has been the rallying cry of a broad social movement for sexual freedom. . . . At the same time . . . gay pride has never been able to separate itself entirely from shame, or to transcend shame. Gay pride does not even make sense without some reference to the shame of being gay, and its very successes (to say nothing of its failures) testify to the intensity of its ongoing struggle with shame.[3]

Similar to this, in *Taking Woodstock*, the protagonist Elliot Tiber experiences a transformational liberation from the repression of his identity under parental/societal authority. Through the microcosm of Elliot's story, Lee reveals the overarching narrative of the sixties: a time of heady optimism and social idealism as young people sought to break away from the restrictions of the older generation, a coming-of-age story in an era of tumultuous change. The title *Taking Woodstock* implies the idea of "taking stock" of one's life and, in a sense, control of one's destiny—and also "taking" the experience of Woodstock, and what that cultural event meant, and preserving that breakthrough moment as a milestone for the rest of one's life.

It is natural that Lee would be drawn to the story of a somewhat tormented gay man who only comes to know himself fully in the liberating atmosphere of Woodstock's heady days.[4] Tiber in the book tells a darker story than the one that ultimately made it to screen—as a teenager he frequented pornographic cinemas and had countless anonymous sexual encounters on a regular basis that left him plagued by internal shame. This is elided in the film—instead, a single phone call from New York City from a gay friend who is heading to San Francisco suggests Elliot's (Demetri Martin) sexual leanings, but Elliot does not embrace his sexuality fully until he meets a handsome electrician/handyman, Paul (Darren Pettie), at the Woodstock festival. As they bond over Judy Garland, an intense mutual attraction sparks between them, and Elliot has his first full-on male-male kiss in a liberating scene in the hotel's bar, in full view of Elliot's father. At first Elliot is fearful of his father's reaction, but his father's burgeoning friendship with a male cross-dressing veteran, Vilma (Liev Schreiber), lays Elliot's fears to rest as he realizes that formerly rigid attitudes are changing with the times.

Changing Attitudes—the Father, the Mother, the Friend

Elliot's relationship with his father is especially significant in this film and provides a hint as to why this material captured the director's interest so intently. In this film more than any other in Lee's oeuvre, walls come tumbling down as the father, Jake Teichberg (Henry Goodman), bares his soul to his son and expresses open approval of him. This happens, in the film, in the final conversation between the two, as the son is packing and preparing to leave the family business (in Tiber's account, this conversation occurs when his father is on his deathbed). The father initiates the conversation, asking if he can talk to his son for a minute. Subsequently, it seems that his sole purpose is to bless his son, to give him a blessing and good wishes for his future. The father confirms the son's identity (in the book, Elliot's father says, "I know about your friends"). However, he goes a step further, to thank his son for waking him up, bringing him to life again. This is the ultimate fatherly commendation—gratitude for the effect of one's offspring upon one's life—the blessing has come full circle. "Because of you, I'm alive," the father says. This relationship is given even more resonance due to Elliot's identity as the son of Eastern-European Jewish immigrants. Elliot's "American-style" liberation echoes that of Wai-Tung as he faces his conservative parents in *The Wedding Banquet*.

Elliot's relationship with his mother, Sonia (Imelda Staunton), is much more complicated. His mother, damaged from traumatic experiences in war-torn Russia before she immigrated to America, is troubled by a pathological fear of poverty, and thus becomes a hoarder of the family fortune and a manipulative liar in the way she runs her business. (In the book, she further damages her son's future by withholding the tuition funds she could have easily used to send him to a good college—she also throws away priceless artwork given to her son as a gift from Mark Rothko because she thinks it is ugly.) Woodstock has a pleasantly transformative effect on Mrs. Teichberg in the film. She becomes more generous, sharing blankets and helping out with enthusiasm in a way that surprises her son. Elliot even sees a soft side of his mother when she inadvertently takes drugs through "special brownies" and ends up dancing and cavorting in the rain with Elliot's father. Elliot's mother's neuroses are eventually fully revealed, however, when, after the drug trip, she is found nuzzling her stash of US$97,000 in crumpled bills on the floor of her closet. Elliot is especially horrified by this deception because he had been pouring his own life savings into helping his parents. In this lust and avarice, Elliot's mother is a pathetic figure who needs to be helped to her feet by her son.

The character of the young Vietnam War veteran Billy (Emile Hirsch) from the very first panicky, PTSD-induced appearance in the bed of the pickup truck, to the stripping off of his own clothes with the Earthlight Players, to the exuberant mudsurfing scene where he shouts, "I love this hill!" tells a story of liberation that is significant to the history of the period. Both Billy and Elliot discuss how they feel out of place in their small, conservative town. Billy tells Elliot he was "normal" in Vietnam—shattered, anxious, crazed, delusional: these were normal traits in Vietnam—but he feels out of place in White Lake. He tells Elliot he would like to return to Vietnam and suggests Elliot join up, too, but Elliot confesses he would be rejected from the military because of his flat feet. The two friends laugh together at the idea that Elliot is not "normal" enough to go to Vietnam—a telling commentary on normalcy. Billy finally begins to come alive when the Earthlight Players, the resident theater artists at the El Monaco, perform their adaptation of Anton Chekhov's *The Three Sisters*, with this prologue:

> Artifice and imagination! Truth and fiction!
> The players play!
> But you, the audience, you sit and judge.
> You sit and judge. You sit and judge.
> But the revolution requires the roles must be reversed!
> The players are the judges now.
> Your revelry must end, and your souls will be bared for all to see.

"The players are the judges" who use their physical nakedness to "bare" the souls of the audience, hinting at the idea of performance and liberation so often reexamined by Lee.

Liberation of Identity through the Woodstock Experience

In *Taking Woodstock*, Elliot Tiber is portrayed as a character who suppresses his identity, including his homosexuality, by hiding within a deep sense of inferiority and shame. This shame is given a context in Tiber's book, in which the author is very transparent and forthcoming about early experiences that shaped his sexual development. While these experiences are not included in the film, a phone call from one of Elliot's New York City friends demonstrates his deep bond to a male friend, and Elliot's sadness is palpable when this friend tells him he is moving away with another man. Elliot's response is silence; his friend thinks he is no longer on the telephone line. "Elliot?" the friend asks, "Are you there?" Elliot can barely speak; his desolation is complete. Abandoned by the one friend he can share intimately with in New York City, Elliot now faces the closed-minded small-town community of White Lake, with its prejudice and intolerance, alone.

As the film progresses, Elliot's body language changes to reveal his shifting interior character. At first, head down, bangs in eyes, shoulders stooped, he runs awkwardly like a girl, and he has trouble meeting people's eyes. There is a rigidity and reticence in his movements, conveying his deep sense of insecurity and lack of self-acceptance, even self-loathing. This can be contrasted with the transvestite ex-Marine Vilma's fluid movements—her easy embraces, her open countenance. Elliot, stunned by the growing relationship between Vilma and his father, asks, "Does my father know what you are?" Vilma, unfazed, thinks for a moment before delivering the line that sums up the film, as well as Tiber's book: "I know what I am. That does make it easier for everyone else, doesn't it?" The meaning is clear—Vilma believes that owning up to one's true self is the key to this confidence. There is a twinkling in Vilma's eye—she is almost amused by the fact of her difference being an affront to convention.

Yet this very freedom itself is captivating and contagious—this is the essence of the spirit of Woodstock, itself a beautiful experience of the happiness of acceptance, recognition, and liberation.

Based on a similar character, the free-spirited lesbian "Georgette," in Tiber's original autobiography, Vilma has qualities that lead to the transformation of others. Tiber's book explains the character this way:

> Within five minutes of meeting Georgette, people knew she was a homosexual—even those who were most in denial. Georgette, meanwhile, was nice to everyone. She wasn't angry; she didn't need to force-feed lesbianism to other people. On the contrary, she was completely relaxed about her orientation, which allowed others to be relaxed, too. . . . People gathered around her in large part because they could freely be themselves. In fact, without any overt effort, her very presence demanded it. She was so honest, so open, and so relaxed, that she made you act the same way.[5]

Elliot's transformation begins with receiving love from this woman, whose acceptance of him helps him accept himself. "She had seen me, even the darkest parts of me, and she loved me. That was healing enough."[6] The implication is that the character's love and acceptance has a transformative power over Eliott, a shared intimacy that leads to a strengthening of Elliot's character.

Throughout the film, Elliot learns to "loosen up"—to throw off the shackles of his conventional role in society (as an obedient son, as a heterosexual rather than a homosexual or bisexual). The scene where he takes LSD with the couple in the VW van at the concert demonstrates this transformation. At first, Elliot is hesitant to join the young couple (played by Paul Dano and Kelli Garner), despite their welcoming and reassuring manner—he has never done anything so "wild" in his life. Finally, however ("What the heck"), he opens his mouth and lets the girl place the drug on his tongue like a communion wafer. (This "wild" behavior later contrasts with his dutiful nature, the next morning when he says, "I'm the only kid here having breakfast with his parents.") Elliot's body language changes during the drug trip—at first he sits rigidly and self-consciously, waiting for something to happen, waiting to experience the rush of the drug, even questioning whether the drug is going to take effect. Eventually, as the scene progresses, the combination of the ethereal music ("The Red Telephone" by Love), the colors on the hanging tapestry that melt into a psychedelic haze, and the fluidity of the movements of Elliot and the other two as they enter into a sexual experience, all combine through Lee's composition of these elements to demonstrate Elliot's liberation from social constraint, and his new experience in the untamed experimentation with his identity. The harmonious acceptance of the sexual experiences of both male and female are reflected by Lee's focus on the Chinese yin-yang symbol on the tapestry—an indication of two oppositional poles (Elliot's conservative past and his new liberated identity) coming together in perfect resolution, a harmony achieved between his interior and exterior worlds.

A second scene that reveals Elliot's transformation is the scene in the hotel bar, where Elliot is pulled reluctantly into a group dance. He tries to resist the efforts of the group to enter into the liberated, joyful environment—such an uncontrolled atmosphere scares him. He glances back at his father—the judge of his identity. Elliot's father in this scene plays the role of Foucault's "panopticon"—the gaze or eye that constrains social behavior (Foucault explains the full allusion as the surveillance system in a modern prison, where the prisoners are never certain whether or at which time the guards are watching them—thus, they constrain their own behavior).[7] In this scene, Elliot is eventually pulled into an embrace with a beautiful girl, who kisses him fully on the lips—the crowd cheers and Elliot grins with unexpected pleasure. As the crowd continues its undulating dance, Elliot is next faced with the handsome carpenter/electrician with whom the audience already knows he shares a connection. The man pulls Elliot into a kiss and the two embrace hungrily, again to the cheers of the crowd, voicing their approval. When the kiss ends, Elliot, with a newfound boldness, pulls the man into a second kiss, initiated by Elliot himself. Clearly, Elliot's passion has momentarily overtaken his need to conform to the established norms. However, when the kiss ends, Elliot regains his self-consciousness and self-regulation; he looks back over his shoulder to the place where his father, the watching eye, Foucault's "gaze," was sitting. The chair is ominously empty, indicating that either Elliot has gotten away with the behavior unseen, or that his father has left the room in disgust. This casts an uneasy look over Elliot's face.

Elliot's relationship with his father is further elucidated by his changing body language toward his dad. When Elliot's dad encourages him to go off to the Woodstock festival for some free time, Elliot and his father exchange an awkward embrace. This is clearly one of the first embraces they have ever shared in their lives. Elliot's dad clearly does not know how to hug him. However, in the final father/son scene at the end of the film, Elliot's dad has learned how to love and accept his son, and he demonstrates this with an easy, warm embrace. The end of Tiber's book, *Taking Woodstock*, further illustrates the emotion shared between the father and son. Instead of the conversation taking place when Elliot leaves home, however, the book reveals that the father does not grant his son acceptance until Elliot's father is on his deathbed. In the book, Elliot's father assures him of his love, saying the following:

> "My little boy, my son," he began. I love you. I know about you. I know what you do. I know about your life, your friends. I just want you should know it's okay by me. I hope you find somebody and you can be happy." He looked deeply into my eyes and nodded his approval and love. He paused before starting again. "I have just one thing to ask you. When I go, I want to be buried facing Woodstock. You know that little Jewish cemetery just near Max's farm? That's where I want to be. The festival was the best time of my whole life, and you did it."[8]

This speech, made by Elliot's father on his deathbed, indicates two interior shifts in the father's character. First, the father's acceptance of his son is complete—he does not reject the son's life choice, nor does he condemn him. Instead, he seeks to understand the boy through the son's own love and happiness. For a homosexual or an alienated person in society, this acceptance and validation is extraordinarily powerful. In addition, Elliot's father validates the effect of the Woodstock festival on his and his son's life, recognizing with gratitude the magnitude of the event's effect by seeking to be buried in a place that honors this significance. Elliot's father sees that his life has been given meaning and transcendence by the effect of the Woodstock concert, and he expresses that gratitude.

The following exchange also takes place further in the same conversation:

> In the silence that followed, I found the question that, on so many occasions, had begged for an answer. "Pop," I said. "Why did you stay with Momma all these years? You were so tired. Why didn't you ever tell her to stop her demands?"
>
> "I love her," he whispered. Those were the last words I heard him speak. The next day he was dead. [9]

This exchange is shortened in the film and moved forward in time so that Elliot's father does not speak these words on his deathbed (which would have been too maudlin), but instead take place in a yearning, tentative talk between Elliot and his father immediately following the concert, when his father is still very much alive. Jake Techberg says, "Because of you, I'm alive—and what should I want now, but for you, my son, to live, too?" and he encourages Elliot to go out in the world and make a new life for himself, as an independent adult apart from his parents.

Ultimately, *Taking Woodstock* is about freedom—the freedom to be loved for who one really is, to be liberated to live fully in the moment. It is about the love that Elliot experienced through those three days of Woodstock, and how that love and acceptance of who he really was called him out of himself. He had been limited by his own thinking and his own ideas of who he was and what he could be. Even his perspective on other people, such as his own father, was limited and rigid. A line from Elliot's new friend Tisha (Mamie Gummer) expresses this notion: "We're all trapped in our little 'perspectives.' It keeps the love out."

Back to the Garden

As Elliot plans his exit from his parents' motel, he doesn't quite have a destination at the end of the film. Elliot has a final, decisive conversation with Woodstock Ventures organizer Michael Lang (Jonathan Groff), in which Lang tells Elliot that he will be heading to California to work on a concert—a free concert—with the Rolling Stones. Lang indicates that this concert will be even more spectacular than Woodstock, because it will be "truly free"; it will be "beautiful." For those standing in the muddy aftermath, the hope of what was going to happen next was palpable for a whole generation, but the next event, Altamont with the Rolling Stones, ended it all. The Rolling Stones concert at Altamont Speedway in California, where Hell's Angels were hired as security, resulted in violent fighting during which the 18-year-old Meredith Hunter was stabbed to death in front of the stage. This suggests a dark ending to the otherwise happy and peaceful legacy of free concerts in America—Altamont as the dark twin of Woodstock. Apart from the ominous reference to Altamont, the ending of *Taking Woodstock* is lyrical and ethereal, as crews of young people roam the hillside together to clear the trash and debris left by the masses of humanity after the concert. The sunlight casts a heavenly glow over Woodstock's natural amphitheater as Lang appears, symbolically, on a white horse. The final words spoken by Elliot, as he observes the scene, are, "Beautiful . . . beautiful . . . " The word "beautiful" refers to the scene itself, in which Elliot is reminded of the freedom this scene represents for him personally; in addition, the word "beautiful" refers to the ethos of Woodstock and the 1960s youthful idealism at its height. Lee says of the film:

> After making several tragic movies in a row, I was looking to do a comedy—and one without cynicism. It's also a story of liberation, honesty, and tolerance—and of a 'naïve spirit' that we cannot and must not lose."[10]

Lee's description of the film underscores these very elements that make the narrative of Elliot Tiber's life so poignant: "liberation, honesty, and tolerance." Both Lee and James Schamus took as their mission the retelling of this tale of 1960s idealism and naïveté. Schamus notes the emphasis on the transformative nature of Woodstock: "Underneath all the comedy in this movie are emotions, and meditations on what it means for people to transform themselves."[11]

In the end, it is this very idea of falling outside the social norm, of finding solidarity in difference, that enables Elliot's transformation in *Taking Woodstock*. As noted, Eve Sedgwick, David Halperin, and Valerie Traub among others have posited the interdependence and tension between queerness and "normalcy"; this is elucidated by the centrality of the alienated versus the accepted, the outsider/insider dichotomy, that made Woodstock a place for the misfit, the outcast, the disreputable "different" to come together. Lee's film suggests that Woodstock is an "idea," a powerful memory, a loving tribute to an incandescent moment in time, a conduit to self-identity, and a potent piece of nostalgia. The transformative liberation highlighted by the three days of peace and music at Woodstock was a landmark in American history influencing an entire generation.

FOURTEEN

Storytelling and Truth in Life of Pi: *A Spiritual Journey*

ANG LEE HESITATED for two months before he agreed to take on Yann Martel's complex book, *Life of Pi*, which charts a young boy's journey across the Pacific Ocean and his struggle with despair, faith, and a ravenous 450-pound Bengal tiger. The narrative is imaginative, fantastical, and philosophical due to Martel's themes of the quest for meaning and the search for truth; by making his protagonist a young boy whose open-mindedness helps him view the world in an unusual way in order to survive, Martel is able to disarm his readers and prepare them for an exploration of soul-searching depths. The book weaves a complex metaphysical puzzle from the story of Piscine Molitor "Pi" Patel from Pondicherry, India, who survives a shipwreck during which he loses his family, and survives for 227 days adrift on a lifeboat with a tiger, a zebra, a hyena, and an orangutan, and who at the end of the narrative gives two differing accounts in relating what actually happened. Adapting *Life of Pi* had been considered by other directors since Fox Studios acquired the film rights to the book in 2003 (including M. Night Shyamalan and Alfonso Cuarón). Possible challenges to the filming included long stretches during which nothing happens, as well as the fact that the book is open to many interpretations, literal and metaphorical. In addition, Lee chose to work with 3D technology for the first time, also using CGI, which had plagued him during *Hulk*. The story is also complex in the telling, involving Indian, French, Japanese, Taiwanese, Mexican, and Canadian cultural elements—the narrative concerns national identity as well as personal identity. Finally, there was the author Yann Martel's own assertion that the book was "unfilmable."

Despite the fact that Martel's book was published in more than forty countries and won the 2002 Man Booker Prize, A. O. Scott claimed in his review that the story of a boy trapped on a lifeboat with a Bengal tiger for 227 days is a difficult read, in which virtually nothing happens.[1] The book is set up as a "true story" tale in Yann Martel's prologue, a fictional "Author's Note" that precedes the novel's text—indeed, this is one of the deliberately disorienting aspects of the book, that the author sets up the narrative as a true story even though the book's cover clearly claims that this is "A Novel." The "Author's Note" is purportedly related in the voice of Martel himself, who explains his "background" as a failed Canadian writer who heads to India to find inspiration for his novel set in 1930s Portugal. The idea of a failed writer is an interesting premise for this story because the writer has undergone a spiritual "death"; he goes to India because he is looking for inspiration for his writing and an outlet for his malaise, noting that "A stint in India will beat the restlessness out of any living creature."[2] While in India, the writer initially fares no better; he abandons his novel on Portugal, accusingly calling it "dead."[3] His reaction is to take the novel to a local post office and mail it to a fictional address in Siberia (with an equally fictional return address in Bolivia)—literally sending it to "no-man's-land." It is interesting then, in a fateful twist, that he is attracted to the story about the "life" of Pi—the implication being that Pi has made his discoveries of the meaning of life before he reaches the age of seventeen.

A second challenge to making the film had to do with its overtly religious content. After sending off the failed novel, the writer heads south, to Pondicherry, where he happens to meet Pi's "family uncle" Mamaji, at a local café. His new friend Mamaji claims: "I have a story that will make you believe in God."[4] Critical response to films that have faith or religion as a central topic are indicative that such films are often considered offensive—therefore, this is the second aspect of the book that challenges the reader and makes filming the work for commercial success somewhat untenable. Author Yann Martel in the book itself also concedes that both zoos and religion are out of fashion: "I know zoos are no longer in people's good graces . . . religion faces the same problem . . . certain illusions about freedom plague them both."[5] While Pi makes a case for both zoos and religion in the book, modern environmentalists balk at the unnaturalness of shutting animals up in zoo enclosures, while religion is not a popular topic by any means. Lee has also commented on the impossibility of making a movie about religion.[6] And yet the film dares to bring the topic of religion—and not just one, but three of the world's most populous religions—to the forefront, in early boyhood scenes with Pi as he explores matters of faith and his love for God. The basic ideas behind Hinduism, Christianity, and Islam are explored by Pi as he is introduced to them as a young boy, with his brother's mocking remarks and his "rationalist" father's questioning serving as a counterbalance in the film. Pi's father is portrayed as logical, stern, and realistic—a realist who can say with confidence, "There is no God." Indeed, in the modern world, the more cynical version of events is considered the more "true." However, in *Life of Pi*, Lee challenges the viewer to consider a fantastic journey as a viable story.

A third challenge to the film was Lee's choice to use 3D technology for the first time. Lee claims to have used 3D technology in an innovative way in this film to create an "intimate" connection with the viewer.[7] He wanted to explore the use of new technology to invite and include and create a bridge; this is especially apparent in the opening montage scenes where birds seem to hover near the viewer, or animals seem to protrude and extend themselves into the viewer's space (such as the monitor lizard who marches right up to the edge of the screen and then dashes away in a lightning-fast maneuver) in a way to invite participation in the Edenic scene. (For example, one of the zoo images contains, in the extreme foreground, a zoo worker napping on a wooden cart, suggesting a peaceful coexistence between the animal and human worlds.) In fact, Lee's own early training as an actor and a stage director allowed him to view the space created by three-dimensional viewing as a "stage" upon which he could now "place" the actors within the shot, just as on a physical stage, and extend the performance space forward toward the viewer. This opening up of the performance space gave Lee entirely new possibilities, but for the classically-trained director, the learning curve must have been immense. The groundbreaking use of 3D technology in this film—usually reserved for action films but considered highly experimental for this kind of serious, meditative drama—is one of the aspects of the film that ultimately received the highest praise from viewers and critics.[8]

A fourth challenge facing the filmmaker was the multicultural and multilingual aspect of the narrative—the setup of the story could have been hopelessly confusing with its multiple localities and many cultures represented, including 1950s Paris and French-colonial India, 1970s India/Mexico, and present-day Canada (Toronto).[9] In the book, the adult Pi describes the racism he experienced in 1970s Canada; however, he also describes his own conflicted love for his adopted Canadian homeland:

> I love Canada. I miss the heat of India, the food, the house lizards on the walls, the musi-cals on the silver screen, the cows wandering the streets, the crows cawing, even the talk of cricket matches, but I love Canada. It is a great country much too cold for good sense, inhabited by compassionate, intelligent people with bad hairdos.[10]

Some of the unique cultural combinations include the following: The boy Pi grows up on a zoo in Pondicherry, India, which was a French colonial territory until 1954 (this is conveyed in a flashback); 1970s Pondicherry contains Hindu, Christian, and Muslim influences. A French cook, Japanese officers, and a Taiwanese crew serve on the ship that is transporting Pi and his family. Later, Japanese representatives from the shipping company come to interview Pi at the Benito Juárez Infirmary in Tomatlán, Mexico: "We are here because a Japanese cargo ship [*Tsimtsum*] owned by Oika Shipping Company, flying the Panamanian flag, sank in the Pacific."[11] It is this hodge-podge, "melting pot" aspect of the story that makes the narrative more complex, with each character naturally reverting in times of stress to the ethnocentric preferences of his own familiar culture.[12] This is highlighted in the film by the heated argument about vegetarian food on the ship between the French cook and the Indian family, where a compromise about gravy is suggested by a Taiwanese sailor, "happy Buddhist."[13]

The opening moments of *Life of Pi* are an early indicator that this film will be unusual. The opening credits hearken back to a grander period in filmmaking, a more leisurely time in Hollywood, where actors were introduced one by one in the film's opening credits, and films took their own time getting started. This opening is already a signifier of the film's epic reach and extravagantly slow pacing. These credits are very creative and humorous, with some of the letters of actors' names swinging like monkeys in a tree, or in the case of the director's name, floating breezily in a reflecting pool that reflects a tiger (here Lee self-identifies with the tiger, slyly cluing the viewer in to his own role). The film opens with unusual pairings of animals—for example, a giraffe and a fox in the first scene, or a hummingbird and a sloth in the second. These incongruous pairings foreshadow the film's main relationship between Pi and the tiger. At the same time, the opening montage is meant to suggest a uto-pian perfection, as suggested by Isaiah 11:6, in which "The wolf will live with the lamb, the leopard will lie down with the goat, the calf and the lion and the yearling together; and a little child will lead them."[14] Pi describes growing up on the zoo grounds as similar to a magical kingdom in the book, and Lee's filmmaking seeks to represent this as a heavenly vision, a paradise untouched by human depravity and weakness. Another unique and quite noticeable aspect of the book and film is that colors are very important in the narrative, with the color orange being a harbinger of hope and survival: the orange whistle around Pi's neck, the orange tarpaulin (in the book), the orange-tipped pen which Pi uses to mark the route to Canada on a map (in the book), the orangutan's name "Orange Juice," and the orange cat "Moccasin" held by Pi's four-year-old daughter in the book are just a few examples.[15]

Confusion of Identity/Names

Pi's (Suraj Sharma) full given name is Piscine Molitor Patel. He was named after a French swimming pool, the Piscine Molitor, in Paris, recalled with fond nostalgia by his uncle Mamaji. Because the French pronunciation of his name can be twisted in English, especially by his cruel and unimaginative classmates, Pi undergoes a dreadful teasing as a child: " 'Where's Pissing? I've got to go.' Or: 'You're facing the wall. Are you Pissing?' "[16] In an act of rechristening that is given full telling in the film, Piscine renames himself "Pi" to avoid this teasing, writing on the blackboard for all his classmates and teachers to see: $\pi = 3.14$. As Pi himself explains in the novel: "And so, in that Greek letter that looks like a shack with a corrugated tin roof, in that elusive, irrational number with which scientists try to understand the universe, I found refuge."[17] Other motifs from the film associated with pi include the 227 days that Pi is on the ocean in the lifeboat: pi can also be read as the fraction $22/7$; in addition, the association of roundness and completeness in the film—such as the roundness of a pool, the ocean, the world, the *bindi* (dot) on an Indian woman's forehead, the mandala sign from Hinduism, the yin-yang sign from Taoism,[18] and a journey that begins and ends in the same place—reflect the idea of "pi" as both a complete number and an abstract and infinitely complex concept.[19]

The origin of the name "Richard Parker," the name given to the Bengal tiger at the Pondicherry Zoo, also has complex implications. First, the name was originally bestowed upon the animal by mistake; as explained in the book the tiger once was given the name "Thirsty" as a cub, but when he escaped and the man who found him was signing the release form, the man's name, "Richard Parker," was given to the tiger, while the man's own name was listed as "Thirsty." The family liked the name, so the tiger became Richard Parker. This confusing origin of the name also points to the identity confusion that troubles Pi (the Catholic priest's first remark to Pi in the church is "You must be thirsty!"). However, the name "Richard Parker" also has haunting significance in nautical history. A number of earlier shipwreck narratives mysteriously contain similar accounts of acts of cannibalism committed by a mysterious figure who is named "Richard Parker." The name "Richard Parker," for example, occurs in Edgar Allan Poe's nautical adventure novel *The Narrative of Arthur Gordon Pym of Nantucket* (1838), a highly elusive text that is at once a nonfictional exploration narrative and a spiritual allegory. This work shares intertextual elements with Pi's narrative, and indeed many of the narratives involving a cannibalistic "Richard Parker" follow a story arc similar to *Life of Pi*.[20]

Many characters in *Life of Pi* are given a deliberately ambiguous identity confusion, often blurred in association with another character in the story. For example, there is the character of Anandi (Shravanthi Sainath), a love interest for Pi, who does not exist in Martel's narrative but was invented for the film. When Pi follows her through a market, he asks her the meaning of some dance steps: "Why would a lotus flower hide in a forest?" (a sexual metaphor) and Anandi is silent in response. Also, Pi says of the day he leaves her, "It's funny . . . I remember everything else about our last day, but I don't remember saying goodbye." This is reminiscent of the unresolved parting with Richard Parker. Similarly, this unresolved parting is evoked by Pi's admission at the end that he would have liked to say goodbye to his own father (Adil Hussain), and to thank him for the lessons he instilled that saved Pi's life. In addition, the tiger and the father and God are conflated. This is also apparent in the scene where Pi's father teaches him the lesson at the zoo by feeding the tiger a sacrifice—the scapegoat that takes Pi's place. Finally, both Richard Parker and Pi on the ocean at times play the role of God, and in other ways they symbolize God for each other.

There is also confusion about the meaning of the "floating island," which could stand for the god Vishnu who both "gives life and takes it away." In the morning the island is a fragrant and fertile oasis that provides Pi with fresh food and pure water, but by evening the island is a death trap—the fresh water turns to acid, killing the fish within it, while the ground becomes carnivorous (Pi finds a human tooth in a lotus flower; in the book he finds an entire set of human teeth in a tree). Both the fact that the flower is a lotus, and the fact that the island is shaped like a woman, suggest strongly that the island is related to Pi's boyhood love interest, Anandi. In addition, Pi takes off the bracelet that Anandi tied on his wrist (as a love token) when they parted, and ties it to a large tree root on the island. Is the island, then, somehow representative of Anandi? The significance of this action of tying the now-faded string to the banyan tree (which Pi once guarded so jealously on his wrist, shielding it from his mother's gaze in the scene on the boat's deck) is to alert the viewer to Pi's emotional state—it is both a leaving-behind of the past, and an honoring of it. At first, when Pi ties the string to the tree root, it seems to suggest that he has come "home," and that he will stay on the island. He is happy there until he realizes that the island is more menacing than it first appeared. Pi says to himself that he must continue his journey or he would "die on this island." At some level, as well, Pi is parting from his memories of his mother (Tabu), and his family as a whole, moving on to his mature purpose as a grown man. Ultimately this scene serves to remind the viewer of the plight of man in the world—one must make one's way in the world independently—we are all fundamentally alone, living alone and dying alone, and cannot find escape in human ties and relationships—if we try to do so, we will find those same relationships become stultifying and dead.

Finally, Pi's identity confusion is also highlighted by his loss. On the ocean, Pi gradually loses his humanity and social structures. From the beginning of his ordeal, when he loses his parents, brother, and the comforts of the ship, of civilization and human contact, Pi's shipwreck strips all human ritual and routine from his life, all of the human social conventions that humans normally cling to for security. For example, Pi takes charge at first by ordering and numbering his supplies from the lifeboat. He is glad to find the "Lifeboat Manual and Navigational Guide," and he finds refuge (and humor: "Community singing is another surefire way to lift the spirits") in the manual's scientific instructions; he keeps track of the days he has spent on the lifeboat by a tally system; he also begins keeping a diary. However, over time, Pi loses even more of these supplies (he says, "I never thought a small piece of shade could bring me so much happiness . . . that a pile of tools—a bucket, a knife, a pencil—might become my greatest treasures"); he finally also loses these one by one: they are scattered and lost during the fantastic and somewhat supernatural leaping of the whale, which shatters his carefully organized human system—a metaphor for the unpredictability of nature, with its storms and cataclysms, and man's inability to control or "tame" it. Also, he finds solace in the human ritual of keeping a journal and recording his thoughts in an orderly manner—a measure of control—but eventually his pencil runs out of lead. He is reduced, toward the end, to simply repeating the endless sequence of the numbers of pi to keep from going insane (the juxtaposition of Pi repeating pi also demonstrates how he is tenuously keeping hold of his own identity through this ritual).

A third stage of Pi's loss of identity is his loss, during the storm, of his "safety instructions" booklet—which had been psychologically anchoring him to the civilized, human world. The friendly, upbeat tone of the instruction booklet had comforted him like a companionable voice, a voice speaking his own language of calm, reasonable English, giving him a sense of security, of human contact. When he loses his "guide" in the chaos of a storm, this is another instance of nature overpowering man and stripping him of his humanity and "civilization." (He had previously recognized "Words are all I have to hold onto," but with the loss of the book, he loses the "companionship" of another voice in the conversation—he is utterly alone). With the human rituals gone, Pi is then "free" in a sense—this is when he has the extraordinary experiences of "intimacy" with the tiger—he asks Richard Parker what he is thinking; he begs Richard Parker to talk to him. When the storm comes, Pi finally "enters" Richard Parker's lair under the tarpaulin, and utterly exhausted by the storm, the two lie in the bow of the boat in an intimate sort of embrace, tiger fur against wet human skin. In the end, in a gesture of intimacy and friendship, Pi cradles the dying tiger's head on his lap and strokes his fur after feeding him a few precious drops of water, finally voicing to the big cat that they will die together.

Pi also gradually loses his humanity and through hunger becomes more "animal," saying that "Hunger can change everything you ever thought you knew about yourself." This is underscored when Pi begins to eat fish although he was formerly a strict vegetarian, disliking even to kill a fish for the feeding of the tiger. There is also a gradual breakdown of the social structure. When Pi originally "trains" Richard Parker, he promises to respect the tiger's space, marking the tiger's home under the tarpaulin. However, later, during the fateful storm, Pi enters the tiger's space to save his own life, snapping down the tarpaulin over both of them. It is significant that these social barriers break down: this "respect" for each other's space is lost just as both their lives are threatened, and instead the tiger ends up floating helplessly side by side with the human in the bilgewater—like lovers their bodies touch in shared intimacy. Later, when Pi concludes that they will soon die, he speaks to Richard Parker like a human, "Can you feel the rain?" and finally, breaks all barriers between man and animal by putting the tiger's head on his thigh and stroking him lovingly as one would comfort a child in one's lap.

It is striking in the film that the adult Pi, in his conversation with the writer, sheds tears only once. He speaks about not being able to say goodbye, not being able to find closure. He never had a chance to say goodbye to his father, or to thank him for teaching him the life-giving skills he needed to survive on the ocean. Most poignantly, Pi never has the "goodbye" he longs for with Richard Parker—he says that he would have liked to tell Richard Parker "Thank you for saving my life . . . I love you . . . You'll always be with me." The flashback of Pi being carried by his Mexican rescuers, while he wails with sorrow over the loss of his "friend" Richard Parker, is utterly arresting—recalling other devastating partings in film survival stories.[21] It is interesting that the film does not cater to a Hollywood ending, in which the tiger would have come bounding back to affectionately lick Pi's face. Instead, Richard Parker walks up to the edge of the jungle, pauses without looking back, and then steps into the underbrush and disappears. This ending is highlighted by the end of the film when the camera rests on the jungle itself, first vivid and green, and then grayish to black-and-white, becoming a faded memory.

Pi's identity confusion is troubled by his lack of closure, his anger at God: "What more do you want from me?" There is also the theme of hope represented by Pi's initial "message in a bottle," that he tosses out with a note asking for rescue (one sees that the bottle floats a few feet away and rests there), and the flare gun and the ship on the horizon that fails to spot them. He nearly loses hope until the appearance of the dreamlike flying fish, which become sustenance (manna in the desert) for them. However, when a great storm comes and washes away Pi's life raft, he is finally stripped of everything he owns. The end seems near as Pi begins to hallucinate from heat and thirst. It is when he says he is ready to die ("Thank you for my life, God—I am ready now") and longs to join his father, mother, and brother in Heaven, that he encounters the island.

Storytelling/Truth-telling, Story and Truth

Ang Lee has said that *Life of Pi* is about the value of storytelling and how it "brings structure and wisdom to life."[22] Thus, included in Pi's coming-of-age odyssey are some of the stories and narratives that shaped him in childhood: young Pi reads Jules Verne's *L'Île mystérieuse* (*The Mysterious Island*, 1874); the restless teenage Pi reads Dostoevsky's *Notes from Underground* (1864) and Camus' existentialist novel *L'Étranger* (1942). In addition, Pi's simultaneous embrace of Hinduism, Christianity, and Islam seems to satirize the fact that every religion claims to have the "truth." What is provable truth? Even the scientific method is suspect. Martel's book ends with the transcript of Pi's interview in the Mexican hospital, where the representatives from the Japanese shipping company are interviewing Pi to try to determine the cause of the sinking of the *Tsimtsum*. At one point, the Japanese investigators claim that Pi is inventing his story because "Bananas don't float." In Martel's book, the investigators conduct a scientific experiment to "prove" that Pi is lying—but it turns out that the two investigators are proven wrong when they fill a hospital sink with water and the bananas rise to the surface. In other words, the focus of Martel's narrative rests on the distinction of fact and fiction, or the relationship between storytelling and truth-telling.

The Japanese shipping company representatives who visit Pi in the Mexican hospital are frustrated by his tale, because they say that they will look "like fools" if they are forced to tell their superiors the story that Pi told. They ask for something "believable," something "without animals." This leads them to question the meaning of the word "story" itself. Pi confronts them, saying:

"Doesn't the telling of something always become a story?"

"Uhh . . . perhaps in English. In Japanese, a story would have an element of *invention* in it. We don't want any invention. We want 'straight facts,' as you say in English."

"Isn't telling about something—using words, English or Japanese—already something of an invention? Isn't just looking upon this world something of an invention?"[23]

The climax of Yann Martel's book, at its very end, is the report from the Japanese investigators, which takes up an entire chapter. The end of the report states: "As an aside, the story of sole survivor, Mr. Piscine Molitor Patel, Indian citizen, is an astounding story of courage and endurance. . . . Very few castaways can claim to have survived so long at sea as Mr. Patel, and none in the company of an adult Bengal tiger." This last sentence is also the final line of the novel, indicating that Martel considered this the key to the story. (By contrast, this is not the ending of the film, although it is close to the end.) Why did the Japanese shipping company employees write on their report the story with the tiger rather than the "truth"? This shows that the Japanese investigators, who had previously asked for a story with "just the facts," so that they wouldn't look like "fools," captured the vision of Pi and of faith, and reported the tiger story as the true one, the one they "believed." The two investigators initially ask for a story that "we can tell our superiors," because they are unwilling to look like "fools." However, in the end of the book, they have become "fools." They "believed" him. The tiger story is the one recorded on the company report as the "truth."

This conclusion of the film troubles viewers who struggle with the ambiguous ending: the questions of which story is the true one—the story with the tiger or the story of brutal murder and cannibalism? This question is addressed in the film when the Canadian writer (Rafe Spall) seems to be at a loss for words, saying after the first story is told, "I don't know what to say," and "It's a lot to take in." The writer matches up the characters in both stories as the viewer himself has also doubtless begun to do: the broken-legged sailor with the lamed zebra, the female orangutan Orange Juice with Pi's mother, the hyena with the French cook, and the tiger himself with Pi. Is that the explanation? Is that the "truth," the "hard facts"? But perhaps it is better not to ask such questions, as the film suggests, not settling the question as one story or another, but instead asking "Which is the better story?" The writer answers (as anyone would presumably answer) "The one with the tiger." The grown-up Pi (Irrfan Khan) then responds with a warm confidence, "So it goes with God." What does he mean by this statement? If it is viewed as consistent with what the film has already presented, the meaning is that whether it was the tiger tale or cannibalism that took place, it was nevertheless a miracle that the young man survived the shipwreck; and Pi's comment "So it goes with God" means that regardless of one's understanding of God, He is operating, and it is up to the individual to make a choice of how to best understand Him. Thus, the meaning of the question of which is the better story is simply a matter of which story reveals God most directly and clearly. In this case, the "one with the tiger" was the story that the Canadian writer preferred as a revelation of God's divine power. Therefore, when the writer is asked which story he prefers, and he makes a choice, Pi replies, "So it goes with God"—both stories tell of God, both are stories to "make you believe in God."

In a number of places, the film underscores this idea of God. As mentioned previously, there is the sacrifice of the goat tied to the tiger's cage, killed and eaten in Pi's place. This is a metaphorical representation of Christ's sacrifice on the cross. The narrative repeatedly reiterates this idea of sacrifice—animals die for the sake of another animal living. Pi bludgeons the dorado fish to death, with the dorado's eye watching him. After this sacrifice of a life, Pi thanks God for sending the fish to keep them alive. Then there is Pi's own self-sacrifice: this is emphasized by Pi's position when he lies on the sand of the beach in Mexico, with arms outstretched like Christ on the cross, and the tiger leaps over him, metaphorically suggesting the sacrifice that Pi has made to keep the tiger alive. However, the tiger does not turn around to give thanks, but instead disregards the sacrifice and ignores the giver, seemingly forgetting Pi in his hurry to return to his activities in the animal world—so humans treat God in Christ's sacrifice. The film explores the metaphorical connection between animals and people and between God and man. At times in the film, Richard Parker seems to symbolize God to Pi: in his might, his majesty, and his remoteness. "Talk to me, Richard Parker," Pi begs. He wants God to talk to him. The montage that follows is one of the most beautiful and breathtaking sequences in the film, as the tiger's thoughts and memories of the shipwreck and the scattered predator/prey relationships of the animal kingdom meld with the boy's own thoughts of the lost Anandi/mother, the meaning of life, and the very strands of DNA. At the end of the scene, the viewer realizes that Pi and the tiger are "sharing" these thoughts, that their thoughts are one and the same. And yet ultimately, Pi cannot "make" Richard Parker become human any more than humans can "make" God become human.

Pi's meaning and purpose for life come from being able to care for someone else, the shifting of his focus from self-preservation to self-sacrifice. Only through reaching out to others can one find meaning in one's pain, find purpose for one's struggles, and find a reason for living that goes beyond oneself. This is illustrated in the film by the beautiful backlit tableau of the animals fighting each other as natural predators on the "lifeboat," also known as "Pi's ark," while Pi helplessly commands them to stop. The orangutan, the zebra, and the other animals didn't have to talk;

A wounded zebra, a bloodthirsty hyena, and a weary orangutan fight in dramatic silhouette on "Pi's Ark" as Pi (*far right*) helplessly attempts to restore order.

the expressions on their faces and in their eyes became a window into their souls. This is especially clear when Pi saves Richard Parker, instead of killing him, by letting him back into the lifeboat after seeing his face. Both the humans and the animals in the film feel pain, make sacrifices, and bond to other creatures, as friend or prey. Pi in a lifeboat forces the viewer to realize that no man's life is wasted, and no animal is unimportant. The connection between humans and animals reflects the larger theme of the connection between God and man. One leaves the film not asking "Why did the Japanese freighter have to sink?" but "Why do any of us have to experience such pain?"

At the end of Pi's story, the writer asks "What does it all mean?" This question addresses the human need to put facts into an orderly narrative in order to produce meaning and justify a conclusion. Tellingly, Pi doesn't see an orderly explanation for what happened in his story. He replies "If it happened, it happened. Why should it have to mean anything?" In the novel version of *Life of Pi*, Yann Martel divides the story into 100 chapters and three parts. The ending of the first part concludes with the adult Pi introducing his family and embracing his young daughter, and Martel confidently asserts, "This story has a happy ending."[24] That Pi was able to triumph over his grievous loss and build his own stable nuclear family is a "happy ending," and Lee chooses to end the film with this emphasis. The end of the film is a Happy Ending, with the final scene highlighting the wholeness and fulfillment of Pi's family. The infinitely unresolved fraction is at last complete: "Pi" the abstract number, seemingly random with no digits in a repeating sequence, is also a precise number.

A 3D feast, *Life of Pi* has an unusual cinematic voluptuousness, exposing the viewer to a beauty that resonates for a long time after seeing it. *Life of Pi* is not simply another award-winning Ang Lee movie masterpiece; instead, it is a doorway into contemplating the meaning of art, narrative, and life. The film communicates through three levels: on the sensual level, it communicates through beauty; on the parabolic level, it communicates through its narrative; and on an overt level, it communicates through its dialogue. This sets it apart from an ordinary moviegoing experience, because it is not a movie to be simply "seen," it is a movie to experience (it actually feels physical at points, such as the flying fish scene where one can almost feel the slippery fish squirming at the tiger's feet, or the slap of the wet scales against Pi's skin) and to meditate on—the film simply cannot be taken in by a single viewing. The unfamiliarity of this experience poses a challenge to some viewers. Lee elevates his films to a moral and spiritual level, and cinema to art. The director strips himself emotionally bare in every scene, so that he not only brings the story to life, but reveals the "life" behind the story.

FIFTEEN

Conclusion: The Dream of Cinema

SINCE HIS 2006 win of the Best Director Academy Award for *Brokeback Mountain*, followed again in 2013 by a second Best Director Academy Award for *Life of Pi*, Ang Lee's position in world cinematic history has been firmly established; he is now considered one of the world's leading directors. From the beginning, his career has been one of surprises. Since his earliest beginnings, with the Chinese trilogy of *Pushing Hands*, *The Wedding Banquet*, and *Eat Drink Man Woman*, he has explored the themes of cultural identity and globalization with unabashed honesty. In these films, Lee probes the dilemma of the "father figure" with unflinching intensity that foreshadows his sensitive handling of future controversial topics. In his second "trilogy" of English-language films, he deals with opposition and resolution in Jane Austen's *Sense and Sensibility*, fragmented identities and "cubist" narrative in *The Ice Storm*, and race, gender, class, and cultural identity in the American Civil War drama *Ride with the Devil*. These films each represent a brave foray into uncharted territory for the director, from his nuanced rendition of Jane Austen's Britain, to his take on Connecticut suburbia during Watergate and Vietnam, to a bemused look at the Confederate side of the Civil War. The release of *Crouching Tiger, Hidden Dragon* in 2000 was a stunning critical and commercial success; following on its heels was the film about the ultimate outsider, *Hulk* (expected to be a blockbuster, but considered his only major commercial failure). Following that was *Brokeback Mountain*, a film that literally changed history. No one could anticipate his next three choices: *Lust/Caution*, an unexpected return to his Chinese roots, *Taking Woodstock*, a look at 1960s hippie culture and a return to the topic of homosexuality, and finally, his most recent film *Life of Pi*, a spiritual journey in 3D that again propelled Lee into new challenges and risks.

Lee's *Brokeback Mountain* was unquestionably the most stunning reversal of the director's career thus far. Following the discouraging experience of making *Hulk*, Lee returned to make what he considered a small-budget art-house film that, to everyone's surprise, quickly became a global cultural phenomenon. Annie Proulx, author of the original short story, was skeptical when she first heard Lee was being considered as a possible director for the film version of *Brokeback Mountain*. She reminisces in an essay about their first meeting:

They were suggesting Ang Lee as the director, and I thought, here we go again. Could a Taiwanese-born director, probably a thorough-going urbanite, who had recently re-created the Hulk, understand Wyoming and the subterranean forces of the place? [. . .] I was nervous about meeting Ang Lee despite his reputation as brilliant and highly skilled. Would we have anything to say to each other? Were the cultural gaps insurmountable? We smiled and made small talk for a while and then, reassured by something in his quietness, I said that I was very afraid about this story, that making stories sometimes took me into off-limits places and that I feared the film would not follow that path. He said that he was afraid, too, that it would be extremely difficult to make into a film. He said he had recently lost his father. I remembered from my mother's death a few years earlier the vast hole in the world that opened and could not be pulled closed. I had a glimmering that Ang Lee might use his sorrow creatively, transferring a personal sense of loss to this film about two men for whom things cannot work out, that he might be able to show the grief and anger that builds when we must accept severe emotional wounding. I felt we both knew that this story was risky and that he wanted to take the story on, probably for the creative challenge and perhaps (though he didn't say so) for the gasping euphoria when you get into unknown but hard-driving imaginative projects. However slender, there was a positive connection.[1]

Ang Lee's relationship to "the father" is the leitmotif of his work. In each of his films, he revisits the theme of the father; even in the films that are not overtly father-centered, Lee never stops dealing subconsciously with the issue. He said in 2005, "All through my work, I always tend to think that making films was a way of getting away from my past, but you always end up going back to your roots. You try to get as far away as you can, but somehow you always come back. That is the impact of my father."[2] While this is most apparent in Lee's early Chinese-language Father-Knows-Best trilogy, as well as his presentation of Kevin Kline's flawed patriarch in *The Ice Storm* and Nick Nolte's mad-scientist father in *Hulk*, each of Ang Lee's films shows this influence. For example, in the opening scene of *Sense and Sensibility*, the family patriarch's death impacts the entire course of the film and the Dashwood family's future. Absence of the father in *Lust/Caution*, who abandons his daughter after his immigration and remarriage in England, also deeply affects the Electra-complex relationship that is the center of the film. The father's presence is a strong force to be grappled with in *Taking Woodstock* as the son deals with his own identity issues—in this film, it is the ultimate acceptance—and in *Life of Pi*, as teenage Pi contends with his father's atheistic rationalism versus his own faith. In *Ride with the Devil*, Jake Roedel's father image is not his own father—it is his friend Jack Bull Chiles' father, who is the master of the property and the true patriarchal figure in that film. In a more indirect and psychologically complex way, Li Mu Bai is a father figure to young Jen in *Crouching Tiger, Hidden Dragon*. And finally, there is the long shadow cast by the father to Ennis in *Brokeback Mountain*, who, in the film's shocking flashback, treats his son to an early exposure of bigotry and hatred that haunts him for the rest of his life. Looking back at the father theme in each of his films in 2005 while making *Brokeback Mountain*, Ang Lee said: "I never really stopped dealing with [the theme of the father]. . . . Making a movie can really hurt. But unless it hurts, you don't usually get anything fresh."[3]

The films of Ang Lee as a whole are characterized by silence, which emphasizes emotional repression with a spare and severe beauty. This is what gives his films— *Brokeback Mountain*, *The Ice Storm*, *Ride with the Devil*, and *Life of Pi* (the most silent of Lee's films, essentially an extended "conversation" between a boy and a tiger in which the tiger cannot speak)—such a lyrical, meandering quality. The camera does not impose itself on the narrative; it does not so much "tell" the story as let it unfold. A subtle glance or a glare of passion are silent signifiers through which the viewer can construct the underlying meaning of the narrative. This demonstrates that the language of the films of Ang Lee is more visual than verbal. Through these visual signifiers, the viewer is drawn into the drama as a participant, as Roland Barthes explains, actively engaging in the construction of a "writerly" text, in contrast to the "readerly" texts on display in traditional Hollywood movies and conventional literature, which proffer easily-understood meanings and allow the viewer a more passive role as an observer.[4] This also explains why Ang Lee's films lodge in the memory so powerfully and become a part of the viewer's own sense of *nostalgia*. James Agee wrote:

> And so in this quiet introit, and in all the time we have stayed in this house, and in all we have sought, and in each detail of it, there is so keen, sad, and precious a *nostalgia* as I can scarcely otherwise know; a knowledge of brief truancy into the sources of my life, whereto I have no rightful access, having paid no price beyond love and sorrow.[5]

This ineffable sense of nostalgia colors the viewer's own memory, in which the filmic world of Ang Lee lingers far beyond the viewing experience. Some of these unforgettable scenes include: a father carrying his teenage daughter through a gray, bare forest; a mournful Hulk hanging pathetically from a fighterjet's fuselage before plummeting back to earth; an impossible battle at the top of a green bamboo grove; two chairs drawn side by side observed in a lingering gaze by the camera; the slap of a newspaper on a front step; the silent sadness on Jack's face as Ennis undresses and bathes just beyond his line of vision; Richard Parker's unceremonious parting with Pi which haunts him in memory; Mr. Yee's devastation as he contemplates the rumpled sheets on the bed after the death of his lover; Piu Piu glancing back over her shoulder at the Statue of Liberty, which represents the freedom she longs for but which (for her) remains out of reach.

Lee's films' transcendence of cultural and gender boundaries—as well as language barriers—leads to a unique "transcendence" in his films. As noted, one of the challenges that Ang Lee presents is his categorization within national or transnational cinema, Chinese or Hollywood cinema, independent art-house or big-budget blockbuster. Lee resists easy categorization; his position in world cinema underscores the slippery terrain of modern academic terminology, as well as shifting conceptualization of national identity in a globalized society. One thing is certain, however: he brings a Chinese sensibility to his films which adds uniquely to their transcendence. Lee's dramas do not aim for a standard Hollywood "happy ending." On the whole, Chinese dramas do not reach such a state of "closure"—there is a much greater tolerance of unresolved sadness and pain. This is why his films, with this Chinese aesthetic, have such an appeal to the Hollywood-saturated English-speaking world.

He brings the tension of unresolved tragedy to his work in, for example, the ending of *Crouching Tiger, Hidden Dragon* in which the viewer is not informed whether the female lead lives or dies, or the ending of *Brokeback Mountain* which leaves the main character with unresolved heartache in a dilapidated trailer home. Lee carries this unresolved tension, which is an element of Chinese sensibility, into his films and makes it accessible and appealing to the non-Chinese viewer. The phrase "huai jiu" or "nostalgia for the past" is a big part of the melancholic element in Chinese culture. The Chinese sense of the word "nostalgia" is not quite the same as the Western meaning; the word "nostalgia" in Chinese carries with it an almost unbearable yearning, a sense of unfulfilled desire—in other words, a longing for things to be not as they are. This nostalgic yearning characterizes Chinese art and literature, especially poetry.

Ang Lee ends his 2002 Chinese-language autobiography, "A Ten-Year Dream of Cinema," with the text of an English poem entitled "The Dreame" by seventeenth-century poet Ben Jonson, a contemporary of Shakespeare. "The Dreame" with music by Patrick Doyle was also performed by Jane Eaglen over the *Sense and Sensibility* end titles. The fact that this literary work appears twice in Ang Lee's oeuvre demonstrates the importance of this particular poem to the director. Below is the poem's text.

The Dreame

> Or Scorne, or pittie on me take,
> I must the true Relation make,
> I am undone to Night;
> Love in a subtile Dreame disguis'd,
> Hath both my heart and me surpris'd,
> Whom never yet he durst attempt t' awake;
> Nor will he tell me for whose sake
> He did me the Delight,
> Or Spight,
> But leaves me to inquire,
> In all my wild desire
> Of sleepe againe; who was his Aid,
> And sleepe so guiltie and afraid,
> As since he dares not come within my sight.

Like the desire that "dares not come within my sight" in this poem, Lee's films express the unknown and unrealized desires of the heart. He uses the example of Marianne, who loved not Willoughby but the fascination of her own romantic interest in him; and Jen, who leapt into the clouds into an unknown state, caught in an endless reverie, preferring this to her real-life lover, Lo. Lee uses this poem as a metaphor to express his own experience of living in the "world of film," the "world within the screen." For Ang Lee, film is like a "subtile Dream disguis'd," the elusive and fleeting sense captured by Jonson's poem.

He closes his book "A Ten-year Dream of Cinema" with these words: "I would like to live inside the film and observe the world from the other side of the screen—perhaps it is even more beautiful."[6]

NOTES

I. INTRODUCTION: *ANG LEE—A HISTORY*

1. Ang Lee, quoted in Anne Thompson's "Ang Lee's 'Brokeback' explores 'last frontier,'" *Reuters/Hollywood Reporter/Yahoo News*, November 11, 2005; see http://news.yahoo.com/s/nm/20051111/en_nm/brokeback_dc (accessed November 11, 2005).

2. Jake Gyllenhaal, quoted in Bruce Shenitz's "Kissin' Cowboy," *Out* (October 2005): 94.

3. One of the actors from this group has since received this honor; Heath Ledger posthumously won the Academy Award for Best Supporting Actor for his role in *The Dark Knight* (2008).

4. Ang Lee quoting his father in Gregory Ellwood's "Top of the 'Mountain,'" *Msn.com*, November 29, 2005; see http://movies.msn.com/movies/hitlist/11–29–05_2 (accessed November 30, 2005). Lee adds, "[For my conservative] father to encourage me, and it happened to be a gay movie, it was kind of strange. I didn't tell him what I was going to make."

5. Ang Lee, quoted in Michael Berry's *Speaking in Images*, 336.

6. Ang Lee, quoted in Elwood (2005).

7. Further capitalizing on this success, the Weinstein Company is producing a sequel entitled *Crouching Tiger, Hidden Dragon II: The Green Destiny*, directed by Yuen Wo Ping, with Michelle Yeoh reprising her role as Yu Shu Lien, based on the fifth and final book of the Crane-Iron Pentalogy entitled *Iron Knight, Silver Vase*.

8. *Crouching Tiger, Hidden Dragon* held the record for the most successful foreign-language film until 2004, when it was surpassed by the release of Mel Gibson's *The Passion of the Christ*.

9. *Crouching Tiger, Hidden Dragon* went down in Academy Awards lore when Steve Martin cracked his classic joke: "I saw *Crouching Tiger, Hidden Dragon* and I didn't see any tigers and dragons and then I realized why. They were hiding and crouching." Steve Martin, host of the 73rd Annual Academy Awards Ceremony in 2001, where Lee's *Crouching Tiger, Hidden Dragon* won four awards.

10. A poster of Ang Lee now honors the Chin Men Theater's most famous "alumnus."

11. With the small number of universities in Taiwan in the 1970s, only the educated elite had the opportunity to attend college. In that period, only 30 to 40 percent of eligible high school students passed the difficult Joint College Entrance Examination. Nevertheless, the son of a principal failing the exam would be stigmatized, and doubly so since students of theater school were known chiefly for physical beauty rather than for academic prowess.

12. Ang Lee, in Zhang Jingpei, ed., *Shinian yijiao dianying meng* [A ten-year dream of cinema], 34.

13. During his time in the military, Ang Lee also made his second work, *A Day in the Life of Maquan Chen (Chen Maquan de yitian, 1978)*, a 9-minute film about a fisherman and his son out fishing for the day.

14. In his father's last-ditch attempt to secure academic status for his son, Lee Sheng allowed his son to continue his studies at the Taiwan Academy of Arts only if he promised to pursue graduate study in the United States. No doubt Lee Sheng had hoped his son would choose a more respectable major, but it was not to be. Also, because the Academy was a vocational school rather than a university, as a transfer undergraduate Ang Lee had to begin his studies in the United States as a university underclassman although he was old enough to be a graduate student.

15. John Lahr, "Becoming the Hulk," *The New Yorker*, June 30, 2003, 76.

16. Ang Lee, quoted in Lahr (2003:76).

17. Jane Lin, quoted in Lahr (2003:76).

18. Ibid.

19. Ang Lee, quoted in Stephen Lowenstein, ed., *My First Movie*, 367.

20. Ang Lee, quoted in Zhang (2002:52).

21. Lahr (2003:77).

22. Neil Peng, quoted in Ho Yi's "Family and Friends Praise Ang Lee's Quiet Dedication," *Taipei Times*, March 7, 2006, 4.

23. Lahr (2003:77–78). Lahr records the memorable sentence pronounced by Lee when he first met Ted Hope and James Schamus: "If I don't make a movie soon, I think I'll die." Quoted in Lahr (ibid., 77).

24. Lee describes it: "When I sent those scripts, that was the lowest point of my life. We'd just had our second son, and when I went to collect them from hospital, I went to the bank to try and get some money to buy some diapers—the screen showed I've got $26 left." Ang Lee, interviewed in "Ang Lee and James Schamus: The Guardian/NFT Interview," *Guardian Unlimited*, November 7, 2000; see www.guardian.co.uk/film/2000/nov/07/3 (accessed August 29, 2003).

25. Xu Ligong (Hsu Li-kong) was the production manager of Taiwan's Central Motion Pictures Corporation until 1997; his desire to support young cinematic talent was largely responsible for the launch of Ang Lee's career. Xu also produced newcomer Tsai Ming-liang's first two films, *Rebels of a Neon God* (1992) and *Vive L'Amour* (1994).

26. Schamus also lent a hand on Lee's first two screenplays to flesh out the American characters and bring a more authentic flavor to scenes set in New York City. Without Schamus' expertise, the American characters—particularly the gay character "Simon" played by Mitchell Lichtenstein in *The Wedding Banquet*—would have seemed underdeveloped and lacked wider appeal.

27. Ti Wei, "Generational/Cultural Contradiction and Global Incorporation: Ang Lee's *Eat Drink Man Woman*," in Chris Berry and Feii Lu, eds., *Island on the Edge: Taiwan New Cinema and After*, 102.

28. *The Wedding Banquet* lost to the Spanish film *Belle Epoque* (*The Age of Beauty*, 1992).

29. Ang Lee, speaking on "A Feast for the Eyes: Ang Lee in Taipei," the making-of featurette for *Eat Drink Man Woman* (MGM World Films Home Video, 2002).

30. Ang Lee, speaking in ibid.

31. "We overuse sex in the movies—why not food?" Ang Lee, speaking in ibid.

32. *Eat Drink Man Woman* lost to the Russian film *Utomlyonnye solntsem* (*Burnt by the Sun*, 1994).

33. Ang Lee, quoted in Wei (2005:110).

34. Lindsay Doran notes that the Columbia and Mirage studios had been pushing for Thompson to play the lead for some time; Lee's decision confirmed how apposite this choice was. See the introduction to Emma Thompson's *The Sense and Sensibility Screenplay and Diaries*, 15.

35. Interview in the dossier on Ang Lee edited by the Taipei Golden Horse International Film Festival Executive Committee, *Dianying dang'an: Li An* [Cinedossier: Ang Lee], 14.

36. From "Ang Lee and James Schamus: The Guardian/NFT Interview," *Guardian Unlimited*, November 7, 2000.

37. Ang Lee, quoted in Winnie Chung, "The Reel Winner," *East* 3.4 (2001): 60.

38. Anon., 2001a, "Ang Lee: Dreaming Up an Everchanging Destiny," in a CNN Special Report on Ang Lee; see www.cnn.com/SPECIALS/2001/americasbest/pro.alee.html (accessed November 5, 2003).

39. Tad Friend, "Credit Grab," *The New Yorker*, October 20, 2003, 160.

40. Lahr (2003:81).

41. Jim Poniewozik, quoted in a 2001 CNN Special Report on Ang Lee, "Ang Lee: Dreaming Up an Everchanging Destiny."

42. In 1994, early in Lee's career, Schamus wrote this tribute to the director: "In a business where self-effacement and modesty are not exactly valued character traits, Ang has succeeded precisely because of his gentle yet determined demeanor. While the persona of the average producer or director is akin to something like a car salesman on an acid trip, it's difficult not to listen seriously to Ang because he speaks so softly and gestures so gently. On the film set during production Ang is, like the emotions his films elicit, everywhere and nowhere—his crews revere him even when they hardly notice that he's there giving the orders and providing the vision that's keeping them working night and day. For anyone even vaguely familiar with the norms of behavior in the film industry, Ang is a genuine anomaly." James Schamus, "Introduction," *Eat Drink Man Woman and The Wedding Banquet: Two Films by Ang Lee*, x–xi.

43. While making *Sense and Sensibility* in 1995, Ang Lee was overheard muttering: "No more sheeps. Never again sheeps." See Emma Thompson (1996:229). *Brokeback Mountain* revealed that he did not get his wish.

44. Lynn Lin, quoted in "Taiwanese Cheer Lee's Win, But Some Question Subject Matter," *Taipei Times*, March 7, 2006, 4.

45. However, not all Taiwanese were uniformly happy about the win. While many legislators applauded Ang Lee's success, the independent legislator and social critic Li Ao was quoted as saying, "I do not understand gay movies and I dislike the idea of homosexuality. . . . *Brokeback Mountain* is simply a nuisance to me." Li Ao, quoted in ibid.

46. Ang Lee, quoted at the postshow interview at the 78th Academy Awards ceremony, March 5, 2006.

47. Annie Proulx, "Blood on the Red Carpet," *Guardian Unlimited*, March 11, 2006; see http://books.guardian.co.uk/comment/story/0,,1727309,00.html (accessed March 11, 2006).

48. Annie Proulx, quoted in "'Brokeback' author: We Were Robbed," CNN, March 16, 2006; see edition.cnn.com./2006/SHOWBIZ/Movies/03/15film.proulx.ap/index/html (accessed March 16, 2006).

49. Kathleen Murphy, "Blue State vs. Red State: Oscar's Civil War," MSN Movies website, no date; see http://movies.msn.com/movies/oscars2006/civilwar (accessed March 20, 2006).

50. Stephen D. Greydanus, "Review of *Brokeback Mountain*," *Decent Films Guide*; see www.decentfilms.com/sections/reviews/brokebackmountain.html (accessed March 20, 2006).

51. Murphy (2006).

52. Ibid.

53. Ibid.

54. Chavasse Turnquest-Liriano, quoted in Paco Nuñez, "Bahamas 'Brokeback Mountain' Ban Draws Ire," *Associated Press*, March 30, 2006; see www.breitbart.com/news/2006/03/30/D8GM5K30C.html (accessed April 2, 2006).

55. Steve Gorman, "Randy Quaid sues studio over 'Brokeback Mountain,'" *Reuters*, March 24, 2006; see http://go.reuters.com/newsArticle.jhtml?type=entertainmentNews&storyID=11644132 (accessed March 24, 2006).

56. Diana Ossana, "Climbing Brokeback Mountain," in Annie Proulx, Larry McMurtry, and Diana Ossana's *Brokeback Mountain: Story to Screenplay*, 149.

57. Jon Stewart, host of the 78th annual Academy Awards in Los Angeles, March 5, 2006.

58. Other scholarly works that have appeared on *Brokeback Mountain* include Eric Patterson's *On Brokeback Mountain: Meditations about Masculinity, Fear, and Love in the Story and the Film* (2008), and Gary Needham's *Brokeback Mountain* (2010). There are also a host of nonacademic books containing personal responses to the film, as well as a *Brokeback Mountain* trivia book.

59. Karen Kingsbury, quoted in "*Lust, Caution* Cast Named," Twitchfilm, July 19, 2006; see www.twitchfilm.net/archives/006894.html (accessed October 9, 2006). For academic articles on selected works by Eileen Chang, see Peng-hsiang Chen and Whitney Crothers Dilley, eds., *Feminism/Femininity in Chinese Literature* (2002). For translations of Eileen Chang's early writings, see Eileen Chang, *Love in a Fallen City*, trans. Karen S. Kingsbury (2006).

60. The full quotation is as follows: "I made two big mistakes. I put 'Woodstock' in the title, and I put his name on the poster. Because, you know, everybody who goes to an Ang Lee movie, you want to be sublimely depressed by the end of the film. And if you have 'Woodstock' in the title, you think you're going to be seeing Joe Cocker screaming onstage." James Schamus, quoted in Jada Yuan, "Ang Lee and James Schamus Discuss the Mistakes They Made with *Taking Woodstock*," Nymag.com, November 20, 2009; see http://nymag.com/daily/entertainment/2009/11/ang_lee_and_james_schamus_talk.html (accessed November 20, 2009).

61. Stephen Holden, "What I Saw at the Countercultural Revolution," *New York Times*, August 26, 2009, C1.

62. Ang Lee, quoted in Edward Douglas, "Oscar-Worthy: *Life of Pi* Director Ang Lee," November 15, 2012. http://www.comingsoon.net/news/weekendwarriornews.php?id=96684, accessed November 20, 2012.

63. Ibid.

64. Ibid.

65. Ang Lee, quoted in Zhang (2002:6).

66. Ang Lee, quoted in Lahr (2003:80).

67. Ang Lee, quoted in "Ang Lee: Biography" on the Internet Movie Database (IMDb), no date; see www.imdb.com/name/nm0000487/bio (accessed February 19, 2006).

68. Ang Lee, quoted in an interview with Anupama Chopra, "Adrift with a Tiger and the Film God," *New York Times*, September 9, 2012, AR44.

2. ANG LEE AS DIRECTOR: *HIS POSITION IN ASIAN AND WORLD CINEMA*

1. The term "Fifth Generation," referring to China's new direction in filmmaking beginning in the mid-1980s, is derived from a periodization of Chinese directors trained since the end of the Cultural Revolution in 1976.

2. James Clifford, "Diasporas," in *Routes: Travel and Translation in the Late Twentieth Century* (1997), 266, 269 (Clifford's emphases).

3. Stephen Teo, *Wong Kar-wai* (2005), 99.

4. Emma Thompson notes in her journal account of the film: "I very much like the fact that there are four generations represented in this film—from Margaret's twelve-year-old perspective through Elinor and Marianne's twenties and Mrs. Dashwood's forties to Mrs. Jennings' sixties. Not a thirty-something in sight." See Emma Thompson's *The Sense and Sensibility Screenplay and Diaries* (1996), 241.

5. Ang Lee, quoted in Michael Pye's "Austen Viewed from Mars," *Daily Telegraph*, January 27, 1996, A1.

6. Chris Berry and Mary Farquhar, "From National Cinemas to Cinema and the National: Rethinking the National in Transnational Chinese Cinemas," *Journal of Modern Literature in Chinese* 4, no. 2 (2001):109–122.

7. *Chinese Films in Focus II* (2008) updates and expands its predecessor, providing, in total, 35 in-depth readings of individual Chinese films from China, Taiwan, Hong Kong and other parts of the diaspora.

8. Sheldon H. Lu and Emilie Yueh-yu Yeh, "Introduction: Mapping the Field of Chinese-Language Cinema," in Lu and Yeh, eds., *Chinese-Language Film: Historiography, Poetics, Politics* (2005), 1.

9. Chris Berry explores the topic of transnationalism and Chinese cinema further in "What Is Transnational Cinema?: Thinking from the Chinese Situation," *Transnational Cinemas* 1.2 (2010): 111–27, in which he argues for understanding transnational cinema as growing out of the conditions of globalization, shaped by neoliberalism, free trade, and the collapse of socialism.

10. See Gina Marchetti, "*The Wedding Banquet*: Global Chinese Cinema and the Asian American Experience," in Darrell Y. Hamamoto and Sandra Liu, eds., *Countervisions: Asian American Film Criticism* (2000), 291–92.

11. Ang Lee, quoted in ibid., 291.

12. Even Ang Lee's name reflects his desire to retain a Chinese identity. His name rendered in pinyin romanization is Li An. Considering his options Li An or Lee An too feminine, Ang Lee did not choose to adopt an English name (such as "David") to clarify his gender. Instead, he added a "g" to his Chinese name to lessen the possibility of confusing it with a woman's name ("Lee An," or the given name "Anne"). The name he selected for himself (Lee Ang) was both neutral in gender and still "Chinese" in appearance. For more on Lee's preservation of his Chinese identity, see Emilie Yueh-yu Yeh and Darrell W. Davis, *Taiwan Film Directors: A Treasure Island* (2005), 188–89.

13. Ang Lee, quoted in Michael Berry's *Speaking in Images* (2005), 352.

14. For a complete study of Chinese cinematic history from its earliest beginnings in Shanghai, see Yingjin Zhang's *Chinese National Cinema* (2004). A transnational history of Chinese film, the volume covers the film industries in China, Hong Kong, and Taiwan.

15. Kwai-Cheung Lo, *Chinese Face/Off: The Transnational Popular Culture of Hong Kong* (2005), 248.

16. Bruce Lee died on July 20, 1973, in the apartment of actress Betty Ting Pei, who had given him her own prescription drug, Equagesic, to cure his headache. He lay down for a nap and never woke up again. The circumstances involving Bruce Lee's death have never been adequately explained, despite a special investigation team called in from London. It was concluded that Bruce Lee had already been suffering from excessive water pressure in his brain due to a stunt accident two weeks prior to his death, and that the drug had exacerbated the condition, causing a cerebral edema. However, conspiracy theorists still debate this, even more intensely after Lee's only son, Brandon, was killed in a freak accident by a dummy bullet while filming *The Crow* in 1993. For biographical studies of Lee, see Linda Lee (1989) and Bruce Thomas (1994). For his influence, see Lou Gaul (1997).

17. The four films Bruce Lee made in Hong Kong in the last three years before his death were *The Big Boss* (1971), *Fist of Fury* (also entitled *The Chinese Connection*, 1972), *The Way of the Dragon* (1972), and *Enter the Dragon* (1973).

18. Jackie Chan was also in the remake of *The Karate Kid* (2010), playing kung fu master Mr. Han in his first dramatic role in American film, costarring Jaden Smith.

19. Steve Fore, "Jackie Chan and the Cultural Dynamics of Global Entertainment," in Sheldon Hsiao-peng Lu. ed., *Transnational Chinese Cinemas: Identity, Nationhood, Gender* (1997), 240.

20. Peggy Hsiung-ping Chiao, "The Emergence of the New Cinema of Taiwan," *Asian Cinema* 5.1 (March 1990): 9.

21. Jeff Yang, *Once Upon a Time in China: A Guide to Hong Kong, Taiwanese, and Mainland Chinese Cinema* (2003), 178.

22. Ibid., 82.

23. Both from Fredric Jameson, "Remapping Taipei," in Browne et al., eds., *New Chinese Cinemas* (1994), 147.

24. Ang Lee, quoted in Stephen Schaefer, "Mr. Showbiz Interview: Ang Lee," March 5, 2001; see http://mrshowbiz.go.com/interviews/572_1.html (accessed August 27, 2005).

25. Nineteen directors have been honored more than once with a Best Director Academy Award, including John Ford (four wins), Frank Capra (three wins), and William Wyler (three wins), while Oliver Stone, Steven Spielberg, and fourteen others have two wins apiece.

26. Ang Lee in Zhang Jingpei, ed., *Shinian yijiao dianying meng* [A ten-year dream of cinema] (2002), 37.

27. See Feii Lu, *Taiwan dianying: zhengzhi, jingji, meixue* [Taiwan cinema: politics, economics, aesthetics] (1998), 103–108, 271–77.

28. Ang Lee, quoted in Rick Lyman's "Watching Movies with Ang Lee: Crouching Memory, Hidden Heart," *New York Times*, March 9, 2001, E27.

29. Yingjin Zhang documents the 1963 popularity of *The Love Eterne*: "Fans went to see the film repeatedly, some up to 100 times. After the movie won several major prizes at the second Golden Horse Awards, 200,000 fans crowded the airport and its adjacent streets when the actress Ling Po, who was given an acting prize for her cross-dressing role as Liang Shanbo, arrived for the award ceremony. For safety reasons, Ling Po was secretly escorted out of the airport in a police vehicle, but to satisfy her fans, she was paraded in a car the next day to 180,000 people lining the streets." Yingjing Zhang, *Chinese National Cinema* (2004:138).

30. Ang Lee, quoted in Lyman (2001:E1).

31. Ang Lee, quoted in ibid., E27.

32. Ang Lee, quoted in ibid.

33. Shu-ching Shih, "Zhuanfang Li An: Cong Buolin, Weinisi dao Haolaiwu" [Interview with Ang Lee: From Berlin and Venice to Hollywood], *Yinke wenxue shenghuo zhi* [Ink Literary Monthly] 1.5 (January 2006): 26.

34. Ang Lee, quoted in Robert Hilferty Bloomberg's "Taiwan's Ang Lee Discusses Gay Cowboys and Sheep Wrangling," *The China Post*, December 13. 2005; see www.chinapost.com.tw/p_detail. asp?id=73561&GRP=h&onNews= (accessed December 13, 2005).

35. James Schamus, interviewed by Andy Towle, "Behind *Brokeback Mountain*," January 25, 2006; see http://towleroad.typepad.com/towleroad/2006/01/interview_with_.html, (accessed April 2, 2006).

36. Ang Lee adds to his description of James Schamus: "And on a personal level: he helps me decide which ties to wear." Ang Lee, quoted in Michael Berry (2005:333–34).

37. James Schamus, "*Brokeback Mountain*: An Exchange," *New York Review of Books*, April 6, 2006, 32.

38. Asked why he did not work with Schamus on *Life of Pi*, Lee replied: "I just thought it was time to try something on my own and see what happens at least once. To grow up a little bit, so to speak (chuckles), just to see what it was like. I just felt like doing it, and he was very nice and encouraging about it and it just happened to be the most difficult movie I've made. (Laughs) So I'll go back to James—we're good friends. We've been working for a long time so a change was good for both of us." Ang Lee, quoted in Edward Douglas, "Oscar-Worthy: *Life of Pi* Director Ang Lee," November 15, 2012; see www.comingsoon.net/news/weekendwarriornews.php?id=96684 (accessed November 20, 2012).

39. Ang Lee, quoted in David M. Halbfinger, "The Delicate Job of Transforming a Geisha," *New York Times*, November 6, 2005, 4.

40. Ang Lee, quoted in ibid.

3. CONFUCIAN VALUES AND CULTURAL DISPLACEMENT
IN *PUSHING HANDS*

1. Ang Lee, quoted in Chris Berry, "Taiwanese Melodrama Returns with a Twist in *The Wedding Banquet*," *Cinemaya* 21 (Fall 1993): 54.

2. See Sheng-mei Ma, "Ang Lee's Domestic Tragicomedy: Immigrant Nostalgia, Exotic/Ethnic Tour, Global Market," *Journal of Popular Culture* 30.1 (1996): 191–201.

3. Wei Ming Dariotis and Eileen Fung, "Breaking the Soy Sauce Jar: Diaspora and Displacement in the Films of Ang Lee," in Sheldon Hsiao-peng Lu, ed., *Transnational Chinese Cinemas: Identity, Nationhood, Gender* (1997), 217.

4. Shu-mei Shih, "Globalization and Minoritization: Ang Lee and the Politics of Flexibility," *New Formations* 40: 89.

5. Possibly an homage to King Hu, one of the most influential Chinese directors in the 1970s, whose *A Touch of Zen* (1969) was a distinct source of inspiration for *Crouching Tiger, Hidden Dragon*. Toward the end of his career, King Hu fell out of favor with Chinese producers because of his slow and meticulous working habits, particularly after spending four years making *A Touch of Zen*, and his career never recovered. In the last years before his death, he struggled unsuccessfully to find investors for his film on Chinese-American railway workers.

6. Ang Lee, speaking on "A Forbidden Passion," a special feature on the DVD *The Wedding Banquet* (MGM Home Video, 1993).

7. Ang Lee, quoted in Zhang Jingpei, ed., *Shinian yijiao dianying meng* [A ten-year dream of cinema] (2002), 17.

8. See Ray Wood, "Pushing Hands," at *taichido.com* (2000, revised 2005); see www.soton.ac.uk/~maa1/chi/taichi/push.htm (accessed May 6, 2005).

9. Ibid.

10. "During my first two movies, I felt like an old lady babbling on and on about her life! (Laughs) That is because *it was my life*." Ang Lee, quoted in Michael Berry's *Speaking in Images* (2005), 337–38 (emphasis mine).

11. "Foreigner" is Ang Lee's own word choice; he characterizes himself as a foreigner in the United States. "Looking back, I realize that I have always had identity problems. People like me, second-generation mainlanders from Taiwan, are a rare breed. They last only about two generations and account for a very small portion of people among Chinese, but we have a very unique experience. . . . Many of us came from Taiwan to the States, where we are foreigners. So all our lives we have identity problems." Ang Lee, quoted in Michael Berry (2005:331–32).

12. Ang Lee, *Pushing Hands* (*Tuishou*) (1991a:45).

13. Ang Lee, interviewed in Berry (2005:331).

4. TRANSGRESSING BOUNDARIES OF GENDER AND CULTURE IN *THE WEDDING BANQUET*

1. James Schamus, speaking on "A Forbidden Passion," a special feature on the DVD *The Wedding Banquet* (MGM Home Video, 1993).

2. Much of the score was composed by the Taiwanese musician Mader; however, the pop song playing on the tape-player that Wai-Tung refers to as "a racket" is actually May Chin's (who played Wei Wei) bestselling duet "Diamond and Stone," performed with fellow Taiwanese artist Ang-Go Tong.

3. Ang Lee, speaking on "A Forbidden Passion," 1993.

4. Ang Lee, speaking on "A Forbidden Passion," 1993. James Schamus adds: "I think that Ang having a father who was a high school principal and somebody who really stressed traditional Chinese values—and that gentleman having a son who ends up going to theater school in the United States . . . There's a lot of autobiography that gets coded into these stories."

5. Ang Lee, "A Forbidden Passion," 1993.

6. Ang Lee and Peng Guangyuan (Neil Peng), *The Wedding Banquet* (screenplay, 1993), 146–47.

7. See Dariotis and Fung, "Breaking the Soy Sauce Jar," in Lu, ed., *Transnational Chinese Cinemas* (1997), 204–205.

8. Marchetti, "*The Wedding Banquet*: Global Chinese Cinema and the Asian American Experience," in Hamamoto and Liu, eds., *Countervisions* (2000), 279.

9. Ibid., 279.

10. Ibid. For more on the political allegory in *The Wedding Banquet*, see Marchetti (2000:276–80).

11. Dariotis and Fung (1997:202).

12. Lee and Peng (1993:69–70).

13. For more on the film's ambivalent stance toward homosexuality, see Dariotis and Fung (1997:199–202).

14. See Marchetti (2000:286).

15. Information about the origin of *The Wedding Banquet* is from Neil Peng [Peng Guangyuan], "Preface," in Lee and Peng (1993:21–26).

16. Ang Lee, in a cameo appearance as "Guest C" in *The Wedding Banquet*, in *Eat Drink Man Woman and The Wedding Banquet: Two Films by Ang Lee* (1994), 177.

17. Ang Lee, "A Forbidden Passion," 1993.

5. GLOBALIZATION AND CULTURAL IDENTITY IN *EAT DRINK MAN WOLMAN*

1. From Ang Lee, Wang Huiling, and James Schamus, *Yinshi nannü: dianying juben yu paishe guocheng* [Eat drink man woman: screenplay and shooting process], ed. Central Motion Pictures Corporation (1994), 166.

2. See Yeh and Davis, *Taiwan Film Directors* (2005), 210–13.

3. See Steve Fore's "Jackie Chan and the Cultural Dynamics of Global Entertainment" (1997), 241.

4. Yeh and Davis (2005:209).

5. Andrew Tudor, *Theories of Film* (1973), 139.

6. Ti Wei, "Generational/Cultural Contradiction and Global Incorporation" (2005), 111.

7. Ang Lee, quoted in Zhang Jingpei, ed., *Shinian yijiao dianying meng* [A ten-year dream of cinema] (2002), 133–34.

8. Sheng-mei Ma, "Ang Lee's Domestic Tragicomedy," *Journal of Popular Culture* 30.1 (1996): 195.

9. Arjun Appadurai, *Modernity at Large: Cultural Dimensions of Globalization* (1996), 38.

10. Ibid., 31.

11. Slavoj Žižek, *The Sublime Object of Ideology* (1989), 97.

12. "Japanese-style" indicates the style of architecture of official residences built during the Japanese occupation of Taiwan; the style includes common features such as slanted, black-tiled roofs, nailed shingles, and elegant wooden interiors.

13. For extensive coverage of the culinary and filming techniques used in *Eat Drink Man Woman*, see Yeh and Davis (2005:205–209).

14. Quote from John Anderson, film critic at *New York Newsday*, as it appears on the 2002 DVD cover of *Eat Drink Man Woman*, issued in the World Films series by Metro-Goldwyn-Mayer.

15. From an anonymous internet discussion of *Brokeback Mountain*.

16. Yeh and Davis (2005:209).

17. Ibid., 210.

18. James Schamus, in the introduction to *Eat Drink Man Woman and The Wedding Banquet, Two Films by Ang Lee* (1994), xi.

19. Ang Lee, in Zhang Jingpei (2002:128).

20. Yeh and Davis (2005:210).

21. Ibid.

22. Ibid., 211.

6. OPPOSITION AND RESOLUTION IN *SENSE AND SENSIBILITY*

1. Ang Lee, quoted in Emma Thompson's *The Sense and Sensibility Screenplay and Diaries* (1996), 15.

2. Meenakshi Mukherjee, *Jane Austen* (1991), 26–27.

3. Jane Austen, *Sense and Sensibility* (1811) (1996:33).

4. Ibid., 34.

5. Ibid.

6. Edward Neill, *The Politics of Jane Austen* (1999), 33.

7. Lindsay Doran, in Emma Thompson (1996:15).

8. Ang Lee, in ibid.

9. Anthony Giddens, *The Consequences of Modernity* (1990), 21.

10. Ibid., 64.

11. Malcolm Waters, *Globalization* (1995), 10.

12. Ibid., 9.

13. Mukherjee (1991:49).

14. Austen (1996 [1811]: 67).

15. Mukherjee (1991:53).

16. Emma Thompson (1996:34).

17. Ibid., 43–44.

18. Ibid., 47–48.

19. Ibid., 49–50.

20. Ibid., 74.

21. A complete list of film adaptations of Austen's work can be found in the appendix of Linda Troost and Sayre Greenfield, eds., *Jane Austen in Hollywood* (1998), 188–90.

22. M. Casey Diana, "Emma Thompson's *Sense and Sensibility* as Gateway to Austen's Novel" in Troost and Greenfield, eds., *Jane Austen in Hollywood* (1988), 140.

23. Lindsay Doran, producer of *Sense and Sensibility*, relates the story this way: "It became a matter of which of us had the nerve to suggest the idea first: a Taiwanese director for *Sense and Sensibility*? Were we crazy?" At the time of the studio's offer, Lee had never before read Jane Austen's work. See Lindsay Doran in Emma Thompson (1996:15).

24. Ang Lee, quoted in Michael Berry's *Speaking in Images* (2005), 338.

25. Emma Thompson (1996:220).

26. Ibid., 226.

27. Ibid., 220.

28. Ibid., 240.

29. The notes are recorded on the following pages in Emma Thompson (1996): for Kate Winslet, 238; for Emma Thompson, 219; for Alan Rickman, 232; for Greg Wise, 240.

30. Emma Thompson (1996:232).

31. Ibid., 216–17.

32. Ibid., 237.

33. Ibid., 247.

34. Ibid., 253.

35. Ang Lee, quoted in "Adapting Jane Austen's *Sense and Sensibility*," on the Hampshire County Council website, 1995; see www.hants.gov.uk/austen/story.html#adaptingjane, 1 (accessed September 21, 2002).

36. Ibid.

7. FRAGMENTARY NARRATIVES/FRAGMENTED IDENTITIES IN *THE ICE STORM*

1. James Schamus, in the introduction to *The Ice Storm: The Shooting Script* (1997), 3.

2. Ibid.

3. Ang Lee, in his preface to Schamus (1997:vii).

4. Ibid.

5. Review by Charles Taylor, "Baby, It's Cold Outside," *Salon.com*, October 17, 1997; see www.salon.com/ent/movies/1997/10/17ice.html (accessed May 8, 1999).

6. Ang Lee, quoted in Michael Berry's *Speaking in Images* (2005), 337.

7. Ang Lee, in an interview with Jennie Yabroff, *Salon.com*, October 17, 1997; see www.salon.com/ent/int/1997/10/17lee.html (accessed May 8, 1999).

8. The quoted sections of dialogue in this chapter are taken from James Schamus' original screenplay to demonstrate this quality of fragmentation and foreshortening.

9. Schamus (1997:16–17).

10. Ibid., 27–28.

11. Ibid., 51–53.

12. Ibid., 50.

13. Ibid., 55–57.

14. Ibid., 2–3.

15. Les Daniels, *Marvel: Five Fabulous Decades of the World's Greatest Comics* (1991), 126.

16. Ang Lee, in Schamus (1997:vii).

17. Schamus (1997:148).

18. Ang Lee, in Schamus, (1997:viii).

19. Ang Lee, in Jennie Yabroff, "Stranger in a Strange Land," *Salon.com*, October 17, 1977; see www.salon.com/ent/int/1997/10/17lee.html (accessed May 8, 1999).

20. Interview with Winnie Chung, "The Reel Winner," *East* 3.4 (2001): 60.

8. RACE, GENDER, CLASS, AND SOCIAL IDENTITY IN *RIDE WITH THE DEVIL*

1. *Ride with the Devil* was recut and shown as a director's cut for the first time at a retrospective hosted by the Film Society of Lincoln Center from August 1–11, 2009. As reported by Larry Rohter in the *New York Times*, Lee was unusually young to be honored as the subject of an 11-day film retrospective. See Larry Rohter, "Chasing Society's Hidden Dragons," *New York Times*, August 1, 2009, C1.

2. See Liz Rowlinson, "A Quick Chat with Daniel Woodrell," *The Richmond Review*, (1999); see www.richmondreview.co.uk/features/woodrell.html (accessed March 6, 2001).

3. James Gleick, *Faster: The Acceleration of Just About Everything* (2000), 21.

4. H. Arthur Scott Trask, "Review of *Ride with the Devil*," *Dixienet* website, 1999; see www.dixienet.org/spatriot/vol7no2/special.html (accessed June 13, 2002).

5. From Stephen Schaefer, "Mr. Showbiz Interview: Ang Lee," March 5, 2001.

6. Ibid.

7. Michael Berry, *Speaking in Images* (2005), 339.

8. Schamus, quoted in Zhang Jinpei, ed., *Shinian yijiao dianying meng* [A ten-year dream of cinema] (2002), 264.

9. Ang Lee, quoted in Berry (2005:339).

9. *Wuxia* NARRATIVE AND TRANSNATIONAL CHINESE IDENTITY IN *CROUCHING TIGER, HIDDEN DRAGON*

1. Ang Lee, "Foreword," in Linda Sunshine, ed., *Crouching Tiger, Hidden Dragon: Portrait of an Ang Lee Film, Including the Complete Screenplay* (2000), 7.

2. Wang Dulu (1909–1977), born into a Manchu family in Beijing, was a Chinese author working in the early part of the twentieth century. His principal occupation was teaching at an elementary school, but in order to supplement his income, he took up the job of authoring serialized novels on the side. His writing, mainly in the form of social realist drama and martial arts novels, is known for its strong tragic sentiment. In 1956, Wang was appointed as the People's Representative of Shenyang. Following the outbreak of the Cultural Revolution (1966–1976), he underwent persecution due to the "bourgeois elements" in his writing. He died in 1977 of Parkinson's disease. From Pei Xiaoxiong, "Wang Dulu," in Ma Liangchun and Li Futian, eds., *Zhongguo wenxue da cidian* [Dictionary of Chinese Literature], and David Bordwell, "Wang Dulu," in Sunshine (2000a:75).

3. See Jennifer Jay, "*Crouching Tiger, Hidden Dragon*: (Re)packaging Chinas and Selling the Hybridized Culture and Identity in an Age of Globalization," *The Canadian Review of Comparative Literature* 30.3–4 (2003): 702–703; and Yeh and Davis, *Taiwan Film Directors*, 197–98.

4. Yeh and Davis (2005:198).

5. Ang Lee, quoted in Winnie Chung's "The Reel Winner," *East* 3.4 (2001): 60.

6. James Schamus in an interview with Eric Wittmershaus, describing the process of writing *Crouching Tiger, Hidden Dragon*, in "James Schamus: Interview," *Flakmag*, June 14, 2001; see http://flakmag.com/features/schamus.html (accessed November 5, 2005).

7. Ibid.

8. Ang Lee, quoted in Chung (2001:60).

9. Ang Lee, in Zhang Jingpei, ed., *Shinian yijiao dianying meng* [A ten-year dream of cinema] (2002), 305–306.

10. In Jay (2003:707).

11. Rey Chow, *Primitive Passions: Visuality, Sexuality, and Ethnography in Contemporary Chinese Cinema* (1995), 195.

12. See Chris Berry and Mary Farquhar, *China on Screen: Cinema and Nation* (2006), 69.

13. Ibid.

14. Ang Lee, "The *Wuxia* According to Ang Lee XE "Ang Lee" ," in Sunshine (2000b:137).

15. See Lo, *Chinese Face/Off* (2005), 246.

16. Yeh and Davis (2005:190).

17. For more on this argument, see Berry and Farquhar, (2006:69–70).

18. From the complete screenplay, in Sunshine (2000:113).

19. Ibid., 40–41.

20. Jen's name in the original novel and in the Mandarin version of the film, Yü Jiaolong, means "delicate dragon." Lo's full Chinese name is Luo Xiaohu, which means "little tiger."

21. From the complete screenplay, in Sunshine (2000:82).

22. Ibid., 86.

23. Ibid., 110.

24. Ibid., 84.

25. Ibid., 82–3.

26. Ibid., 132.

27. Ibid., 120.

28. See Fran Martin's "The China Simulacrum: Genre, Feminism, and Pan-Chinese Cultural Politics in *Crouching Tiger, Hidden Dragon,*" in Chris Berry and Feii Lu, eds., *Island on the Edge* (2005), 159.

29. Ang Lee, quoted in Stephen Schaefer, "Mr. Showbiz Interview: Ang Lee," March 5, 2001.

30. Ibid.

31. Ibid.

32. Ang Lee, quoted in Kar Law, ed., *Transcending the Times: King Hu and Eileen Chang* (1998), 107.

33. David Bordwell, "Hong Kong Martial Arts Cinema," in Sunshine (2000a:20).

34. Ibid., 20–21.

35. Ang Lee, quoted in Anon. (2001b), "'*Tiger*' Pounces But Misses Big Oscars," CNN website, March 26, 2001; see http://archives.cnn.com/2001/WORLD/asiapcf/east/03/26/china.oscar.miss/index.html (accessed September 23, 2005).

36. Anthony Lane, "Come Fly with Me," *The New Yorker*, December 11, 2000, 131.

37. Ibid.

38. Ibid.

10. THE ULTIMATE OUTSIDER: *HULK*

1. Ang Lee, quoted in John Lahr, "Becoming the Hulk," *The New Yorker*, June 30, 2003, 76, before the release of the film.

2. Interestingly, both origin stories have since been remade, *The Incredible Hulk* in 2008 and *The Amazing Spider-Man* in 2012, demonstrating the continuing lucrative trend of this genre.

3. Joe Kubert, *Superheroes: Joe Kubert's Wonderful World of Comics* (1999), 7.

4. *The Incredible Hulk* was originally gray, but the color was changed to green after it was discovered that a consistent shade of gray could not be supplied by the printer. For more on the history of the comic, see Tom DeFalco's *Hulk: The Incredible Guide* (2003), 28.

5. Stan Lee, quoted in Les Daniels, *Marvel: Five Fabulous Decades of the World's Greatest Comics* (1991), 9.

6. Ibid.

7. Stan Lee also used the alias "Neel Nats" (a pseudo-inversion of his name) in issues where he had written two stories. Stan Lee, quoted in Daniels (1991:41).

8. Ibid.

9. DeFalco (2003:7).

10. Stan Lee, quoted in ibid.

11. Stan Lee, quoted in Daniels (1991:10).

12. Daniels (1991:89–94).

13. Stan Lee would have been on hand to concur with these references because he had a cameo in Ang Lee's *Hulk*. He reportedly improvised his lines in the cameo he shares with Lou Ferrigno (The Hulk in the original television series *The Incredible Hulk*, 1978), who plays the Head of Security in this film. More *Hulk* history can be found at the Internet Movie Database website for *Hulk*, IMDb, n.d.; see www.imdb.com/title/tt0286716/trivia (accessed November 7, 2005).

14. Lahr (2003:75).
15. Ibid., 80.
16. "Hulk," IMDb, n.d.; see www.imdb.com/title/tt0286716/taglines (accessed August 20, 2004).
17. Ang Lee turned down *Terminator 3: Rise of the Machines* (2003) to make *Hulk*. The main role played by Eric Bana was originally offered to Tom Cruise, who turned it down. Billy Crudup, who also turned it down, was Ang Lee's first choice for the role. Other actors tested were Steve Buscemi, David Duchovny, and Jeff Goldblum. The composer Mychael Danna (*The Ice Storm*) was hired for *Hulk*, but was replaced by Danny Elfman during filming. This is evidence that the production process was not entirely a smooth one. Information from the *Hulk* website on the Internet Movie Database, IMDb, n.d.; see www.imdb.com/title/tt0286716/trivia (accessed August 20, 2004).
18. Lahr (2003:75).
19. Daniels (1991:89).
20. James Schamus, John Turman, and Michael France, *Hulk: The Illustrated Screenplay* (2003), 91–92.
21. Ibid., 93–96.
22. Ibid., 97.
23. Ibid., 106.
24. Ibid., 141.
25. James Schamus, quoted in Tad Friend's "Credit Grab," *The New Yorker*, October 20, 2003, 169.
26. Schamus, Turman, and France (2003:96).
27. Daniels (1991:89).
28. Ang Lee, quoted in Rick Lyman's "Watching Movies with Ang Lee: Crouching Memory, Hidden Heart," *New York Times*, March 9, 2001, E27.

11. TRANSCENDING GENDER IN *BROKEBACK MOUNTAIN*

1. Anne Thompson, "Ang Lee's 'Brokeback' explores 'last frontier,'" *Reuters/Hollywood Reporter/Yahoo News*, November 11, 2005.
2. Eve Sedgwick, *Shame and Its Sisters: A Silvan Tompkins Reader* (1995), 35.
3. Judith Halberstam, "Queer Studies," in Philomena Essed, David Theo Goldberg, and Audrey Kobayashi, eds., *A Companion to Gender Studies* (2005b), 63.
4. The story "Brokeback Mountain" was published in the *New Yorker* (1997) without the italicized prologue, which was included in the later version published in 1999 in *Close Range: Wyoming Stories*, a collection of Annie Proulx's short stories.
5. Annie Proulx, "Brokeback Mountain," in *Close Range* (1999 [1997]: 262).
6. Proulx (1999 [1997]: 278).
7. James Schamus, quoted in Thompson (2005).
8. James Schamus, quoted in Sean Smith, "Forbidden Territory" in *Newsweek*, November 21, 2005; see http://msnbc.msn.com/id/10017716/site/newsweek/page/2/ (accessed November 21, 2005).
9. Anon., "Town Not Big Enough for Gay Cowboy Heath," *The Daily Telegraph*, January 10, 2006; see www.dailytelegraph.news.com.au/story/0,20281,17771006–50001026,00.html (accessed January 12, 2006).
10. Choire Sicha, "Chokeback Mountain," *New York Observer*, November 21, 2005, 15.
11. *Brokeback Mountain* ironically produced a heterosexual romance between two actors paired as husband and wife in the film; after wrapping the film, Heath Ledger had a baby with and became engaged to his costar, Michelle Williams. Although the two never married, they shared a home in Boerum Hill, Brooklyn, from 2005 to 2007, and continued to share parenting responsibilities of their daughter Matilda until Ledger's death in 2008.
12. Jake Gyllenhaal, quoted in Karen Durbin's "Cowboys in Love . . . With Each Other," *New York Times*, September 4, 2005, 9.
13. Frank Rich, "Two Gay Cowboys Hit a Home Run," *New York Times*, December 18, 2005, 13.
14. Ibid.

15. Proulx (1999 [1997]: 283).
16. Ibid., 268–69.
17. Ibid., 277.
18. Ibid., 280.
19. Ibid., 278.
20. Ibid., 276.
21. Ibid., 284.
22. Ibid., 268.
23. Ibid., 278–9.
24. Ang Lee, in Carlo Cavagna, "Interview: Ang Lee," *Aboutfilm.com*, December 15, 2005; see www.aboutfilm.com/movies/b/brokebackmountain/lee.htm (accessed May 20, 2006).
25. Ang Lee, quoted in Durbin (2005:9).
26. Cinematographer Rodrigo Prieto in an uncredited performance—this again demonstrates the low-budget atmosphere within which the film was made. Rodrigo Prieto had worked on another Focus Features production, *21 Grams* (2003), with director Alejandro Gonzáles Iñárritu; Focus Features brought Prieto together with Ang Lee, who was searching for an up-and-coming cinematographer who could shoot quickly.
27. Proulx, 1999 [1997], 278.
28. Ang Lee, quoted in Thompson (2005).
29. Ang Lee, quoted in Durbin (2005:15).

12. EROTICISM AND PERFORMANCE IN *LUST/CAUTION*

1. James Schamus, "Introduction," in Eileen Chang et al., *Lust, Caution: The Story, The Screenplay, and The Making of the Film* (2007), xi.
2. Ibid., xii.
3. Although the film was not popularly received in the West, in Asia it generated an overwhelming response, both positive and negative. While the film was received with unprecedented enthusiasm in Taiwan and Hong Kong, it was castigated in China for its anti-patriotic portrayal of Wang Chia-chih's disloyalty and sexual obsession with a traitor, leading to the actress Tang Wei being banned from the film industry until late 2010. In addition, the most crucial line in the film, when Wang Chia-chih tips off Mr. Yee in the jewelry store, "Go, now!" [*kuai zou*] was changed to "Let's go!" [*zou ba*] to make Wang Chia-chih seem less of a traitor herself. This highly charged and controversial reception of the film is explored in detail in Chinese scholarship on *Lust/Caution*. For further reference, see also Leo Ou-fan Lee's 2008 article "Ang Lee's *Lust, Caution* and Its Reception," *Boundary 2* 35.3: 223–38, and Peng Hsiao-yen and Whitney Crothers Dilley's *From Eileen Chang to Ang Lee: Lust/Caution* (2014).
4. For example, the technique of employing explanatory text in the film's opening frames was used to introduce the central conflict between the Bushwhackers and Jayhawkers at the beginning of Lee's American Civil War drama *Ride with the Devil*. Presumably, for the native English speaker the conflicts of war in China would have an even greater need for explanation.
5. Georges Bataille, *The Accursed Share*, trans. Robert Hurley (1993), 2.48.
6. Georges Bataille, *Eroticism: Death and Sensuality*, trans. Mary Dalwood (1986), 48.
7. Bataille (1993:2.119).
8. Bataille (1986:129).
9. Ibid., 20.
10. Bataille (1993:2.104).
11. Wang Huiling and James Schamus, "*Lust, Caution*: A Screenplay," in Eileen Chang et al., *Lust, Caution: The Story, The Screenplay, and The Making of the Film* (2007), 196.
12. Eileen Chang, "Lust, Caution: The Story," trans. Julia Lovell, reprinted in Eileen Chang et al., *Lust, Caution: The Story, The Screenplay, and The Making of the Film* (2007), 21.
13. Ibid., 23.

14.   Ibid.

15.   The title of the film *Lust/Caution* contains a pun on the word "caution," because the same Chinese character can also mean "ring"—signifying the ring that Mr. Yee gives to Wang Chia-chih. In addition, "lust" and "caution" are presented in a symbiosis common to Lee's work: "lust" is "sense" and "caution" is "sensibility."

16.   Eileen Chang (2007:3).

17.   Ibid., 8.

18.   Ibid., 3–4.

19.   Ibid., 3.

20.   Ibid., 7.

21.   Nick James, "Cruel Intentions: Ang Lee," *Sight & Sound* 18.1 (January 2008): 50.

22.   Moira Macdonald, "Ang Lee and the Power of Performance," *Seattle Times*, October 2, 2007, 11 (italics mine).

23.   James Schamus (2007:xv).

13. MEMORY, NARRATIVE, AND TRANSFORMATION IN *TAKING WOODSTOCK*

1.   Opening lines of the chorus from the song "Woodstock," written one month after the event by Joni Mitchell, and first performed at the Big Sur Folk Festival in 1969. The song was released on Mitchell's third album, *Ladies of the Canyon*, in 1970. Joni Mitchell, "Woodstock," copyright (c) 1969 Siquomb Publishing Corp., New York (BMI).

2.   While the memoir was published under the Americanized name "Tiber," Elliot's original family name "Teichberg" is used in the film.

3.   David Halperin and Valerie Traub, eds., *Gay Shame* (2010), 3–4.

4.   The generation of the film came about when Ang Lee was scheduled on a West Coast television interview program as a guest on the same day as Elliot Tiber. In the green room before the interview, Tiber discussed his autobiography of the Woodstock period and handed Lee a copy of the book with the suggestion that Lee might want to make a movie out of it. When Lee eventually did read it, he was captivated by the story and decided he wanted to make the film. Rachel Abramowitz, "Ang Lee—Hippie?" in the *Los Angeles Times*, August 27, 2009; see http://articles.latimes.com/2009/aug/27/entertainment/et-lee27 (accessed June 16, 2012).

5.   Elliot Tiber, with Tom Monte, *Taking Woodstock: A True Story of a Riot, a Concert, and a Life* (2007), 164.

6.   Ibid.,166.

7.   Michel Foucault, *Discipline and Punish: The Birth of the Prison*, trans. Alan Sheridan (1995), 201–205.

8.   Tiber (2007:212).

9.   Ibid.

10.   Ang Lee, interviewed in "*Taking Woodstock* Production Notes," *festival-cannes.com*, May 15, 2009; see www.festival-cannes.fr/assets/Image/Direct/029702.pdf, 2 (accessed October 12, 2010). Lee saw *Taking Woodstock* as following naturally from his previous work. If his 1973-set movie *The Ice Storm* was, as he says, "the hangover of 1969, then *Taking Woodstock* is the beautiful night before and the last moments of innocence" (2).

11.   James Schamus, interviewed in ibid., 3.

14. STORYTELLING AND TRUTH IN *LIFE OF PI*: *A SPIRITUAL JOURNEY*

1.   The book has been described as "arguably readable" by A. O. Scott, film critic of the *New York Times*, who gave the film one of its early lukewarm reviews. Scott claimed himself too cynical to be moved by the "wonder" in the film. A. O. Scott, "Plenty of Gods, But Just One Fellow Passenger: *Life of Pi*, Directed by Ang Lee," *New York Times*, November 21, 2012, C1.

2.   Yann Martel, "Author's Note," in *Life of Pi* (2001), v.

3. Ibid., vii.

4. Ibid., ix.

5. Martel (2001:24).

6. Lee's entire quote is as follows: "I loved the book, but it's very hard to crack. I thought you can't make a movie about religion but it can be a movie about the value of storytelling and how that brings structure and wisdom to life. This is a coming-of-age story. It's about taking a leap of faith." Ang Lee, quoted in an interview with Anupama Chopra, "Adrift with a Tiger and the Film God," *New York Times*, September 9, 2012, AR44.

7. "There is a certain perception about 3-D, but just because nobody has made an intimate movie with it doesn't mean it can't be done." Lee, quoted in ibid.

8. The special effects technology used in *Life of Pi* was a topic not without controversy, however, as the company Rhythm and Hues filed for bankruptcy after making this film.

9. These multilingual and multicultural aspects reflect Yann Martel's own spiritual and cultural journey toward defining his own identity as an author who was born in Spain, raised in Costa Rica, France, Mexico, and Canada, and who as an adult spent time in Iran, Turkey, and India.

10. Martel (2001:7).

11. Ibid., 379.

12. This relationship between ethnocentrism and the semiotics of culture is also highlighted by Pi's mother in the novel where she asks her husband if they can buy a pack of cigarettes right before their departure. When her husband replies that neither of them smokes, and that they have tobacco in Canada, Pi thinks: "'Yes, they have tobacco in Canada. But do they have Gold Flake cigarettes? Do they have Arun ice cream? Are the bicycles Heroes? Are the televisions Onidas? Are the cars Ambassadors? Are the bookshops Higginbothams?' Such, I suspect, were the questions that swirled in Mother's mind as she contemplated buying cigarettes." Martel (2001:115).

13. Another passage which highlights this ethnocentric yearning is when Pi is looking for help on the disabled *Tsimtsum* during the storm: "I ran for the bridge. Up there was where the officers were, the only people who spoke English, the masters of our destiny here, the ones who would right this wrong. They would explain everything. They would take care of my family and me." Here a godlike status is conferred upon these English speakers. Quoted from Martel (2001:130).

14. *The Holy Bible: New International Version* (1984), 354.

15. Some colors were also altered in the film; for example, the crunchy, tubular seaweed Pi bites into on the floating island is white on the inside (in the book); this is changed to a vibrant purple in the film. Purple is the color of taro, a popular tuber vegetable in Taiwan. Taro refers to a family of root vegetables native to Southeast Asia, and is believed to be one of the earliest cultivated plants.

16. Martel (2001:26).

17. Ibid., 30.

18. Chinese-language studies of this film make much use of Lee's symbolism of both *pi* as an infinite number (metaphorically linked to the endless repetition of the cycle of life-and-death, i.e., Pi's birth occurs at the same time that the zoo's monitor lizard escapes and is trampled to death; the roundness of the pool and bodies of water; the spherical shape of the earth and the secret laws of the universe), as well as the "tiger" as a representative of the filmmaker himself. For further insight see Ye Jigu, *Li An dianying de jingyu biaoda* [Frame imagery expression in Ang Lee's films] (2012).

19. Pi himself makes reference to this at the end of the novel, in reference to his unceremonious farewell with Richard Parker: "I'll tell you, that's one thing I hate about my nickname, the way that number runs on forever. It's important in life to conclude things properly. Only then can you let go." Martel (2001:360).

20. Martel's book captures the reader's imagination in its presentation of human alienation, isolation, and the hope and meaning that can be gained through philosophical inquiry—the work shares these and other intertextual elements (such as the name "Richard Parker" given to the tiger) with other historical shipwreck narratives.

21. Specifically, this moment recalls the loss of "Wilson" in *Cast Away* (2000).

22. Ang Lee, quoted in an interview with Anupama Chopra (2012:AR44).

23. Martel (2001:380).

24. Ibid., 117.

15. CONCLUSION: *THE DREAM OF CINEMA*

1.   Annie Proulx, "Getting Movied," in Annie Proulx, Larry McMurtry, and Diana Ossana, *Brokeback Mountain: Story to Screenplay* (2006), 135.
2.   Ang Lee, in Michael Berry's *Speaking in Images* (2005), 329.
3.   Ibid., 357.
4.   Roland Barthes, *S/Z: An Essay*, trans. Richard Miller (1974), 4.
5.   James Agee and Walker Evans, *Let Us Now Praise Famous Men* (1960, 2d ed.), 415.
6.   Ang Lee, in Zhang Jingpei, ed., *Shinian yijiao dianying meng* [A ten-year dream of cinema] (2002), 467.

BIBLIOGRAPHY

Abbas, Akbar. 1994. "The New Hong Kong Cinema and the Déjà Disparu." *Discourse* 16.3: 65–77.
——. 1996. "Cultural Studies in a Postculture." In Cary Nelson and Dilip Parameshwar Gaonkar, eds., *Disciplinarity and Dissent in Cultural Studies*, 289–312. New York: Routledge.
——. 1997. *Hong Kong: Culture and the Politics of Disappearance*. Hong Kong: Hong Kong University Press.
Abramowitz, Rachel. 2009. "Ang Lee—Hippie?" *Los Angeles Times* [online], August 27. See http://articles. latimes.com/2009/aug/27/entertainment/et-lee27 (accessed June 16, 2012).
Agee, James, and Walker Evans. 1960. 2d ed. *Let Us Now Praise Famous Men*. Boston: Houghton Mifflin.
Anagnost, Ann. 1997. *National Past-Times: Narrative, Representation, and Power in Modern China*. Durham, NC: Duke University Press.
Anon. 1995. "Adapting Jane Austen's *Sense and Sensibility*." Hampshire County Council website. See www. hants.gov.uk/austen/story.html#adaptingjane, 1 (accessed September 21, 2002).
——. 2000. "Ang Lee and James Schamus: The Guardian/NFT Interview," *Guardian Unlimited*, November 7. See www.guardian.co.uk/film/2000/nov/07/3 (accessed August 29, 2003).
——. 2001a. "Ang Lee: Dreaming Up an Everchanging Destiny." CNN Special Report. See www.cnn. com/SPECIALS/2001/americasbest/pro.alee.html (accessed November 5, 2003).
——. 2001b. "'*Tiger*' Pounces But Misses Big Oscars," CNN website, March 26. See http://archives.cnn. com/2001/WORLD/asiapcf/east/03/26/china.oscar.miss/index.html (accessed September 23, 2005).
——. 2005. "Hulk" Internet Movie Database (IMDb) website. See www.imdb.com/title/tt0286716/trivia (accessed November 7, 2005).
——. 2006a. "Ang Lee: Biography." Internet Movie Database (IMDb) website. See www.imdb.com/ name/nm0000487/bio (accessed February 19, 2006).
——. 2006b. "'Brokeback' author: We Were Robbed," *CNN*, March 15. See http://edition.cnn. com./2006/SHOWBIZ/Movies/03/15film.proulx.ap/index/html (accessed March 16, 2006).
——. 2006c. "*Lust, Caution* Cast Named." Twitchfilm. July 19. See www.twitchfilm.net/archives/006894. html (accessed October 9, 2006).
——. 2006d. "Town Not Big Enough for Gay Cowboy Heath." *The Daily Telegraph*, January 10. See www.dailytelegraph.news.com.au/story/0,20281,17771006–50001026,00.html (accessed January 12, 2006).
——. 2009. "*Taking Woodstock* Production Notes," *festival-cannes.com*, May 15. See www.festival-cannes. fr/assets/Image/Direct/029702.pdf (accessed October 12, 2010).
Appadurai, Arjun. 1996. *Modernity at Large: Cultural Dimensions of Globalization*. Minneapolis: University of Minnesota Press.
Armstrong, Nancy. 1987. *Desire and Domestic Fiction: A Political History of the Novel*. New York: Oxford University Press.

Arp, Robert, Adam Barkman, and James McRae, eds. 2013. *The Philosophy of Ang Lee*. Lexington: The University Press of Kentucky.

Austen, Jane. 1996 [1811]. *Sense and Sensibility*. Oxford: Oxford University Press.

Barthes, Roland. 1973. *Elements of Semiology*. Trans. Annette Lavers and Colin Smith. New York: Hill and Wang.

——. 1974. *S/Z: An Essay*. Trans. Richard Miller. New York: Hill and Wang.

Bataille, Georges. 1986. *Eroticism: Death and Sensuality*. Trans. Mary Dalwood. San Francisco: City Lights.

——. 1993. *The Accursed Share*, vol. 2. Trans. Robert Hurley. New York: Zone.

Berry, Chris. 1993. "Taiwanese Melodrama Returns with a Twist in *The Wedding Banquet*." *Cinemaya* 21 (Fall): 52–54.

——. 2003. "*Wedding Banquet*: A Family (Melodrama) Affair." In Chris Berry, ed., *Chinese Films in Focus*, 183–190.

——. 2010. "What Is Transnational Cinema?: Thinking from the Chinese Situation," *Transnational Cinemas* 1.2: 111–27.

Berry, Chris, ed. 1991. *Perspectives on Chinese Cinema*. London: British Film Institute.

——, ed. 2003. *Chinese Films in Focus: 25 New Titles*. London: British Film Institute.

——, ed. 2008. *Chinese Films in Focus II*. New York: Palgrave MacMillan.

Berry, Chris, and Mary Farquhar. 2001. "From National Cinemas to Cinema and the National: Rethinking the National in Transnational Chinese Cinemas." *Journal of Modern Literature in Chinese* 4.2: 109–122.

——. 2006. *China on Screen: Cinema and Nation*. New York: Columbia University Press.

Berry, Chris, and Feii Lu, eds. 2005. *Island on the Edge: Taiwan New Cinema and After*. Hong Kong: Hong Kong University Press.

Berry, Michael. 2005. "Ang Lee: Freedom in Film." In Michael Berry, ed., *Speaking in Images: Interviews with Contemporary Chinese Filmmakers*, 324–61. New York: Columbia University Press.

Bersani, Leo. 1996. *Homos*. Cambridge: Harvard University Press.

Bloomberg, Robert Hilferty. 2005. "Taiwan's Ang Lee Discusses Gay Cowboys and Sheep Wrangling." *The China Post* [online], December 13. See www.chinapost.com.tw/p_detail .asp?id=73561&GRP=h&onNews= (accessed December 13, 2005).

Bordwell, David. 1997. "Aesthetics in Action: Kung Fu, Gunplay, and Cinematic Expressibility." In Kar Law, ed., *Fifty Years of Electric Shadows*, 81–89. Hong Kong: Urban Council.

——. 2000a. "Hong Kong Martial Arts Cinema." In Sunshine, ed., *Crouching Tiger, Hidden Dragon: Portrait of an Ang Lee Film*, 14–21.

——. 2000b. *Planet Hong Kong: Popular Cinema and the Art of Entertainment*. Cambridge: Harvard University Press.

Braester, Yomi, and James Tweedie. 2010. *Cinema at the City's Edge: Film and Urban Networks in East Asia*. Hong Kong: Hong Kong University Press.

Braudy, Leo. 2004. *Film Theory and Criticism*. New York: Oxford University Press.

Browne, Nick, Paul G. Pickowicz, Vivian Sobchack, and Esther Yau, eds. 1994. *New Chinese Cinemas: Forms, Identities, Politics*. New York: Cambridge University Press.

Buell, Frederick. 1994. *National Culture and the New Global System*. Baltimore: Johns Hopkins University Press.

——. 1998. "Nationalist Postnationalism: Globalist Discourse in Contemporary American Culture." *American Quarterly* 50.3: 548–91.

Castelli, Jean-Christophe. 2012. *The Making of Life of Pi: A Film, a Journey*. New York: Harper Collins.

Cavagna, Carlo. 2005. "Interview: Ang Lee." *Aboutfilm.com*, December 15. See www.aboutfilm.com/ movies/b/brokebackmountain/lee.htm (accessed May 20, 2006).

Chan, Felicia. 2003. "*Crouching Tiger, Hidden Dragon*: Cultural Migrancy and Translatability." In Chris Berry, ed., *Chinese Films in Focus*, 56–64.

Chan, Kenneth. 2009. *Remade in Hollywood: The Global Chinese Presence in Transnational Cinemas*. Hong Kong: Hong Kong University Press.

Chang, Eileen (Zhang Ailing). 2006. *Love in a Fallen City*. Trans. Karen S. Kingsbury. New York: New York Review Books Classics.

——. 2007. "Lust, Caution." In *Lust, Caution: The Story, The Screenplay, and The Making of the Film.* Trans. Julia Lovell. New York: Pantheon.

Chang, Hsiao-hung. 1996. "Taibei qingyu dijing" [An erotic map of Taipei]. In *Yuwang xin ditu: xingbie, tongzhixue* [Queer desire: Gender and sexuality], 78–109. Taipei: Lianhe wenxue.

Chen, Peng-hsiang, and Whitney Crothers Dilley, eds. 2002. *Feminism/Femininity in Chinese Literature.* New York: Rodopi.

Cheshire, Ellen. 2001. *The Pocket Essential: Ang Lee.* Harpenden: Pocket Essentials.

Chiao, (Peggy) Hsiung-ping. 1990. "The Emergence of the New Cinema of Taiwan." *Asian Cinema* 5.1: 1–19.

——. 1991. "The Distinct Taiwanese and Hong Kong Cinemas." In Chris Berry, ed., *Perspectives on Chinese Cinema,* 155–65.

Chiao, (Peggy) Hsiung-ping, ed. 1988. *Taiwan xindianying* [Taiwan New Cinema]. Taipei: Shibao.

Chopra, Anupama. 2012. "Adrift with a Tiger and the Film God." *New York Times,* September 9: AR44.

Chow, Eileen Cheng-yin. 1997. "Food, Family, and the Performance of 'Chineseness' in Ang Lee XE "Ang Lee" 's Father-Knows-Best Trilogy." Paper presented at the North American Taiwan Studies Conference, University of California—Berkeley.

Chow, Rey. 1995. *Primitive Passions: Visuality, Sexuality, and Ethnography in Contemporary Chinese Cinema.* New York: Columbia University Press.

——. 2007. *Sentimental Fabulations, Contemporary Chinese Films: Attachment in the Age of Global Visibility.* New York: Columbia University Press.

Chow, Rey, ed. 2000. *Modern Chinese Literary and Cultural Studies in an Age of Theory: Reimagining a Field.* Durham, NC: Duke University Press.

Chung, Winnie. 2001. "The Reel Winner." *East* 3.4: 54–60.

Clark, Robert, ed. 1994. *New Casebooks: Sense and Sensibility and Pride and Prejudice.* London: Macmillan.

Clifford, James. 1992. "Traveling Cultures." In Lawrence Grossberg, Cary Nelson, and Paula Treichler, eds., *Cultural Studies,* 96–112. New York: Routledge.

——. 1997. "Diasporas." In *Routes: Travel and Translation in the Late Twentieth Century,* 244–78. Cambridge: Harvard University Press.

Cohen, Robin. 1997. *Global Diasporas: An Introduction.* Seattle: University of Washington Press.

Connell, R. W. 1987. *Gender and Power: Society, the Person, and Sexual Politics.* Cambridge: Polity Press.

Cui, Shuqin. 2003. *Women Through the Lens: Gender and Nation in a Century of Chinese Cinema.* Honolulu: University of Hawaii Press.

Daniels, Les. 1991. *Marvel: Five Fabulous Decades of the World's Greatest Comics.* New York: Harry N. Abrams.

Dannen, Fredric. 1995. "Hong Kong Babylon." *The New Yorker,* August 7: 30–38.

Dannen, Fredric, and Barry Long. 1997. *Hong Kong Babylon: An Insider's Guide to the Hollywoood of the East.* New York: Miramax Books.

Dariotis, Wei Ming and Eileen Fung. 1997. "Breaking the Soy Sauce Jar: Diaspora and Displacement in the Films of Ang Lee." In Sheldon Hsiao-peng Lu, ed., *Transnational Chinese Cinemas,* 187–220.

Davis, Darrell William, and Ru-shou Robert Chen, eds. 2007. *Cinema Taiwan: Politics, Popularity and State of the Arts.* London: Routledge.

DeFalco, Tom. 2003. *Hulk: The Incredible Guide.* New York: DK Publishing.

Deppman, Hsiu-Chuang. 2010. *Adapted for the Screen: The Cultural Politics of Adaptation in Modern Chinese Fiction and Film.* Honolulu: University of Hawaii Press.

Desser, David. 2000. "The Kung-Fu Craze: Hong Kong Cinema's First American Reception." In Poshek Fu and David Desser, eds., *The Cinema of Hong Kong: History, Arts, Identity,* 19–43. New York: Cambridge University Press.

Diana, M. Casey, "Emma Thompson's *Sense and Sensibility* as Gateway to Austen's Novel." In Troost and Greenfield, eds., *Jane Austen in Hollywood,* 140–48. Lexington: University of Kentucky Press.

Dilley, Whitney Crothers. 2003. "Fragmentary Narratives: Globalization and Cultural Identity in the Films of Ang Lee." *Canadian Review of Comparative Literature/Revue Canadienne de Littérature Comparée* 30.3–4: 688–97.

Dilley, Whitney Crothers, and Peng-hsiang Chen. 1998. "Comparative Studies of Chinese and Western Feminism/Femininity." *The Tamkang Review* 29.1: 1–18.

Dilley, Whitney Crothers, and Peng-hsiang Chen, eds. 2002. *Feminism/Femininity in Chinese Literature*. New York: Rodopi.

Dissanayake, Wimal, ed. 1993. *Melodrama and Asian Cinema*. London: Cambridge University Press.

——, ed. 1994. *Colonialism and Nationalism in Asian Cinema*. Bloomington: Indiana University Press.

Douglas, Edward. 2012. "Oscar-Worthy: *Life of Pi* Director Ang Lee," November 15. See www.comingsoon.net/news/weekendwarriornews.php?id=96684 (accessed November 20, 2012).

Duckworth, Alistair M. 1971. *The Improvement of the Estate: A Study of Jane Austen's Novels*. Baltimore: Johns Hopkins University Press.

Durbin, Karen. 2005. "Cowboys in Love . . . With Each Other." *New York Times*, September 4: 15.

Ehrlich, Linda C., and David Desser, eds. 1994. *Cinematic Landscapes: Observations on the Visual Arts and Cinema of China and Japan*. Austin: University of Texas Press.

Ellwood, Gregory. 2005. "Top of the 'Mountain.'" *Msn.com*, November 29. See http://movies.msn.com/movies/hitlist/11–29–05_2 (accessed November 30, 2005).

Featherstone, Mike. 1993. "Global and Local Cultures." In Jon Bird, Barry Curtis, Tim Putnam, George Robertson, and Lisa Tucker, eds., *Mapping the Futures: Local Cultures, Global Change*, 169–87. London: Routledge.

Ferguson, Roderick A. 2004. *Aberrations in Black: Toward a Queer of Color Critique*. Minneapolis: University of Minnesota Press.

Fore, Steve. 1997. "Jackie Chan and the Cultural Dynamics of Global Entertainment." In Sheldon Hsiao-peng Lu, ed., *Transnational Chinese Cinemas*, 239–62.

Foucault, Michel. 1995. *Discipline and Punish: The Birth of the Prison*. Trans. Alan Sheridan. New York: Vintage Books.

Friedman, Susan Stanford. 1998. *Mappings: Feminism and the Cultural Geographies of Encounter*. Princeton: Princeton University Press.

Friend, Tad. 2003. "Credit Grab." *The New Yorker*, October 20: 160–69.

Frodon, Michel, ed. 1999. *Hou Hsiao Hsien*. Paris: Cahiers du Cinéma.

Fu, Poshek and Desser, David, eds. 2000. *The Cinema of Hong Kong: History, Arts, Identity*. New York: Cambridge University Press.

Fuery, Patrick. 2000. *New Developments in Film Theory*. New York: St. Martin's.

Gaul, Lou. 1997. *The Fist That Shook the World: The Cinema of Bruce Lee*. Baltimore: Midnight Marquee Press.

Giddens, Anthony. 1990. *The Consequences of Modernity*. London: Polity Press.

Gleick, James. 2000. *Faster: The Acceleration of Just About Everything*. New York: Vintage Books.

Gopinath, Gayatri. 1995. "'Bombay, UK, Yuba City': Bhangra Music and the Engendering of Diaspora." *Diaspora* 4.3: 303–22.

Gorman, Steve. 2006. "Randy Quaid sues studio over 'Brokeback Mountain.'" *Reuters*, March 24. See http://go.reuters.com/newsArticle.jhtml?type=entertainmentNews&storyID=11644132 (accessed March 24, 2006).

Greydanus, Stephen D. 2005. "Review of *Brokeback Mountain*," *Decent Films Guide*, n.d. See www.decentfilms.com/sections/reviews/brokebackmountain.html (accessed March 20, 2006).

Halberstam, Judith. 2005a. *In a Queer Time and Space: Transgendered Bodies, Subcultural Lives*. New York: New York University Press.

——. 2005b. "Queer Studies." In Philomena Essed, David Theo Goldberg, and Audrey Kobayashi, eds., *A Companion to Gender Studies*, 62–72. Oxford: Blackwell.

Halbfinger, David M. 2005. "The Delicate Job of Transforming a Geisha." *New York Times*, November 6: 4.

Hall, Stuart. 2003. "Cultural Identity and Diaspora," in Jonathan Rutherford, ed., *Identity: Community, Culture, Difference*, 222–37. London: Lawrence and Wishart.

Halperin, David, and Valerie Traub, eds. 2009. *Gay Shame*. Chicago: University of Chicago Press.

Hamamoto, Darrell Y., and Sandra Liu, eds. 2000. *Countervisions: Asian American Film Criticism*. Philadelphia: Temple University Press.

Handley, William R., ed. 2011. *The Brokeback Book: From Story to Cultural Phenomenon*. Lincoln: University of Nebraska Press.

Harvey, David. 1990. *The Condition of Postmodernity*. Cambridge: Blackwell.

Higbee, Will, and Song Hwee Lim. 2010. "Concepts of Transnational Cinema: Towards a Critical Transnationalism in Film Studies." *Transnational Cinemas* 1.1: 7–21.

Ho, Yi. 2006. "Family and Friends Praise Ang Lee's Quiet Dedication," *Taipei Times*, March 7, 4.

Holden, Stephen. 2009. "What I Saw at the Countercultural Revolution," *New York Times*, August 26: C1.

The Holy Bible: New International Version. 1984. Grand Rapids, MI: Zondervan.

Huang, Jianye. 1994. *Yang Dechang dianying yanjiu* [Cinematic studies of Edward Yang]. Taipei: Yuanliu.

Huang, Jianye, ed. 2005. *Kua shiji Taiwan dianying shilu (1898–2000)* [The chronicles of Taiwan cinema (1898–2000)]. Taipei: Xingzhengyuan wenhua jianshe weiyuanhui.

Huang, Ren, and Liang Liang, eds. 2002. *Li An yu huashang yingren jingying* [Ang Lee and the Chinese film industry elite]. Taipei: Yatai.

Huang, Ren, and Wang Wei, eds. 2004. *Taiwan dianying bainian shihua* [One hundred years of Taiwan cinema]. 2 vols. Taipei: Zhonghua yingpingren xiehui.

Hunt, Leon, and Leung, Wing-fai, eds. 2008. *East Asian Cinemas: Exploring Transnational Connections on Film*. London: I. B. Tauris.

James, Nick. 2008. "Cruel Intentions: Ang Lee." *Sight & Sound* 18.1 (January): 50.

Jameson, Fredric. 1992. *The Geopolitical Aesthetic: Cinema and Space in the World System*. Bloomington: Indiana University Press.

——. 1994. "Remapping Taipei." In Browne et al., eds., *New Chinese Cinemas*, 117–50.

Jay, Jennifer. 2003. "*Crouching Tiger, Hidden Dragon*: (Re)packaging Chinas and Selling the Hybridized Culture and Identity in an Age of Globalization." *Canadian Review of Comparative Literature/Revue Canadienne de Littérature Comparée* 30.3–4: 698–713.

Kam, Tan See, and Annette Aw. 2003. "*Love Eterne*: Almost a (Heterosexual) Love Story." In Chris Berry, ed., *Chinese Films in Focus*, 137–43.

Kellner, Douglas. 1998. "New Taiwan Cinema in the 80s." *Jump Cut* 42 (December): 101–15.

Kim, L. S. 2006. "*Crouching Tiger, Hidden Dragon*: Making Women Warriors—A Transnational Reading of Asian Female Action Heroes." *Jump Cut* 48, n.d. See www.ejumpcut.org/archive/jc48.2006/womenWarriors/index.html (accessed December 10, 2007).

Kimmel, Michael. 1992. "Reading Men: Men, Masculinity, and Publishing." *Contemporary Sociology* 21.2: 162–71.

King, Anthony, ed. 1997. *Culture, Globalization, and the World-System: Contemporary Conditions for the Representation of Identity*. Minneapolis: University of Minnesota Press.

Klein, Christina. 2004. "*Crouching Tiger, Hidden Dragon*: A Diasporic Reading." *Cinema Journal* 43.4: 18–42.

Kubert, Joe. 1999. *Superheroes: Joe Kubert's Wonderful World of Comics*. New York: Watson-Guptill.

Kuhn, Annette. 1993. *Womenn's Pictures*. New York: Verso.

Kuoshu, Harry H. 2002. *Celluloid China: Cinematic Encounters with Culture and Society*. Carbondale: Southern Illinois University Press.

Lahr, John. 2003. "Becoming the Hulk." *The New Yorker*, June 30: 72–81.

Lane, Anthony. 2000. "Come Fly with Me." *The New Yorker*, December 11: 129–31.

Lau, Jenny Kwok Wah, ed. 2003. *Multiple Modernities: Cinemas and Popular Media in Transcultural East Asia*. Philadephia: Temple University Press.

Law, Kar, ed. 1998. *Transcending the Times: King Hu and Eileen Chang*. Hong Kong: Provisional Urban Council.

Lee, Ang. 1991a. *Tuishou* [Pushing Hands]. Taipei: Zhongyang dianying gongsi; Li An dianying gongsi.

——. 1991b. *Tuishou* [Pushing Hands]. Taipei: Xingzhengyuan xinwenju.

——. 1991c. *Tuishou* [Pushing Hands]. In Peng Guangyuan [Neil Peng], ed., *Tuishou: yibu yingpian de dansheng* [Pushing Hands: The birth of a film], 143–221. Taipei: Yuanliu.

——. 1994. *Eat Drink Man Woman and The Wedding Banquet: Two Films by Ang Lee*. Woodstock, NY: The Overlook Press.

——. 2000a. "Foreword." In Sunshine, ed., *Crouching Tiger, Hidden Dragon: Portrait of an Ang Lee Film*, 7.

——. 2000b. "The *Wuxia* According to Ang Lee." In Sunshine, ed., *Crouching Tiger, Hidden Dragon: Portrait of an Ang Lee Film*, 137.

Lee, Ang, and Peng Guangyuan [Neil Peng]. 1993. *Xiyan* [The Wedding Banquet: screenplay]. Taipei: Shibao wenhua.

Lee, Ang, Wang Huiling, and James Schamus. 1994. *Yinshi nannü* [Eat drink man woman]. In Central Motion Pictures Corporation, ed., *Yinshi nannü: dianying juben yu paishe guocheng* [Eat drink man woman: screenplay and shooting process], 19–142. Taipei: Yuanliu.

Lee, Leo Ou-fan. 2008. "Ang Lee's *Lust, Caution* and Its Reception." *Boundary 2* 35.3: 223–38.

Lee, Linda. 1989. *The Bruce Lee Story*. Santa Clarita, CA: Ohara.

Lent, John A. 1990. *The Asian Film Industry*. Austin: University of Texas Press.

Leung, William. 2001. "Crouching Sensibility, Hidden Sense." *Film Criticism* 26.1: 42–55.

——. 2008. "Sex, China, and Propaganda: Ang Lee's *Lust Caution*." *Metro* 156.3: 50–56.

Leyda, Jay. 1972. *Dianying: An Account of Films and the Film Audience in China*. Cambridge: MIT Press.

Li, Taifang. 1996. *Nüxing dianying lilun* [Theory of women's cinema]. Taipei: Yangzhi wenhua.

Li, Tianduo. 1997. *Taiwan dianying, shehui yu lishi* [Taiwan cinema, society, and history]. Taipei: Yatai.

Liang, Shouzhong. 1990. *Wuxia xiaoshuo hua gujin* [Martial art-chivalry novels in the past and present]. Hong Kong: Zhonghua shuju.

Lim, Song Hwee. 2006. *Celluloid Comrades: Representations of Male Homosexuality in Contemporary Chinese Cinemas*. Honolulu: University of Hawaii Press.

Lim, Song Hwee, and Julian Ward, eds. 2011. *The Chinese Cinema Book*. London: British Film Institute.

Liu, Cynthia. 1995. "To Love, Honor, and Dismay: Subverting the Feminine in Ang Lee's Trilogy of Resuscitated Patriarchs." *Hitting Critical Mass: A Journal of Asian American Cultural Criticism* 3.1: 1–60.

Liu, Kang. 2004. *Globalization and Cultural Trends in China*. Honolulu: University of Hawaii Press.

Liu, Xiancheng. 1997. *Taiwan dianying, shehui, yu guojia* [Taiwanese cinema, society, and state]. Taipei: Taiwan dianying yanjiu congshu.

Lo, Kwai-Cheung. 2005. *Chinese Face/Off: The Transnational Popular Culture of Hong Kong*. Chicago: University of Illinois Press.

Lowenstein, Stephen, ed. 2001. "Ang Lee's *Pushing Hands*." In Lowenstein, ed., *My First Movie: Twenty Celebrated Directors Talk About Their First Film*, 361–81. New York: Pantheon.

Lu, Feii. 1998. *Taiwan dianying: zhengzhi, jingji, meixue* [Taiwan cinema: politics, economics, aesthetics]. Taipei: Yuanliu.

Lu, Sheldon Hsiao-peng. 2001. *China, Transnational Visuality, Global Postmodernity*. Stanford, CA: Stanford University Press.

——. 2005. "Crouching Tiger, Hidden Dragon, Bouncing Angels: Hollywood, Taiwan, Hong Kong, and Transnational Cinema." In Sheldon H. Lu and Emilie Yueh-yu Yeh, eds., *Chinese-Language Film*, 220–33.

Lu, Sheldon Hsiao-peng, ed. 1997. *Transnational Chinese Cinemas: Identity, Nationhood, Gender*. Honolulu: University of Hawaii Press.

Lu, Sheldon H., and Emilie Yueh-yu Yeh, eds. 2005. *Chinese-Language Film: Historiography, Poetics, Politics*. Honolulu: University of Hawaii Press.

Lu, Tonglin. 2001. *Confronting Modernity in the Cinemas of Taiwan and Mainland China*. New York: Cambridge University Press.

Lyman, Rick. 2001. "Watching Movies with Ang Lee: Crouching Memory, Hidden Heart." *New York Times*, March 9: E1, 27.

Ma, Sheng-mei. 1996. "Ang Lee's Domestic Tragicomedy: Immigrant Nostalgia, Exotic/Ethnic Tour, Global Market," *Journal of Popular Culture* 30.1: 191–201.

Macdonald, Moira. 2007. "Ang Lee and the Power of Performance." *Seattle Times*, October 2: 11.

Manalansan, Martin. 2003. *Global Divas: Filipino Gay Men in the Diaspora*. Durham, NC: Duke University Press.

Marchetti, Gina. 1993. *Romance and the "Yellow Peril": Race, Sex, and Discursive Strategies in Hollywood Fiction*. Berkeley: University of California Press.

——. 1998. "Chinese and Chinese Diaspora Cinema—Plural and Transnational: Introduction." *Jump Cut* 42: 68–72.

——. 2000. "*The Wedding Banquet*: Global Chinese Cinema and the Asian American Experience." In Hamamoto and Liu, eds., *Countervisions*, 275–97.

Martel, Yann. 2001. *Life of Pi*. New York: Harcourt.

Martin, Fran. 2003. *Situating Sexualities: Queer Representation in Taiwanese Fiction, Film, and Popular Culture*. Hong Kong: Hong Kong University Press.

——. 2005. "The China Simulacrum: Genre, Feminism, and Pan-Chinese Cultural Politics in *Crouching Tiger, Hidden Dragon*." In Chris Berry and Feii Lu, eds., *Island on the Edge*, 149–59.

McDougall, David. 1998. *Transcultural Cinema*. Princeton, NJ: Princeton University Press.

Messner, Michael A. 1997. *Politics of Masculinities: Men in Movements*. Walnut Creek, CA: Alta Mira Press.

Monaghan, David. 1980. *Jane Austen: Structure and Social Vision*. London: Macmillan.

Moody, Rick. 1994. *The Ice Storm*. New York: Warner Books.

Mukherjee, Meenakshi. 1991. *Jane Austen*. London: Macmillan.

Murphy, Kathleen. 2006. "Blue State vs. Red State: Oscar's Civil War," MSN Movies website, no date. See http://movies.msn.com/movies/oscars2006/civilwar (accessed March 20, 2006).

Needham, Gary. 2010. *Brokeback Mountain*. Edinburgh: Edinburgh University Press.

Neill, Edward. 1999. *The Politics of Jane Austen*. New York: St. Martin's.

Ng, Maria N. 2006. *Reading Chinese Transnationalisms: Society, Literature, Film*. Vancouver: University of British Columbia Press.

Nuñez, Paco. 2006. "Bahamas 'Brokeback Mountain' Ban Draws Ire." *Associated Press*, March 30. See www.breitbart.com/news/2006/03/30/D8GM5K30C.html (accessed April 2, 2006).

Ossana, Diana. "Climbing Brokeback Mountain." In Proulx, McMurtry, and Ossana, *Brokeback Mountain: Story to Screenplay*, 143–51.

Patterson, Eric. 2008. *On Brokeback Mountain: Meditations about Masculinity, Fear, and Love in the Story and the Film*. New York: Lexington Books.

Pei, Xiaoxiong. 1991. "Wang Dulu." In Ma Liangchun and Li Futian, eds., *Zhongguo wenxue da cidian* [Dictionary of Chinese literature]. Tianjin: Tianjin renmin chuban she.

Peng, Guangyuan [Neil Peng]. 1993. "Preface." In Ang Lee and Neil Peng's *Xiyan* [The Wedding Banquet], 20–43. Taipei: Shibao wenhua.

Peng, Guangyuan [Neil Peng], ed. 1991. *Tuishou: yibu yingpian de dansheng* [Pushing Hands: The birth of a film]. Taipei: Yuanliu.

Peng, Hsiao-yen, and Whitney Crothers Dilley, eds. 2014. *From Eileen Chang to Ang Lee: Lust/Caution*. London: Routledge.

Person, Ethel S. 1989. *Dreams of Love and Fateful Encounters: The Power of Romantic Passion*. New York: Viking Penguin.

Poe, Edgar Allan. 1838. *The Narrative of Arthur Gordon Pym of Nantucket*. New York: Harper.

Proulx, Annie. 1997. "Brokeback Mountain." *The New Yorker*, October 13: 74–85.

——. 1999. "Brokeback Mountain." In *Close Range: Wyoming Stories*. New York: Scribner.

——. 2006a. "Blood on the Red Carpet." *Guardian Unlimited*, March 11. See http://books.guardian.co.uk/comment/story/0,,1727309,00.html (accessed March 11, 2006).

——. 2006b. "Getting Movied." In Proulx, McMurtry, and Ossana, *Brokeback Mountain: Story to Screenplay*, 129–38.

Proulx, Annie, Larry McMurtry, and Diana Ossana. 2006. *Brokeback Mountain: Story to Screenplay*. London: Harper Perennial.

Pye, Michael. 1996. "Austen Viewed from Mars." *The Daily Telegraph*, January 27: A1.

Rich, Frank. 2005. "Two Gay Cowboys Hit a Home Run." *New York Times*, December 18: 13.

Robertson, Roland. 1992. *Globalization*. London: Sage.

Robin, Diana, and Ira Jaffe, eds. 1999. *Redirecting the Gaze: Gender, Theory, and Cinema in the Third World*. New York: State University of New York Press.

Rogin, Michael. 1996. *Blackface, White Noise*. Berkeley: University of California Press.

Rohter, Larry. 2009. "Chasing Society's Hidden Dragons." *New York Times*, August 1: C1.

Rojas, Carlos, and Eileen Chow, eds. 2013. *The Oxford Handbook of Chinese Cinemas*. New York: Oxford University Press.

Rowlinson, Liz. 1999. "A Quick Chat with Daniel Woodrell." *The Richmond Review*. See www.richmondreview.co.uk/features/woodrell.html (accessed March 2001).

Said, Edward. 1979. *Orientalism*. New York: Random House.

——. 1994. *Culture and Imperialism*. New York: Vintage.

Sales, Roger. 1994. *Jane Austen and Representations of Regency England*. New York: Routledge.

Sam, Robert. 2000. *Film Theory*. New York: Blackwell.

Sarris, Andrew. 2003. "Ang Lee's Angst-Ridden Hulk: The Not-So-Jolly Green Giant." *New York Observer*, July 7: 14.

Schaefer, Stephen. 2001. "Mr. Showbiz Interview: Ang Lee." March 5. See http://mrshowbiz.go.com/interviews/572_1.html (accessed August 27, 2005).

Schamus, James. 1994. "Introduction." In *Eat Drink Man Woman and The Wedding Banquet: Two Films by Ang Lee*, 9–13. Woodstock, NY: The Overlook Press.

——. 1997. *The Ice Storm: The Shooting Script*. New York: Newmarket Press.

——. 2006. "*Brokeback Mountain*: An Exchange." *New York Review*, April 6: 32.

——. 2007. "Introduction." In *Lust, Caution: The Story, The Screenplay, and The Making of the Film*, xi–xv. New York: Pantheon.

Schamus, James, Ang Lee, David Bordwell, and Richard Corliss. 2001. *Crouching Tiger, Hidden Dragon: A Portrait of the Ang Lee Film*. New York: Faber and Faber.

Schamus, James, John Turman, and Michael France. 2003. *Hulk: The Illustrated Screenplay*. With a foreword by Ang Lee. New York: Newmarket Press.

Scholes, Robert. 1998. *The Rise and Fall of English*. New Haven: Yale University Press.

Scott, A. O. 2012. "Plenty of Gods, But Just One Fellow Passenger: *Life of Pi*, Directed by Ang Lee." *New York Times*, November 21: C1.

Sedgwick, Eve. 1995. *Shame and Its Sisters: A Silvan Tompkins Reader*. Durham, NC: Duke University Press.

Server, Lee. 1999. *Asian Pop Cinema: Bombay to Tokyo*. San Francisco: Chronicle Books.

Shen, Shiao-ying. 1995. "Where Has All the Capital Gone: The State of Taiwan's Film Investment." *Cinemaya* 30: 4–12.

Shenitz, Bruce. 2005. "Kissin' Cowboy." *Out* (October): 92–99, 124.

Shih, Shu-ching. 2006. "Zhuanfang Li An: Cong Buolin, Weinisi dao Haolaiwu" [Interview with Ang Lee: From Berlin and Venice to Hollywood], *Yinke wenxue shenghuo zhi* [Ink Literary Monthly] 1.5 (January): 26–40.

Shih, Shu-mei. 1999. "Gender and a Geopolitics of Desire: The Seduction of Mainland Women in Taiwan and Hong Kong Media." In Mayfair Mei-hui Yang, ed., *Spaces of Their Own*, 278–307.

——. 2000. "Globalization and Minoritization: Ang Lee and the Politics of Flexibility." *New Formations* 40: 86–101.

Sicha, Choire. 2005. "Chokeback Mountain." *New York Observer*, November 21: 15.

Simon, Sherry. 1996. *Gender in Translation: Cultural Identity and the Politics of Transmission*. London: Routledge.

Smith, Murray. 1995. *Engaging Characters: Fiction, Emotion, and the Cinema*. New York: Oxford University Press.

Smith, Sean. 2005. "Forbidden Territory." *Newsweek* [online], November 21. See http://msnbc.msn.com/id/10017716/site/newsweek/page/2/ (accessed November 21, 2005).

Stacy, Jim, ed. 2007. *Reading Brokeback Mountain: Essays on the Story and the Film*. Jefferson, NC: McFarland.

Staff Writer. 2006. "Taiwanese Cheer Lee's Win, But Some Question Subject Matter." *Taipei Times*, March 7: 4.

Stokes, Lisa Odham, and Michael Hoover. 1999. *City on Fire: Hong Kong Cinema*. London: Verso.

Stoler, Ann Laura. *Race and the Education of Desire: Foucault's History of Sexuality and the Colonial Order of Things*. Durham, NC: Duke University Press, 1995.

Sunshine, Linda, ed. 2000. *Crouching Tiger, Hidden Dragon: A Portrait of the Ang Lee Film, Including the Complete Screenplay*. New York: Newmarket Press.

Taipei Golden Horse International Film Festival Executive Committee, eds. 1991. *Dianying dang'an: Li An* [Cinedossier: Ang Lee]. Taipei: Shibao wenhua.

Tam, Kwok-kan, Terry Yip, and Wimal Dissanayake, eds. 1999. *A Place of One's Own: Stories of Self in China, Taiwan, Hong Kong, and Singapore.* New York: Oxford University Press.

Taylor, Charles. 1997. "Baby, It's Cold Outside." *Salon.com.* October 17. See www.salon.com/ent/ movies/1997/10/17ice.html (accessed May 8, 1999).

Teo, Stephen. 1997. *Hong Kong Cinema: The Extra Dimensions.* London: British Film Institute.

——. 2005. *Wong Kar-wai.* London: British Film Institute.

Thomas, Bruce. 1994. *Bruce Lee: Fighting Spirit.* Berkeley, CA: Frog.

Thompson, Anne. 2005. "Ang Lee's 'Brokeback' explores 'last frontier.'" *Reuters/Hollywood Reporter/Yahoo News,* November 11. See http://news.yahoo.com/s/nm/20051111/en_nm/brokeback_dc (accessed November 11, 2005).

Thompson, Emma. 1996. *The Sense and Sensibility Screenplay and Diaries.* New York: Newmarket Press.

Tiber, Elliot, with Tom Monte. 2007. *Taking Woodstock: A True Story of a Riot, a Concert, and a Life.* New York: Square One Publishers.

Tomlinson, John. 1999. *Globalization and Culture.* Chicago: University of Chicago Press.

Towle, Andy. 2006. "Behind *Brokeback Mountain*: An Interview with Producer James Schamus." *Towleroad,* January 25, 2006. See http://towleroad.typepad.com/towleroad/2006/01/interview_with_. html (accessed April 2, 2006).

Trask, H. Arthur Scott. 1999. "Review of *Ride with the Devil.*" *Dixienet* website. See www.dixienet.org/ spatriot/vol7no2/special.html (accessed June 13, 2002).

Troost, Linda, and Sayre Greenfield, eds. 1998. *Jane Austen in Hollywood.* Lexington: University of Kentucky Press.

Tudor, Andrew. 1973. *Theories of Film.* New York: Viking.

Wakeman, John, ed. 1988. "King Hu." In *World Film Directors, Volume Two, 1945–1985,* 438–42. New York: H. W. Wilson.

Wang, Dulu. 2000. *Wohu canglong* [Crouching tiger hidden dragon.] Hong Kong: Tiandi tushu youxian gongsi.

Wang, Huiling, Ang Lee, and James Schamus, eds. 1994. *Yinshi nannü: dianying juben yu paishe guocheng* [Eat drink man woman: screenplay and shooting process]. Taipei: Yuanliu.

Wang, Huiling, and James Schamus. 2007. "*Lust, Caution*: A Screenplay." In *Lust, Caution: The Story, The Screenplay, and The Making of the Film,* 51–228. New York: Pantheon.

Wang, Huiling, James Schamus, and Cai Guorong (Tsai Kuo-jung). 2000. "*Crouching Tiger, Hidden Dragon*: The Illustrated Screenplay." In Sunshine, ed., *Crouching Tiger, Hidden Dragon: Portrait of an Ang Lee Film,* 29–139.

Warner, Michael. 1993. *Fear of a Queer Planet: Queer Politics and Social Theory.* Minneapolis: University of Minnesota Press.

——. 2000. *The Trouble with Normal: Sex, Politics and the Ethics of Queer Life.* Cambridge: Harvard University Press.

Waters, Malcolm. 1995. *Globalization.* London: Routledge.

Wei, Ti. 2005. "Generational/Cultural Contradiction and Global Incorporation: Ang Lee's *Eat Drink Man Woman.*" In Chris Berry and Feii Lu, eds., *Island on the Edge,* 101–112.

Wittmershaus, Eric. 2001. "James Schamus: Interview." *Flakmag,* June 14. See http://flakmag.com/features/schamus.html (accessed November 5, 2005).

Wood, Ray. 2000 (rev. 2005). "Pushing Hands," *taichido.com.* See www.soton.ac.uk/~maa1/chi/taichi/ push.htm (accessed May 6, 2005).

Woodrell, Daniel. 1987. *Woe to Live On.* London: No Exit Press.

Xing, Jun. 1998. *Asian America Through the Lens: History, Representations, and Identity.* Walnut Creek, CA: Alta Mira Press.

Yabroff, Jennie. 1997. "Stranger in a Strange Land." *Salon.com,* October 17. See www.salon.com/ent/ int/1997/10/17lee.html (accessed May 8, 1999).

Yang, Jeff. 2003. *Once Upon a Time in China: A Guide to Hong Kong, Taiwanese, and Mainland Chinese Cinema.* New York: Atria Books.

Yang, Mayfair Mei-Hui, ed. 1999. *Spaces of Their Own: Women's Public Sphere in Transnational China.* Minneapolis: University of Minnesota Press.

Yang, Yuanying, ed. 2000. *Huayu dianying shi daoyan* [Ten Chinese film directors]. Hangzhou: Zhejiang sheying chuban.

Yau, Esther, ed. 2001. *At Full Speed: Hong Kong Cinema in a Borderless World.* Minneapolis: University of Minnesota Press.

Ye, Jigu. 2012. *Li An dianying de jingyu biaoda* [Frame imagery expression in Ang Lee's films]. Taipei: Showwe Information.

Yeh, Emilie Yueh-yu, and Darrell W. Davis. 2005. *Taiwan Film Directors: A Treasure Island.* New York: Columbia University Press.

Yip, June. 2004. *Envisioning Taiwan: Fiction, Cinema, and the Nation in the Cultural Imaginary.* Durham, NC: Duke University Press.

Yuan, Jada. 2009. "Ang Lee and James Schamus Discuss the Mistakes They Made with *Taking Woodstock*," *Nymag.com*, November 20. See http://nymag.com/daily/entertainment/2009/11/ang_lee_and_james_schamus_talk.html (accessed November 20, 2009).

Zhang, Jingpei. 2004. *Cai Mingliang yu Li Kangsheng* [Tsai Ming-liang and Lee Kang-sheng]. Singapore: Bafang wenhua chuangzuoshi.

Zhang, Jingpei, ed. 2002. *Shinian yijiao dianying meng* [A ten-year dream of cinema]. Taipei: Shibao wenhua.

Zhang, Yingjin. 2004. *Chinese National Cinema.* London: Routledge.

Zhang, Yingjin, ed. 2012. *A Companion to Chinese Cinema.* London: Wiley-Blackwell.

Žižek, Slavoj. 1989. *The Sublime Object of Ideology.* London: Verso.

——. 1990. "The Limits of the Semiotic Apporach to Psychoanalysis." In Richard Feldstein and Henry Sussman, eds., *Psychoananalysis and . . .* , 89–110. New York: Routledge.

——. 1999. *The Ticklish Subject: The Absent Center of Political Ontology.* London: Verso.

——. 2000. "Da Capo senza Fine." In *Contingency, Hegemony, Universality: Contemporary Dialogues on the Left*, 213–62. London: Verso.

INDEX

Initial articles in all languages (e.g., The, La, L', Die) are ignored in sorting titles.